The Role of Religion in Marriage and Family Counseling

The Family Therapy and Counseling Series

Consulting Editor

Jon Carlson, Psy.D., Ed.D.

The Role of Religion in Marriage and Family Counseling

Edited by
Jill Duba Onedera

Routledge
Taylor & Francis Group
New York   London

Routledge
Taylor & Francis Group
270 Madison Avenue
New York, NY 10016

Routledge
Taylor & Francis Group
2 Park Square
Milton Park, Abingdon
Oxon OX14 4RN

© 2008 by Taylor & Francis Group, LLC
Routledge is an imprint of Taylor & Francis Group, an Informa business

Printed in the United States of America on acid-free paper
10 9 8 7 6 5 4 3 2 1

International Standard Book Number-13: 978-0-415-95499-0 (Hardcover)

Library of Congress Cataloging-in-Publication Data

Onedera, Jill D., 1975-
    The role of religion in marriage and family counseling / Jill D. Onedera.
        p. cm. -- (The family therapy and counseling series)
    Includes bibliographical references and index.
    ISBN 0-415-95499-1 (hardcover)
    1. Marriage counseling. 2. Marriage counselors. 3. Family counseling. 4. Family counselors. 5. Marriage--Religious aspects. 6. Family--Religious aspects. I. Title.

HQ10.O54 2006
616.89'156--dc22   2006039777

Visit the Taylor & Francis Web site at
http://www.taylorandfrancis.com

and the Routledge Web site at
http://www.routledge.com

My Grandmothers,
Marcella Duba and Helen Krzesniak,
Who epitomize faith, hope, and love through their
faith in God, works, and dedication to others.

And to Mrs. Yvonne Greenwalt,
May you forever be reminded of how much Bill loves you.

Contents

SECTION III: RELIGION AND RELATIONSHIPS

SECTION IV: Religion and the Counselor

The Editor

Jill D. Onedera, Ph.D., LPCC, NCC, MFTA is an assistant professor in the marriage and family therapy program at Western Kentucky University. She is a licensed professional clinical counselor and marriage and family therapist associate in the Commonwealth of Kentucky. She is also licensed as a professional counselor in Illinois and Ohio. She presently serves as an editorial board member for *The Family Journal* and the *Journal of Counseling & Development*. In addition, Dr. Onedera is currently serving as board member-at-large and co-membership chair of the International Association of Marriage and Family Counselors (IAMFC). She is acting co-chair for the ACA Professional Standards Committee, the Chi Sigma Iota Advocacy Committee, and the Association of Counselor Education and Supervision Advocacy Interest Network. She has co-authored numerous articles and book chapters including "Teaching Gerontology in Counselor Education"; "Depression Among Older Persons"; "Creating a Multicultural Family Practice"; "Cultivating Alliances With Other Helping Professionals"; "Interprofessional Training Within The Curriculum"; "Counseling Flora: Adjusting, Grieving, Dating, and Moving On." Dr. Onedera was recently awarded a faculty grant for her research study entitled "Marital Satisfaction and Coping Strategies of Couples Married Over 40 Years."

Contributors

Belkeis Altareb, Ph.D., is a graduate of Ball State University's Counseling Psychology Program. She is a limited licensed psychologist who currently lives and works in Dubai, the United Arab Emirates (UAE). She is assistant professor at Zayed University, Dubai, and teaches psychology, health education and promotion, research methods, and global studies to female UAE undergraduate students. Dr. Altareb also supervises student research and clinical practice. Her interests are in working with diverse populations, most notably Muslim individuals. Her previous publications have dealt with counseling Muslims and attitudes toward Muslims.

Gord Bruyere is Anishnabe, originally from the Couchiching First Nation in northwestern Ontario, Canada. He currently works in Merritt, British Columbia, on the traditional territory of the Nlaka'pamux peoples where he is coordinator of social work at the Nicola Valley Institute of Technology, an Aboriginal public post-secondary institution. He has taught, developed curricula, and coordinated programs at seven different mainstream and Aboriginal post-secondary institutions in social work, Aboriginal law and advocacy, political science, indigenous learning, and early childhood education. He has made national and international presentations on Aboriginal education and social work issues. He has published journal articles, book chapters, and reviews that focus on Aboriginal issues in education, child welfare, traditional Anishnabe family beliefs, and anti-racism. He is currently developing a book on Aboriginal social work practice, and is a member of the Board of Accreditation of the Canadian Association of Schools of Social Work.

Anthony J. Centore, Ph.D., serves as executive assistant to the president for the 50,000-member American Association of Christian Counselors, is associate director of the Christian Care Network (a membership of clinical professionals), and is adjunct graduate professor for the Center for Counseling and Family Studies at Liberty University. He has written numerous book chapters and articles, and is a columnist for *Christian Counseling Today* magazine. Anthony is also founder and director of an up-and-coming company that provides a venue for Internet and telephone psychotherapy, at eCounseling.com.

Tim Clinton, Ph.D., is president of the 50,000-member American Association of Christian Counselors (AACC). He serves as executive director of the Liberty University Center for Counseling and Family Studies and is a professor of counseling and pastoral care. Tim has authored over 150 articles, chapters, notes, and columns on Christian counseling, counselor education and development, and on marriage, family life, and parenting issues. His newest book, *Turn Your Life Around: Break Free From Your Past to a New and Better You*, was just released in November 2006.

Carol J. Cook is associate professor of pastoral care and counseling at Louisville Presbyterian Theological Seminary in Louisville, KY. She is a fellow of the American Association of Pastoral Counselors (AAPC) and an approved supervisor of the American Association of Marriage and Family Therapists (AAMFT). Dr. Cook is a member of the Reformed Church in America and serves as a contributing editor of *Perspectives: A Journal of Reformed Thought*. She has devoted much of her writing and research to issues in psychosocial human development and the way they intersect with growth in faith.

Richard Deaner, Ph.D., is an educator, researcher, and consultant in the field of counselor education. Deaner has extensive clinical experience in both school and mental health settings with children and families. As a graduate of the University of South Carolina, his scholarly interests include transcultural counseling, religion/spirituality, supervision, counselor training, and wellness. Deaner has authored and co-authored publications regarding couples counseling, spirituality, wellness, and transcultural issues; and is actively involved in research, teaching, service, and presentations within state, national, and international arenas.

Elliot N. Dorff, Ph.D., was ordained a Conservative rabbi by the Jewish Theological Seminary of America in 1970 and earned his Ph.D. in philosophy from Columbia University in 1971. Since then he has directed the rabbinical and master's programs at the University of Judaism, where he currently is rector and distinguished professor of philosophy. He was awarded the *Journal of Law and Religion*'s Lifetime Achievement Award, and he holds three honorary doctoral degrees. Rabbi Dorff is vice-chair of the Conservative Movement's Committee on Jewish Law and Standards and served on the editorial committee of *Etz Hayim*, the new Torah commentary for the

Conservative Movement. He has chaired two scholarly organizations, the Academy of Jewish Philosophy and the Jewish Law Association and currently chairs the Society of Jewish Ethics. In spring 1993, he served on the Ethics Committee of Hillary Rodham Clinton's Health Care Task Force. In March 1997 and May 1999, he testified on behalf of the Jewish tradition on the subjects of human cloning and stem cell research before the President's National Bioethics Advisory Commission. In 1999 and 2000 he was part of the Surgeon General's commission to draft a Call to Action for Responsible Sexual Behavior; and from 2000 to 2002 he served on the National Human Resources Protections Advisory Commission, charged with reviewing and revising the federal guidelines for protecting human subjects in research projects. He is also a member of the Ethics Advisory Committee for the $3 billion California Stem Cell Project.

Virginia Todd Holeman received her Ph.D. from Kent State University and an M.A. from Ashland Theological Seminary as well as an M.A. from Wheaton College and is a professor of counseling at Asbury Theological Seminary. She is also a licensed marriage and family therapist (Kentucky) and a licensed psychologist (Ohio). She authored *Reconcilable Differences: Hope and Healing for Trouble Marriages* (2004, InterVarsity Press) and has contributed a variety of journal articles and book chapters on the topics of forgiveness, repentance, and reconciliation.

Joshua N. Hook, B.S., is a doctoral student in the counseling psychology program at Virginia Commonwealth University (VCU). He is also the director of research at the MATE (Marital Assessment, Treatment, and Enrichment) Center at VCU. His research interests include cultural differences in forgiveness, marital and family therapy, marital enrichment, the integration of religion and therapy, and men's issues.

Aaron Kindsvatter received his Ph.D. from Kent State University. He is currently serving the profession of counseling as a faculty member in the Department of Counseling and Student Affairs at Western Kentucky University. His research interests pertain to the study of factors associated with therapeutic change. Specifically, Dr. Kindsvatter is interested in investigating the question of how counselors can assist clients to explore possibilities, and to utilize unrealized (or perhaps forgotten) strengths in the context of challenging situations.

David R. Koepsell earned his Ph.D. in philosophy as well as his law degree from the University of Buffalo. He has authored numerous articles as well as authored and edited several books, including *Searle on the Institutions of Social Reality*, co-edited with Laurence Moss (Oxford UK: Blackwell, 2003); *Reboot World* (New York: Writer's Club Press, 2003) (fiction); and *The Ontology of*

Cyberspace: Law, Philosophy, and the Future of Intellectual Property (Chicago: Open Court, 2000). He has lectured worldwide on issues ranging from civil rights to philosophy, science, ontology, intellectual property theory, society, and religion.

Tracy M. Lara, Ph.D., LPCC, is an assistant professor in the Department of Counseling and Student Affairs at Western Kentucky University. She is a licensed professional clinical counseler (Kentucky). Lara acknowledges the role of family, relationships, and spiritrality in her works as a career counselor. Her interests revolve around wellness, prevention, and human development.

Jayamala (Mala) Madathil, Ph.D., joined the Department of Counseling at Sonoma State University in Fall 2006, where she teaches in the Community Counseling/MFT track. Prior to taking this position, she was an assistant professor in the Department of Counseling and Human Services at the University of Colorado at Colorado Springs. She received her Ph.D. in counseling and counselor education from the University of North Carolina at Greensboro. Clinically, Dr. Madathil has experience in community mental health agencies, working with children, adolescents, and families on a wide variety of mental health concerns. Her research areas include multicultural counseling and working with families.

John McFadden, Ph.D., NCC, LPCS, is a leader in counselor education regarding cultural diversity and transcultural counseling. As the Benjamin Elijah Mays Distinguished Professor Emeritus and the director of the African American Professors' Program at the University of South Carolina, John McFadden has edited, authored, and co-authored multiple publications regarding marriage and family counseling, counselor training, culture, spirituality, and transcultural issues. Dr. McFadden actively contributes to research, teaching, service, and presentations within state, national, and international arenas.

Denise Mercurio-Riley earned her B.A. in psychology at the University at Buffalo where she is currently a master's degree candidate in the Rehabilitation Counseling Program. She is employed by the Council for Secular Humanism and additionally works as research assistant to David Koepsell.

Andrea J. Miller, M.S., is a doctoral candidate at Virginia Commonwealth University. She studies forgiveness, interventions, marriage enrichment, and religion.

Neresa Minatrea, Ph.D., LPCC, NBCC, NCC, CADC, earned degrees include a doctorate from the University of South Carolina, 1996, master's from Boston University, 1985, and bachelor's from M. H. Baylor University,

1982, and has worked for 22 years in various organizations utilizing counseling, supervisory, and presentation skills. During her work with the U.S. Armed Forces, she established, coordinated, and participated in many collaborative ventures between religious leaders and mental health providers. These were instrumental in increasing quality of life, providing crisis intervention, and re-establishing homeostasis after crises. Her current work involves research, teaching, and supervising counselors-in-training at Western Kentucky University.

Kara Pechersky, Ed.S., is a doctoral candidate in the counselor education program at the University of South Carolina where she works as a mental health therapist. Ms. Pechersky has extensive clinical experience as a mental health therapist with children and families in South Carolina. Her educational background is in marriage and family counseling and she has co-authored a publication regarding couples counseling. Kara Pechersky continues to be an active member of the counseling profession as she presents on topics regarding counseling couples in the military, spirituality, supervision, and transcultural issues on state, national, and international platforms.

Daya Singh Sandhu, Ed.D., NCC, is former chairperson (1996–2004) and professor in the Department of Educational and Counseling Psychology at the University of Louisville. He has a doctorate in counselor education from Mississippi State University and has taught graduate courses in counseling and counseling psychology for more than 20 years. In addition to more than 50 refereed journal articles, Dr. Sandhu has authored or edited 15 books. He has received several distinguished awards, including a Fulbright Senior Research Scholarship Award, Fulbright Senior Specialist Award, President's Distinguished Faculty Award for Outstanding Scholarship, Research and Creative Activity, Association of Multicultural Counseling and Development Research Award, Kentucky Counselor Educator of the Year Award, and Mississippi State Alumnus of the Year Award. He is recognized as one of the twelve pioneers in multicultural counseling for which Sage published his autobiographical account in the *Handbook of Multicultural Counseling* (2001).

Jhampa Shaneman is one of the first Western Buddhist monks in the Tibetan tradition of Mahayana Buddhism. He lived in India for 14 years and studied the tenets of all schools of Buddhist thought. By 1980 he had completed six years of study of the sutras and tantras and four years of short retreats. Jhampa then entered an isolated retreat for three years. He now lives and teaches in Canada and Mexico.

Constance B. Sharp is a Ph.D. candidate at Virginia Commonwealth University. She holds an M.S. in counseling psychology from Virginia Commonwealth University, an M.S. in clinical psychology from San Francisco State

University, and a master of divinity from the Graduate Theological Union in Berkeley. She currently lives in British Columbia where she teaches at Trinity Western University.

Nathaniel G. Wade, Ph.D., is an assistant professor of psychology at Iowa State University and a licensed counseling psychologist. His primary research interests are the psychology of forgiveness and religion, particularly as they intersect with psychotherapy. He is the director of the Center for Group Counseling and Research, a research clinic that provides group counseling and conducts state-of-the-art process and outcome research.

Everett L. Worthington, Jr., Ph.D., professor of psychology at Virginia Commonwealth University, is also a licensed clinical psychologist in Virginia. He studies forgiveness, and claims as his life mission, "To promote forgiveness in every willing heart, home, and homeland." He also studies an approach called hope-focused marriage enrichment and therapy, both within the Christian context and within secular society.

Daniel W. Zink, Ph.D., joined the full-time faculty of Covenant Theological Seminary in 1995 after serving for five years as adjunct professor in counseling and director of student services, and for 11 years as a family counselor, caseworker, and supervisor of public children's services. In addition to his teaching responsibilities, Dr. Zink was the founding director and the five-year head of New Hope Counseling Services, a ministry of nearby Chesterfield Presbyterian Church (PCA). He has also been involved in the Christian education programs of four churches and has served as assistant pastor. His doctoral research focused on the enduring marriages of adult children of divorce.

Series Editor's Foreword

If you talk to God, you are praying; if God talks to you, you have schizophrenia.

—Thomas Szasz

At a time when scientists are stating that people are brainwashed by religion, over 90% of Americans still believe in a god or higher power. Science versus religion is not a new debate and will likely never be completely settled. Whatever the truth, religion and spirituality seem to be well accepted by society and an important part of each person's subjective reality.

No single volume can do justice to the range and depth of human faith and devotion to religious and spiritual phenomena, nor can the possibilities for healing be described in full (Richards & Bergin, 1997). Psychology and counseling, in their attempts to be a science, have historically avoided the topic altogether. However, this is changing as the number of books and journal citations has grown markedly this past decade. As Richards and Bergin (2000) state, "The alienation that has existed between the mental health professions and religion for most of the 20th century is ending."

It is now being mandated that all therapists must become "spiritually sensitive." There is a need to become competent in religious and spiritual diversity. This will allow therapists to gain a further understanding of each client's core beliefs and values.

Jill Duba Onedera and Bill Greenwalt have assembled an impressive group of contributors to enrich your knowledge in this area. You will be able to understand and appreciate many of the world's most popular religions and see how this knowledge is important for therapists.

In closing, remember what Plato stated, "He was a wise man who invented God."

Jon Carlson, Psy.D., Ed.D.
— Series Editor

REFERENCES

Richards, P. S., & Bergin, A. E. (1997). *A spiritual strategy for counseling and psychotherapy*. Washington, DC: APA Books.

Richards, P. S., & Bergin, A. E. (2000). *Handbook of psychotherapy and religious diversity*. Washington, DC: APA Books.

Acknowledgments

I would like to thank to my husband, Sonny. Throughout this process, he provided me with confidence and support. With each hour I spent working on this project, he gave another hour of encouragement and appreciation for my endeavor. I have so appreciated his partnership in prayer, charity work, and in our relationship with God. I am grateful to him, my best friend.

A spirit of hope, determination, and passion about religion and its place in the lives of families and individuals close to me has carried me throughout this process. To my parents, Robert and Christine, I am most grateful. Throughout my life, they have parented me with God as their co-pilot. So much of my own faith and desire to become a person marked with integrity and mercy come from the spirit that shined from within them. I am grateful to my mother who has never faltered in practicing and living out her faith in all that she does. She has been an angel and inspiration to me and has given me further reason to pursue this project. My mother exemplifies "true christianity" or a relationship with Christ, by living a life encompassed by integrity, warmth, compassion, forgiveness, understanding, and nonjudgmental love toward others. I would like to thank my godmother, Diana, who has kept the relationship promise she made when I was an infant. She continues to illustrate what it means to try to live a life with spiritual and religious meaning. I am also grateful to my other set of parents, Joe and Helen. They have encouraged me from the moment I began this project. Their strong Catholic faith and dedication to their family continue to inspire me.

Two of my greatest religious teachers have been my grandmothers, Helen and Marcella. In action, word, and intention, they have lived out their religious faith gracefully through stewardship, dedication, and selflessness. My grandmother Marcella has taught me through her recent struggles with cancer that despite moments when she could not move or speak, her faith is her stronghold. During one moment in particular, as I knelt beside her bed, she reached across and grabbed my hand and said, "Let's pray." They, too, have provided me with the incentive to pursue this project.

I would like to thank other members of my family who expressed interest in my project, as well as understanding when I was unable to partake in family time. I am thankful for the support of Kim, Aunt Bev, Uncle Chick, Aunt Jackie, Uncle Todd, Lola, Heart, Christie, Bobby, Jason, and Ken. I love them all very much. I would like to thank my friends who also have provided support and encouragement. I am indebted to Tracy, Neresa, and Aaron for stepping in when I needed them most. I appreciate the effort they put into making this project happen. I am thankful for my good friends Alison, Louisa, Tammy, and Tracy for being friends despite my hectic work schedule. I am grateful for the unconditional relationship I have with each one of them. My friend Susan helped me with some of the finishing touches to this project. As always, she was there. Also, I am grateful to Deacon Bob and Dr. Tracy Lara for the wonderful, faith-forming discussions we have had. They have been instrumental in my own spiritual and religious growth. I am thankful once again for Dr. Jon Carlson who has provided me with the opportunity and the means to bring something so important to me alive. He continues to make differences in my life.

With much gratitude, I am indebted to my contributing authors. I have enjoyed the review of their writings to the fullest. I am confident that readers will be as touched, enlightened, and moved as I was. In addition, I am grateful to my reviewers who provided insightful and helpful feedback, as well as encouragement.

Finally, I want to thank my very dear friend, the late Bill Greenwalt. I know that he was somewhere watching. He has been watching all along. Bill continued to co-edit this book with me even when he was not physically present. I suppose that is what faith is really all about. Although I could not rely on his humanly consult, I learned to trust his spirit. When I had writer's block or when I wondered how I would complete this endeavor without him, Bill was there. Through this, he taught me the true meaning of faith, hope, and trust.

Thank you, Bill.

Editor's Note

Due to the varied backgrounds and professional affiliations of the contributing authors, terminology may vary from one chapter to the next. For example, titles such as marriage and family counselor, marriage and family therapist, or mental health professional are used interchangeably throughout the book. However, my hope is that the material presented in this book will be helpful to many other mental health practitioners and educators across the professional spectrum.

A Tribute

BY JILL D. ONEDERA

Bill Greenwalt will forever stand out in my mind as one of the greatest mentors in my personal and professional development. I imagine that there are others who feel the same way.

My professional relationship with Bill began when I started my first professional position as a counselor educator at Western Kentucky University. He welcomed me warmly by sharing his wisdom and lending his ears. Bill's way of mentoring was certainly antithetical to advice giving. Because he believed so greatly in people and their own capacities, his way was to provide questions for deeper reflection. I remember how he would often look to the side when I would ask him a philosophical question about teaching or even about life. He took a few moments to think. Typically he responded with a story. Bill had a wonderful way of telling stories; he captured his audience in a way that was engaging and thought-provoking. It was through his stories that I found the wisdom that brought me the answers to my questions on my own.

In the brief two years that I knew Bill, we spent hours of discussion comparing our different religious backgrounds. Although we noted many differences between my Catholic background and upbringing and his Presbyterian background, we also laughed about the numerous similarities. However, so often I went away from our discussions realizing how little I knew about what it was that I was practicing and incorporating into my daily life. Needless to say, Bill served as the impetus for my further study into my own Catholic faith. This also has lead to my interest in how religious doctrine and faith play out in relationships, specifically those within families and marriages. Further more, with Bill's support, my relationship with God has been enriched and increasingly attended to.

When the opportunity came for me to write this book, I could not think of anyone who would be a greater co-editor. Bill and I already had many deep conversations about religion and mental health. I also had spent hours of supervision under Bill for my marriage and family therapist associate license talking about families and couples. It seemed perfect; and it was perfect while it lasted. During the months before Bill died, we constructed an outline, engaged our fantastic contributors in the project, and submitted the manuscript proposal. Even prior to the acceptance of the proposal, Bill and I worked on and completed the first chapter of this book. We believed the story of religion in peoples' lives was very important. We also were convinced that mental health professionals working with couples and families needed a background for such stories present in the lives of their clients.

Bill was never one to condemn, judge, or interrogate those different from him. To me, he modeled everything good about being religious. The spiritual nature of his religious faith was modeled in the way he handled life's conflicts, routine, and how he handled the precious moments (such as times in the garden with his grandson). By watching and working with Bill I was invited to see religion and spirituality in their most alive forms. It was not something he simply practiced on Sunday mornings or during silent moments of meditation. The practice of his religion, and thus his spiritual nature, were reflected in how he lived each day and each moment. He moved through his life with integrity and godly intentions. He hoped and he had faith in even the most futile of situations. His hope was infectious. He believed in God, he believed in others, and he acted accordingly. And more importantly, he modeled the most important element of religious faith, a relationship with God.

So on January 7, 2006 when Bill left us, I was shocked, extremely sad, and for a brief time, desperately alone. However, I knew that the book had to go on and that I had to look for Bill's spirit in the work ahead of me. I was also determined to follow through with the task of providing readers with additional information related to religion and its place in the lives of couples and families. I have witnessed the "religious" and "spiritual" in my friend. Through knowing Bill, I have a greater appreciation for how others work toward living a life within God's shadow and under the premise of their religious beliefs. Many of these persons will walk through our professional counseling doors. We must seek out ways to understand and appreciate them. We must make an effort to understand how religion shapes the lives of our clients, individuals, couples, and families.

They are not gone who live in the hearts they leave behind.

— **Native American Proverb**

SECTION I

The Opening Dialogue:
Identifying the Holy Elephant
in the Counseling Room

Multicultural diversity has become increasingly prevalent in the United States. As mental health providers, we can expect the same growth in diversity amongst our clientele. This book will address a particular area of diversity, specifically that of religious faith, doctrine, and values. The first two chapters of the book will provide a foundation highlighting the relevance of this topic in the work of mental health professionals.

The first chapter will provide a brief overview of how religion has been embraced within the field of mental health, as well as how religious beliefs affect the culture of America. Finally, recent statistics related to religious diversity and the importance of religion within the lives of persons living in America is presented. In chapter two, Worthington and his colleagues introduce issues related to how the mental health practitioner's religious beliefs and commitment might effect therapeutic decisions and relationship. In addition, the authors discuss ways in which client factors impact the therapeutic relationship.

The goal of the first two chapters is to prepare mental health practitioners to be aware of and able to "identify the holy elephant in the counseling room." What follows in the book is information about particular religious faith perspectives, as well as ideas about how to actually work inside the counseling room, and in the counseling community at large.

CHAPTER 1

Introduction to Religion and Marriage and Family Counseling

JILL D. ONEDERA AND BILL C. GREENWALT

Religion plays an important role in the lives of many people. They live their lives based on religious principles and beliefs. All aspects of their lives from play to work to relationships are affected by their religious beliefs. With something as pervasive as this, one would assume that counselors would consider religion an integral part of the counseling process. However, very few counselors will raise religious issues or consider them when assessing client strengths or symptoms (Harper & Gill, 2005). Part of the reason counselors are reluctant to raise religious issues is the lack of understanding of the various religions and even the lack of agreement on definitions.

DEFINITIONS

Two terms need to be defined and differentiated: *spirituality* and *religion*. The terms are sometimes used interchangeably even though some find them to be exclusive of one another. Some individuals define their spirituality by their adherence to a particular religion, while others develop their spirituality apart from an organized religion (Cashwell & Young, 2005). For example, a person may be spiritual without being religious, religious without being spiritual, or both religious and spiritual by integrating the two (Wiggins-Frame, 2005). The first of the nine spiritual competencies for counselors states: "The professional counselor can explain the relationship between religion and spirituality, including similarities and differences" (Association for Spiritual, Ethical and Religious Values in Counseling [ASERVIC], 1999). Since considerable differences occur on the relationship of spirituality and religion, counselors have a challenge to meet the first competency.

Authors, in their efforts to define spirituality, have referred to the word for spirit in various languages: Latin (*spiritus* meaning breath, courage, vigor, or life), Greek (*pneuma* meaning wind, breath, life, and spirit), or Hebrew (*ruach* meaning wind, breath, life, and spirit) (Ingersoll, 1995; Roth, 1990; Sheldrake, 1992; Wiggins-Frame, 2005). The first three definitions of *spiritual* in *Webster's New Universal Unabridged Dictionary* (1996) are

1. of, pertaining to, or consisting of spirit; incorporeal. 2. of or pertaining to the spirit or soul as distinguished from the physical nature: *a spiritual approach to life*. 3. closely akin in interests, attitude, outlook, etc.: *the professor's spiritual heir in linguistics*. (p. 1840)

The next two definitions relate to spirits or the supernatural. Then the next four definitions include religious qualities:

6. of or pertaining to the spirit as the seat of the moral or religious nature. 7. of or pertaining to sacred things or matters; religious; devotional; sacred. 8. of or belonging to the church; ecclesiastical: *lords spiritual and temporal*. 9. of or relating to the mind or intellect. (p. 1840)

The first group of definitions may be interpreted to demonstrate a separation between spirituality and religion. If one takes all of the definitions into consideration, then spirituality is connected with religion.

Some find *religion* to be easier to define (Cashwell & Young, 2005; Wiggins-Frame, 2005) because it is more institutionalized with particular beliefs and practices. *Webster's New Universal Unabridged Dictionary* defines religion as

1. a set of beliefs concerning the cause, nature, and purpose of the universe, esp. when considered as the creation of a superhuman agency or agencies, usually involving devotional and ritual observances, and often containing a moral code governing the conduct of human affairs. 2. a specific fundamental set of beliefs and practices generally agreed upon by a number of persons or sects: *the Christian religion, the Buddhist religion*. 3. the body of persons adhering to a particular set of beliefs and practices. (p. 1628)

In his book on world religions, W. C. Young (1995) challenges the dictionary definition as too narrow because some of the major world religions do not meet the definition. Instead he poses the following as a working definition: "Religion is human transformation in response to perceived ultimacy" (p. 4). Three words are essential to this definition: human, transformation, and ultimacy. First, religion is a human activity and not an activity of a supreme being and includes some understanding of what it means to be human. Second, religion involves a transformation. A change occurs from one state to another state by some means espoused by the religion. Third, religion is a response to some perceived ultimacy such as God in Christianity or Nirvana in Buddhism (Young, 1995). This definition, while objectionable to some religions, enables one definition to fit the varied religions in the world. In order to include all of the major world religions in the discussions of this book, this is the definition that will be accepted for our use. This book will focus on organized religions and not spirituality. All contributors will be writing from their own religious beliefs and values.

HISTORICAL PERSPECTIVE

Over the past few years the counseling profession has started to address spiritual and religious issues. Books have been written with both spirituality and religion in the title; however, within these books the discussion of religion is typically from a general perspective and not from any particular religious perspective (Cashwell & Young, 2005; Kahle & Robbins, 2004). The authors raise important issues for counselors to consider and offer suggested strategies when working with religious clients, but they do not help the counselor understand some of the basic beliefs of clients from a specific religion on issues that might enter the counseling room. This information is important for counselors to know in order to understand the client's worldview and problems.

Other authors such as Burke and Miranti (1995) and Hinterkopf (1998) approach the topic almost totally from a spiritual viewpoint. While both books contain some mention of religion, the real focus is on spirituality. For example, a central theme seems to be the development of one's own spirituality as more important than adhering to a particular religion. While this may sound good from a humanistic perspective, followers of particular religions may perceive this as a threat to an individual's "spiritual growth" within the religion. For example, many Christian groups follow the Apostle Paul's admonition to Timothy: "For the time will come when men will not put up with sound doctrine. Instead, to suit their own desires, they will gather around them a great number of teachers to say what their itching ears want to hear" (2 Tim. 4:3).

Counselors who encourage clients to develop their own beliefs apart from the teachings of the stated religion unintentionally may be leading the client out of the religion. While people have the freedom to move from one religion to another, is it ethical behavior for a counselor to lead clients away from their religion? This is a very tough ethical dilemma that involves many of our ethical principles and needs considerable debate within our field. Clergy and other religious leaders will not have confidence in referring clients to counselors without assurances that counselors will respect religious beliefs and practices. Further, counselors find themselves in difficult positions when clients have beliefs significantly different from their own.

Psychology and counseling have not been completely friendly to the religious community (Kahle & Robbins, 2004). Freud saw religion as something harmful that can be traced to infancy (Freud, 1973). Later B. F. Skinner (1953) thought religion was nothing more than fiction held in place by negative reinforcement and threats of punishment. More recently, Albert Ellis (1980) wrote, "Religiosity, therefore, is in many ways equivalent to irrational thinking and emotional disturbance … The less religious they are, the more emotionally healthy they will tend to be" (p. 637). Although these are quotes from leaders within the field of psychology and counseling, the editors of this book wonder if these types of statements show respect to religion or nurture the acceptance of counseling within the religious communities.

On the other hand, many religious schools have instituted training programs in psychology and counseling. A quick review of the Council for Accreditation of Counseling and Related Education Programs (CACREP) list of accredited programs revealed 30 programs associated with religious colleges, universities, and seminaries. Some of the leaders in the Christian counseling movement, such as James Dobson, Larry Crabb, Timothy Clinton, Paul Meier, Frank Minnerth, and Everett Worthington, are well known and have gained prominence in the counseling field. The American Association of Christian Counselors (AACC) is a very large organization attesting to the interest of many in obtaining continuing education and association with people who take religion seriously.

RELIGIOUS DIVERSITY

Traditionally religious scholars identify seven major world religions: Judaism, Christianity, Islam, Hinduism, Buddhism, Confucianism, and Taoism (Young, 1995). In addition to these, many indigenous and folk religions have been identified. Humanism now is recognized as one of the major religions in many texts (Young, 1995). Furthermore, each religion has many different subgroups with very distinctive beliefs and practices. This results in a very complex field of study.

Since most people reading this text will probably have some background in Christianity, that particular religion will be used as an example of the diversity within subgroups of an individual religion. Christianity is divided into several large groups, which are then divided into many smaller groups. The large groups consist of Catholics, Protestants, and Orthodox. Most people are familiar with the Roman Catholic Church and may not be familiar with some of the lesser known Catholic churches such as the American Catholic Church, Liberal Catholic Church, Mariavite Old Catholic Church, or some of the other small Catholic denominations (Mead & Hill, 2001). Distinct Protestant denominations are numerous ranging from the small Independent Churches to the larger mainline denominations such as Baptist, Methodist, or Presbyterian. Mead and Hill (2001) identify 14 different Orthodox churches within the United States. Each major denomination is also divided into numerous smaller groups. For example, 19 Baptist denominations, 12 Methodist denominations, and nine Presbyterian denominations are listed in Mead and Hill's handbook. Further, they provide the mailing addresses and web sites for 208 different religious groups.

Because of the principle of religious freedom, the United States has great diversity in its religious practices and beliefs. One only has to look at all of the independent churches who do not affiliate with any of the major religions and groups to see that religious diversity is valued within the country. Within each religion and major denomination one also will find a range from the very conservative to the very liberal. Therefore, just because a person identifies a religious preference, one cannot assume to know what the individual might believe. Every individual develops an understanding of his/her religious traditions that may be slightly different from the stated beliefs of the religion. Therefore, counselors cannot assume that a particular client who professes to be a member of the Roman Catholic Church will believe and follow all of the principles of that Church. A counselor needs to be aware of the teachings of the professed religion and sensitive to individual differences and practices. Respecting the individual and respecting the religion have to be taken together. Stressing one over the other may result in unethical behavior. These are issues similar to multicultural treatment implications.

RELIGION AND CULTURAL DIVERSITY

Does religion adapt to the culture or does culture adapt to the religion? Sometimes that is a very difficult question to answer. Often culture and religion are so integrated that one has difficulty knowing which influenced the other. For example, Asian cultures are known for their family values and proper decorum (McGoldrick, Pearce, & Giordano, 1982). The principles of "filial piety" and respect for authority are key beliefs of Confucianism, which was the official doctrine of China for centuries until about 1913 (Fellows, 1979). The Chinese educational system taught the principles of Confucianism until it was banned in 1949 (Young, 1995). Here, in all probability, religion impacted culture significantly over time. In order to fully understand Chinese and other Asian cultures, one must have some understanding of Confucianism. Since the religion was outlawed in 1949, many people studying culture may not see the influence of the religion on the present-day society.

The impact of Christianity on American culture is very prevalent. Because of the principle of religious freedom, one can see both the impact of religion on the culture and the impact of culture on religion. For example, we can see the impact of religion on culture within the Protestant work ethic of working six days and then honoring the Sabbath, which resulted in a culture where work was done Monday through Saturday with Sunday being a day off. For many years "Blue Laws" prohibited businesses from operating on Sunday. Even today with a greater interest in diversity and the recognition of other religious holy days such as Friday for Muslims and Saturday for the Jews, our culture still thinks in terms of the Christian calendar.

The influence of religion on society is evident in many areas. During the 2004 elections several news agencies reported that some Catholic bishops and priests were considering refusing the sacraments of the Church to politicians who supported legislation such as abortion or gay marriages (Garber, 2004; Pinsky, 2004). The impact of clergy refusing the sacraments to political leaders who espouse or support positions contrary to church doctrine cannot be assessed at this time. Religious leaders want practitioners of a religion to be faithful to the principles of the religion. To do otherwise may cause the individual to suffer spiritual harm and/or result in others being led astray and suffering spiritually. Some politicians said they separated their religious beliefs from their political responsibilities. This raises some mental health issues. Will political leaders follow their religion or will they create a dichotomy within themselves where they believe one thing but do something different? Will this result in individuals seeking counseling because of the dichotomy?

Current culture can be seen impacting some religious practices as well. For example, many churches now have women clergy. While this remains a very controversial issue in the Catholic and many Protestant churches, some denominations have changed remarkably over time. The same may be said about some other social issues of our time, such as abortion, divorce, and homosexuality. While the issues remain very controversial, culture has influenced some beliefs and practices.

The second spirituality competency states, "The professional counselor can describe religious and spiritual beliefs and practices in a cultural context" (ASERVIC, 1999). Since cultures are influenced by the predominant religion of the culture, counselors need to be able to understand the integration of the culture and the predominant religion(s). White Anglo Saxon Protestants are often lumped together without considering the impact of their various religious backgrounds (McGoldrick, et al., 1982). German-American Lutherans, Irish Presbyterians, Dutch Reformed, and Southern Baptists have unique beliefs and practices that impact cultural activities.

Nancy Boyd-Franklin (1989) says that therapists who do not remember that the church plays an extremely important role in the lives of Black people may have clients terminate therapy because of the differences in values. Sue and Sue (1990) and later Paniagua (1998) stressed the importance of the Catholic Church in the lives of many Hispanic families. However, it should be noted that Irish Catholicism is very different from Latin Catholicism (Fukuyama, Siahpoush, & Sevig, 2005). Finally, one cannot overlook religion in the study of multiculturalism. Paul Tillich (1959), a leading Protestant theologian in the mid-twentieth century, said that man's quest for the ultimate is what gives meaning to culture.

To understand the numbers involved in religious diversity both within the United States and the world, the number of adherents to the major world religions is listed in Table 1.1 for both the United States and the world. While the American Religious Identity Survey (ARIS) provides reliable numbers for the United States, no such survey is available for adherents throughout the world. The number of adherents varies considerably from source to source. In addition, the various sources combine similar religions. For example, in our primary source, Adherents.com, Confucianism, Taoism, and Chinese Buddhism are combined to form Chinese Traditional Religion. Therefore, a secondary source was used to find the number of adherents for Taoism.

According to the ARIS data Christianity is the dominant religion with approximately 77% of the population stating Christianity as their religion of choice. Except for Confucianism, which is frequently combined with Taoism and/or Buddhism and seldom is practiced solely (Young, 1995), all of the major world religions are found within the United States to some degree. From 1990 to 2000 Hinduism grew by 237%; Buddhism grew by 170%; and Islam grew by 109%. This compares to a 5% growth rate for Christianity

Table 1.1 Adherents to the Major World Religions Within the United States and World[a]

Religion	United States[b]	World[c]
Christian	159,980	2,100,000
Jewish	2,831	14,000
Muslim/Islamic	1,104	1,300,000
Buddhist	1,082	376,000
Unitarian/Universalist/Humanist	668	800
Hindu	766	900,000
Native American	103	
Taoist	40	2,700[d]
Sikh	57	23,000
No religion specified	29,481	1,100,000

[a]Numbers represent thousands. For example, 40 represents 40,000.
[b]Kosmin, Mayer, & Keysar, 2001.
[c]Adherents.com, 2005.
[d]Robinson, 2005.

(Kosmin, Mayer, & Keysar, 2001). While the raw numbers are small, the percentage increases indicate an unprecedented changing of the landscape of religious diversity within the country. Counselors need to become familiar with these religions to provide effective treatment for individuals, couples, and families.

People clearly consider religion to be important in their lives. The AP/Ipsos Poll (2005) reported that 84% of the American people consider religion important in their lives. Religion provides meaning, connectiveness, and support for individuals (Shafranske, 1996). With religion playing such a high prominence in the lives of individuals who are potential clients, how can counselors justify not placing a greater focus on it? Are counselors as religious as the general population?

RELIGION AND COUNSELORS

One might assume that the percentage of counselors who are religious is parallel to that of the rest of the population. Based on several studies done on the spirituality and religiosity of mental health professionals, the contrary has been found. Bergin (1983) reported a survey of the studies that indicated that counselors were less committed than the rest of society. Later Bergin and Jensen (1990) surveyed mental health professionals and found that 80% reported some type of religious preference. While this is a significant number, it is below the general public's 92%. Kelly (1995) surveyed 479 members of the American Counseling Association (ACA). Although 90% of the respondents indicated some type of spiritual or religious orientation, spiritual values were more widely held than religious values. This seems to follow what is available in the literature. One can find more written about spirituality than about religion.

How can the profession be so close to the general public in a professed connection to religion, but then be reluctant to discuss religion in treatment? Kahle and Robbins (2004) discuss how religion was suppressed in their own training programs. Some counselors believe that religious issues should be referred to religious counselors or clergy and should not be considered part of the counselor's domain (Kahle & Robbins, 2004) even though 58% of the general public believe that religion can answer all or most of today's problems (Gallup Poll, 2005). The editors of this book wonder how something so important to the potential client can not be considered important in counseling.

Kelly (1994) reported that in a study of 343 counselor education programs, 287 programs had no course specifically addressing spiritual or religious issues. The vast majority (250 programs) did not have religion or spirituality as a part of any course. As one would expect, Kelly reported state institutions included them less than private schools. Since thirty religious affiliated schools have counselor training programs accredited by CACREP, one wonders if the programs that do address religion within their programs do so out of their own religious affiliation. In other words, do those students get training in the treatment of clients from all religious backgrounds or only from their own tradition? Further, is some religious training better than no religious training or does it result in a narrowed perspective with students prepared to treat only those from their religious heritage?

When one does not receive training in a particular area, then professionals are left to seek training on their own. Since our ethical standards require us to practice only within the area of our expertise, then it would seem logical that people would seek some type of religious training. However, some (if not many) may not see a need for training because they do not think religion has a place in treatment. Others may attend workshops or read books on the subject. The scarcity of meaningful literature and training workshops on religious issues may make that a difficult task. One can find significant literature on Christian counseling or some other religious tradition, but finding literature on counseling people from various religious backgrounds is more difficult.

PURPOSE OF BOOK

The purpose of this book is to further the dialogue between spirituality and religion and to convey some importance to studying the various world religions. To be true to our ethical guidelines, counselors have to demonstrate a respect of all religions, whether we agree with them or not. One can be in total disagreement with a client's religious beliefs and still respect the dignity of the client and his/her religion. The editors want to begin a dialogue on the effect religion has within the counseling room. That is, we would like to begin a discussion around the question of how religion affects the way clients view their problems and/or view the type of treatment they want. We also want the book to provide significant information on how various religions view specific issues related to marriage and family counseling. This material will allow therapists to see differences and similarities within religions. Lastly, we want to provide material to encourage skill development for working with clients who view religion as important and who see religion as a vital ingredient in personal growth.

The book is divided into four sections: (1) "The Opening Dialogue: Identifying the Holy Elephant in the Counseling Room"; (2) "Religious Context Within Marriage and Family Counseling"; (3) "Religion and Relationships"; and (4) "Religion and the Counselor." Contributors have been selected based upon their expertise on the given topic and are not all counselors.

"The Opening Dialogue" contains two chapters. Besides this introductory chapter, the second chapter will address how religion affects the marriage and family counselor. For example, how the counselor's theory of choice, view of human nature, problem development and treatment approaches are affected by religious beliefs will be addressed.

The second section on religious context within marriage and family counseling is the largest section, including chapters 3–11. Contributors with specific religious backgrounds write on how religious beliefs and practices affect marriages and families. Contributors were asked to write on the following topics from their own specific religious backgrounds: definition of marriage; roles within marriages and families, child bearing, birth control, abortion, and teenage pregnancy; finances; dissolving relationships, divorce, and annulment; managing the family after separation and/or divorce; death and dying; and homosexuality in couples and families. The following six religions are represented in these chapters: Christianity, Judaism, Islam, Buddhism, Hinduism, Sikhism, Native American religions, and humanism. As is the case when some group is left out of anything, some may object to the fact that a particular religion is not represented. However, space is limited and the choice of these groups was made on the prominence of the religion within the United States.

The editors of the book asked contributors of the chapters to write from their own understanding of the religious tradition. This may mean that a contributor's understanding may differ from some of our readers' knowledge of the religion. Consequently, we encourage everyone to seek additional knowledge on all religions. Doing so will emphasize the importance of finding out an individual's own personal belief instead of relying on either a religion's stated position or one's own understanding of the religion. To emphasize this point further there are three contributors writing from the Christian perspective: Catholic, conservative Christian, and liberal Christian. One could find similar divisions within any of the religious traditions.

Section 3 contains chapters 12–14. Chapter 12 includes a discussion of studies on the effect of religion on recovery from relationship problems. Studies on such things as prayer, religious support groups, and other religious activities have reported significant benefits of religion on all areas of one's life. Researchers studying healthy marriages report that spirituality and religious activity are strengths of a healthy marriage.

Chapter 13 is a discussion of the role of forgiveness in religious life and within marriage and family relationships. Conflict and disagreements within relationships are common. Being able to forgive an offending partner often is tied to one's religious commitment. The various religions have differing beliefs about forgiveness. The counselor will be able to understand better the client's issues around forgiveness by understanding the individual's religious beliefs about forgiveness.

Many marriages include individuals from more than one religion, because of the increasing religious diversity within the United States and the increased mobility of our society. This is the topic of chapter 14. Individuals often enter into mixed marriages at a time when one, or both, of the individuals was not active in their religion. As a result the difficulties of maintaining a relationship with significantly different religious beliefs and practices were not foreseen. The contributors discuss some of the typical family developmental points during which religious issues result in increased conflict.

Section 4 is a discussion of religion and the counselor and begins with a chapter on ethnicity. This chapter outlines how ethnicity and culture impacts religious beliefs and practices and then impacts marriages and families. One cannot take religion away from culture nor culture away from religion. Counselors have to be able to integrate their understanding of both in a way that is beneficial to the client.

In chapter 16 the contributors discuss the relationship between mental health professionals and religious leaders. This relationship is often one lacking trust, because of the hostility of some individuals within the profession toward religion. When the mental health professional takes the time to develop a working relationship with religious leaders who can serve as resources for information on religious beliefs and practices, the clients benefit the most. Clients have very special relationships with their clergy or other religious leaders and develop special relationships with their counselors. Counselors should establish clear boundaries with both clients and religious leaders to provide effective treatment.

In the final chapter, the contributor discusses how religion is currently incorporated in counseling training programs. How can counselors be trained better to handle religious issues within the counseling setting? Should programs develop courses that provide an overview of the world's religions or should material be included in other courses? Since religion plays such an important role in the lives of our clients, we need to train our professionals in such a way that they are comfortable in identifying and treating religious issues.

CONCLUSION

Religion plays an important role in the lives of many people. In order to understand fully the worldview of one's clients, the counselor needs to attend to the beliefs and practices of the religion to which a client belongs. This book will help one become familiar with important religious principles that affect marriage and family counseling. The contributors hope to increase the counselor's understanding of the various religious beliefs and practices to facilitate assisting clients in solving their problems and remaining true to their religious principles.

REFERENCES

Adherents.com (2005). *Major religions of the world ranked by number of adherents.* Retrieved September 20, 2005, from http://adherents.com/Religions_By_Adherents.html

AP/Ipsos Poll (2005). *Religious attitudes.* Retrieved September 20, 2005, from http://wid.ap.org/polls/050606religion.html

Association for Spiritual, Ethical, and Religious Values in Counseling (1999). *Competencies for integrating spirituality into counseling.* Retrieved September 24, 2005, from http://www.aservic.org/guidelines%20for.htm

Bergin, A. E. (1983). Religiosity and mental health: A critical reevaluation and meta-analysis. *Professional Psychology: Research and Practice, 14,* 170–184.

Bergin, A. E., & Jensen, J. P. (1990). Religiosity of psychotherapists: A national survey. *Psychotherapy, 27,* 3–7.

Boyd-Franklin, N. (1989). Five key factors in the treatment of black families. *Journal of Psychotherapy and the Family, 6,* 53–69.

Burke, M. T., & Miranti, J. G. (1995). *Counseling: The spiritual dimension.* Alexandria, VA: American Counseling Association.

Cashwell, C. S., & Young, J. S. (2005). Integrating spirituality and religion into counseling: An introduction. *Integrating spirituality and religion into counseling: A guide to competent practice.* Alexandria, VA: American Counseling Association.

Ellis, A. (1980). Psychotherapy and atheistic values: A response to A. E. Bergin's "Psychotherapy and Religious Values." *Journal of Counseling and Clinical Psychology, 48,* 635–639.

Fellows, W. J. (1979). *Religions east and west.* Chicago: Holt, Rinehart and Winston.

Freud, S. (1973). *The future of an illusion.* (W. D. Robson-Scott, Trans.; J. Strachey, Ed.). London: Hogarth Press.

Fukuyama, M. A., Siahpoush, F., & Sevig, T. D. (2005). Religion and spirituality in a cultural context. In C. S. Cashwell & J. S. Young (Eds.), *Integrating spirituality and religion into counseling: A guide to competent practice* (pp. 123–142). Alexandria, VA: American Counseling Association.

Gallup Poll (2005, April 18–21). *Mid-April economic poll.* Retrieved on September 20, 2005, from http://brain.gallup.com/documents/question.aspx?question=152830 &Advanced=0&SearchConType=1&SearchTypeAll=problems

Garber, P. (2004, October 1). Bishop tackles communion issue—Discipline, not politics, behind decision to deny rite to abortion supporters, Jugis says. *Winston-Salem Journal,* p. B1

Harper, M. C., & Gill, C. S. (2005). Assessing the client's spiritual domain. In C. S. Cashwell & J. S. Young (Eds.), *Integrating spirituality and religion into counseling: A guide to competent practice* (pp. 31–62). Alexandria, VA: American Counseling Association.

Hinterkopf, E. (1998). *Integrating spirituality in counseling: A manual for using the experiential focusing method.* Alexandria, VA: American Counseling Association.

Holy Bible, New International Version. (1978). Grand Rapids, MI: Zondervan Bible Publishers.

Ingersoll, R. E. (1995). Spirituality, religion, and counseling: Dimensions and relationships. In M. T. Burke & J. G. Miranti (Eds.), *Counseling: The spiritual dimension* (pp. 5–18). Alexandria, VA: American Counseling Association.

Kahle, P. A., & Robbins, J. M. (2004). *The power of spirituality in therapy: Integrating spiritual and religious beliefs in mental health practice.* Binghamton, NY: Haworth Pastoral Press.

Kelly, E. W., Jr. (1994). The role of religion and spirituality in counselor education: A national survey. *Counselor Education and Supervision, 55,* 227–237.

Kelly, E. W. (1995). *Spirituality and religion in counseling and psychotherapy: Diversity in theory and practice.* Alexandria, VA: American Counseling Association.

Kosmin, B. A., Mayer, E., & Keysar, A. (2001). *American religious identification survey.* Retrieved September 16, 2005, from The Graduate Center of the City University of New York Web site: http://www.gc.cuny.edu/faculty/research_studies/aris.pdf

McGoldrick, M., Pearce, J., & Giordano, J. (1982). *Ethnicity and family therapy.* New York: Guilford Press.

Mead, F. S., & Hill, S. S. (2001). *Handbook of denominations in the United States* (11th ed., Craig D. Atwood, Rev.). Nashville, TN: Abingdon Press.

Paniagua, F. A. (1998). *Assessing and treating culturally diverse clients: A practical guide* (2nd ed.). Thousand Oaks, CA: Sage Publications.

Pinsky, M. I. (2004, November 3). Kerry takes communion during visit to Orlando — Some say he should not receive the sacrament because he backs abortion rights. *The Orlando Sentinel,* p. A14.

Robinson, B. A. (2005). *Religions of the world: Number of adherents; names of houses of worship, names of leaders, rates of growth.* Retrieved September 20, 2005, from http://www.religioustolerance.org/worldrel.htm

Roth, N. (1990). *The breath of God: An approach to prayer.* Cambridge, MA: Cowley.

Shafranske, E. P. (1996). Religious beliefs, affiliations, and practices of psychologists. In E. P. Shafranske (Ed), *Religion and the clinical practice of psychology* (pp. 149–162). Washington, DC: American Psychological Association.

Sheldrake, P. (1992). *Spirituality and history: Questions of interpretations and method.* New York: Crossroad.

Skinner, B. F. (1953). *Science and human behavior.* New York: Macmillan.

Sue, D. W., & Sue, D. (1990). *Counseling the culturally different: Theory and practice.* New York: John Wiley and Sons.

Tillich, P. (1959). *Theology of culture.* New York: Oxford University Press.

Webster's New Universal Unabridged Dictionary (1996). New York: Barnes and Noble Books.

Wiggins-Frame, M. W. (2005). Spirituality and religion: Similarities and differences. In C. S. Cashwell & J. S. Young (Eds.), *Integrating spirituality and religion into counseling: A guide to competent practice* (pp. 11–30). Alexandria, VA: American Counseling Association.

Young, W. C. (1995). *The world's religions: Worldviews and contemporary issues.* Englewood Cliffs, NJ: Prentice-Hall.

CHAPTER 2

The Effects of a Therapist's Religion on the Marriage Therapist and Marriage Counseling

EVERETT L. WORTHINGTON, JOSHUA N. HOOK,
NATHANIEL G. WADE, ANDREA J. MILLER, CONSTANCE B. SHARP

In the complex situation of marital counseling, many factors can contribute to its implementation, success, and course. One such factor is the therapist's religion. The therapist's degree of religious commitment (especially) and, for highly committed therapists, religious beliefs and values affect many therapeutic decisions. Interactions between the religion of the therapist and the client's religion (or lack of it) add another level to the influence of the therapist's religion on the marriage therapist and thus on marriage counseling.

THERAPISTS' RELIGIOSITY AFFECTS MARRIAGE COUNSELING

Religion and Spirituality Defined

Spirituality is defined as a person's search for the sacred (Hill & Hall, 2002). *Religion* is defined as a person's search for the sacred within an organized worldview of specified beliefs and values that are lived out within a community of faith (Hill & Hall, 2002). In the present chapter, we are concerned with the religious commitment, beliefs, and values of a therapist rather than a more generic spirituality. However, Zinnbauer, Pargament, and Scott (1999) have shown that spirituality and religion are highly related for religious people. In recent years, religion has been addressed with increasing frequency within the literature on marriage and families (Carlson, Kirkpatrick, Hecker, & Killmer, 2002).

RELIGIOUS COMMITMENT GENERALLY DETERMINES WHETHER RELIGION WILL PLAY ANY ROLE

Religious commitment is the extent to which a person's religious beliefs and values affect his or her everyday life (Call & Heaton, 1997). Worthington (1988) has argued that people with high religious commitment—greater than or equal to one standard deviation above the mean—tend to see the world more often in religious terms and thus to hold different values than do people who are less religiously committed. According to Worthington, religious commitment can manifest as positions along three value dimensions. These include value on (a) the authority of scriptures/sacred writings; (b) the authority of ecclesiastical leaders; and (c) identification with a particular religious group, denomination, or religion. Neither religious commitment nor position in the three-dimensional value space determines religious beliefs. A consequence of the centrality of high religious commitment is that therapists with high religious commitment are more likely to integrate religion into their therapy through choice of religiously compatible theories, assess their clients' religiosity, attend to religious verbalizations of clients and follow up on them, choose techniques that have associations or origins in formal religion or ecclesiastical practice, and make recommendations to or guide clients toward religious behavior.

Religious commitment is not what one believes or values, but the degree of impact on and interpenetration of these beliefs and values on everyday life. It is therefore possible for a person to hold religious beliefs and affirm those beliefs strongly, but if the person is not highly religiously committed, then he or she will not allow those religious beliefs to affect his or her daily life. Because counseling is part of daily life we would anticipate that the therapist with moderate or low religious commitment would be unlikely to allow his or her beliefs and values to affect therapy substantially. According to this working definition of religious commitment, people who keep their religious beliefs separate from other aspects of their lives, such as relationships or politics or counseling practice, would be considered lower in religious commitment than those whose religious beliefs influence many areas of their lives, even if low religiously committed people had very religious beliefs and values.

These distinctions between religious commitment, beliefs, and values were examined in a series of analogue studies on response to individual therapy (McCullough & Worthington, 1995; McCullough, Worthington, Maxie,

& Rachal, 1997; Morrow, Worthington, & McCullough, 1993). In videotapes of a therapy role-play, a female client expressed a conflict among the following: (a) her desire to have sexual intercourse with a male friend, (b) her religious beliefs, and (c) her parent's wishes. The strengths of these three motivations were portrayed as equal in intensity. Participants watched the videotaped interaction between the therapist and client in which the therapist treated the problem as either a family problem, a religious problem, or a problem of self-control. Participants' religious beliefs (as measured by the Shepherd Scale, a measure of conservative Christian beliefs, or Glock and Stark's Religious Inventory) did not predict response to the therapist. Instead, the religious commitment of the participants predicted response to the therapist's actualized case conceptualization. The more highly religiously committed participants strongly preferred therapists who treated the religion of the client seriously. Religious beliefs of the participants did not predict reaction to the therapist. Worthington (1988) had predicted that religious commitment was a key variable in determining both therapist and client behavior. As hypothesized, in these three studies, religious commitment was a better predictor of clients' response to therapist conceptualization than were particular religious beliefs.

There are many reasons that a therapist might not discuss religious issues in therapy unless the client raises the issue. Among those are low or moderate religious commitment of the therapist. But even if the therapist is highly religiously committed, he or she might avoid discussing religion because therapeutic values or theory might suggest that the therapist should not initiate discussion of value-oriented topics (for instance, psychoanalytically informed approaches). Furthermore, therapeutic settings, such as employment at an agency whose policy does not encourage therapists to initiate religious exploration, can inhibit therapists from initiating religious discussions. Finally, surveys suggest that often clients attending counseling in secular agencies are intimidated from initiating religious discussions. They might believe that secular therapists or therapists in secular agencies are opposed to religion, that such discussions are prohibited by separation of church and state, or that the therapist will dismiss or deflect such discussions. If therapists believe that clients must initiate discussions of religion before it is acceptable to address religious issues, then therapists might engage in infrequent discussions of religion.

Religious Beliefs

Although in many situations religious commitment might be a better predictor of the admission of religion into therapy, the specific religious beliefs and values of the therapist can influence the direction of therapy and the interaction between therapist and clients around religion (and sometimes other issues). Denominations have strong opinions about a variety of issues that affect couple counseling. For instance, religious beliefs might affect a therapist's personal opinions on issues such as gay marriage, cohabitation, abortion, artificial insemination, child rearing practices, and divorce. The therapist's religious beliefs will affect how he or she counsels couples dealing with these specific issues, especially if the therapist is highly religiously committed.

THERAPISTS' PERSONAL RELIGION-RELATED DISPOSITIONS AFFECT MARRIAGE COUNSELING

Virtue Orientation

A therapist's religious commitment and beliefs are interdependent with his or her personal dispositions. It is impossible to determine which aspects are most causal in the relationship among these variables. For example, people vary in their orientation toward virtue (Worthington & Berry, 2005). People with a strong orientation toward virtue are concerned about behaving virtuously and promoting it in others. They embrace virtuous actions, beliefs, and expressions of virtuous emotions such as gratitude. They eschew hatred, arrogance, prejudice, and other vices. Worthington and Berry (2005) identified two types of virtue. Conscientiousness-based virtues include truth, justice, responsibility, accountability, honesty, and self-control. Warmth-based virtues include love, forgiveness, empathy, sympathy, compassion, and mercy. People who are oriented toward virtue usually express a distinct preference for either conscientiousness-based virtues or warmth-based virtues. They usually consider both sets of qualities to be virtuous, but one set occupies the thought and energy of the person more than the other set does.

Virtue orientation is related to religious commitment and beliefs. People who have a dispositional orientation toward justice, self-control, and other conscientiousness-based virtues will likely choose religious denominations and personal religious beliefs that emphasize such virtues. Similarly, people who value the warmth-based virtues will likely choose religious denominations and personal religious beliefs that emphasize those warmth-based virtues. On the other hand, religious institutions can affect the virtue orientation of their members. Religious communities extol the virtues consistent with their beliefs and values, and they encourage people to embrace community-consistent virtues in their private life. Thus, the causal influence is hypothesized to be bi-directional.

In most marital therapy, the therapist gives little conscious attention to the virtues he or she most strongly advocates. Nevertheless, therapists' personal sense of virtue will often shape some of their therapeutic behaviors. Therapists who are oriented toward the conscientiousness-based virtues will likely push couples toward demonstrating truth, responsibility, honesty, and self-control. Therapists who are oriented toward warmth-based virtues will push their clients to manifest forgiveness, compassion, mercy, and sympathy.

Religious traditions place different values on forgiveness, mercy, and grace as opposed to justice. Depending on the relative emphasis on each of these polarities, the marital therapist might seek different solutions for marital conflict. The therapist who comes from a faith tradition that emphasizes forgiveness, grace, and mercy will support reconciliation, forgiveness, and tolerance between the partners. The therapist who values forgiveness might be less tolerant of divorce and more highly motivated to promote healing and reconciliation within the relationship. The therapist who comes from a faith tradition that highly values justice might emphasize truth, fairness, responsibility, and accountability. This therapist might employ interventions that promoted truth and fairness. The therapist who values justice might be more supportive of divorce in marriages that seem inequitable. That therapist might emphasize individual truths and if those truths disagree, then see the marriage as involving irreconcilable differences, making divorce a healthy option. Consciousness-based virtues do not determine a predilection toward divorce; nor do warmth-based virtues predetermine marital stability. A therapist who emphasizes keeping rules (such as promising to stay together until death) might encourage the couple to stay together when a therapist who emphasizes forgiveness of mistakes (such as broken marriages) might be more tolerant of divorce. Individual applications of theological beliefs might vary from therapist to therapist. Regardless, the attraction to virtues and religion interpenetrate each other.

Therapists' View of Marriage

The therapist's view of marriage also affects how marital therapy is conducted. Religions usually highly value marriage and commitment to the marriage vows. To the extent that the therapist belongs to a faith community that emphasizes the importance of marriage and marital longevity, the therapist is likely to strive toward preserving marriages and making them better. To the extent that the therapist belongs to a faith community that emphasizes the importance of personal and marital happiness or protection from harm, the therapist will likely be more accepting of divorce, especially if the marriage seems to be causing pain.

Religious traditions can look at marital social values differently. Some religions view marriage as a contract. Each partner makes certain agreements and has an individual responsibility to adhere to those agreements, implicit or explicit. Similar to a business contract, if the agreements are broken, the relationship can be terminated. On the other hand, some religious communities view marriage more as a covenant, in which each partner promises to be committed regardless of the other partner's behavior. A covenantal agreement promotes devotion between partners. Thus, partners *expect* to stay together. Those denominations suggest that marriage is an agreement for life. Therapists who hold a covenantal view of marriage are likely to try to preserve that relationship in their married clients.

Marital commitment is also understood differently by different therapists. Marital commitment has historically been seen as a statement of intention to remain faithful for life. Recent views of commitment, however, have focused more on the exclusivity of romantic relationships. This modern view of marital commitment does not imply a lifelong bond, but rather leads to serial monogamy. A person is committed to a relationship as long as the love endures. Therapists who have a traditional view of commitment will likely work harder to help couples preserve their marriage and will be more negatively affected if their clients divorce.

RELIGION AFFECTS THE WAY THERAPISTS CONDUCT COUPLE THERAPY

The Stance of the Therapist Toward Integration

The therapists' religious beliefs arise from their theology or life spent in a religious community. These can affect the stance of the therapist toward integrating psychology and theology. In a survey of 1,200 randomly selected members of the American Association for Marriage and Family Therapy (AAMFT), 62% of the therapists reported themselves to be religious (Carlson et al., 2002). However, about half of those did not identify with organized religious groups. Among the therapists who considered themselves to be religious, there were substantial differences in their method of integration of theology and psychology. Therapists from denominations that are more theologically conservative or fundamentalist tend to rely on their sacred scriptures and their church ecclesial practices to inform people about how to cope with psychological problems. Therapists from denominations that are more oriented toward social action tend to rely more strictly on psychological approaches. Some denominations place a high value on the way society and theology interact with each other. Those denominations are likely to promote more integration of one's faith beliefs and practices into one's therapy.

One's theology and faith practices are not always constant. Each can change over time. Theology, of course, is modified continually, and faith practices can also change. Let us take as an example the fundamentalist Christian movement. Historically, Christian fundamentalists embraced the idea that people were not to be of this world. That idea led fundamentalists to separate from the world and have their own schools, social events, and holidays. Within the recent decades, however, the rise of fundamentalist leaders such as Pat Robertson and Jerry Falwell changed fundamentalist Christian groups. They advocated political involvement while maintaining a conservative theological stance. Today, many fundamentalists are socially and politically active. This change in the understanding of Christian fundamentalism has affected the counseling conducted by fundamentalist therapists. No longer do all fundamentalists repudiate secular counseling theories and techniques. Many fundamentalist therapists do mostly secular counseling and integrate ecclesiastical practices into these secular counseling approaches.

The Therapist's Religion Affects Choice of Counseling Theory

There is no direct correlation between one's theology and choice of counseling theory. Data do not exist regarding the relationship between the two. So, knowing that we are over-generalizing, we propose hypotheses that might account for some variance in this relationship.

In individual psychotherapy, the Evangelical Christian tradition has tended to embrace cognitive therapies more than other more experiential types of therapy (see McCullough, 1999). Both traditions share an emphasis on making a profession of beliefs and the impact of that profession on one's daily decisions. However, many theologically conservative therapists also embrace psychoanalytic formulations. Perhaps this association occurs because the two systems share an emphasis on the internality of beliefs and conscience. Calvinist theology (i.e., Jesus is Lord of the conscience) and Southern Baptist theological distinctives (i.e., sole accountability and priesthood of the believer) emphasize the integrity of conscience of the Christian believer.

In couple therapy, the effect of religion on choice of theory is even less predictable than in individual psychotherapy. Family systems theories dominated during the 1970s in most couple therapy situations. Many religious therapists were drawn to family therapy because of religion's and family therapy's shared value on the family. However, in the 1990s, solution-focused therapy, integrated behavior therapy, emotion-focused therapy, and insight-oriented couple therapy became prominent. With the exception of solution-focused therapy, these approaches became empirically supported theories of couple therapy (Baucom, Shoham, Mueser, Daiuto, & Stickle, 1998). Religious therapists have followed this trend and have relied on theories that have been proven to work, rather than simply adopting approaches that are consistent with their theology. Most religious couple therapists tend to modify secular therapy into a faith-tailored brand of the secular therapy. This is not to say, however, that religious beliefs do not have any effect on choice of therapy.

Many religions have recently become more emotionally expressive in worship and individual spiritual practice. Reasons include, in traditional Christendom, a post-modern rejection of rationality and, in the Southern hemisphere, an integration of Christianity and Islam with emotionally expressive folk religious traditions. We suspect that people from expressive religious traditions will be increasingly drawn to emotion-focused therapy. Second, we suspect that Evangelical Protestants, Baptists, theologically conservative Muslims, and other religions that are belief-focused will be drawn toward cognitive or insight-oriented couple therapies. Third, we suspect that therapists of Roman Catholics and Orthodox faith might be drawn toward insight-oriented approaches due to the emphasis of history in those religions. Furthermore, Roman Catholics have been more comfortable than Protestants with acceptance of evolutionary theory (e.g., see theological works by theologians Teillhard de Chardin and John Haught). This embrace of change, chance, and evolving nature of life might predispose therapists who embrace such faith toward eclecticism.

The Therapist's Religion Affects a Therapist's Stance Toward Empirically Supported Therapies

There are only four empirically supported couple therapies, and none are explicitly faith-based (Baucom et al., 1998). One might wonder why. Many people seek religiously oriented couple therapy. In fact, more people seek explicitly Christian couple therapy than any other type of couple therapy (Wylie, 2000). Nevertheless, no form of Christian couple therapy has met the criteria for an empirically supported treatment (EST). Chambless and Hollon (1998) believe that empirical support should include the following:

1. Comparison with a no-treatment control group, alternative treatment group, or placebo (a) in a randomized control trial, controlled single case experiment, or equivalent time-samples design and (b) in which the EST is statistically significantly superior to no treatment, placebo, or alternative treatments or in which the EST is equivalent to a treatment already established in efficacy, and power is sufficient to detect moderate differences.
2. These studies must have been conducted with (a) a treatment manual or its logical equivalent; (b) a population, treated for specified problems, for whom inclusion criteria have been delineated in a reliable, valid manner; (c) reliable and valid outcome assessment measures, at minimum tapping the problems targeted for change; and (d) appropriate data analysis.
3. For a designation of efficacious, the superiority of the EST must have been shown in at least two independent research settings (sample size of three or more at each site in the case of single case experiments). If there is conflicting evidence, the preponderance of the well-controlled data must support the EST's efficacy.
4. For a designation of possibly efficacious, one study (sample size of three or more in the case of single case experiments) suffices in the absence of conflicting evidence.
5. For a designation of efficacious and specific, the EST must have been shown to be statistically significantly superior to pill or psychological placebo or to an alternative bona fide treatment in at least two independent research settings. If there is conflicting evidence, the preponderance of the well-controlled data must support the EST's efficacy and specificity (Chambless & Hollon, 1998, p. 18).

No religious treatments meet these criteria.

There are several reasons for this lack of empirically supported Christian couple therapies. First, religious therapists and academicians have not published much research on couple therapies. Perhaps faith communities place relatively less value on empirical research, perhaps because revelation is elevated over empiricism in religious epistemology. It also may be that federal agencies have been reluctant to grant research funding to explicitly study religious therapies. Each of these reasons reinforces the other. A lack of smaller studies provides little justification for federal agencies to grant money for larger studies. Unwillingness to grant money for larger studies discourages smaller studies from being done.

A second reason for the lack of empirically supported religious therapies involves the source of demand for the theories. Most secular theories have been articulated by practitioners or academician-clinicians. They tend to articulate a secular approach and then conduct empirical studies that seek to test the efficacy of the approach. In contrast, religious or faith-based approaches to couple therapy have developed as a result of a demand by the religious community for faith-based approaches. Religious therapists responded to the demand, by adapting secular therapeutic theories. This has inhibited the articulation and investigation of religious therapies.

A third reason for the lack of empirically supported religious therapies is that many religious practices are simply adaptations or spin-offs of established secular practices. Practitioners who have been trained in secular approaches have attempted to tailor the secular approaches to Christian audiences. Each practitioner has tailored the approach according to his or her own assumptions and presuppositions. The approach to religious couple therapy, therefore, is extremely eclectic and diverse because of the idiosyncratic tailoring by diverse clinicians.

Fourth, one of the defining issues in Christianity and often in Islam as well has been the role of authority. Roman Catholics and Orthodoxy had a falling out over who or what constituted legitimate authority. Protestants branched off from Roman Catholicism over authority (among other issues). Tension exists through the Muslim world over whether authority for religious and political leadership should be united or separate. Western religion has often been concerned with authority. ESTs are a form of authority. We might suggest tentatively that people of faith traditions that do not value authority, and in fact bristle against worldly authority, would resist the imposition of ESTs into their practice of marital therapy.

The Therapist's Religion Affects Case Conceptualization

Case conceptualization tends to be either propositional or narrative in nature. Case conceptualizations that are largely propositional are founded on well articulated theories that are governed by beliefs about how the clients behave and how they should behave. Narrative approaches seek to discern the story that the partners tell and then construct between the partners a new story that is more likely to promote positive interactions. Those narrative stories tend to be more ad hoc than the more structured propositional case conceptualizations.

Propositional case conceptualization centers around three constructs: diagnostic, clinical, and treatment formulations (Sperry, 2005a, 2005b). Sperry has been articulate in systematizing such conceptualizations and identifying some roles of both spirituality and religion in each formulation (Sperry & Shafranske, 2005). He argues forcefully for congruent and evidence-based conceptualization across the three domains.

Faith commitment can affect the way that problems are conceptualized, diagnosed, and treated by the therapist. For example, it will determine to what degree a problem is seen as a spiritual problem rather than a psychological problem. If a client's affair is seen as a psychological problem, a therapist might focus on addiction or interpersonal work. If, on the other hand, a client's affair is seen as a spiritual problem, the therapist might focus on confession or restoring the client's relationship with God.

The Therapist's Religion Affects Goals of Couple Therapy

The values of the therapist as well as the values of the client interact to result in both a covert goal of couple counseling and a stated goal of couple counseling. Often the stated and the covert goals are the same. However, in many instances, they will differ. For example, a therapist may value the stability or permanence of marriage. The clients might not be committed to such a view of marriage. Thus, to permit a good working relationship, the stated goal of marriage therapy will likely be an agreed-upon goal such as to work to give the marriage the chance to succeed. However, in reality, the therapist might hold a covert goal of preserving the marriage at all costs.

The goal of marriage counseling is also affected by factors such as the view of marriage held by the therapist and client. This view of marriage may depend on religious traditions. For example, Islamic tradition permits up to four wives for a single husband. The goals of therapy in a household with one husband and four wives are clearly different than a household with one husband and one wife.

Another factor that affects the goal of couple therapy is the definition of a good marriage. Some religious traditions emphasize hierarchical marriages, whereas others emphasize egalitarian marriages. Again, the faith commitments of the therapist and client might lead to a different view of a "good" marriage.

The Therapist's Religion Affects Treatment Planning

Treatment planning differs widely across types of therapists and therapies (see Sperry, 2005b). Some therapists prefer to use theory-based assessments at the outset of therapy. They will formulate a treatment plan based upon a systematic assessment. Assessment will preferably be a multi-model assessment involving inventories, observation, interviews, and perhaps even structured behavioral tasks. Other therapists will assess the couple as therapy takes place. They tend to modify their treatment plans as they learn more about the clients. The choice of style of treatment planning is probably heavily influenced by the personality and training of the therapist, but it can also be affected by the therapist's religious beliefs.

People who believe in one of the more literal religions might be drawn more toward structured assessment prior to beginning therapy. People who belong to religious traditions in which free worship and momentary guidance by the Divine are valued might be more drawn toward approaches to treatment planning that are open to revision under quick notice.

In treatment planning, therapists must decide how much of their faith to introduce into therapy, under which conditions, and at which times (Carlson et al., 2002). Some therapists are less inclined to modify their approach; others are more flexible. For example, some therapists behave essentially the same regardless of the client's commitment to religion. Therapists might adhere to a secular approach regardless of the faith commitments of the clients, or they might adhere to a faith-based approach even when clients are not of that faith persuasion.

CLIENT FACTORS INTERACT WITH THE THERAPIST'S RELIGION

Religious Techniques Are More Effective With Religious Clients

The therapist's religion is also likely to affect the techniques used in the therapy. Initial research on religious techniques in individual therapy indicates that for those clients with greater religious commitments, therapy accommodating religious beliefs and practices is more effective (McCullough, 1999; Wade, Worthington, & Vogel, in press). For example, in a study of over 200 clients and 50 therapists in primarily Christian therapy, Wade et al. (in press) found an interaction effect between the client's religious commitment and the use of religious techniques. When the client was high in religious commitment, the therapist's use of religious techniques resulted in greater therapeutic alliance and more change in the presenting problem than when the religious techniques were not used. Furthermore, they found that clients working with highly religious therapists were more likely to report receiving religious interventions. Therapists who are comfortable with and use religious interventions are often themselves religious. Most academic programs do not include training on religious diversity. Therapists without a personal religious background are often unprepared to intervene with highly religious clients. This is unfortunate given the growing data that suggest that religious clients do better in therapy when they receive interventions aligned with their religious beliefs and practices (see Wade et al., in press).

Religious Values of Therapists Interact With Those of Clients

Both therapists and clients who are highly religious evaluate social interactions according to their religious values. Worthington (1988) has suggested an interpersonal theory describing the role religious values play in counseling, especially for clients and therapists with high religious commitment. He suggested that people have a zone of toleration for interacting and working with others who have different values on the three religious dimensions (i.e., authority of sacred writing, authority of leaders, and identification as a religious person). People's religious values can be characterized from high to low on each dimension, creating a three-dimensional space within which each person's values are located. Thus people can have high or low toleration for interacting and working with people who have different values.

A few therapists have a zone of toleration that is narrowly centered on their own values. They tolerate few differences with others. Most therapists—by selection and by training—have a wide zone of toleration. Wide zones of toleration are necessary if therapists are to (a) thrive professionally given the wide variety of values they face in general practice and (b) conform to ethical guidelines of accrediting agencies and state licensing boards. Most therapists have some limits to their tolerance. Often these limitations arise from religious beliefs and values.

Worthington (1988) suggested that, if the values of the therapist and client are widely discrepant, the relationship will be impaired. When the therapist detects people to fall outside of the therapist's zone of toleration, then the therapist either will (a) not help the person effectively or (b) refer the person to someone who is more value congruent. If the client's values fall inside the therapist's zone of toleration, religious differences in belief will affect therapy.

In secular therapy, it can be easier to counsel someone with different religious beliefs. Neither therapist nor client is sensitized to religion. Neither evaluates therapy through a grid of religious values. In fact, Beutler (1979) and colleagues (Beutler & Bergan, 1991) have shown that non- or moderately religious clients tend to move their religious values closer to those of the therapist in secular therapy—even though the issue of religion was rarely, if ever, addressed.

So, client-therapist religious-value discrepancy results in termination in religious therapy and value change in secular therapy. Worthington (1991) has argued that religious clients' heightened salience of religious values drives them away from religiously different therapists, but religious differences don't make much difference to secular clients, so their values are changed. To the extent that this theorizing is correct (see Worthington, Kurusu, McCullough, & Sandage, 1996, for empirical support), religious therapists would be more likely to attract clients with a particular religious affiliation. Thus, even before counseling begins, the explicitly religious therapist might have an impact on the types of clients who seek help. This self-selection could have implications for the way therapy is conducted. Knowing that their clients are seeking a specifically religious professional, these counselors may be more open to integrating religious or spiritual interventions into the typical therapy.

Client Religiosity

Clearly, one strong situational cue that affects how therapists address religion is the couple's religious stance (Mahoney et al., 1999). In couple therapy, by virtue of homogony in mate selection (Call & Heaton, 1997), most partners agree on fundamental religious issues and commitment. Sometimes, religious differences exist or conflict and power struggles culminate in religious differences. Occasionally, religious differences are the focus of the conflict.

Conflict

Almost every couple that comes to counseling will be in the midst of conflict. Some couples attend counseling because they have disagreements about intimacy or simply feel that the relationship is too distant. But for most couples, conflict over longstanding issues or acute issues, such as a recently discovered affair, will be the focal point of therapy, at least in the beginning. One of the most frequently observed patterns of conflict in couple behavior is an embedded *power struggle* between partners. Haley (1963) suggests that a power struggle is a disagreement over who has the power to decide an issue. It is not over the content of the issue. Both partners believe that they perceive the truth. They demand vindication from the partner. Often when they come to therapy each will demand vindication of their positions from the therapist. Philosophers (Foucault, 1988) and theologians (Volf, 1996) have argued that there is power in who has the "correct" version of the truth. Perceptions of the truth are used to sustain power (Foucault, 1988). Both clients and therapists use "truth" as a weapon. A therapist's religious convictions about truth can interact with the client's perceptions of truth. Each might believe his or her view of truth is correct. If the therapist believes that he or she has a sense of God's truth, the therapist will attempt to gently, but firmly, lead both partners to agree with the therapist. The therapist's view of truth is used as a cohesive power. Presumably the cohesion is benign and not malevolent, but it is an instrument of power nonetheless.

Volf (1996) has argued that a negotiated truth is necessary to resolve such power struggles. In a negotiated "double vision" of truth, each partner is encouraged to see things from his or her own perspective, then see things from the other person's perspective, and finally bring that perspective back into a modification of one's own perspective. This is a recursive process that eventuates in a negotiated truth that is shared among the participants.

When the therapist has a third version of truth (different from each partner), the negotiation may be even more complex. Couple therapy seeks a way of resolving the issue without resorting to an imposed cohesive power (i.e., "My way of looking at this is God's way, and you both need to come into line with God's way of understanding truth."). By coming to agree on a negotiated truth, partners and therapist together create a version of negotiated truth that can guide the behavior of the couple in their interactions with each other. Couples begin therapy believing that truth is power over the partner. A religious therapist can help them see that there is power in negotiated truth. But if a therapist uses his or her religious beliefs to coerce cooperation, the therapist merely perpetrates the truth-is-power dynamic.

REMAINING QUESTIONS

Should the Therapist Bring Up Religion?

Therapists differ as to whether they believe that religion has a place in therapy at all. Most therapists who adhere to the ethical guidelines of the American Psychological Association or American Association of Marriage and Family Therapy (AAMFT) consider religion important, requiring some assessment (Haug, 1998). In one survey, 68% of surveyed AAMFT members agreed that it is appropriate for a family therapist to ask clients about their spirituality (Carlson et al., 2002). Twenty percent were neutral. Only 13% thought spirituality had no place in therapy. Many therapists believe that, even if religion is deemed to be important to the client, it does not necessarily need to be addressed in therapy *unless* the issue at hand explicitly refers to religion, faith, or differences in religion.

For highly religiously committed therapists, however, religion is the essence of life, and the therapist will be inclined to introduce consideration of religion within therapy. This is typically done by asking clients whether religion plays a part in various issues and accepting the client's answer at face value (Hoogestraat & Trammel, 2003). Almost all therapists would agree that it is unethical to impose a religious framework of counseling when the client does not value religion (Haug, 1998). What constitutes imposing religion, however, can be perceived in many ways. The highly religious therapist might ask about the religious aspect of a marital issue, believing it would not be ethical or moral to withhold even asking a religious question that is potentially important. That action, though, might be perceived by nonreligious or anti-religious therapists as an attempt of the therapist to impose religious beliefs and values on the client.

In religious counseling, therapists often face the opposite problem. The client may be referred to a therapist *because* the therapist is known to be of a particular religion. Such clients often expect religion to be the focal point of therapy. The client might even give the therapist a "theology test." The therapist must respond non-defensively and take the religious client's questions seriously. Clients who believe that they are mismatched with the therapist will often terminate the relationship quickly. Therapists are advised to be honest and straightforward when answering questions of a client instead of treating a client's questioning of the therapist's religious beliefs as a defensive maneuver or interpreting the client's questions as pathology.

For a religious therapist, a related decision is to know when *not* to deal with religion in counseling. Couples can spiritualize issues and use scriptural positions to argue with each other. For example, a Christian man might quote from the New Testament that wives are to be submissive to their husbands (Eph. 5:22) to try to control his wife. Or, a Christian wife might quote the same verse to her husband to try to force the husband to take more responsibility in the relationship. At times, religious beliefs can be used by clients as weapons in a battle for power. The therapist can unwittingly err if such questions arise early in therapy—especially if the issue is contentious and one partner (or both) pushes for an answer to the "theology test" before the therapist understands the partner dynamics and issues. The therapist, regardless of his or her theological beliefs about such Scriptures, must resist empowering one spouse over the other systematically by consistently agreeing with that spouse's interpretations of Scripture. This is usually easier to do if the therapist can tactfully postpone an answer until after assessment.

Can a Religious Therapist Counsel a Person Highly Committed to a Different Religion?

People highly committed to different religious persuasions often share many similarities—e.g., a strong belief in God or that their scriptures are not merely well thought out philosophical statements but are in fact important truths that guide people's lives. However, the therapist should probably not attempt to use specific Scriptures to counsel a person with a completely different religious framework. Clients often do not consider a therapist from a divergent tradition to be qualified to interpret their own Scriptures, so they usually question the therapist's judgment. A therapist can counsel people of different religious persuasions but must be scrupulous about his or her limits. If religion is important to the client, the therapist can ask about the client's religious beliefs and values, but should listen actively rather than try to help clients reframe their theological understanding.

What Is Religious Counseling?

Actually, there is no clear consensus about what religious counseling is. Some people believe that religious counseling is counseling that is done by a believer of a particular faith employing the beliefs and practices of that faith with the client. For other therapists, religious counseling is counseling done by a religious counselor even if the client does not understand that the therapist is religious. The answer probably lies somewhere between these two extremes. Whether the therapist uses religious techniques or addresses religion specifically is thus flexible and depends on the beliefs, values, and desires of the client.

CONCLUSION

A therapist's religion affects the marriage therapist and hence affects marriage counseling in numerous ways, including the therapist's virtue-orientation and understanding of marriage. Generally, religious commitment determines whether religion will play a part in therapy, but it does not determine what parts religion will play. That depends more often on religious beliefs and values. When therapists are highly committed to their religion, their particular religious beliefs and values interact to affect almost every part of counseling. Decisions involve the exclusion or inclusion of religion in therapy. The highly religious therapist, therefore, is advised to make decisions about therapy with couples conscientiously and intentionally. When therapists are moderately or less strongly committed to their religious beliefs and values, the religious issues in therapy either tend to be implicit or are more strongly driven by the client.

Clients who are highly religious may either militantly demand the inclusion of religion in their therapy or be intimidated about bringing up religion even though they may consider it to be integral to their problem. Or they might be conflicted about religion, either because of different beliefs or values or because this is one of many areas of conflict within the relationship. The therapist is advised to discern the couple's issues behind their stance to religion.

Religion can be considered an area of multicultural competency. Almost every therapist will, at times, have to deal with couples of different religious beliefs, values, or commitment than his or her own. To best help clients of all religious backgrounds (specifically those seeking religious counseling), therapists should seek training in religious counseling competence. Training programs should also include more training. Because religion is powerful and can affect most of therapy, therapists are cautioned to be thoughtful about their own religious commitment, beliefs, and values and to anticipate the likely effects of their own religion on their practice. In the present chapter, we have sought to provide a jumping-off point for such an analysis.

REFERENCES

Baucom, D. H., Shoham, V., Mueser, K. T., Daiuto, A. D., & Stickle, T. R. (1998). Empirically supported couple and family interventions for marital distress and adult mental health problems. *Journal of Consulting and Clinical Psychology, 66,* 53–88.

Beutler, L. E. (1979). Values, beliefs, religion and the persuasive influence of psychotherapy. *Psychotherapy, 16,* 432–440.

Beutler, L. E., & Bergan, J. (1991). Value change in counseling and psychotherapy: A search for scientific credibility. *Journal of Counseling Psychology, 38,* 16–24.

Call, V. R., & Heaton, T. B. (1997). Religious influence on marital stability. *Journal for the Scientific Study of Religion, 36,* 382–392.

Carlson, T. D., Kirkpatrick, D., Hecker, L., & Killmer, M. (2002). Religion, spirituality, and marriage and family therapy: A study of family therapists' beliefs about the appropriateness of addressing religious and spiritual issues in therapy. *American Journal of Family Therapy, 30,* 157–171.

Chambless, D. L., & Hollon, S. D. (1998). Defining empirically supported therapies. *Journal of Consulting and Clinical Psychology, 66,* 7–18.

Foucault, M. (1988). In L. D. Kritzman (Ed.), *Politics, philosophy, culture: Interviews and other writings, 1977–1984.* Translated by A. Sheridan. New York: Routledge, Chapman & Hall.

Haley, J. (1963). *Strategies of psychotherapy.* New York: Grune & Stratton.

Haug, I. E. (1998). Including a spiritual dimension in family therapy: Ethical considerations. *Contemporary Family Therapy, 20,* 181–194.

Hill, P. C., & Hall, T. W. (2002). Relational schemas in processing one's image of God and self. *Journal of Psychology and Christianity, 21,* 365–373.

Hoogestraat, T., & Trammel, J. (2003). Spiritual and religious discussions in family therapy: Activities to promote dialogue. *American Journal of Family Therapy, 31,* 413–426.

Mahoney, A., Pargament, K. I., Jewell, T., Swank, A. B., Scott, E., Emery, E., & Rye, M. (1999). Marriage and the spiritual realm: The role of proximal and distal religious constructs in marital functioning. *Journal of Family Psychology, 13,* 321–338.

McCullough, M. E. (1999). Research on religion-accommodative counseling: Review and meta-analysis. *Journal of Counseling Psychology, 46,* 92–98.

McCullough, M. E., & Worthington, E. L., Jr. (1995). College students' perceptions of a psychotherapist's treatment of a religious issue: Partial replication and extension. *Journal of Counseling and Development, 73,* 626–634.

McCullough, M. E., Worthington, E. L., Jr., Maxie, J. L., & Rachal, K. C. (1997). Gender in the context of religious counseling: An example of the interactive framework for gender in counseling. *Journal of Counseling Psychology, 44,* 80–88.

Morrow, D., Worthington, E. L., Jr., & McCullough, M. E., (1993). Observers' perceptions of a counselor's treatment of a religious issue. *Journal of Counseling and Development, 71,* 452–456.

Sperry, L. (2005a). Case conceptualizations: The missing link between theory and practice. *Family Journal: Counseling and Therapy for Couples and Families, 13,* 71–76.

Sperry, L. (2005b). Case conceptualization: A strategy for incorporating individual, couple, and family dynamics in the treatment process. *American Journal of Family Therapy, 33,* 189–194.

Sperry, L., & Shafranske, E. P. (2005). Approaches to spiritually oriented psychotherapy: A comparative analysis. In L. Sperry & E. P. Shafranske (Eds.), *Spiritually oriented psychotherapy* (pp. 333–350). Washington DC: American Psychological Association.

Volf, M. (1996). *Exclusion and embrace: A theological exploration of identity, otherness, and reconciliation.* Nashville, TN: Abingdon Press.

Wade, N. G., Worthington, E. L., Jr., & Vogel, D. L. (in press). Effectiveness of religiously-tailored interventions in Christian therapy. *Psychotherapy Research,* in press.

Worthington, E. L., Jr. (1988). Understanding the values of religious clients: A model and its application to counseling. *Journal of Counseling Psychology, 35,* 166–174.

Worthington, E. L., Jr. (1991). Psychotherapy and religious values: An update. *Journal of Psychology and Christianity, 10,* 211–223.

Worthington, E. L., Jr., & Berry, J. W. (2005). Character development, virtues, and vices. In W. R. Miller & H. D. Delaney (Eds.), *Human nature, motivation, and change: Judeo-Christian perspectives on psychology* (pp. 145–164). Washington, DC: APA Books.

Worthington, E. L., Jr., Kurusu, T., McCullough, M. E., & Sandage, S. J. (1996). Empirical research on religion and psychotherapeutic processes and outcomes: A ten-year review and research prospectus. *Psychological Bulletin, 119,* 448–487.

Wylie, M. S. (2000, January/February). Soul therapy. *Family Therapy Networker, 24,* 26–37, 60–61.

Zinnbauer, B. J., Pargament, K. I., & Scott, A. B. (1999). The emerging meanings of religiousness and spirituality: Problems and prospects. *Journal of Personality, 67,* 889–919.

SECTION II

Religious Context Within Marriage and Family Counseling

Chapters 3 through 11 focus on issues related to marriage and the family from the standpoint of specific religions. Authors of these chapters speak to philosophies and principles embedded in their respective religion that will provide counselors with a deeper conceptualization and understanding of their religious clients. The following issues are addressed as they pertain to each religion: (a) definition of marriage; (b) dating and cohabitation; (c) roles within marriages and families; (d) child bearing, birth control, abortion, teenage pregnancy; (e) finances; (f) dissolving relationships, divorce, annulment; (g) managing family after separation and/or divorce; (h) death and dying; and (i) homosexuality in couples and families.

Readers are encouraged to consider that due to limited space in this book, not all religious perspectives have been included. The choice of particular religious groups presented in this book were made on the prominence of this religion within the United States. In addition, authors of each chapter wrote from their own understanding of their affiliated religious tradition. Thus, it is possible that an author's understanding may differ from that of the reader.

CHAPTER 3

The Practice of Marriage and Family Counseling and Catholicism

JILL D. ONEDERA

"No theological principle … is more characteristic of Catholicism or more central to its identity than the principle of sacramentality" (McBrien, 1994, p. 1196). Through the intervention and power of the Holy Spirit, the Catholic Church recognizes sacraments as unique signs that are meant to build up the kingdom of God (Pennock, 1998). The seven sacraments include Baptism, Confirmation, the Eucharist, Penance, the Anointing of the Sick, Holy Orders, and Matrimony. The sacraments also represent *outward signs* of Christ's presence and God's relationship with his people. Through these *signs*, Christians are able to see God in all things (Groome, 2002). For example, it is through the sacrament of marriage that partners can see an outward sign of God in the behaviors of the other partner. The sacrament of marriage also behooves each spouse to consider how one's own behaviors promote the love of Jesus Christ through interacting with each other. Even still, through the exchange of marriage vows and the process of matrimony, couples celebrate Christ's presence between each other, while also among family and friends at the wedding ceremony.

According to the *Catechism of the Catholic Church* (Catholic Church, 2003), sacraments also are efficacious. That is, Christ Jesus works Himself through the sacraments. For example, in marriage, Christ promises to sustain the couple throughout their life journey and to sanctify their sexual love, and to empower them to be signs of love to each other. Through the sacrament of marriage, the Holy Spirit enters and provides the couple with power to maintain their relationship "till death do them part." Finally, sacraments also hold persons accountable. Through the receiving of a sacrament, persons respond faithfully and work toward carrying out the gifts that God has provided. Consequently, married couples are expected to exercise their virtues given to them by Christ, namely by nurturing their relationship with kindness, faithfulness, humility, love, and a forgiving heart.

Counselors can work better with Catholic couples and families when they consider the basic underpinnings of Catholicism and its sacraments, as well as how this foundation provides guidance for families as they carry out even the most mundane of daily tasks. It is through particular life cycle stages (i.e., marriage, death) that couples and individuals become in touch with the spiritual, namely, how Christ is revealed through such experiences. Pope John Paul II noted that "willed by God in the very act of creation, marriage and the family are interiorly ordained to fulfillment in Christ" (1981, p. 2). Couples and families whom are rooted in their Catholic faith will strive to live their lives through their actions, words, and deeds based within this faith. The purpose of this chapter is to highlight some of these basic truths grounded within Catholic marriages and families and how counselors might best work with such clients.

DEFINITION OF THE MATRIMONIAL COVENANT

In the sacrament of marriage, a baptized man and woman mutually and exclusively give themselves to each other in an act of irrevocable consent. Through their vows, they are joined by Christ in union that will be marked forever by respect, concern, compassion, and commitment (Lawler, Boyle, & May, 1998). Marriage, as described by John Paul II (1997) or the sacrament of creation, can be traced back to a passage found in Genesis: "A man ... cleaves to his wife and they become one flesh." It is through this passage that Catholics believe marriage is reflected as an unbreakable union of two different lives that become "one flesh" (Catholic Church, 2003, no. 1605).

The Catholic Church draws on other passages within the Bible to further explain the meaning of marriage. For example, in Ephesians 5:22–25, it is written:

> Wives, be subject to your husbands as to the Lord. For the husband is the head of the wife as Christ is the head of the Church, his Body, and is himself its Savior. As the Church is subject to Christ, so let wives also be subject in everything to their husbands. Husbands, love your wives, as Christ loved the Church and gave himself up for her ...

Later in Ephesians, "For no man ever hates his own flesh, but nourishes and cherishes it, as Christ does the Church, because we are members of his body" (5:29–30).

Needless to say, it is important for mental health professionals to understand the symbolism between marriage and the relationship between Christ and the Church. The sacrament of marriage is compared to this very special relationship that Christ has with members of his Church. St. Thomas Aquinas suggested that the union of Christ with His Church is signified through marriage (Weisheiple & Larcher, 1980). In other words, a groom's relationship with his bride should emulate the love that Christ has for his Church. As Christ devotes, cherishes, and nourishes the Church, so should husbands and wives do within their marriage (John Paul II, 1997). The Catholic Church does not leave couples to guess how this love should permeate their relationship, however. Through the teachings and *Catechism of the Catholic Church* (Catholic Church, 2003), couples are provided with ample guidance and direction for improving and/or maintaining a healthy marriage. Some of the basic teachings will be addressed in the following subsections. Counselors are behooved to consider such teachings when working with couples who are struggling to maintain love and commitment in their marriage. Couples who are struggling to keep their marriage grounded in the Catholic belief system might struggle with feelings of failure or guilt. Counselors might address such feelings, as well as encourage them to lean on the guidance the Catholic Church provides. In addition, couples should be encouraged to consider and make meaning of Christ's forgiving nature in the context of their marriage for healing and recovery.

THE GOODS AND REQUIREMENTS OF MARRIAGE

"I promise to be always faithful to you, in joy and in sadness, in sickness and in health, and to love you and honor you all the days of my life." It is through a couple's marriage vows that they make a matrimonial consent, proclaiming through words and body their new life in Christ and in the Church (John Paul II, 1997; May, 2000). By the means of marriage as a sacrament, both the man and woman are called to bear witness by acting in ways that portray conjugal love. The *Catechism of the Catholic Church* (Catholic Church, 2003) states:

> Conjugal love involves a totality, in which all the elements of the person enter—appeal of the body and instinct, power of feeling and affectively, aspiration of the spirit and will. It aims at a deeply personal unity, a unity that, beyond union in one flesh, leads to forming one heart and soul; it demands *indissolubility* and *faithfulness* in definite mutual giving; and it is open to *fertility*. In a word it is a question of the normal characteristic of all natural conjugal love, but with a new significance which not only purifies and strengthens them, but raises them to the extent of making them the expression of specifically Christian values. (no. 1643)

The Unity and Indissolubility of Marriage

Marriage is not a human-made relationship, but a covenant "completed by communion in Jesus Christ, given through the sacrament of Matrimony" (Catholic Church, 2003, no. 1644). Furthermore, this relationship is seen as a commitment for life and a moral obligation for two persons to remain together as long as one's partner is alive. As previously mentioned, the relationship between husband and wife should be symbolic of their relationship with Christ (John Paul II, 1997).

The Fidelity of Conjugal Love

Married couples are called to remain faithful to each other, as Christ is faithful to His Church. However, the Catholic Church does not take the position that couples will remain in marital bliss and will feel love throughout their relationship. Its position is quite the contrary; however, the Church believes that God's grace, as well as the Church community, is upon all married couples keeping them sustained and encouraged in all difficult times.

Consequently, infidelity is not an option. The Church teaches that maintaining fidelity, even in tempestuous times, is sustained through a couple's love and friendship. This love and friendship beget self-sacrifice, mutual help, support, and cooperation within the marriage (Lawler et al., 1998). In addition, this marital love and fidelity can be fostered through marital intercourse.

The Openness to Fertility

The Catholic Church teaches that every marital act (intercourse) should be one that is open to new life. However, that is not to say that the function of the marital act of intercourse is only for reproduction. It is the act by which both partners become one loving organism where each is giving oneself freely to the other. It is a freeing act that is open to love and life. Thus, any intentional impediment to procreation during the marital act is considered to be both an antilife as well as an antilove choice (May, 2000). It is within such an act that husband and wife are not giving themselves freely to each other and the sexual union is no longer considered a conjugal act, or one that leads to the forming of both hearts and souls (Catholic Church, 2003, no. 1643).

Marriage Preparation

Couples seeking marriage in the Catholic Church usually are required to participate in Pre-Cana, or a formal marriage preparation process (Drinan, 2003). It is through this preparation process that couples are educated about the goods and requirements of Catholic marriage. This marriage preparation can be in the form of a conference, retreat, or workshop. It is lead by a priest, as well as by other married couples who are living out the sacrament (Pennock, 1998). During the preparation, engaged couples learn about the seriousness of the marriage sacrament, specifically what their new responsibilities will be as they enter this permanent contract with each other. Other issues examined in Pre-Cana are interpersonal in nature, namely, communication skills, the role of faith in the marriage, finances, parenting issues, value and belief systems, and plans for the actual marriage ceremony. Professional counselors who are working with engaged or married couples might talk to them about their experiences and discussions during this process. In addition, counselors might inquire about issues that the couple wished they had more time to discuss during the marriage preparation.

DATING AND COHABITATION

The Catholic Church provides clear guiding principles about dating and cohabitation. It is imperative that professional helpers understand these basic tenets when working with practicing Catholics who are dating and/or cohabitating. Chances are that clients are aware of these principles and either have chosen to disregard them or are struggling with living out their Catholic faith while at the same time behaving in ways that are contrary to it. With such knowledge, professional counselors can help clients make meaning out of their decisions and present situations in the context of what the stances of the Catholic Church are. In no way should helpers condemn divergent behaviors; rather, clients should be heard and allowed to come to peace with the decision that they have made or will make after careful consideration of their Catholic belief system.

The Catholic Church understands that human sexuality is a part of basic human nature. In fact, sexual feelings, thoughts, and desires are considered natural. However, the Church teaches that any type of sexual expression (i.e., intercourse, petting, masturbation) is special and should be a sign of one's commitment to another person (Singer-Towns, Claussen, & vanBrandwijk, 2004). Further, such commitment cannot be assumed in a temporary situation such as dating or engagement.

Chastity, or the "successful integration of sexuality within the person and … the inner unity of man in his bodily and spiritual being" (Catholic Church, 2003, no. 2337) is required of all non-married Catholics. By practicing chastity, persons become apprentices in self-mastery and are neither victims nor slaves to their sexual passions or appetites. The virtue of chastity allows persons to reach inner peace, self-determination, and self-control. Furthermore, a relationship based in chastity allows persons to love freely without selfishness, aggression, or unwarranted expectations (Lawler et al., 1998). The beauty of chastity, as seen in the Catholic Church, is that this virtue allows all persons, married and unmarried, to more fully live out the Christian life, specifically in their interactions with others (Flaman, 1999).

As might be suspected, cohabitation is not supported within the Catholic Church (John Paul II, 1981). More specifically, the Catholic Church's stance is that "human love does not tolerate 'trial marriages'" (Catholic Church, 2003, no. 2391). In fact, some Catholic dioceses have formal policies regarding cohabitating couples who want to be married. For example, one diocesen policy requires cohabitating couples to settle for a more simplistic marriage ceremony. Another policy requires cohabitating couples to split their living arrangements for at least six months prior to the marriage (Schaeffer, 1996).

ROLES WITHIN MARRIAGES AND FAMILIES

Catholic families (and couples) are considered to be members of the "domestic church" (Catholic Church, 2003, no. 2204). It is within this community that members of the domestic family are called to proclaim, serve, and celebrate the Gospel of Life (John Paul II, 1995). Further, all members are responsible in bringing action to the Gospel through his or her individual gifts, charisms, and ministry. Within the family, the love of spouses and the full acceptance of children is one way to celebrate and proclaim the Gospel of Life. Parents also proclaim the Gospel of Life by raising children to honor God, to understand the depths and effects of suffering, and to respect others, specifically those whom are sick and elderly (Catholic Church, 2003, no. 92; Pope Benedict XVI, 2006). Parents are encouraged to enroll children in formal religious education throughout elementary school.

Members of Catholic families are called to initiate themselves within society through the provision of care, support, and help given to other families whether they are Catholic or not. More specifically, family members are responsible for taking care of and supporting the old, the young, the handicapped, the sick, and the poor within society (Catholic Church, 2003, no. 2208). It is the responsibility of parents to teach their children to be socially responsible and alert at early ages. Children are taught to be respectful of the dignity of others and the importance of carrying out relationships with all persons in good will (no. 2213).

Duties of Children

The Catholic Church teaches that children should be held responsible for two basic duties including respect for parents and as adult children, being responsible for parents. Young and adult children should exercise filial piety or respect for their parents. Children are called to express gratitude toward parents for their love, their work, and the freedom they expounded in allowing them to grow. Adult children are called to be responsible in the care of their older parents by providing moral support in times of loneliness, illness, or distress (Catholic Church, 2003, no. 2218). In fact, John Paul II (1995) asserted that all members of the family from birth to death should be cared for. Further, elderly family members should be treated with dignity and be given places within the family in which their wisdom and experiences are held in high regard (no. 94). Biblical support for the Catholic teaching on roles within families can be found in Sirach (3:12–13, 16):

"O son, help your father in his old age, and do not grieve him as long as he lives; even if he is lacking in understanding, show forbearance; in all your strength do not despise him ... Whoever forsakes his father is like a blasphemer, and whoever angers his mother is cursed by the Lord."

Duties of Parents

A primary duty and responsibility of Catholic parents is to educate their children in the faith (Pope John Paul II, 1981). Through their example and evangelizing, parents educate children at a very early age about virtues, responsibility, and ways to live the faith. Marriage and family counselors working with Catholic parents might best understand their goals of their parenting within Catholic parameters through the following three key elements of parental duties (May, 2000). First, parents are called to provide their children with a sense of values. Children should be able to distinguish between the desires of the heart and material and instinctual desires. Secondly, children should be initiated into the faith in such a way that they develop personal and interpersonal dispositions reflective of the gospel. Finally, parents are obliged to respect their children as God's children. Part of this respect is expressed in their devotion in providing children with their spiritual and physical needs (Catholic Church, 2003, no. 2228).

CHILD BEARING, BIRTH CONTROL, ABORTION, TEENAGE PREGNANCY

Child Bearing

The purpose of marriage is twofold. First, partners are bonded together through a communion of life where there is mutual self-giving and sacrifice (Catholic Church, 2003, no. 1644). The second purpose of marriage is procreation, namely for partners to be open to new life (Catholic Church, 2003, no. 1652; May, 2000). Children are not seen as products of a couple, rather children are "begotten" (May, 2000; Vatican Council II, 1965). That is, husbands and wives do not "make" a baby, as a baby is not a considered to be a product that is made. Rather, children are begotten through a giving act of conjugal love where both partners also are open to the gift of human life. The marital act is then one of "procreation" rather than reproduction. In cases where partners are not blessed with children, they may be called to express a spiritual fatherhood or motherhood through acts of hospitality, charity, and sacrifice (Catholic Church, 2003, no. 1654; May, 2000).

Professional counselors might apply the above information when working with a couple who is struggling with fertility and is feeling that their infertility is somehow *caused* by their previous use of contraception. Counselors should note that there is no such correlation mentioned anywhere in the teaching of the Catholic Church. Guiding couples to come to terms with this misconception might be helpful in their struggle. Furthermore, partners whom are not blessed with children might be reminded of where their place is in God's plan, specifically in terms of their dedication to hospitality, charity, and sacrifice.

Birth Control

The Catholic faith teaches that every marital act must remain true to its purposes; namely, the unitive and procreative significances (Pope Paul VI, 1978). Married partners should "cooperate with the love of God the Creator" by being open to the transmission of human life (Catholic Church, 2003, no. 2367). Contraception is considered antilife, antilove, and as directly violating the very nature of marriage (John Paul II, 1981). It supposes antilife because it impedes the beginning of new human life. Through the use of contraception, the possibility of new human life is treated as something to be opposed and rid of (Lawler et al., 1998). The use of contraception also is considered an act of antilove because it prevents full mutual self-giving that is a cornerstone in the marital act (John Paul II, 1997).

Professional counselors should understand that the Church supports couples who have "reasonable grounds for spacing births" (Paul VI, 1978). For example, such reasonable grounds may include physical or psychological conditions of each partner or from other external circumstances. Upon these grounds the Church teaches that married people may take advantage of the reproductive system's natural cycle. It is through this natural family planning (NFP) that couples can control births without committing sins against moral principles. Marriage and family counselors might consider maintaining a list of resources in the community that provide information on NFP for interested couples.

Counselors unfamiliar with the differences between NFP and contraceptives might heed John Paul II's (1997) distinction of the two, specifically regarding intent and choice. The intent of contraception is to impede new human life, a basic contradiction to Catholic teaching. Natural family planning, on the other hand, includes both a choice and intent as well. In this case, the intent is the same: to not conceive. However, the choice is to refrain from the marital act. The object chosen is chastity. It is through this virtue of chastity or choice of self-discipline that partners are given the opportunity to grow together spiritually (Paul VI, 1978).

Marriage and family counselors working with Catholic families should resist suggesting contraception as a "healthy" means of family planning or safeguard to sexual activity. Instead, counselors might first ask the family or clients what their personal position on birth control is before engaging in any long-term discussion on the topic.

Abortion

The Catholic Church teaches that abortion or an act that is intended as an end or as a means to an end of life is "gravely contrary to the moral law" (Catholic Church, 2003, no. 2271). More specifically, an embryo "must be defended in its integrity, cared for, and healed like every other human being" (no. 2323). Any direct, willful act of ending this life is contrary to moral law (John Paul II, 1995). In addition, a prenatal diagnosis that does not fall in the parameters of "normal" physical well-being and development does not in any way legitimize infanticide.

The Church relies on several biblical scriptures to support its stance. For example, in Genesis, it is written, "From man in regard to his fellow man I will demand an accounting for human life" (9:5). Jeremiah writes, "Before I formed you in the womb I knew you, and before you were born I consecrated you" (1:5). Further, "My frame was not hidden from you, when I was being made in secret, intricately wrought in the depths of the earth" (Ps. 139:15). Finally, "You shall not kill" (Ex. 20:13; Dt 5:17).

Many Catholics who have had abortions are dealing with the ramifications of their choice by experiencing guilt, remorse, and alienation from other family members. Professional counselors can best understand and empathize with such a range of feelings by considering the teachings of the Catholic Church. Through this understanding, better rapport can be developed along with increased possibilities of helping such persons deal with after-emotions of the abortion. Counselors are behooved to take a nonjudgmental stance. The Church teaches that Christ is a forgiving Christ, and anyone remorseful can be forgiven. Either consulting or providing a referral to a priest also might be a helpful intervention.

Teenage Pregnancy

In the case of teenage pregnancy, the Catholic teaching regarding birth control and abortion are the same. Marriage and family counselors should resist suggesting abortion as an option to teenage pregnancy unless they know the family's position is contrary to that of the Church. Similarly, counselors should be cautious in suggesting to sexually active teenagers that they use contraception. The basic stance on sex education for teenagers is abstinence and chastity (Flaman, 1999). Understanding the parents' position on this issue is absolutely essential.

FINANCES

Discussion of finances within the Catholic Church might best be explained through the Church's six precepts or guidelines regarding how persons can grow in love of their neighbor and of God through prayer and moral effort. In regards to finances or giving, one of the precepts states that "The faithful are obliged to assist with the material needs of the Church, especially according to his own ability" (Catholic Church, 2003, no. 2043). The Catholic *Code of Canon Law* states that "The Christian faithful are obliged to assist with the needs of the Church so that the Church has what is necessary for divine worship for apostolic works and works of charity end for the decent sustenance of ministers" (Catholic Church and Canon Law Society of America, 1983, no. 222). The Church does not mandate a particular percentage of income or other amount; rather, Catholics are called to make a financial decision for the Lord first while keeping the needs and wants of oneself and one's family second. It is through this sacrificial nature and need for trust in the Lord's providential support during times of tithing that brings Catholics closer to God and allows them to really practice their faith.

Marriage and family counselors working with Catholic persons in financial need should be considerate of particular perspectives on the issue. First, Catholics can use this financial strain and burden as a time to trust in the Lord and actually practice their faith. Instead of focusing on desperation, counselors might best help families by encouraging them to focus on the spiritual nature of the situation. Also, whether a family or couple is in dire financial situations, they still may give to the church. This is something that should be respected by all counselors. Persons should not be encouraged to cut this part of their giving in order to help the financial situation. Finally, counselors might work with couples or families to make meaning out of financially difficult times. Such meaning can be placed in the context of their faith and hope for God's mercy.

DISSOLVING RELATIONSHIPS, DIVORCE, ANNULMENT

Marriages in the Catholic Church are seen as a permanent communion between two persons. The Church expects spouses who come together in one flesh through the power and grace of God to rely on the Holy Spirit for strength and guidance throughout their marriage. Marriage vows should and must be taken seriously. Further, Keane (1977) suggested that "marital indissolubility is the goal or norm under which the Catholic approach to marriage must operate" (p. 141) except by the death of one spouse.

Since many Catholic marriages reach points of separation, divorce, and remarriage, it is important to address how these processes are seen through the lens of the Catholic Church. In the case of marital separation, the *Catechism of the Catholic Church* (Catholic Church, 2003, no. 1649) states that there may be "some situations in which living together becomes impossible for a variety of reasons." In such extraordinary cases, physical separations are allowed, however the couple still is considered married and is not allowed to contract a new union with another partner. The Church emphasizes the importance of intervention by the Christian community. Members of the community are called to help couples who are struggling to reconcile and live according to their indissoluble marriage bond.

Divorce is not an option that is favored or supported within the Catholic Church. It is considered immoral and gravely sinful for several reasons. It is immoral because it is seen as being harmful to the family and to society (Catholic Church, 2003, no. 2385). Divorce is considered gravely offensive because it goes against the natural law, namely, the sacramentality of marriage (no. 2384). Hence, remarriage or the contracting of a new civil union also adds to the seriousness of the split, especially if the first union or marriage was recognized as valid. The Church relies on Jesus' words noted in scripture to sustain its view: "Whoever divorces his wife and marries another, commits adultery against her; and if she divorces her husband and marries another, she commits adultery" (Mark 10:11-12). Remarried couples in such situations are living in direct conflict with God's law (Catholic Church, 2003, no. 1650). Although they are not separated from the Church, couples in such situations cannot receive Eucharistic communion, nor take part in any ecclesial activities.

It should be noted that the Catholic Church is sensitive to spouses who have sincerely tried to work through their marriage. It recognizes that in many cases, one spouse may be the victim of unjust abandonment and the perpetrations of the other spouse. It is in such cases where the grave faults of one spouse "destroys a canonically valid marriage" (Catholic Church, 2003, no. 2386). Of course, spouses are encouraged to exert conscious effort in working at the marriage, such as consultation with church elders and individual and marital counseling.

As readers might suspect, marriage and family counselors should be sensitive to the Catholic Church's position on the seriousness of marriage promises. Practicing Catholics may make desperate measures to keep their marriage intact. Counselors should help couples clarify what a successful marriage would mean to them. Outlining and having descriptive goals can help counselors and couples work together more efficiently. Hopeful attitudes on the part of counselors should match the attitudes of the couple, unless there is reason for concern (i.e., violence, unrepented pattern of affairs). Counselors might ask couples if they have consulted with their parish priest for additional guidance and prayer.

Annulment

The Catholic Church takes the position that there is no authority that can dissolve a marriage (Catholic Church, 2003, no. 1640). However, the Church does not ignore the fact that some marriages fail. The annulment process is the Catholic Church's official declaration that what seemed to be a valid Christian marriage was in fact not one at all (Anderson, 1997; Pennock, 1998).

The process is meant to establish reasons the marriage broke down and whether critical elements were absent from the start. An annulled marriage means that the "failed" marriage was never a Christian marriage to begin with. Consequently, if the marriage can be shown to be invalid, the individuals are allowed to enter into a true marriage in the future.

In order for a marriage to be considered annulled, one or both of the partners must submit his or her situation to the diocesan marriage tribunal or court for judgment and examination regarding the nullity of the marriage (Catholic Church, 2003, no. 1629; Pennock, 1998). The process can be a lengthy and exasperating one but is meant to help divorced Catholics come to a deeper understanding of what failed in their previous marriages. In addition, it provides a medium from which persons can reflect on themselves in potential future marriages. The annulment process is one that requires persons to take a psychological, emotional, and spiritual reflection of their lives (Califano, 2004). It can be healing, as well as reconciling (Paquette, 2002). Marriage and family counselors who have clients going through annulments are encouraged to invite clients to talk about this process. Counseling can provide a medium from which persons can further explore themselves in the context of their past marriage versus the context of a future one.

MANAGING FAMILY AFTER SEPARATION AND/OR DIVORCE

The Catholic Church encourages all divorced individuals to remain close to the Church. One way of beginning this new relationship with the church is through the Sacrament of Reconciliation (Catholic Church, 2003, no. 1650). Through this sacrament, persons who have been divorced have the opportunity to reconcile their faith to God with genuine sorrow for any fault involved in the divorce. Furthermore, confession of sins associated with the divorce allows persons to work at expanding their consciences, fight against any evil tendencies in the future, and healing (no. 1458).

Above all, the Catholic Church does not ignore or scorn persons who have divorced. They are welcome to return to the church by attending daily or weekly services and by the Sacrament of Reconciliation. In fact, parents who are divorced are strongly encouraged to continue in their faith so as to model a Christian lifestyle for their children. Marriage and family counselors can incorporate the above mentioned philosophy of Catholicism when working with divorced persons or their families. They can provide a medium from which single or divorced parents can talk about how they can live up to their Catholic belief system. When working with blended Catholic families, counselors can rely on the coping strategies and strengths that the family has developed through wrestling with the crisis associated with the break-up of their families (Wood, 2001). Furthermore, counselors are encouraged to help families find strength and support with their church community (Hornik, 2001).

DEATH AND DYING

Death

Catholics believe that when someone dies, he or she will face God's grace or the rejection of it (Catholic Church, 2003, no. 1021). There also are three possible places persons who have died will enter: heaven, purgatory, and hell. The receiving of God's grace can come immediately or through purification. Living a life faithful to God's will, remaining hopeful and believing, and loving unconditionally are possible grounds in which to die in God's grace while moving immediately to heaven (Groome, 2002). On the other hand, the "imperfectly purified" are still assured of eternal salvation, but may undergo purification to achieve a state of holiness required to enter heaven (Catholic Church, 2003, no. 1030).

Hell is a different story. The Church maintains its beliefs based in scripture. John 3:14-15 states: "He who does not love remains in death. Anyone who hates his brother is a murderer, and you know that no murderer has eternal life abiding in him." God also expects persons to live a life that is attentive to the needs of the poor, as well as the needs of younger people (Matt. 25:31–46). Finally, someone who has willfully turned himself or herself from God and has committed a grave sin without repenting and accepting God's love may find themselves as the door of hell. It should be noted that the underlying desire of the Catholic Church is for all persons to receive God's grace and blessings in heaven (2 Pet. 3:9). It is for this reason that marriage and family counselors working with victims of someone who has died from suicide or someone who has died after living a criminal life should still help clients keep this message of hope and forgiveness alive in their thoughts.

Dying

In Pope John Paul II's *Evangelium Vitae,* he sums up the Catholic perspective on dying: "Absolute respect for every innocent human life also requires the *exercise of conscientious objection* in relation to procured abortion or euthanasia" (1995, p. 141). Further, Pope John Paul II explains that any neglect of an elderly person is inexcusable. Even so, as caretakers, friends, or family members of an ailing person, Catholics are expected to adopt the viewpoint that the person under care is not a victim or the source of another job to do. Above all, elderly or sickly persons are to be respected for their wisdom, as well as their roles in witnessing love and hope.

Marriage and family counselors may work with persons who are juggling their careers and the caretaking responsibilities of a parent or elderly family member. They may feel stressed and even guilty because they do not "feel like" caring for an older family member. Counselors should keep in mind that encouraging persons to cut down on the number and time of their responsibilities may be taken offensively or with guilty reservation. Instead counselors can help Catholics who are in such predicaments find some peace in their activities, time for prayer, and ways to mentally and emotionally challenge their stress. Clients also might benefit from simple validations of their feelings.

Euthanasia

Actions of good or evil nature are conceptualized within the Catholic Church by considering the will and the methods used (John Paul II, 1997). In the case of euthanasia, both passive and active, the will (or intention) always is to terminate life. In passive euthanasia, the method is the withholding or withdrawing (also known as omission) treatments that could preserve life. The intent is to terminate one's life. The will in active euthanasia also is to terminate life; however, the method used to do so is different. In this case, termination of life is conducted through commission, or taking a definite action such as administration of a legal injection (Munson, 1996). Both actions are based on the judgment of someone (either the patient or someone else) that the person to be killed is either too burdensome, useless, or "better off dead than alive" (May, 2000, p. 240). Further, both passive and active euthanasia are morally wrong in the eyes of the Catholic Church.

May (2000) refers to an exception to euthanasia that he labels "benemortasia." Benemortasia refers to the act of refraining from unnecessary treatment modalities on a dying person, specifically if such treatments are ineffective. The intent of benemortasia is respect for one's human life in the present condition (as debilitating as it is) as something good. The method used would be the withdrawing or withholding of treatments. However, such action would be taken *only* if the person was not benefiting from treatment and if the current treatment actually was more burdensome than relieving or helping.

Suicide

Suicide is seen as an evil choice; one that is in direct opposition to God's sovereignty and grace over life and death (Ws. 16:13; Tb. 13:2). Catholics believe that it is not the right of individuals to choose to dispose of their lives. Not only is this an antilove choice for self, it is one against one's family and friends and against God. There are unique exceptions. The Catholic Church does consider possible involuntary situations or settings in which one's responsibility in choosing to commit suicide is slightly diminished (Catholic Church, 2003, no. 2282). For example, in cases where the person was afflicted with psychological disturbances, anguish, or fear of suffering, hardship, or torture, suicide may have been seen as the only reasonable choice.

As in all cases, marriage and family counselors will benefit from assessing if their Catholic clients adhere to the previously mentioned Catholic teachings. Only after doing so will counselors have clearer perspectives on where to proceed. When clients are presenting issues related to any of the above circumstances, consultation with a priest or deacon might provide better understanding on the part of the counselors, as well as a deeper understanding for the issues on the part of the clients. Situations should be treated as unique. For example, in the case of suicide, no one will know what that victim's last prayers or confessions were. Perhaps he or she asked God for forgiveness minutes before death. In such a case, Catholics might wonder if God extended his grace to this person for eternal life. Again, counselors might encourage clients to find hope or peace in any situation related to death.

HOMOSEXUALITY IN COUPLES AND FAMILIES

There are two basic stances that the Catholic Church takes that might best describe its position on homosexuality. First, every person is believed to have a fundamental identity and one that is explicitly intertwined with God and eternal life (Lawler et al., 1998). Furthermore, the terms or descriptions related to persons being either heterosexual or homosexual are not words you will find being used in the Catholic Church. (For the sake of clarity, however, such words will be used in this section.) Secondly, the Catholic Church does not judge persons on their sexual orientation; rather, it is the sexual acts that are judged as immoral or moral. That is, the stance in the Church is that homosexual inclinations may not be a matter of choice.

The Catholic Church does assert that homosexual acts are gravely wrong. This position is based in scripture throughout the Bible. The *Catechism of the Catholic Church* (Catholic Church, 2003, no. 2357) states that homosexual acts are "contrary to the natural law." In addition they "close the sexual act to the gift of life," which is a fundamental principle within Catholic teachings on marriage and family. Furthermore, marriage in the Catholic Church is only possible with a woman and a man. And as previously mentioned, it is only within marriage that any kind of genital sexual expression is normalized (Lawler et al., 1998).

Similar to the Church's acceptance and welcoming of divorced persons into the Church, persons who have homosexual inclinations also are welcome. In fact the Church recognizes that because of such tendencies, such persons may be faced with unique trials, struggles, and crosses to bear (Catholic Church, 2003, no. 2358). Consequently, persons with homosexual inclinations are called to live a life of chastity. It is through this chastity or self-master that individuals have the opportunity to become closer to God and to experience inner freedom (no. 2359). Finally, the Catholic Church holds everyone else to accept persons with "homosexual tendencies" respectfully, in compassion, and with sensitivity. Furthermore, discrimination of any kind is not acceptable.

Marriage and family counselors working with persons who have homosexual tendencies and are Catholics have a twofold task. First, counselors should assess whether the client's sexuality is an aspect of the presenting problem. Secondly, such clients should be asked if they are trying to follow the Catholic Church's teachings on homosexual behavior. Only when this is clear should counselors proceed.

For clients who have homosexual ideations and tendencies and are trying their best to follow the Catholic Church, counselors may need to first debunk any myths about the Catholic Church's stance on homosexuality before proceeding. That is, the Church does not teach that homosexual persons are evil and are doomed to hell. Rather, the Church's position is focused on the homosexual actions. Marriage and family counselors working with Catholics involved in homosexual lifestyles might do best by listening and helping clients weigh their beliefs in Catholic teaching with their desire to live this lifestyle. Helping clients build a support system of other nonjudgmental Catholics also might help them work through any issues they are struggling with.

CONCLUSION

This chapter incorporates the basic teachings, truths, and guidelines of the Catholic Church. The contributor attempted to provide a broad, encompassing view of how family and marital issues of Catholic families might be conceptualized. The Catholic Church provides guidelines and moral tenets about almost every aspect of family and marital life. Although it may seem constraining and restricting to non-Catholics, persons practicing Catholicism have a rich foundation to rely on in their daily routine, as well as in crisis. It is a faith perspective, if understood completely, that can permeate and shape families and couples with hope and anticipation for better lives. The author encourages marriage and family counselors to see Catholicism for what it can do in the lives of clients, rather than what it forbids. Counselors also are encouraged to assess their clients' degree of practice in the Catholic Church, as well as what faith teachings they subscribe to.

REFERENCES

Anderson, G. M. (1997). Marriage annulments. *American, 177*(9), 10–15.

Benedict XVI, Pope. (2006). *God is love: Deus Caritas Est.* (Encyclical Letter). Washington, DC: U.S. Conference of Catholic Bishops.

Califano, J. A. (2004, November 15). The annulment: One Catholic's journey of reconciliation. *America, 191*(15), 10–14.

Catholic Church. (2003). *Catechism of the Catholic Church* (2nd ed.). New York: Doubleday.

Catholic Church and Canon Law Society of America. (1983). *Code of Canon Law: Latin-English Edition.*

Drinan, R. (2003, December 19). The mystery of marriage. *National Catholic Reporter, 40*(8), 17.

Flaman, P. J. P. (1999). *Premarital sex and love: In the light of human experience and following Jesus.* Edmonton, Canada: University of Alberta Printing Services.

Groome, T. H. (2002). *What makes us Catholic: Eight gifts for life.* San Francisco: HarperSanFrancisco.

Hornik, D. (2001). Can the church get in step with stepfamilies? *U. S. Catholic, 66*(7), 30–34.

John Paul II, Pope. (1981). *On the family: Familiaris Consortio.* Washington, DC: U.S. Catholic Conference.

John Paul II, Pope. (1995). *The gospel of life: Evangelium Vitae* (Encyclical Letter). Boston: Daughters of St. Paul.

John Paul II, Pope. (1997). *The theology of the body: Human love in the divine plan.* Boston: Pauline Books & Media.

Keane, P. S. (1977). *Sexual morality. A Catholic perspective.* New York: Paulist Press.

Lawler, R., Boyle, J., & May, W. E. (1998). *Catholic sexual ethics: A summary, explaination, & defense* (2nd ed.). Huntington, IN: Our Sunday Visitor.

May, W. E. (2000). *Catholic bioethics and the gift of human life.* Huntington, IN: Our Sunday Visitor.

McBrien, R. P. (1994). *Catholicism* (rev. ed.). San Francisco, CA: HarperSanFrancisco.

Munson, R. (1996). *Intervention and reflection: Basic issues in medical ethics* (5th ed.). Belmont, CA: Wadsworth Publishing.

Paquette, J. (2002, December). Disentwining souls. *U. S. Catholic, 67*(12), 38–40, 65.

Paul VI, Pope. (1978). *Humanae Vitae* (Encyclical Letter on the Regulation of Births). San Francisco: Ignatius Press.

Pennock, M. F. (1998). *This is our faith: A Catholic catechism for adults.* Norte Dame, IN: Ave Maria Press.

Schaeffer, P. (1996, May 3). Cohabitating may trip up trip to the altar. *National Catholic Reporter, 32*(27), p. 3–5

Singer-Towns, B., Claussen, J., & vanBrandwijk, C. (2004). Winona, MN: Saint Mary's Press.

Tyndale House Publishers. (1997). *Life application Bible.* Carol Stream, IL.

Vatican Council II. (1965). *Gaudium et Spes (GS)* (The church in the modern World).

Weisheipl, J. A., & Larcher, F. (1980). *Translation of Commentary on the Gospel of Saint John (St. Thomas Aquinas).* Albany, NY: Magi Books.

Wood, C. (2001). A homily for the feast of the blended family. *U. S. Catholic, 66*(7), 32.

CHAPTER 4

The Practice of Marriage and Family Counseling and Conservative Christianity

DANIEL W. ZINK

A central purpose of this chapter is to explain conservative Christian views on key marriage and family issues. These issues are the definition of marriage; views on dating and cohabitation; roles within marriages and families; positions related to child bearing such as birth control, abortion, and teenage pregnancy; views on finances; homosexuality in couples and families; dissolving relationships through divorce; managing the family after divorce; and beliefs about death and dying. This chapter is an attempt to clearly delineate the *content* of the beliefs of conservative Christians in these identified areas.

A companion purpose of this chapter is to delineate the *process* conservative Christians utilize to arrive at their beliefs. Understanding this process will help make sense of conservative Christian thought, particularly when such thought appears diverse, fractured, or disconnected from reason. Different groups among conservative Christians arrive at different interpretations of the Bible and recognize different principles from the biblical data. As a result, those outside Christian circles can be confused by the disparate views of various Christian subgroups. It is hoped that explanation of the process of how conservative Christians think about marriage and family issues will aid those who are working with conservative Christians so they will be better equipped to understand, dialogue with, and enter into helping relationships with conservatives.

55

CONSERVATIVE CHRISTIANS DEFINED

Christian Defined

Christians are participants of the religious tradition established by follow-ers of Jesus, who was also called The Christ. Christian is a broad term that identifies people historically, theologically, culturally, and socially. Some Christians place an emphasis on cultural and social meanings with less emphasis on theological implications. Others place the priority on theologi-cal meaning. There are many today who identify themselves as Christians, sharing common historical roots, but there is much diversity within this broad group. For this reason, other labels are used to clarify and emphasize distinctions from one Christian subgroup to another. Conservative is one such label.

Conservative Christians

Conservative Christians, also known as conservative Protestants or as evan-gelicals, are those who maintain certain views on God, the Bible, the nature of salvation, and the historic doctrines of the Christian faith (Cairns, 2002). Evangelicals emphasize the reality of God "with a stress on the sovereignty of God, the transcendent, personal, infinite being who created and rules over heaven and earth" (Elwell, 2001, p. 406). Christians believe God spoke into the human context, inspiring the authors of the Bible to write what they did. As a result, the Bible is considered to be the authoritative word of God (Cairns, 2002). Erickson, focusing on the nature of salvation, concisely defines evangelical as "a movement in modern Christianity emphasizing the gospel of forgiveness and regeneration through personal faith in Jesus Christ" (Erickson, 1986, p. 52). For the evangelical, "salvation is preeminently a matter of personal relationship with God through Jesus Christ" (Cairns, 2002, p. 169). This salva-tion is the result of God's work which man receives, not through earning it in some way, but as a gift graciously given by God. Conservatives do not believe completely different things than other Christians, but put special emphasis on certain doctrines. Conservative evangelicals are distinguished from other Christian groups by the special emphasis they place on retaining their faith in its purity. This includes an unusually high priority on the doctrine of God, the nature of Scripture as the authoritative and inspired word of God, and on salvation as God's work through Jesus Christ.

HOW CONSERVATIVE CHRISTIANS THINK

God Is the Source of Truth

Conservative Christians hold strong convictions that God exists and acts in human history. God as creator established what is good and right. The Bible includes law, expressions of what is right and wrong, which is consistent with

God's moral nature. For conservatives, God is, therefore, the source of all that is true and right.

The Nature of Truth

What God has established as true is objective in the understanding of conservative Christians. What God has established as good and right is not dependent on a subject believing it, but is true even if it is not believed. It stands on its own because God has established it.

Conservative evangelicals assume that truth is revealed by God both through the Bible and through creation, which can be observed by human persons. This assumption divides the conservative Christian from many others in today's culture who assume that truth is constructed through social process. Such truth is ultimately personal and subjective, so truth may vary from person to person. This fundamental difference in perspective on the nature of truth can hinder understanding between conservative Christians and those ascribing to more postmodern assumptions. Dialogue, to be as productive as possible, needs to include discussion to clarify what is meant by truth and other key concepts to avoid conversation in which each party uses the same words without realizing there is not agreement on the meaning of these words. Therapists working with conservative Christians need to assure clarifying dialogue occurs to enhance understanding and effectiveness in the helping process.

The Process and Structure of Ethical Thinking

Conservative Christians believe the Bible is foundational for developing ethical positions. Ethical considerations begin by considering what the Bible says that is relevant to the issue. In this way, evangelicals set out to think in accordance with the Bible, and therefore, God. This approach "is distinctive in that it identifies the good with the revealed will of God" (Jones, 1994, p. 13).

It is important to recognize that while this rendering authority to the Bible is foundational, it cannot be the complete process. Making good ethical decisions is not done merely by seeing how the Bible directs on an issue. The Bible, most evangelicals understand, is not a handbook for science or life; the Bible does not address everything and is not exhaustive in all that it does address. The Bible is an account of God's intervention to restore relationship with rebellious mankind. It is a record of God's restorative work, conservative Christians believe, and while speaking authoritatively, it is not intended to speak to every issue of life directly or completely. As Douma points out,

> Rather than functioning as a guide to tell us concretely what is good or bad, scripture functions as a compass to point out the direction we should move to find our answer to the question of what is good or bad in a given situation. (2003, p. 76)

Marriage and family issues, being tangential to the redemptive focus of the Bible, are mostly addressed indirectly in the biblical account. The Bible, while offering some guidance and warnings in reference to marriage and family issues, on many specific aspects of these issues serves mostly as a "compass" in inquiry and decision making.

In the process of making ethical decisions, especially on issues that are outside the direct scope of the Bible's intent, the conservative evangelical must do more than just know and do what the Bible says. A process of discernment is required, taking what is said in the Bible, understanding its meaning in its historical context, and drawing principles from it that apply to the current context. In this way, principles are discerned that are consistent with what the Bible says, even though the Bible did not necessarily state these principles directly. While similar processes may be practiced in other Christian groups, conservative evangelicals are particularly careful to be God honoring, respecting the authority of the Bible by striving to think and act consistently with the message of the Bible even when not guided directly by literal biblical statements.

Jones (1994) suggests that ethics for conservative Christians possesses a threefold structure. Sound Christian ethics are concerned not only about ethical practice but also the purpose for ethics, as well as the person involved. The purpose behind ethical choices for the conservative Christian is to honor God, not gratify human desires. For the conservative evangelical, to decide against God is equal to declaring that the person knows better, does not need God, and is self-sufficient. On the other hand, to decide consistently with what God expects is declaring that he is right and knows what is best.

Evangelical ethics also are concerned with the person involved in the situation. Consideration must be given not only to what is best to do, but also to the ontological issue, what are we to be. "What is God calling us to be and do?" (Jones, 1994, p. 11) becomes the question that shapes ethical pursuit in fundamental ways. To address this question of what people are to be, the motivational, volitional, and rational aspects of the person's ethical decision making must be considered. For the conservative evangelical, the motivation in ethics is to love God and love neighbor through actions resulting from ethical choices (Jones, 1994). Further, it is recognized that the will must be exercised, marked by the courage to do right. Also, ethical choices should be made in informed and reasonable ways. Conservative Christians believe they are called to be God's people, requiring them to be people who love well, choose well, and do so reasonably.

Choices on issues in marriage and family are further complicated for conservative Christians because Christians have been impacted by the monumental changes that have occurred in the culture during the last 50 years. These changes result in important differences across generations. Today's young adults experienced in their formative years different marriage and family forms, attitudes toward gender and roles of men and women, and perspectives on work, than the more traditional environment middle-aged adults experienced. Today's young adult conservative Christian, while holding to

Christian beliefs, may incorporate cultural views to a greater extent into their practical choices than their parents. This results in them holding different views on things such as gender roles, divorce, and parenting (Myers, 2006).

Great weight is attributed to ethical choices for the conservative evangelical, as these choices are believed to be more than mere human choices, but choices that God cares about and has a stake in. Pursuing what God has called one to be and do is not just a choice with private ramifications. It is a choice that impacts one's relationship with God himself, as it is reflective of the honored position one is giving to God, and it impacts upon one's family and community.

A goal for the therapist working with conservative Christians is to aid in the process of growing in maturity, encouraging active interaction between affective and cognitive processes, with higher levels of maturity represented by higher levels of balance between affective and cognitive processes (Bowen, 1994). This will include helping conservative Christians think not only about biblical propositions but also about foundational biblical principles as they consider personal issues. Therapists, when confronted with a client who appears stuck in a legalistic way, can help that client by asking what else the Bible says about the issue. Gently and persistently pursuing such a line of questioning can lead the client to a change in perspective as he or she expands his or her thinking about the related biblical principles.

CONSERVATIVE CHRISTIANS' VIEWS ON MARRIAGE AND FAMILY ISSUES

Views on the Definition of Marriage

Conservative Christians believe the definition of marriage is clearly stated in the Bible. For Christians, the story of creation delineates God's intent for how human relationships, including marriage, work best (Köstenberger & Jones, 2004). In Genesis 1:26, God is quoted as saying; "Let us make man in our image" (English Standard Version). "Us" is significant as God is speaking to himself when he says, "Let us." This is the first hint to the Christian understanding of the nature of God as being one god consisting of three distinct persons. Much is implied in this complicated belief, but the important point here is that God in his essence and being is relational. To create man and woman after his image means mankind will reflect God's essence including this relational element. This is highlighted in the expanded story of mankind's creation in Genesis chapter 2. In verse 18, God says, "It is not good for man to be alone." It is not good because the man and the woman "bear his image in part through loving relationship. So it was not good for man to be alone because God's purpose in creation envisioned a relationship" (Phillips & Phillips, 2006, p. 20). For conservative Christians, the marriage relationship is established by God and is rooted in his creational purposes.

Conservative Christians understand marriage to be a special and unique relationship. The unique nature of the marriage relationship is expressed in the term "covenant". Genesis 2:24 says, "Therefore a man shall leave his father and mother and hold fast to his wife, and they shall become one flesh." The term "hold fast" is used of relationships marked by special affection and loyalty, the kind of bond that occurred in covenant relationships of the day (Jones, 1994). Marriage is the most important relationship into which a person enters. "[Leaving] father and mother to hold fast to his wife" indicates that this new relationship is more important than even that of parents and child. A decision to marry includes a lasting commitment to join oneself with another in a way that supersedes all other connections. These covenant relationships included a special commitment, one that was expected to last a lifetime.

A second unique aspect of the marriage relationship is the level of intimacy and acceptance possible in marriage. In Genesis 2:25, it is stated that "the man and his wife were both naked and were not ashamed." The biblical author recognizes the psychological state of the man and woman; they were free of shame in their nakedness. Christians understand the biblical suggestion that a husband and wife can move toward being completely known, a deep intimacy, and experience acceptance from each other.

A third aspect of the uniqueness of the marriage relationship is a high level of interdependence. Spouses are to enjoy companionship together like each does with no other person. The Bible states that Eve was created to be the "helper" of Adam. Her role while different was complimentary. The woman should not be understood as being subordinate.

> To call a woman a helper is not to emphasize her weakness but her strength, not to label her as superfluous but as essential to Adam's condition and to God's purpose in the world. Helper is a position of dignity given to the woman by God himself. (Phillips & Phillips, 2006, p. 26–27)

Genesis 1:27 states, "So God created man in his own image, in the image of God he created him; male and female he created them." God created both the male and the female in his image. An equality is stated here that must not be set aside because of differences, but differences enhance the interdependence of the man and the woman.

A fourth unique aspect of the marriage relationship is the purpose marriage gives to sexuality. "Be fruitful and multiply," God says to the couple (Gen. 1:28), stating that procreation is one of the purposes of sex in marriage. But the Bible does not stop there, saying the man and woman "shall become one flesh" (Gen. 2:24), implying more than the physical aspect of the relationship. Through connecting the physical aspect of sexual intercourse to the relational aspect of marriage, the understanding of marriage is furthered. Jones states,

> "One flesh" refers to the entire life-union of the couple, of which sexual intercourse is the unique realization and expression. The essential moral problem with nonmarital sexual intercourse is that it performs a life-uniting act without a life-uniting intent, thus violating its intrinsic meaning. (Jones, 1994, p. 158)

Marriage is to be the uniting of two lives. Sexual intercourse is intended, in the understanding of the conservative Christian, to both symbolize this unity and through the mutually shared pleasure and intimacy, strengthen the couple's unity.

Marriage for conservative Christians is a God established, purposeful, and special union between a man and a woman. This relationship is marked by the highest order of commitment, deep intimacy and acceptance, interdependence, and unity in which a new family unit is established, sexuality is experienced to its fullest, and normally, children are born and nurtured.

Views on Dating and Cohabitation

Dating

Conservative Christians' views on dating are shaped significantly by their understanding of marriage. Dating is understood as the process that leads to marriage through which two individuals progressively grow in commitment, intimacy, and interdependence. These factors are interrelated and dynamic; they develop together, but not without order as one is foundational for the next. Conservative Christians believe that commitment comes first, then intimacy and interdependence. The trust that is developed as commitment grows is the necessary context for safety in intimacy and the oneness of interdependence (Phillips & Phillips, 2006).

The conservative Christians' understanding of marriage generally leads to Christian singles making careful choices about dating. For Christians, the choice of a spouse is assumed to be a choice God cares about and has influenced. Christians can fear making the wrong choice, sometimes leading to avoidance of the commitment necessary to pursue marriage. Since many have had parents who divorced, and parental divorce can exacerbate concerns about marriage longevity, this avoidance of commitment can become a significant issue. Help may be needed to identify fears and their sources, and separate the fears from judgments of the potential spouse so the individual can make a well-thought-through decision.

The high view of the purpose of sexuality in marriage limits conservative Christians in sexual behavior in dating. For conservative Christians, sexual intercourse is reserved for those who are married. Because premarital sexual intercourse separates sexual activity from its intended purpose to nurture the marriage relationship, in the mind of conservative evangelicals sex outside marriage reduces sex to a more ordinary activity, one with a less profound purpose.

Not all Christians act consistently with these beliefs about sex before marriage, choosing to engage in premarital sex. Guilt for choices contrary to one's belief system can be intense, and help may be needed, particularly to avoid adopting an over-punitive attitude toward one's own desires, as if sexual desire is the problem. It is important to remind Christians that sex is part of God's creative work, a gift from him, and that a growing desire for sexual experience together as the relationship grows is expected and good.

Cohabitation

The above views on premarital sex guide conservative Christians in their thinking about cohabitation. Since cohabitation usually includes premarital sex, and since conservative Christians view premarital sex as contrary to the purposes for sex, cohabitation is considered to be problematic.

Marriage includes vows that are an explicit expression of the commitment of the woman and man to each other. Traditional vows are made "before God and these witnesses," and are solemn promises to which others can hold the couple accountable. Without marriage, there is no explicit expression of the man and woman's commitment to each other, diminishing the necessary context for the deep intimacy that sexuality entails. Because cohabitation precludes marriage, it changes the order and priority in the commitment-intimacy-interdependence dynamic because of the reduced commitment compared to a marriage relationship.

Many justify cohabitation as a trial for marriage, wanting to be careful because so many marriages end in divorce (Balswick & Balswick, 2000). Since conservative Christians believe cohabitation changes the dynamics of the relationship (primarily through a reduction in commitment) to something different than marriage, cohabitation is not seen as an accurate or effective trial for marriage.

Views on the Roles Within Marriages and Families

Many conservative Christians experience significant confusion about the roles of husbands and wives. Interpretations of the biblical teaching on male and female roles are diverse, ranging from traditional views emphasizing distinctions in male and female roles to egalitarian views. This is in part the result of the influence of the broader culture as "today's couples often base their marriages on the wider cultural ideologies of gender equality more than on their religious ideologies" (Myers, 2006, p. 303). These two factors of a lack of a clear, unified perspective among conservative Christians and the power of the cultural influences result in significant uncertainty and confusion on this issue for conservative Christians.

Conservative Christians usually begin consideration of roles of men and women with Ephesians 5:22-33. Verse 22 states, "Wives, submit to your own husbands, as to the Lord." Later, in verse 33, men are addressed, "Husbands, love your wives, as Christ loved the church and gave himself up for her." Christians, in wrestling with this text, often do not go further in their investigation to include other relevant things the Bible says. Focusing on Ephesians 5 without holding onto the context created by other biblical teaching on marriage usually leads to a distortion of the Bible's overall message on how marriage is to be lived out. With this distortion enters an over-focus on the needs and desires of each individual. This self-focus works against the unity that comes from focusing on the other's needs equally or more than your own. Self-focus is contrary to the Bible's message as "God neither commends or commands selfishness" (Chapell, 1998, p. 10), and selfishness is contrary to the Bible's model of marriage as a unifying relationship in which companionship, intimacy, and interdependence are vital parts.

Christians can be helped to clarify their thinking on roles in several ways. First, Ephesians 5:21 needs to be considered, which says that in their interactions with each other, Christians are to be "submitting to one another, out of reverence for Christ." There is a mutual submission created here for all Christians that precludes understanding the verses that follow as establishing a strict hierarchy with the husband ruling over his wife. Verse 25 can then be better understood. Christ, although head of the church, loved the church sacrificially, giving his life for the church. Husbands also are to love sacrificially for their wives, benefit, a kind of giving that is unlikely if the husband sees himself at the top of a marital hierarchy.

Furthermore, conservative Christians need reminders of the importance of bringing balance to these concepts. Balance can be found by holding the message of Genesis 2 together with the message of Ephesians 5. While Ephesians 5 indicates that husbands have an authority that creates responsibility for the trajectory of the marriage, it is not an autocratic authority. He needs and is provided a helper. While husbands are to have influence in their wives' lives, it is an influence exercised with the wives' good in sight, and does not have control as its goal. Husbands and wives are to struggle together with husbands becoming servant leaders and wives becoming active participants in the marriage. In this way, together husbands and wives bring into practical reality that for a woman to be a helper in the relationship "is not to emphasize her weakness but her strength" and this "is a position of dignity" (Phillips & Phillips, 2006, pp. 26–27). Each couple will work out this balanced relationship of mutual contribution within their distinct roles in their own way. The measure of success of growing such a relationship is not whether one rules and the other follows, but do they love each other well, actively participating together, utilizing their distinct talents for each others' good, she helping him lead with a servants heart, while he gives his life to help her grow to her fullest.

Views on Child Bearing, Birth Control, Abortion, Teenage Pregnancy

Child Bearing and Birth Control

For conservative Christians, bearing children is not an individual decision predicated on the couple's personal desires. This choice connects to God's purposes in creation. "Be fruitful and multiply" (Gen. 1:28) mandates a positive attitude toward having children. Most view children as a blessing to be received, rather than avoided.

Like most Protestants, most conservative Christians believe there is no biblical condemnation of contraception, assuming the method does not involve stopping development of the unborn child. While some may take the mandate to bear children as prohibiting contraception, most believe Christians should choose responsibly in life, including the area of birth control. Considering the couple's ability to support children born to the family, readiness of the couple for the responsibility of raising a child, and potential stress on the physical and emotional health of the mother by the birth of an additional child, among other factors, are considered in making a good, responsible choice.

Abortion

For the conservative Christian, abortion is unacceptable, except in rare circumstances, as it stops the development of an unborn child. The conservative places great value on each individual person as the Bible teaches that God forms each person, and knows each one before they are born (Ps. 139:13; Jer. 1:5). For this reason, abortion is not considered a viable solution for the undesired pregnancy, in or outside of marriage. For the additional reason that the purposes of marriage include raising children, abortion is unacceptable for the married.

Teenage Pregnancy

Conservative Christians see teenage pregnancy as a twofold problem. First, because sexual intercourse is believed to be reserved for the married, the teenagers' sexual involvement is contrary to God's design and command. Second, the expected child will be born outside a marriage relationship, and therefore cannot be expected to receive the usual level of nurturance from a mother and father compared to married parents.

Abortion, unless the mother's life is in danger or perhaps in the case of pregnancy as the result of rape, will usually not be viewed as the answer to teenage pregnancy. Sometimes teens are encouraged to marry as a solution to the pregnancy, but probably less so now than historically. Because conservative Christians recognize both the high level of commitment involved in marriage and the high value placed on marriage, most believe marriage should not be entered into for reasons of expedience. It is usually understood that a poor choice to marry does not improve a prior poor choice to be involved sexually before marriage.

The teenage pregnancy creates an opportunity for the family to come together, sort through the issue, and be supportive to each other. This is difficult, and sadly, is not always the outcome for conservative Christian families. A complicating factor can be the parents' strong negative reaction to their daughter's situation. The intensity of this reaction may be fueled by the parents' shame, which they often do not recognize. Therapists can be of great assistance by helping parents name and own their feelings, especially their fears about their failure in parenting their child. Helping the teenager face the myriad of mixed feelings also will be essential work for the therapist. Ultimately, the therapist can guide the family in the crucial work of growing in connection as they adjust to life as it now is.

Views on Finances

Biblical statements about money such as "for the love of money is the root of all kinds of evils" (1 Tim. 6:10) and "You cannot serve God and money" (Matt. 6:24), along with biblical commands to not worry about provisions but trust God (Matt. 6:25-33), create an important perspective about money. This influences many conservative Christian couples in their lives together. However, specific couple's management of finances will vary greatly.

The delegation of the tasks of managing finances is usually determined by which spouse has the most ability to "do the checkbook" well. Life demands and time constraints, especially as the demands of work and children grow, limit communication about finances for many couples. As a result, one spouse is often acting independently, with only very rudimentary communication with the other about the family finances. Furthermore, power, or who decides what to do and when to do it, then rests with the one who controls the checkbook. This imbalance of power undermines the couple's efforts to develop a unified relationship in which they experience intimacy and interdependence. Over time, this pattern can lead to serious problems.

Resolution of such problems can be difficult as the power dynamic is unrecognized by most couples. It is this dynamic that needs to be addressed to help the couple move toward greater interdependence. Conservative Christian couples might mistakenly believe the heart of the issue is failure in role functioning. For example, if the wife has been in charge of the finances, she may feel the husband's lack of leadership left her on her own to do the finances, setting her up for what she feels is his unfair criticism. On the other hand, if the husband has been responsible for the finances, he may feel the issue is the wife's lack of submission to his decision making, even if he has acted independently. The focus on failure in roles intensifies blaming of each other, preventing the couple from addressing the need to do the finances in a more unified way. Therapists can help by exposing the power issues, and challenging the couple to take responsibility for the system they together have created. As couples come to better understand the unhealthy independence they built into handling finances, they are better able to come together and make changes in this area. This renewed perspective can enable them to move toward a fuller realization of the kind of marriage they desire, one marked by great commitment, intimacy, and interdependence.

Views on Homosexuality in Couples and Families

Conservative Christian views on homosexuality are grounded in the understanding of God's creation purposes for the marriage relationship. Genesis 1:28 says, "God said to them, "Be fruitful and multiply and fill the earth." The obedience God expected was dependent on the natural biological reproductive functions of the man and woman. God's command is addressed to the man and the woman. Homosexuality precludes fulfilling the moral and reproductive obligations inherent in God's command and purpose for marriage. As a result, conservative Christians are opposed to homosexuality for both moral and biological reproductive reasons.

It is understood that multiple factors contribute to one becoming homosexual. In recent years, some have concluded that the primary cause is genetic, that people are born with a significant inclination toward homosexuality. Proponents of this position cite scientific research to support this claim. By and large, conservative Christians are less convinced that the science is clear or conclusive (Jones & Yarhouse, 2000), or that any inherited inclination is as strong as often believed. Conservative Christians are inclined to believe that family dynamics and social pressures are more important causal factors than genetics, while recognizing that not well understood multiple causes have an influence.

The moral aspects of homosexuality are paramount for the conservative Christian. Most conservatives separate homosexual behavior from homosexual inclination. The homosexual, it is assumed, can choose to not do wrong behavior. Christians believe in the possibility of change, while recognizing that change is very difficult for the homosexual.

A real tension develops for the conservative Christian in relating to homosexuals. It is clear to the conservative that homosexuality is against what the Bible says. On the other hand, the Bible expects Christians to love their neighbor, which includes having compassion for others even if they are not obedient to what God says. Conservatives wrestle with how to better love homosexual men and women while holding on to what seems to be clear biblical statements.

This tension has implications for families. Conservative Christian parents can be uncertain on how to relate to their homosexual children. Assumptions that homosexuality includes a moral choice factor can enhance the divide between parents and the gay or lesbian child. The child often does not view his or her sexual orientation as wrong or problematic. He or she may be fighting against others' efforts to change his or her view based on the assumption that homosexuality is part of his or her identity. This fight can be waged between parents and child.

Parent-child relationships can be further complicated because the parent is likely to believe that family dynamics are a contributing cause of homosexuality. Assuming something went wrong within the family relationships, parents may feel responsible for their child's sexual orientation. Parents may feel a great deal of guilt when their child is gay. This becomes an emotionally laden family field that is difficult to navigate for all involved. The child may misunderstand parents' honest expressions of their concerns that they failed the child, believing the parents view her or him as defective. This difference in understanding can become a tangled mismatch of views that prohibits clear and comfortable communication within the family.

Therapists working with these families will be challenged to help diffuse the intensity of the family interactions. Therapists may need to see parents and the child separately to assist them in identifying and sorting through their various feelings of guilt, anger, and shame before bringing the family back together for further work.

Views on Divorce

Conservative Christians hold an array of positions about if and when divorce is an appropriate choice for a Christian couple. Christians recognize that the general voice of the Bible is pro-marriage, and conclude that divorce is usually not an acceptable option for a couple. However, most Christians also see that there are situations in which the Bible permits divorce as a response. What these situations are and when they apply is debated among conservative Christians.

Two biblical exceptions are generally acknowledged in conservative Christian thought. First, Jesus states, "whoever divorces his wife, except for sexual immorality, and marries another, commits adultery" (Matt. 19:9). Jesus established sexual immorality as a reason divorce is permissible. Infidelity by a spouse is accepted by most as clear grounds for divorce, along with other forms of sexual immorality, assuming the offense is of a serious nature.

Christians accept desertion of one spouse by the other, especially if the deserting spouse is not a Christian, as a second possible biblical reason for divorce. 1 Corinthians 7:15 says, "If the unbelieving partner separates, let it be so. In such cases the brother or sister is not enslaved."

Application of these two exceptions for divorce is debated among conservative Christians. Some take these two exceptions literally, believing there are no other biblically mandated and acceptable reasons for divorce. Others interpret the exceptions as broadly as possible, stretching the implications of the exceptions to cover other marriage difficulties, such as physical abuse, substance abuse, or other serious marital complications. In this latter approach, in an effort to remain grounded biblically, equivalency to sexual unfaithfulness or desertion is being sought. Is the physical abuse or substance abuse so severe that it is equal to desertion? Are the other marital offenses equal to desertion or sexual behavior outside of marriage? Such an approach may become problematic. Evaluating a marital circumstance for its equivalence to sexual immorality or desertion turns the consideration toward what similarities the circumstance shares with one of these other two things, and away from the nature of the current circumstance itself. In the process, the physical abuse, substance abuse, or other marital discord is less likely to be evaluated on its own merits and for its impact on the marriage. The state of the marriage as a result of the offender's action is no longer the focus, but rather, the focus has become the effort to redefine the actions as being like something else. This easily slants the spouses and involved helpers away from trying to judge the seriousness of the issues and whether or not they are irremediable, toward a decision in favor of divorce by finding a defense for it.

Divorce is a clear example that the best ethical decision making requires looking beyond the specifics of the reasons found in the Bible that divorce is permissible, to the principle behind these propositions. In this case, there is a common thread of reasoning behind the two exceptions; sexual immorality and desertion result in breaking the marriage covenant in a radical way. "The exceptional circumstance common to both instances is *willful and radical violation of the marriage covenant*" (Jones, 1994, p. 202). One who is sexually unfaithful has broken his or her promise of sexual exclusivity, commitment, and intimacy in the marriage. One who abandons her or his family is breaking the promise of commitment, companionship, and interdependence. Whether or not the current marital difficulties result in a radical break of the marriage covenant becomes the primary consideration, along with whether this breaking of the promises for the marriage relationship is irremediable. Focus is maintained on the nature of the offending behavior, the impact of this behavior on the marriage relationship, and whether these results are so severe that remedy is no longer possible.

Therapists can be helpful to conservative Christian couples caught in the turmoil of marital distress by helping couples identify and clarify their beliefs about the nature of the marriage relationship. Helping couples evaluate their marriage relationship, including the hurts and hardships, in light of whether a radical breaking of the marriage covenant has occurred is often the beginning to finding renewed hope for change.

Therapists can also be helpful to conservative Christian couples that do experience divorce, particularly helping spouses grieve the many losses inherent in the ending of the marriage. Often, conservative Christians are well schooled in the necessity of forgiving those who have done harm. In divorce, a spouse may feel compelled to forgive first and early, moving too quickly past the needed work to grasp the fullness of the consequences of the marital breakdown. Therapists can reassure clients that while forgiveness is desirable and needed, it will be fullest when the work toward an honest grasp of the losses inherent in the divorce has been done. Forgiveness can be more growth producing and lasting when the person has a clearer grasp on what needs to be forgiven.

Divorce can be a time of great confusion for Christians. It is important that therapists encourage clients to talk about the impact of the divorce on their concept of God and their relationship with him. Serious questions can arise for conservative Christians as they wonder why God did not prevent the divorce, or as they question their own history and decision making, and how they can relate to God when they are angry with him. Through questions, therapists can help clients come to a deeper understanding of the nature of life. Conservative Christians often need to be reminded that the Bible does not promise an absence of suffering in life. Brokenness still enters the lives of Christians. God's promise is to be present with the person in such times, using the circumstances to strengthen the person in the midst of the suffering.

Divorce recovery is often complicated by unresolved hurt. For conservative Christians, situations involving infidelity can be particularly intense because the understanding of sexual fidelity is so central to the beliefs about the nature of marriage. Again, rapid forgiveness that precludes grieving the losses inherent in the infidelity prevents working through the sense of betrayal, resultant anger, depression, confusion over responsibility, and other factors that need to be honestly faced in order to forgive. Therapists can be very helpful by doing the hard work of not allowing clients to avoid the pain of the losses in infidelity and divorce. In so doing, therapists increase the chances that losses will be resolved sufficiently enough that the client can move forward in life less burdened by the consequences of divorce.

Views on Managing the Family After Divorce

Conservative Christians face similar challenges to other divorced couples in managing the family after divorce. Many continuing difficulties will revolve around working together as parents. This is a crucial issue. Parents working together peacefully create for children the best chance to adjust favorably to the parents' divorce. This is a very difficult task for most divorced couples. The ability for creative negotiation and compromise necessary to make this work is usually the kind of relationship skill that keeps a marriage functioning well and would have prevented divorce. If parents are to work together peacefully, they will have to improve skills in this area. Divorced conservative Christians can expect to struggle as much in this area as any other couple. To manage the family well post-divorce requires maturity. When this is lacking, growth toward functioning better together is required.

Views on Death and Dying

Death and dying presents complicated issues for all people, and the conservative Christian is no different. In the not too distant past, when a person stopped breathing and their heart stopped beating, they were pronounced dead. Advances in medical science that enable doctors to maintain function of certain vital organs have blurred the definition of death. Today, breathing can be maintained artificially. The body can be supported in any number of ways so that the line between prolonging life and prolonging death is unclear. Decision making for families at the end of life is complicated for all families. The emotional burden for conservative Christians can be heightened because Christians place high value on human life, granting great dignity to the individual because of the belief that God creates the human person, and that individual to some extent is a reflection of God's personhood. Christian families may need help talking about the approaching death of a loved one. Few people find it easy to acknowledge that death is coming. Helping the dying one tell the family of her or his wishes is immensely helpful. Encouraging the family to talk to the dying one about their feelings for their loved ones, offering forgiveness when that is needed, and being honest with each other about the pain of the coming separation are all important assistance that can be offered to families.

Conservative Christians view death as contrary to the original pattern of creation, death entering the world as part of the negative consequences of man's rebellion against God. Grieving the pain from the death of a loved one is proper as death is part of the brokenness of this current world, and not part of God's original creation pattern. Conservative evangelicals, emphasizing a personal relationship with God that results in a current and future relationship with God, have hope that there is life after this life. Conservative Christians should and do grieve, but in light of the message that Christ has secured a future place for them in a life after this one, their grief is accompanied by a sense of hope. Sometimes, conservative Christians resist mourning out of a misguided sense of religious duty. Since the loved one has gone on to a better place, it may seem to some that grieving is equal to selfishness or doubt of one's beliefs. Conservative Christians may need to be encouraged and given permission to grieve. Therapists can help conservative Christians with the mixed feelings that are inevitable in experiencing loss through death while believing there is life with God after this one.

CONCLUSION

Therapists working with conservative evangelical couples and families, whatever the therapist's own belief system may be, should attend to the beliefs of these couples and families in their work together. Discussion of values is beneficial to the therapeutic process and should not be avoided. Doherty (1995) has asserted that good therapists will be willing to use moral language, and "willing to engage in moral discussion about what is fair, right, honest, or responsible. [Such therapists will appear] comfortable talking with you about your values and your religious beliefs and about your sense of right and wrong" (p. 182). Fair, right, honest, and responsible should be understood from the perspective of the client, and to do so requires the therapist to pursue discussion about such moral issues.

Therapists can work effectively with conservative Christian clients, even if therapists do not agree with the beliefs of these clients. Marriage and family therapists understand the complexity of family systems, including the powerful influence on family dynamics of those not visibly present in the system. Recognizing that conservative evangelicals believe in a God who is active and speaks into family life, therapists can be more effective in helping these couples and families by recognizing that their God is part of the family system. Listening well to couples and families express what place God has in their lives and discussing this influence in the system will enhance therapists' effectiveness in working with their conservative Christian clients. Assisting clients to think more consistently with the principles derived from the Bible, while helping clients see ways they can move away from an individual focus to a greater couple focus, developing their eye for the other, can help conservative Christian couples pursue their biblically informed conception of marriage marked by commitment, intimacy, and interdependence.

REFERENCES

Balswick, J. O., & Balswick, J. K. (2000). A Christian response to cohabitation. *Marriage & Family: A Christian Journal, 3*(2), 163–173.

Bowen, M. (1994). *Family therapy in clinical practice*. Northvale, NJ: Jason Aronson Publishers.

Cairns, A. (2002). *Dictionary of theological terms*. Greenville, SC: Ambassador Emerald International.

Chapell, B. (1998). *Each for the other: Marriage as it's meant to be*. Grand Rapids, MI: Baker Books.

Crossway Bibles. *The Holy Bible: English standard version*. (2001). Wheaton, IL: Good News Publishers.

Doherty, W. J. (1995). *Soul searching: Why psychotherapy must promote moral responsibility*. New York: Basic Books.

Douma, J. (2003). *Responsible conduct: Principles of Christian ethics*. Phillipsburg, NJ: P&R Publishing.

Elwell, W. A. (2001). *Evangelical dictionary of theology* (2nd ed.). Grand Rapids, MI: Baker Books.

Erickson, M. J. (1986). *Concise dictionary of Christian theology*. Grand Rapids, MI: Baker Books.

Jones, D. C. (1994). *Biblical Christian ethics*. Grand Rapids, MI: Baker Books.

Jones, S. L., & Yarhouse, M. A. (2000). The use, misuse, and abuse of science in the ecclesiastical homosexuality debates. In Balch, D. L. (Ed.). *Homosexuality, science, and the "plain sense" of scripture* (pp. 73–120). Grand Rapids, MI: William B. Eerdmans Publishing.

Köstenberger, A. J., & Jones, D. W. (2004). *God, marriage, and family: Rebuilding the biblical foundation*. Wheaton, IL: Crossway Books.

Myers, S. M. (2006). Religious homogamy and marital quality: Historical and generational patterns, 1980–1997. *Journal of Marriage and Family, 2,* 292–304.

Phillips, D. P., & Phillips, S. L. (2006). *Holding hands, holding hearts: Recovering a biblical view of Christian dating*. Phillipsburg, NJ: P&R Publishing.

CHAPTER 5

The Practice of Marriage and Family Counseling and Liberal Protestant Christianity

CAROL J. COOK

From the outset of his book entitled *Theology for Liberal Presbyterians and Other Endangered Species*, theologian Douglas F. Ottati reminds readers of liberal Protestantism's "inherent theological plurality" (2006, p. 3). As do others, he further maintains that the wide river of liberal Protestantism, let alone its Reformed and Presbyterian tributaries, cannot be described by a singular, generic set of theological tenets requiring strict adherence. Rather, he outlines a "few characteristics that different liberal and progressive theologies might share" such as being reformed and ecumenical, theocentric and worldly, Christ shaped and generous, realistic and hopeful, ecologically inclined and humane (pp. 3–8). He notes that at their best, liberal Protestants "try to retrieve, restate, rethink, and revise traditional theologies and beliefs in the face of contemporary knowledge and realities. That is what makes them liberal" (p. viii).

Similarly, one can think about liberal Protestantism as a set of recurring themes that theologians throughout church history have traced back to the Bible, and have interpreted in response to particular historical circumstances. These theological commitments received varying degrees of emphasis among the 16th century Reformers (Martin Luther and John Calvin), the late 18th and early 19th century Enlightenment informed thinkers (Friedrich Schleiermacher, Adolf von Harnack, and Walter Rauschenbusch), and various 20th century liberation theologians (Gustavo Gutierrez, Frederick Herzog, James Cone, Rosemary Radford Ruether, Letty Russell, Choan-Seng Song, and Delores Williams; Hensley, 2004; Rieger, 2004).

The recurring themes include the central authority of scripture, which includes scripture critiquing scripture; being reformed, always being reformed, and the accompanying resistance to idolatry; openness to other sources of knowledge including the arts and sciences; sexuality as a good gift from God; absolute dependence on the grace of God for justification and salvation. Additional themes include faith and reason held in creative tension, not opposition (faith-seeking understanding); balance between individual agency and a sense of community—the self is always a self-in-relation; appreciation for diversity; contextual awareness; concern for those on the margins and commitment to social justice.

In line with these recurring theological themes and characteristics, no church doctrine or practice, no interpretation of scripture, no institution, and no established tradition is considered infallible. To claim such would be to commit idolatry. The same approach applies to ethical decision making. Liberal Protestants would maintain that no infallible and acontextual moral blueprint of how to handle the complexity of contemporary life exists in the Bible or in any church confession or book of church order. Nothing removes adherents of the Christian faith from having to make hard ethical decisions. Liberal Protestants do their best to engage in rigorous biblical interpretation and to be open to the ongoing revelation of God's spirit in their own time. This includes listening to voices that did not help shape the historical theology, namely women, the marginalized, the powerless, and oftentimes persons of color. What guides this critical dialogue is an image of God from the Hebrew Bible, revealed in Jesus Christ through the presence of the Holy Spirit, calling followers to a way of justice-love (Ellison & Thorson-Smith, 2003).

It will be shown in what follows that the interpretations of scripture, tradition, and contemporary society that are natural extensions of liberal theology's themes can support, inform, and learn from the culturally-competent practice of marriage and family therapists, which takes into account contextual factors such as gender, race, class, ethnicity, and sexual orientation (McGoldrick, Giordano, & Garcia-Preto, 2005).

DEFINITION OF MARRIAGE

Marriage is not just one thing. Like the family, the institution of marriage has borne many cultural functions and expectations that have changed over time. In *Promising Again*, pastoral theologians Anderson, Hogue, and McCarthy (1995) describe some of these dimensions. Sociologically, marriage is a regulatory social and legal institution; economically, it is a unit of consumption and production; theologically, it is a gift and sign of God's grace. These authors refer to marriage as a "pilgrimage of promising" that is "sustained by courage and self-giving love," emphasizing that marriage "is covenantal in nature and based on the willingness to hold one's partner in abiding seriousness" (pp. 2–3).

Throughout church history, marriage has been defined as a covenant relationship intended to provide companionship, sanctioned sexual intimacy, and a stable context for procreation. Since at least the time of the Reformation, most Protestant understandings of marriage have celebrated sexual intimacy as a good gift from God whether or not it is related to procreation. In recent times, the realities of overpopulation, economics, infertility, and birth control have further "uncoupled" marriage from God's charge to "be fruitful and multiply" (Gen. 1:22). The rise of reproductive technologies and adoption have expanded options for procreation and have created opportunities for couples to raise children—in loving and faithful ways—who have varying degrees of biological relation (including none) to one or both parents.

Whether marriage is defined as an accommodation to human sinfulness or as a preferred state, historically it has been assumed to be between a man and a woman. However, in light of various contemporary realities, many Christians are now asking how intrinsic the language "only between a man and a woman" is to a definition of marriage. The experience of transgender persons challenges binary understandings of what it means to be created "male and/or female" and call for reform of historically accepted interpretations of Genesis 1–3 (see Tanis, 2003). Other theologians are reconsidering traditional biblical interpretations in light of scientific explanations of how sexual orientation develops (Smith, 2006). These new understandings have led some Protestants to argue that marriage should extend to persons experiencing same-sex love and commitment. David Myers and Letha Scanzoni (2005) make a compelling case for this as part of their larger affirmation of faithful marriages and families.

Marriage and family therapists influenced by these theological perspectives evaluate and define marriage primarily in terms of the *quality of relational intimacy* that exists between persons rather than *form* of relationship, and may choose to advocate on behalf of gay, lesbian, bisexual, and transgender persons seeking the right to marry. It may be that the norm of heterosexual marriage has become an idol in our time.

DATING AND COHABITATION

Dating is a social practice that may vary considerably depending on the age of the participants. Parents and adolescents must negotiate together matters that include age, activities, curfews, and perimeters of sexual contact. Research has shown that adolescents benefit from comprehensive education about sexuality and health concerns, open conversation about values, involvement in communities of faith, and preventative awareness around such painful possibilities as date rape (Crooks & Baur, 2005).

Dating can continue throughout the adult life cycle and the adults involved must mutually negotiate the level of sexual intimacy. Ethicist Karen Lebacqz notes that "single sexuality, when it is discussed at all, falls under the category of 'premarital sex'" (1994, p. 256). However, this category has become more complex in a world of the divorced and widowed, gays and lesbians excluded from marriage, and persons marrying at middle age and beyond. Thus, Lebacqz poses a middle ethical category between a legalistic "celibacy in singleness" and "anything goes." This third option has to do with "appropriate vulnerability," which acknowledges both the need for protective structures and for a level of sexual expression that is "commensurate with the level of commitment in the relationship" (p. 260).

Similar issues are at stake in cohabitation patterns. According to Crooks and Baur (2005), "nearly 60% of couples who married in the early 1990s lived with each other before marriage" (p. 402) and about 25% of adults in their mid-20s live together. This trend also exists among adults 65 and older who choose not to marry for a variety of reasons including financial ones. While many couples experience living together as advantageous, there are disadvantages as well. National surveys have found that cohabiting persons are less likely to be monogamous, are legally vulnerable, and may experience increased relational stress due to continuing social disapproval. Overall, research indicates that marriage results in a higher degree of commitment and social stability, which may explain why living together permanently without marriage is uncommon in the United States. About 90% of adult Americans marry at least once (Crooks & Baur, 2005, p. 403). Marriage and family therapists can help families, couples, and individuals sort through their values in relationship to the dating process and cohabitation in light of ongoing research and age-appropriate considerations.

ROLES WITHIN MARRIAGES AND FAMILIES

At least on the surface, most liberal Protestants would disavow the patriarchal patterns of male domination and female subordination that have pervaded much of Western civilization. Feminist biblical scholarship, such as Phyllis Trible's groundbreaking *God and the Rhetoric of Sexuality* (1978), challenged foundational interpretations of Genesis that justified these patterns and accompanying gender roles as God-ordained. In addition, understandings of male headship found in passages such as Ephesians 5:21–33 have been heavily critiqued by feminist scholars of many disciplines. This is especially significant for marriage and family therapists since subjugation of women has been used to legitimate varying degrees of oppression, from silencing women's voices in church to domestic violence.

For liberal Protestants, images of female subservience have been superseded by biblical images of equality and mutuality. Contemporary biblical scholars and historians have highlighted patterns of mutuality found in the Genesis 1 creation narrative, the Song of Solomon, Galatians 3:28, the respect Jesus of Nazareth consistently showed toward women throughout the gospels, and the role of women leaders in the early church and church history. In this shift toward mutuality, "scripture interprets scripture" and traditional role assumptions are in the process of being reformed. Pastoral theologian Edward Wimberly explicates this position clearly (1997).

However, the *practice* of traditional gender roles still pervades much of American society. Even among liberal Protestants, couples tend to internalize traditional role expectations and fall into predictable patterns where women who work outside the home continue to do more than their fair share of child care and housework. Ongoing theological and sociocultural critique and the establishment of alternate practices that free both genders from constraining assumptions and patterns is necessary because research has indicated that "compliance with rigid gender expectations and the resulting power differentials in intimate relationships" contribute to marital unhappiness and are predictors of divorce (Haddock, Zimmerman, & Lyness, 2003, p. 307). The goal in marriage and family therapy is to encourage mutuality and flexibility in relationship roles, as a way for each person to develop their full range of gifts and abilities. This must be done with knowledge of and sensitivity to the ways persons' cultural backgrounds influence their perceptions of gender roles (Boyd-Franklin, 2003; Sue & Sue, 2003).

Historically, the Christian tradition has provided mixed messages about the role or place of children in families. Perceptions have swung between seeing children as repositories of original sin who need to be morally molded through punishment ("spare the rod, spoil the child"), to being idealized, innocent original blessings around which the family should revolve. This mixed legacy remains today. Children can still be viewed as "little adults," private property, economic assets or burdens, gifts, entitlements, or parental caretakers. The hope is that above all, children will be regarded with the respect due to all persons (Anderson & Johnson, 1994) and as "labors of love and as moral and spiritual agents" (Miller-McLemore, 2003, p. 157).

All therapists strive to protect children, the most vulnerable among us, from situations of physical and/or emotional abuse. Depending on the level of one's commitment to feminism and willingness to take an advocacy stance, a marriage and family therapist will work to challenge patriarchal assumptions and roles that make women and children vulnerable to oppressive and abusive men, even if those happen to be husbands and fathers. By law, mental health professionals must report instances of child abuse and neglect whether inflicted by a parent, family member, or stranger. In some states (such as

Kentucky) instances of domestic violence must also be reported. Sadly, strands of Christian teaching have historically sanctioned both of these family sins. Thanks to the work of feminist theologians and counselors, these interpretations have been substantively critiqued and multiple supportive social services, pastoral, and therapeutic resources now exist (Adams & Fortune, 1995).

Initial treatment interventions in the case of either child or spouse abuse prioritize taking the claims of the victims seriously, protecting them from further abuse, and providing a safe, nonjudgmental place for them to express their often contradictory emotions about the abuse. Male abusers also need appropriate treatment referrals, often to men's groups (Poling, 2003).

CHILDBEARING, BIRTH CONTROL, ABORTION, TEEN PREGNANCY

As noted in the earlier section on marriage, most Protestants no longer believe that procreation is an imperative of marriage or the only justification for sexual intercourse. However, many might still consider child bearing an entitlement, an expectation, even a fulfillment of marriage. Others see having children as a call or a sense of vocation to be entered into with intentionality, maturity, and conviction. In general, Protestants embrace matters of family planning as a means of making more responsible choices. Birth control serves as an aid to this larger vocational journey. The 1983 Presbyterian Church (U.S.A.) statement entitled "Covenant and Creation: Theological Reflections on Contraception and Abortion" states that "for the most part, Protestants have affirmed the role of contraception as a responsible exercise of stewardship with regard to procreation" (1998, p. 112).

Similarly, Protestants would denounce interpretations of infertility as a moral failure or a sign of God's punishment. Rather, they would view infertility with compassion and as a condition that can be medically treated through reproductive technologies if a couple chooses to do so. The *Presbyterians and Human Sexuality 1991* report states that "in the Reformed tradition, we understand advancements in medical technology frequently to be instruments of a gracious God for healing and the promotion of well-being." There is an accompanying recognition, however, that "these burgeoning new technologies thrust us into increasingly complex areas of medical ethics, leaving us with fears that even more difficult ethical dilemmas are on the horizon" (Presbyterian Church [U.S.A.], p. 85). Marriage and family therapists can best support couples confronting such decisions by helping them cope with the stresses *as a couple* and by helping them to anticipate future consequences of their present decisions (Peterson, 2006).

Despite the polarization that typifies much of the national debate on abortion, some agreement exists among Christians. Almost no one views abortion to be a completely neutral, let alone optimal option. Yet, liberal Protestants would err on the side of respecting the complexity of such situations and honoring a person's right to make a responsible, prayerful decision that includes termination of pregnancy under certain conditions. The Presbyterian Church (U.S.A.) theological statement on contraception and abortion referred to above articulates this position clearly. Among other thoughtful reflections, it includes the following:

> Abortion can therefore be considered a responsible choice within a Christian ethical framework when serious genetic problems arise or when the resources are not adequate to care for a child appropriately. Elective abortion, when responsibly used, is intervention in the process of pregnancy precisely because of the seriousness with which one regards the covenantal responsibility of parenting.

> ... Even in the face of the most difficult decisions, of which abortion is surely one, the gospel assures us that we can trust in God's Spirit to guide us in our decision ... Only in the knowledge of such grace and guidance could we dare to claim the responsibility and freedom to use modern medical skill to intervene in the process of human procreation (1998, pp. 112–113).

The strongest case any advocate for the life of children can make, including marriage and family therapists, is to establish networks of adequate care and resources of all kinds for the millions of children who already inhabit our planet, one quarter of whom are born into poverty and situations that lack the necessary resources to survive, let alone thrive (Couture, 2000).

Teen pregnancy is a grave social concern given adolescents' incomplete physiological and emotional development. Most adults across the religious spectrum seek a reduction of teen pregnancy for combined health and moral/ religious reasons. The question is how best to reduce that biological and social risk. A liberal Protestant response would tend to focus first on the health and well-being of the teen and promote whatever protects her the most. While abstinence might be the preferred choice of many parents, numerous studies have shown that teaching "abstinence only" has proven to be ineffective. In contrast, there is considerable evidence that comprehensive sex education programs "that stress safer sex and provide accurate information about various contraceptive methods actually increase the use of birth control, reduce teenage pregnancies, reduce high-risk sexual behavior" (Crooks & Baur, 2005, p. 397). Furthermore, such programs do not result in earlier onset of sexual intercourse, an increase in either frequency or number of sexual partners; in some cases they delay onset and reduce partner numbers.

Schools, churches, and marriage and family therapists are in positions to provide thorough contraceptive education along with discussion of values. Embracing comprehensive sex education allows both the teens and parents to make informed decisions that may have the power to override the natural flow of hormones and various social and psycho-social pressures that lead teens to engage in premature sexual intimacy. If persons are primarily concerned about the health and welfare of youth, they must resist the temptation to make teens, especially girls, the "identified patients." Boys are fully implicated in this social concern as is poverty.

Systemically speaking, children and youth in contemporary American culture are bombarded with sexually laden media images, especially in advertising. The juxtaposition of sexuality with consumerism perpetuates the objectification of women and men at multiple levels. Adults, including therapists, must take responsibility for giving youth the critical apparatus to sort through the maze of sexual imagery that saturates our culture and assist them in formulating and inhabiting values that acknowledge the goodness *and* vulnerability of sexual intimacy.

FINANCES

How to manage money and to reckon with its impact on all facets of life, including marriage and family relationships, challenge Christians as much as everyone else. Interestingly, religious admonitions against pride or neediness appear to make Americans reluctant to talk about money (Wuthnow, 1994). Finances continue to be a point of contention and conflict within marriages since "money is symbolic of many emotional needs—such as security and power—and goes to the core of our individual value system" (Gottman, 1999b, p. 194). According to this researcher, the task for couples in relationship to money is "balancing the freedom and empowerment money represents with the security and trust it also symbolizes" (p. 194). By using some of his accessible, basic questionnaires and strategies (1999a & b), therapists can help couples sort out the emotionally laden issues surrounding money and set some joint priorities.

During the last thirty years, feminists have heightened public awareness of the interrelationship between money and power, and of the ways money can be used as a means of controlling others in family life. Research studies have shown that "money buys power in marriage. It buys the privilege to make decisions—concerning whether to stay or leave, what the family will purchase, where they will live, and how the children will be educated. In other words, money talks" (McGoldrick, 1999, p. 113). Therefore, as with the above discussion of roles, feminist-oriented marriage and family therapists focus on encouraging egalitarian relationships and mutuality to prevent either partner from using access to financial resources as a means of exploitation or coercion. Money, like any other resource within a family, is to be shared and treated with appropriate stewardship. In light of the historical reality that males have tended to be higher income earners, many therapists encourage transparency in this area so that women are not placed in a position of naïve dependency.

Focusing on finances exposes class divisions within the United States and ongoing patterns of unequal access to resources throughout the world. The vast majority of persons below the poverty line in America and abroad are women and children; particularly at risk are populations of color. Post divorce, women tend to end up with less money and men with more, and generally women have less power than men in the custody and other negotiations (Ahrons, 1999). These financial imbalances remain linked with systemic retention of predominantly white male privilege and power in and outside of the church. Family therapists are challenged to help heighten families' awareness of how these multiple systemic factors intersect with their financial options in the service of accountability, greater justice, and empowerment where needed.

DISSOLVING RELATIONSHIPS THROUGH DIVORCE

Given all that is involved in marriage, divorce for Christians has complex legal, psychosocial, and theological ramifications. As the 1980 Presbyterian Church (U.S.A.) statement on marriage makes clear, divorce has had legal legitimacy since the time of Moses. Theologically, based on the teachings of Jesus in Mark, divorce and the many forms of brokenness that lead up to and result from it are recognized as manifestations of the reality of human sin.

> Protestant churches, and particularly the Presbyterian church have recognized divorce as legitimate, not only on grounds of adultery (which Jesus sanctioned, according to Matthew 19:9) or desertion (the old terms in the Westminster Confession of Faith) but also "where a continuation of the legal union would endanger the physical, moral, or spiritual well-being of one or both of the partners or that of their children" (Book of Church Order 215:5). (1998, p. 361)

Christian caregivers are called to embody the healing, just, and forgiving character of the church in response to all persons suffering from such broken relationships. Reconciliation within the marriage can be attempted and is sometimes achievable. But where that is not possible—or appropriate as in circumstances of ongoing affairs or violence—members of the divorcing couple and family are to be met with the same level of compassionate, non-punitive pastoral care that is extended toward all members of the Christian community. In the small volume *Promising Again,* co-authors Anderson, Hogue, and McCarthy elucidate occasions in which promises, even those made in a marriage ceremony, "ought to be broken, because keeping them may represent the ultimate infidelity," a destruction of the self as made in the image of God (1995, p. 29).

The role of marriage and family therapists varies in terms of the therapist's values and views about the legitimacy of divorce. Most would see their primary goal as helping the stressed couple "to improve communication and increase mutual understanding ... to help the partners have a better and enduring relationship ... not necessarily to 'save' the relationship at all costs" (Emery & Sbarra, 2002, p. 510). This includes helping the adults accept responsibility for whatever decision they make, being a "reality check" that divorce never fully "dissolves" former marital relationships, and reviewing the impact of a divorce on the children involved. According to a recent research review, the comforting news is that 75–80% of children "who experience the divorce of parents grow up to become healthy, well-functioning adults. Presented from the other perspective, 20 to 25% of children are likely to suffer long-term consequences" (Ahrons, 2006, p. 26). No research can provide definitive answers about how particular children will react to a divorce. Since ongoing, unresolved, interparental conflict (whether the couple is together or apart) has been shown to impact children negatively, it is advisable for therapists to work with parents and children around problem solving and conflict skills to reduce the level of conflict in all family constellations.

MANAGING FAMILY AFTER SEPARATION AND/OR DIVORCE

It is more helpful to view divorce as a process rather than an event. The step of separation may or may not result in divorce. However, a couple and family in distress would benefit from seeking ongoing support during and following this period of family upheaval. The period of separation can be an opportunity for the members of the couple to attempt reconciliation and discern whether a renewed life together is viable. Sadly, by the time many couples seek therapy, at least one member of the couple has overtly or covertly already decided whether she or he wants a divorce. Part of the therapist's task is to help expose each spouse's level of commitment to restoring the marriage and work with emerging realities. While situations of violence and infidelity are extremely difficult to work through, if offending persons truly cease those behaviors, relational repair is occasionally possible (Spring, 1996). Any responsible therapist must be extremely judicious about advocating reconciliation or premature forgiveness of such profound betrayals of the marriage covenant.

While the adults involved require ongoing pastoral and therapeutic care during these family life cycle changes, children must bear the consequences as well and with fewer resources. Research has uncovered vulnerabilities children experience during and for sometime after divorce and also suggests ways to alleviate risk factors and enhance resilience (Emery & Sbarra, 2002, p. 512). It is also helpful to keep in mind that separation and divorce impact extended family members and communities of which the couple and family are a part. Divorce is a public and communal experience as well as a deeply personal and individual one. Grief, loss, anxiety, anger, alliances, judgments, forgiveness, and renewed hope cycle through all of these relationships as well (Townsend, 2000).

DEATH AND DYING

The specter of facing our own death and/or that of one dear to us presents us with perhaps life's greatest challenge. While Christians cling to the promises made throughout scripture that nothing "will be able to separate us from the love of God" (Rom. 8:38–9), death does separate us from the full bodily presence of loved ones and forecloses dreams of a shared future. Christians both lament the loss of life as we know it, and hope in the promise of the resurrection. Despite the biblical witness, the inevitable mystery of death generates anxiety for many and invites questions about the meaning of life. Pastoral caregivers and therapists can provide a safe place for persons to explore medical options and to confront questions of meaning that arise from approaching our own death or the death of others.

Given the complexity of the role of modern medicine, liberal Protestants tend not to make absolutist claims about how end-of-life decisions should be made. The patient (if deemed competent) and family members join doctors and other medical professionals in deciding whether to withhold, withdraw, or continue life-sustaining interventions. Liberal Christians find these heart-wrenching decisions as daunting as any other kind of religious person. What may set them apart is a willingness to engage in an interdisciplinary consultation process. This process takes seriously faith perspectives about the inevitability of death and resurrection hope, studied medical expertise and wisdom, the mystery of human consciousness and personhood, and the acceptance of the responsibility to make such decisions, humbly, prayerfully, and realistically. Therapists have the privilege and burden of sharing this discernment process with families.

The hope is that persons will have an experience of "dying well." Theologian Plantinga Pauw elucidates the various ways the Christian community can provide practical and spiritual forms of support and resources for individuals facing death and all who grieve (1997). And yet, suffering frequently accompanies the dying process, especially for those who die of progressive illnesses (Kleespies, 2004, p. 163). Emotional anguish can also dominate those who bear witness ("secondary sufferers") to such illness and death (Cook, 1991).

Where a death occurs in the family life cycle influences the process as well. The death of an infant or young person differs from that of an adult who has lived a long and satisfying life. Death through acts of violence and despair challenges persons in traumatic ways. Marriage and family therapists can best serve those grieving by knowing as much as possible about the differences and similarities between complicated and uncomplicated mourning. In all circumstances, the therapeutic task is to support persons through the six "R's" of the grief process: recognize the loss, react to the separation, recollect and re-experience the deceased and the relationship, relinquish the old attachments to the deceased and the old assumptive world, readjust to move adaptively into the new world without forgetting the old, and reinvest in life (Rando, 1993, p. 45).

SAME-SEX RELATIONSHIPS AND FAMILY LIFE

The introduction to *Presbyterians and Human Sexuality 1991* redefines "the sexual problem" facing church and society as being in the prevailing unjust social, cultural, and ecclesial arrangements, rather than in persons, their sexual orientation, or in non-marital sex (Presbyterian Church [U.S.A.], p. 17). The authoring committee asserts that normative sexuality is not about whom is sleeping with whom but about the *character* of our sexual and social relationships (p. 28). The moral norm is not heterosexual marriage, but justice-love. This document and its themes have been expounded upon in a follow-up collection of essays entitled *Body and Soul: Rethinking Sexuality as Justice-Love* by Ellison and Thorson-Smith (2003).

Many, but not all, liberal Protestants take a welcoming and affirming posture toward same-sex relationships, seeing in them reflections of the *imago dei* (Larry Kent Graham, 1997). In this view, covenantal same-sex relationships are affirmed and honored as vehicles of God's creation and grace, as are opposite-sex ones. Thus, many Christians and therapists conclude that it is unjust theologically to exclude persons who in the name of God's justice-love seek access to the legal rights, social recognition, and church blessings that come with the institution of marriage.

Marriage and family therapists can play a role in supporting same-sex couples and families by understanding the depth and nature of external and internalized prejudices, and by helping them live as healthily as possible in what is still a relatively hostile cultural and religious environment. They also do well to remember that research indicates that same-sex relationships have far more in common with other forms of family than they have differences and shows that children raised in these relationships are in no way at a disadvantage (Adams & Benson, 2005, pp. 20–23). If anything, due to cultural prejudices that must be dealt with both externally and internally, same-sex couples tend to enter partnership covenants and childbearing and rearing with greater intentionality, mutuality, and commitment. Furthermore, there is a great deal that all families can learn from gay and lesbian couples and families. This includes lessons about "couple satisfaction, egalitarianism, gender and sexual relationships, creative parenting, children raised in nontraditional homes, adaptation to tensions in this society, and especially about strength and resilience" (Laird, 2003, p. 180).

CONCLUSION

Throughout this chapter, it is possible to observe a mutually enriching compatibility between much of liberal Protestantism, especially its liberationist stream, and the practice of culturally-competent marriage and family therapy. Both share concern for those who suffer and are socially marginalized. Marriage and family therapists influenced by liberal Protestantism's emphasis on justice-love seek to empower persons with whom they work to both honor *and* be open to critiquing their religious traditions and inherited traditional assumptions as they wrestle with contemporary issues that do not have specific correlations in scripture or classical theology.

Like other social sciences and fields of study including theology, marriage and family therapy is changing in response to several contemporary challenges (Nichols, 2004). Feminist critiques, the notion that long-held assumptions about gender and family roles are socially constructed, the multiple interpretations persons give to their life narratives, cultural power dynamics, and the ongoing search for meaning encourage persons to "retrieve, restate, rethink, and revise traditional [and psychological] theologies and beliefs in the face of contemporary knowledge and realities" (Ottati, 2006, p. viii).

What is lost in the face of these contemporary challenges are simple answers and the sense of certainty and security that come with the belief that "my family, my church, my religious tradition, my racial group, my gender, and/or my nation know best." *What is gained* is the opportunity to exercise our God-given capacities to engage communally the complexity of contemporary life with eyes, minds, and hearts wide open, to work collaboratively rather than in dominating ways with others as therapists and global citizens, to clarify one's convictions while remaining in respectful dialogue with those who disagree, and to take seriously once again—and in fresh ways—the ancient charge to do justice, to love mercy, and to walk humbly with God and neighbor.

REFERENCES

Adams, A., & Benson, K. (2005). Considerations for gay and lesbian families. *Family Therapy Magazine*. Nov/Dec, 20–23.

Adams, C., & Fortune, M. (Eds.). (1995). *Violence and women and children: A Christian theological sourcebook*. New York: Continuum.

Ahrons, C. (1999). Divorce: An unscheduled family transition. In B. Carter & M. McGoldrick (Eds.), *The expanded family life cycle: Individual, family, and social perspectives* (3rd ed., pp. 381–398). Boston: Allyn and Bacon.

Ahrons, C. (2006). Long-term effects of divorce on children. *Family Therapy Magazine*, May/June, 24–27.

Anderson, H., Hogue, D., & McCarthy, M. (1995). *Promising again*. Louisville, KY: Westminster John Knox Press.

Anderson, H., & Johnson, S. (1994). *Regarding children: A new respect for childhood and families*. Louisville, KY: Westminster John Knox Press.

Boyd-Franklin, N. (2003). *Black families in therapy: Understanding the African-American experience* (2nd ed.). New York: Guilford Press.

Carter, B., & McGoldrick, M. (1999). Overview: The expanded family life cycle: Individual, family, and social perspectives. In B. Carter & M. McGoldrick (Eds.), *The expanded family life cycle: Individual, family, and social perspectives* (3rd ed., pp. 1–26). Boston: Allyn and Bacon.

Cook, J. (1991). *Shared pain and sorrow: Reflections of a secondary sufferer.* New York: Pilgrim Press.

Couture, P. (2000). *Seeing children, seeing God: A practical theology of children and poverty.* Nashville, TN: Abingdon Press.

Crooks, R., & Baur, K. (2005). *Our sexuality* (9th ed.). Belmont, CA: Wadsworth.

Ellison, M., & Thorson-Smith, S. (Eds.) (2003). *Body and soul: Rethinking sexuality as justice-love.* Cleveland, OH: Pilgrim Press.

Emery, R., & Sbarra, D. (2002). Addressing separation and divorce during and after couple therapy. In A. Gurman & N. Jacobson (Eds.), *Clinical handbook of couple therapy* (3rd ed., pp. 508–530). New York: Guilford Press.

Gottman, J. (1999a). *The marriage clinic: A scientifically based marital therapy.* New York: W. W. Norton.

Gottman, J. (1999b). *The seven principles for making marriage work.* New York: Crown Publishers.

Graham, L. K. (1997). Disclosing the image of God. In *Discovering images of God: Narratives of care among lesbians and gays.* Louisville, KY: Westminster John Knox Press.

Haddock, S., Zimmerman, T., & Lyness, K. (2003). Changing gender norms: Transitional dilemmas. In F. Walsh (Ed.), *Normal family processes: Growing diversity and complexity* (3rd ed., pp. 301–336). New York: Guilford Press.

Hensley, J. (2004). Liberal Protestantism. In Hillerbrand, J. (Ed.). *The encyclopedia of Protestantism* (pp. 1086–1090). New York: Routledge.

Kleespies, P. (2004). *Life and death decisions: Psychological and ethical considerations in end-of-life care.* Washington, DC: American Psychological Association.

Laird, J. (2003). Lesbian and gay families. In F. Walsh (Ed.), *Normal family processes: Growing diversity and complexity* (3rd ed., pp. 176–209). New York: Guilford Press.

Lebacqz, K. (1994). Appropriate vulnerability. In J. B. Nelson and S. P. Longfellow (Eds.), *Sexuality and the sacred: Sources for theological reflection.* Louisville, KY: Westminster/John Knox Press.

McGoldrick, M. (1999). Women and the family life cycle. In B. Carter & M. McGoldrick (Eds.), *The expanded family life cycle: Individual, family, and social perspectives* (3rd ed., pp. 106–123). Boston: Allyn and Bacon.

McGoldrick, M., Giordano, J., & Garcia-Preto, N. (Eds). (2005). *Ethnicity and family therapy* (3rd ed.). New York: Guilford Press.

Miller-McLemore, B. (2003). *Let the children come: Reimagining childhood from a Christian perspective.* San Francisco: Jossey-Bass.

Myers, D., & Scanzoni, L. (2005). *What God has joined together? A Christian case for gay marriage.* San Francisco: Harper.

Nichols, M. P., with Schwartz, R. (2004). Chapter 11: Family therapy in the twenty-first century. In *Family therapy: concepts and methods* (6th ed.). Boston: Pearson.

Ottati, D. F. (2006). *Theology for liberal Presbyterians and other endangered species.* Louisville: Geneva Press.

Pauw, A. P. (1997). Dying well. In D. Bass (Ed.), *Practicing our faith: A way of life for a searching people* (pp. 163–177). San Francisco: Jossey-Bass Publishers.

Peterson, B. D. (2006). Advances and complexities: In vitro fertilization (IVF) and embryo freezing. *Family Therapy Magazine,* Jan/Feb., 16–23.

Poling, J. N. (2003). *Understanding male violence: Pastoral care issues.* St. Louis, MO: Chalice Press.

Presbyterian Church (U.S.A.). (1991). *Presbyterians and human sexuality 1991.* Louisville, MO: Office of the General Assembly Presbyterian Church (U.S.A.).

Presbyterian Church (U.S.A.). (1998). *Selected theological statements of the Presbyterian church (U.S.A.) general assemblies (1956–1998).* Louisville, MO: Office of Theology and Worship.

Rando, T. A. (1993). *Treatment of complicated mourning.* Champaign, IL: Research Press.

Rieger, J. (2004). Liberation theology. In Hillerbrand, J. (Ed.). *The encyclopedia of Protestantism* (pp. 1090–1095). New York: Routledge.

Smith, T. A. (2006). (Ed.). *Frequently asked questions about sexuality, the Bible, and the church.* San Francisco: Covenant Network of Presbyterians.

Spring, J. A. (1996). *After the affair: Healing the pain and rebuilding trust when a partner has been unfaithful.* New York: Harper Collins Publishers.

Sue, D. W., & Sue, D. (2003). *Counseling the culturally diverse: Theory and practice* (4th ed.). New York: John Wiley & Sons.

Tanis, J. (2003). *Transgendered: Theology, ministry, and communities of faith.* Cleveland, OH: Pilgrim Press.

Townsend, L. (2000). *Pastoral care with stepfamilies: Mapping the wilderness.* St. Louis, MO: Chalice Press.

Trible, P. (1978). *God and the rhetoric of sexuality.* Philadelphia: Fortress Press.

Wimberly, E. (1997). *Counseling African American marriages and families.* Louisville, KY: Westminster John Knox Press.

Wuthnow, R. (1994). *God and mammon in America.* New York: Macmillan.

CHAPTER 6

The Practice of Marriage and Family Counseling and Islam

BELKEIS ALTAREB

And among His Signs
Is this, that He created
For you mates from among
Yourselves, that you
Dwell in tranquility with them,
And He has put love
And mercy between (your hearts):
Verily in that are Signs
For those who reflect.

—(Quran, 30:21)

Islam is one of the fastest growing religions, with nearly one billion follow-ers; adherents to this faith exist on every continent and nation. There is a plethora of information and more often misinformation that exists about the religion and its followers; unfortunately, this misinformation often con-fuses pertinent issues related to the Islamic belief structure, rituals, values, and how people within this faith system structure their lives. Given that

89

counseling and other social service practitioners will most likely deal with Muslim adherents at some time in their professional careers, it is prudent that human service workers understand how this faith constructs marriage and family, as many of the social issues revolve around religion and family.

The information presented in the following chapter provides a brief synopsis of vast topic areas with volumes of information, law, and interpretations from different Islamic schools of thought. Alongside the enormity of this topic from the legal and scholarly perspectives, there are also differences in the practice of Islam, with variations in practice among Muslims from different cultural backgrounds, socioeconomic statuses, nationalities, religious backgrounds, personal interpretations and preferences, which could be different from what is presented in the chapter. This chapter on the Islamic view of marriage and the family is a theoretical understanding of how marriage *should* be. Though the information presented provides a general overview of the Islamic view on marriage and family, it would be important for these generalities to be compared against the experiences, reality, and practice of the individuals, couples, or families in which practitioners work. One of the realities that exist among many Muslim families is the gap that exists between theory and practice; the way things should be religiously are sometimes at odds with the way things are practically. The present chapter does not really address the discrepancies or try to understand how they have come about, except to say that they exist. The following chapter outlines the most common understanding of marriage and family from an Islamic perspective.

Islam is an Arabic word derived from two root words: one *Salm*, meaning peace, and the other *Silm*, meaning submission. Islam is a complete way of life governing how individuals interact with their creator and to creation. In this system, individuals find peace through submission to the creator's rules. If people accept and follow these rules, peace and tranquility will result (Abdalati, 1993). As a complete way of life, Islam provides guidelines on the relationship between man and God and how people should treat each other. A Muslim is one who submits the self to the Will of the One God (Allah in Arabic; Mawdudi, 1980). Muslims believe that the Quran (holy book of Muslims), Hadith (sayings of the Prophet Muhammad), and Sunnah (behaviors of the Prophet Muhammad) provide instructions on how people should live their lives. In addition to more personal aspects of belief and faith, the many facets of social interactions are described in Islam, most notably within marriage and family. According to Muslims, Islam is a religion that chooses the middle path and is opposed to extreme positions in all affairs, especially those regarding family relationships. God says in the Quran, "We have made you a nation justly balanced" (2:143). The following pages examine more closely how marriage and family relationships function along a middle, balanced path in creating a unifying and workable system for all family members.

DEFINITION OF MARRIAGE

Within Islam, the family is viewed as the foundation of society; as such, there are prescribed rules, roles, expectations, and duties incumbent on family members (Mawdudi, 1980). Islam tends to see the family as ultimately good and almost sacred (Omran, 1994). In addition to providing mutual tranquility, support, and understanding between husband and wife, marriage satisfies sexual desires both culturally and legally, and at the same time allows the next generation to be raised with the necessary moral and social responsibilities (Abdalati, 1993).

According to the Islamic viewpoint, marriage is basic to family formation and Muslims are encouraged to marry (Al-Jibali, 2000). Muslims are advised to marry according to Al-Jibali (2000) because not only was marriage practiced by prophets, but God has instructed people to marry. Also, marriage preserves chastity and lawfully fulfills desire. Furthermore, marriage is considered to be a completion of faith. Though marriage can be postponed for important reasons, celibacy is not the Islamic way and was prohibited by the Prophet Muhammad (Al-Jibali, 2000). It was once reported that people came to the Prophet not wanting to marry because they wanted to devote themselves to worshipping God, but the Prophet (peace be upon him—pbuh) advised that as he worshipped, fasted, worked, and married then his followers should follow a similar way (Al-Qaradawi, 1982). It is considered to be a positive trait to follow in the footsteps of the Prophet's Sunnah. Moreover, the Prophet Muhammad (pbuh) spoke of marriage as being "half the religion": "Whoever has married has completed half of his religion; therefore let him fear Allah in the other half!" (Hadith quoted in Maqsood, 2000).

The Arabic term for marriage is *nikah*, or intercourse (Al-Jibali, 2000). According to Mir-Hosseini (1997), marriage is seen as a contract that makes sexual relations between a man and woman lawful; marriage is also seen as a religious obligation, especially as sexual contact outside of marriage is classified as a crime of *zina* (fornication) and is subject to a heavy punishment. Mir-Hosseini (1997) further contends that marriage takes on a religious dimension, as it preserves morals and chastity through the satisfaction of sexual needs within the limits set by God. Several of the social advantages of marriage outlined by Al-Jibali (2000) are that it safeguards societies from diseases and moral degeneracy, that it preserves kinship ties, and that it establishes the family environment—an environment that is critical to society's function and maintenance.

Muslims marry in a variety of ways depending upon their cultural practice, religious understanding and importance, and family requirements.

Typically, a man or his relatives will come to ask for marriage after hearing about a woman's good character, her beauty, or her family's position. In some societies, marriages are still arranged with couples having little say in the matter; however, this practice is not Islamic. From an Islamic perspective, individuals are allowed to see each other to ensure that neither finds the other unsuitable. Seeing one another does not necessarily mean that the two interact but that they have seen how the other's face looks. Al-Qarawadi (1982) suggests that a man who proposes marriage should be allowed to meet with his betrothed as long as she is accompanied by a *mahram*. A mahram is a male relative that women are prohibited from marrying, such as fathers, stepfathers, fathers-in-law, grandfathers, brothers, uncles, sons, stepsons, sons-in-law, and nephews. Moreover, when it comes to consent, it is the woman's right to make a decision concerning her marriage; her father or guardian is not permitted to ignore her wishes (Al-Qaradawi, 1982). In fact, it is forbidden in Islam for a father to deny a person from marrying his daughter, if the person is of good character and the daughter agrees.

Upon agreement to marry, a contract is signed outlining the specified amount required as a gift to the woman and the amount to be paid in the event of divorce (*mahr*). This amount not only depends upon what the bride's family asks but what the groom can afford. The Islamic view is that the mahr remains with the bride to use in preparation for the wedding; the Prophet Muhammad (pbuh) recommended that the mahr be a token gift to the bride, rather than an excessive amount asked of the groom. Other conditions can be placed in the marriage contract, such as transferring the right of divorce from the husband to the wife. The marriage concludes with a public announcement and celebration of the union; after the community celebration, the marriage is consummated.

Several categories of unions are unlawful in Islamic marriage. Men are not permitted to propose to divorced or widowed women during the time they must wait to determine whether they are carrying a child from their former husbands. Moreover, men must not approach women who are already engaged unless the engagement is broken. When it comes to marriage itself, men are prohibited from marrying their father's wives (whether divorced or widowed), their mothers and grandmothers, mothers-in-law, daughters, stepdaughters, daughters-in-law, granddaughters, aunts, nieces, foster mothers (milk-mothers who have suckled him during infancy), foster sisters, foster aunts, and foster nieces. In a similar vein, women are forbidden from marrying male relations as outlined above.

DATING AND COHABITATION

Marriage is the only legitimate way in which men and women are allowed to be alone together. Unsupervised dating (common among many people where persons of the opposite sex spend time alone together) and cohabitation (living with persons of the opposite sex before marriage) are prohibited in Islam in order to regulate sexual desire and to make any physical contact between individuals lawful (or *halal*; Al-Qaradawi, 1982). Moreover, because Islam regulates strict interactions between the sexes, dating is prohibited because of the belief that this practice leads to deviance and sexual temptation.

The Islamic prohibition of dating rests on the notion that privacy between a man and a woman is not allowed, unless a woman has a mahram with her (Al-Qaradawi, 1982). According to the Prophet Muhammad (pbuh): Whoever believes in Allah and the Last Day must never be in privacy with a woman without there being a mahram (of hers) with her, for otherwise Satan will be the third person [with them] (Al-Qaradawi, 1982). Al-Qaradawi (1982) noted that when Islam prohibits something, it closes all the avenues of approach to it. Hence, as dating and cohabitation could lead to exciting passions, opening ways to illicit sexual relations between a man and woman, and promoting indecency and obscenity, then they would necessarily be forbidden, or *haram*.

Although dating is prohibited, individuals may come to know each other through chaperoned meetings with family and friends for the purpose of marriage. Typically, it is a male or his relatives/friends who approach the family of an eligible female for the intention of marriage. Though some marriage seekers make known to family and friends what they are looking for in a spouse, often family and friends will look for basic criteria of beauty, piety, good manners, and good family reputation, then allow the strictly controlled chaperoned meetings to determine whether the couple like each other, share similar ideas and values, and are compatible for marriage. If a man already knows a woman and wishes to marry her, then he would still need to ask her family or guardians for permission to marry. It is typical for the man and/or his representatives to seek out potential marriage partners on his behalf; it is atypical for a woman or her representatives to do something similar. However, there is precedent within Islamic history for the latter to occur—the Prophet's first wife Khadijah, upon hearing that the Prophet was an honest man, sent a representative to ask him for marriage.

There is a misunderstanding by many that Muslim marriages are arranged in the sense that the couple has no choice in the matter. Although arranged marriages still do occur in some places in the Muslim world, they are neither the norm nor are required by the religion. In contrast, chaperoned meetings that have been arranged by family or friends are common among couples, though the outcome of such meetings is not arranged. Keeping to Islamic guidelines, these arranged and supervised meetings allow the couple to get to know each other under the watchful eye of others but do not commit the couple to anything lasting. After several meetings, couples find whether they share similar ideas, dreams, ways of thinking, etc. from which they can build a life together in marriage, or whether they are not compatible and look elsewhere for a potential spouse. If marriage does not result from these supervised meetings, then the process of seeking out an appropriate spouse begins again. The Islamic process of seeking out potential spouses is clear, objective, and goal-driven. Whether a couple chooses to marry or not is left to them to decide without the complications of emotional attachments and sexual desires clouding judgment.

The preceding discussion on supervised meetings between potential marriage partners is the appropriate Islamic way of meeting others for the intention of marriage, but this is not to say that all Muslims follow this manner. Some Muslims do go out on unsupervised dates; depending upon the cultural group, this practice may or may not be frowned upon by others in society. However, from an Islamic perspective, the practice is not appropriate because it could lead to uncontrolled sexual desires (Abdul-Rauf, 1995). According to Dahl (1997), marriage is the true arena for the divine and lawful sexuality. In Islam, intercourse between unmarried couples, be it premarital or postmarital, is a grave sin that is punishable. Extramarital sexuality threatens family stability and ultimately peace in a society because the activity causes strife for individuals, families, and societies (Al-Qaradawi, 1982). In the Quran God instructs people not to come near adultery because not only is it a "shameful and evil deed" but it also "opens the road to other evils" (17:32). Not only are legitimate rights and responsibilities denied to family members, but there are increased health risks, and any children born from such a union are not socially or legally protected. Children born outside of a lawful marriage are not only socially stigmatized, but they are not given the father's name and are not given their inheritance rights. Moreover, women within these unlawful unions are not fully protected as legitimate wives who have maintenance and inheritance rights (Al-Qaradawi, 1982).

The preceding paragraphs reiterated the Islamic view of keeping male-female interactions regulated so as not to entice sexual desires. The only legitimate manner for a man and woman to come together is in marriage. Islam forbids all means of eliciting sexual desires, whether this means being alone with the opposite gender, dressing provocatively, dating, and/or living together. Cohabitation as a means of living with a person to determine whether the person is a suitable marriage partner is not allowed in Islam because this arrangement does not provide legitimate rights and responsibilities for individuals; it does provide protection from sexual desires and temptations that may arise.

ROLES WITHIN MARRIAGES AND FAMILIES

One of the roles of the Muslim family is to provide financial and emotional support for dependent members (aged, sick, single adults, especially women, children, disabled); in this security of the family, individuals are able to proceed through life. One of the roles of the family is to instill in members loyalty to the group and to society. It is within the family system that Muslims develop religious training, develop moral character, establish close social relationships, and sustain loyalty both to family and society.

Family is not only the cradle of man, but it is also the cradle of civilization (Mawdudi, 1980). A family consists of the husband, the wife, and their children. Rules regarding the Muslim family are explicit, with the man being assigned the responsibility for earning and providing the necessities of life for his wife and children and for protecting them from life's hardships. The woman is assigned the duty of managing the household, training and bringing up the children, and providing her husband and children with comfort and contentment (Mawdudi, 1980). The Islamic view of family also prescribes children the duty of respecting and obeying their parents, and, when they are old, to care for their needs and serve them.

According to Abdul-Rauf (1995), both spouses have equal but separate roles within the family unit, and husbands and wives have duties and responsibilities to each other (Abdalati, 1993). Women and men are equally responsible for treating each other well and bringing up the children and rearing them in a good way, but have different and complementary roles due to their nature. The husband-father and wife-mother roles, though equally important, are not identical but reciprocal. The mother's duty is to provide comfort, care, and relaxation to her home, while the father's role is to shield and protect the family from the outside world and to provide steady guidance and discipline (Abdul-Rauf, 1995). Moreover, a husband's duty is to be kind and equitable to his wife, to care for her and treat her well, and to maintain his wife's needs from what he can afford. In a similar vein, a wife's duty is to keep her husband and home comfortable, to be honest, to keep her husband's property safe, and to make herself sexually desirable to her husband (Abdalati, 1993).

Some Muslim men erroneously believe that women are solely responsible for the housework; however, taking the Prophet Muhammad's actions as an example, then we know that he often assisted his wives in house duties. As a woman is ultimately responsible for making her house run smoothly, then extra thought and effort will need to go into how to do this if she chooses to work outside the home (Maqsood, 2000). Moreover, some writers (Abdalati, 1993; Maqsood, 2000) argue that it is when women and men go against their inherent natures that conflicts arise for individuals and families.

Within the parent-child relationship as well there are duties and responsibilities of both parents and children. Children have the right to life, legitimacy (knowing who their fathers are), good upbringing, and care. The rights of parents are complementary to the rights of children. Children should treat their parents with empathy, patience, gratitude, respect, praying for their souls, giving good counsel, deference, and financial support of parents if they are in need (Abdalati, 1993). In the Quran God refers to how parents should be treated:

Thy Lord hath decreed
That ye worship none but Him,
And that ye be kind
To parents. Whether one
Or both of them attain
Old age in thy life,
Say not to them a word
Of contempt, nor repel them
But address them
In terms of honor.
And out of kindness,
Lower to them the wing
Of humility, and say:
"My Lord! Bestow on them
Thy Mercy even as they
Cherished me in childhood." (17:23–24)

In Islam, children are instructed to give high esteem and devotion to parents. Mothers in particular are given a special status in prophetic traditions. According to numerous Prophetic sayings not only does heaven exist at mothers' feet, but mothers deserve special respect and attention (Al-Mawdudi, 1982). Respect for parents is stressed again when God says in the Quran (46:15): "We have enjoined on man Kindness to his parents: In pain did his mother Bear him, and in pain Did she give him birth."

CHILD BEARING, BIRTH CONTROL, ABORTION, TEENAGE PREGNANCY

The Islamic view on children is that they are a gift from God; as such, procreation is a natural extension of the marital bond (Omran, 1994). In the Quran, God says: "And Allah has made for you mates from yourselves and made for you, out of them, children and grandchildren" (16:72). Having children is encouraged, though there is recognition by Muslims that whether a couple has children and the number of children is determined by God. In the Quran, God says:

To God belongs the dominion
Of the heavens and the earth.
He creates what He wills
(And plans). He bestows
(Children) male or female
According to His Will (and Plan).
Or He bestows both males

And females, and He leaves
Barren whom He will. (42: 49–50)

Birth control as a means of spacing children or preventing financial hardships is permissible according to some Muslim scholars. Moreover, Omran (1994) argued that Muslim couples should also examine whether they have the appropriate time, social support, and environmental conditions to support the demands of additional children. If parents cannot properly raise children according to Islamic guidelines because of their particular situations, many Islamic scholars would support the view of family planning, though not all would agree, noting the unacceptable nature of people undoing what God has planned (Omran, 1994). Family planning and abortion, however, are not the same. In cases of abortion, the consensus is clearer. According to Albar (1989), many Islamic jurists allow abortion, provided there are medical reasons, before the soul enters the fetus at 120 days. All scholars, however, refute abortion after the soul enters the fetus, except in one situation only, when the life of the mother is endangered. Most scholars agree that abortion after 120 days from conception (17 weeks and one day) would amount to taking a life and would not be permissible (Albar, 1989). The soul entering the fetus at this specified time comes from numerous sayings of the Prophet Muhammad and subsequent scholars who have identified embryo stages mentioned by Quran and Hadiths (Albar, 1989). From an Islamic perspective, signs of human life do not begin at conception but when voluntary actions occur, which coincides with when Muslim scholars say the soul is breathed into a fetus by God.

As stated earlier because encounters between the sexes are strictly controlled, unwed teenage pregnancy is prohibited unless the teenagers are married. Sexual encounters are solely within the realm of marital relations only; premarital sex is prohibited.

FINANCES

From an Islamic viewpoint, men are designated as the head of household; as such, they are responsible for providing financially for their families. While men have typically made the money, women have been the ones to manage the home finances. If women have earned income from a job or other investment, they are free to utilize their money for whatever purpose they choose and are not obliged to use the money for household expenses. However, many working women are finding that what they believed to be their own money to use as they wish has turned out to be the sole income supporting the family, while men, instead of providing for household expenses with their income, use their income for other purposes because they can (R. Ibrahim, personal communication, April 2005). Rather than have conflict over whose income gets used to pay for household expenses, women may feel compelled to use their income out of necessity and in order to maintain peace at home (R. Ibrahim, personal communication, April 2005). Although the practice of using a wife's income to support the family may not be Islamic, a wife would have to be willing to have her family or the courts interfere in order to force the husband to honor his financial responsibility. While some women may resort to the courts to guarantee their Islamic rights, others may keep personal matters of finance within the privacy of the marriage. Ultimately, the husband, as the head of the Muslim household, is answerable to God for how the family operates; if he has neglected his Islamic responsibilities, then he alone is held accountable. Also, some Muslim men may expect their wives to work in order to release them from, or help them with, the burden of taking care of their families. Who works in a family, what each person does, and how money is managed are issues to be worked out by a couple. Unfortunately, when financial problems and conflicts are not addressed in a marriage, then these can lead to divorce.

DISSOLVING RELATIONSHIPS, DIVORCE, ANNULMENT

Marriage is a serious responsibility and agreement to marry should not be taken lightly. As described in the preceding paragraphs, a woman's consent for marriage is mandatory in Islam. Unlike a never-married woman whose father or other male guardian must give his own consent for the marriage, a woman who has been married previously can represent herself. The rationale for this is that the unmarried woman because of inexperience must have a male relative also agree with the marriage to ensure that the woman's full rights are protected, but the previously married woman knows what she is embarking upon by getting married and does not need a male guardian to represent her rights. Though marriage should be taken as a serious, permanent bond if it does not work well for any valid reason, then it may be terminated in kindness, honor, equity, and peace (Abdalati, 1993). When there are serious conflicts in the marriage, there are social and religious pressures for the couple to work on the relationship, as marriage is seen as an institution with social, financial, legal, psychological, and moral consequences (Abdul-Rauf, 1995).

Divorce is allowed in Islam when couples no longer are able to live together peacefully; though permissible, divorce is considered to be the least liked of what God has permitted (Al-Qaradawi, 1982). Whether a woman represented herself in marriage or gave a male guardian the authority to do so, the divorce procedure is similar. When couples are in conflict, they should appoint an arbitrator from each side to assist them in reconciliation. Usually family or friends are asked to step in to intervene as arbiters; in many Islamic countries, the courts have gotten involved to ensure that arbitration is used before granting divorces. Needless to say there are many social, religious, and familial constraints in finalizing a divorce; couples are asked to remember God's displeasure of divorce occurring without sufficient grounds (Abdul-Rauf, 1995).

From an Islamic perspective, men are the maintainers of their families and as such they have been given the right to divorce by God though a woman can invoke her right under some circumstances, such as desertion, cruelty, and/or failing to provide maintenance. When a woman invokes her right to divorce this is called *khula*; as a result, she forfeits the amount outlined in her marriage contract. For those women who want the right of divorce transferred to them in the marriage contract, then they can specifically request the provision to be included in their marriage contract. With all rights come responsibilities and consequences; within an Islamic context, when God gives men the right to divorce, then men are held responsible to God for the ensuing divorce and all consequences resulting from the divorce. Some husbands may take this right lightly and divorce their wives without cause, but doing so would mean that they are held responsible and accountable to God for their action.

The marriage process involves several stages from engagement period, contract signing, to the actual wedding party; at any stage, a breaking of the agreement can occur. It should be noted, however, that even though Islam permits divorce, most Muslim groups will have strong cultural oppositions to breaking off a marriage once it occurs, especially if there are children involved. A man can only divorce (and then reconcile) with his wife twice. Thereafter, if he divorces his wife a third time, then the divorce is considered final, and a reconciliation is not possible unless she marries someone else. God says in the Quran (2:229): "A divorce is only permissible twice: after that, The parties should either hold Together on equitable terms, Or separate with kindness." A divorced woman must have a waiting period of three monthly courses (*iddat*) before she can remarry another person in order to determine whether she is carrying a baby from her previous husband (Abdul-Rauf, 1995). If she is pregnant, then she cannot remarry until after she has given birth to her previous husband's baby. The rationale for this provision is to ensure that paternity of the child is clear.

MANAGING FAMILY AFTER SEPARATION AND/OR DIVORCE

As stated earlier, when a couple separates, several steps are recommended in order to reconcile the couple, from each couple trying to persuade the other, to physically separating themselves, and finally family and/or community members stepping in to try to reconcile the couple. Again, pressure is placed on the couple to remain together; unfortunately, there is stigma attached to being divorced, especially for women. For both separated and divorced women, husbands are responsible for financial maintenance, which is considered "a duty on the righteous" (Quran, 2:242).

Typically, in cases of divorce, women can keep young children until they are older; thereafter, they become the responsibility of the father. The exact age at which a mother can keep her child/children, along with specified maintenance, is not specifically mentioned in Islamic jurisprudence and is left to jurists within a particular society to determine age limits depending upon particular circumstances (Al-Qaradawi, 1982). The rationale provided for the practice of young children remaining with their mother is that they need the emotional support of their mother when they are young; then children need their fathers to guide and discipline them into adolescence. However, as children are the financial responsibility of fathers, they are more appropriately placed with him rather than becoming the burden of the mother who may wish to remarry or may find it difficult to financially support them on her own. Additionally, unlike a new husband who is not responsible financially for another man's children in Islam, a new wife to the husband will have little choice but to care for her husband's children. When a Muslim woman agrees to marry a Muslim man who has been previously married and has children, she is agreeing to care for his children. However, when a Muslim man marries a Muslim woman who has children from a previous marriage, he is not expected to be responsible for them. In fact, the previously married woman enters the new marriage free to begin her new life without the added responsibility of former children.

Men are responsible for maintenance of any children in a former wife's care, but some men may ignore this responsibility if women willingly took on their children's care after divorce. To prevent men from avoiding responsibility, then men are compelled to take total responsibility for their children from previous spouses. However, if women choose to care for her children from a former spouse and agree not to remarry, then she may be allowed by the courts to keep her children. The rules that govern Islamic divorce and separation were meant to safeguard family members and to bring about peaceful interactions, recognizing that financial and social hardships for divorced women are greater than for men. Despite the fact that Islam encourages peaceful marriages and in the event of divorce, peaceful separations, the reality is that divorce is a painful experience for individuals and families. Ideally, if the divorce is equitable and amenable, following Islamic guidelines, then both parties will try doing what is best for any children rather than battle over them.

HOMOSEXUALITY IN COUPLES AND FAMILIES

In contrast to the indecision of the scientific community in finding a common understanding of homosexuality, Islam is clear on the matter. As described in the Quran, the People of Lut (Lot) who were engaging in homosexual acts at the time are described with corruption, sin, transgression, ignorance, and crime: "Of all the creatures in the world, will you approach males, And leave those whom Allah has created for you to be your mates? Nay, you are a people transgressing (all limits)!" (Quran 26:165–166).

According to Al-Qaradawi (1982), homosexuality is a deviation from Allah's original rule that men and women should be attracted to each other and should propagate. Moreover, as sexual acts are private manners that should not be disclosed to anyone, vocalization of sexual preferences is not allowed. Instead, the Islamic view on committing sins is that persons should keep their sins secret, ask for forgiveness, and stop repeated offenses (El-Awady, 2003). Globally, there has been a push to reinterpret *Sharia* or Islamic jurisprudence, and in many countries it is no longer acceptable to publicly denounce homosexuality.

When people are confused about their sexual identity and are Muslim, the Islamic view is that they must seek treatment to prevent transgression. Dr. Yusuf Al-Qaradawi claimed that homosexuality is not a genetic disposition; instead, he noted that homosexuals, similar to drug addicts, need treatment. He noted that homosexuality is a "disease that needs a cure" (as quoted in Maqsood, 2003). According to Al-Qaradawi (1982), homosexuality deprives those who practice it of morality and decency; homosexuality disrupts society of its natural order. Earlier it was noted that the natural or God-given plan for human beings rested on the peace that was created by following God's plan. According to Islam, homosexuality is a perverted act that goes against what God ordained for human beings.

Feelings and actions are separated in Islam and have different obligations and consequences. For example, persons may feel a particular way and are obligated to themselves alone to seek Allah's guidance and help. However, if persons act on a feeling to commit a sin, then there are both social and legal consequences for the action. Using homosexuality as an example, a person may have unnatural urges, which would need treatment; they may never act on them because Islam forbids sexual relations, sexual experimentation, and other forms of sexual contact outside of marriage. To rid themselves of these private urges, they could try getting closer to God. If, however, they were to ever act on these urges, then the action is now considered a crime that requires punishment. However, Al-Qaradawi (1982) acknowledged the debate among Islamic jurists as to whether individuals who perform this act should receive death or whether the punishment should be the same as those who commit adultery (a number of slashes).

For Muslim people and societies, the degree to which secular and religious laws are understood, interpreted, and then judged worthy of punishment are often in conflict. Moreover, many Muslim societies and individuals are left to judge for themselves the degree of punishment warranted for particular behaviors described as crimes in Islamic law. For example, in cases of adultery, individuals may not receive an earthly punishment from government, but the Islamic understanding is that the offense would be punishable by

God on the Day of Judgment. In fact, many Muslims believe that receiving the earthly punishment would be far less painful than one received later, and some have reported wanting to receive the former rather than the latter. This being said, Al-Qarawadi (1982) stressed that even though Islamic law may seem severe, eliminating segments of a society for engaging in particular behaviors is in the interest and health of everyone in society.

Islamic society, family, and interactions are not about individuals but the group; as such, Muslims choose what God has prescribed for them that accounts for others in the group. With individual choices for Muslims come responsibilities and obligations to one's self, society, family, and ultimately God. Muslims are free to act or be any way they choose as long as they are within the parameters set by God; this is the Islamic balance. Muslims have rights to themselves, to others, and to God; they must balance these rights and responsibilities appropriately. If Muslims choose to transgress the limits set by God, then they accept the consequences of such actions. One such consequence is the belief in the Hereafter and that all individuals will be judged on their actions in this world. For many Muslims, the consequences of the Hereafter are enough to maintain a particular order and peace in society; for others, the finality of earthly death is a reminder of one day meeting their creator and answering to their deeds.

DEATH AND DYING

The Islamic view on death and dying is that the process is a natural continuum of the life cycle; as such, death is not seen as the end of life, but merely as a point of transition from the physical world to the next world. Death is not, therefore, something for Muslims to fear; instead, Muslims see death as bringing them a step closer to God.

All living things must die; as such, human beings are judged by how well they have lived according to Islamic principles. Muslims believe the life on this earth is only a transition period that precedes a life in the Hereafter. Winning the latter life is the goal of every Muslim, which is achieved through gaining God's satisfaction through believing in Him and following His commands and prescriptions (Sedki, n.d.). The reward for those who gain God's satisfaction and forgiveness is Heaven, and that for those who disobey God is Hell. Muslims are advised by Prophet Muhammad to work for this life as if they are living forever, and work for the latter life as if they are dying tomorrow. This saying highlights the balance that Muslims try to achieve for both this world and the Hereafter.

When death approaches, the close family and friends try to support and comfort the dying person through supplications as well as remembrance of God and his will; those near the dying person will help the person utter the declaration of faith, or shahadah. Upon death, the person's eyelids are closed, the body is covered, and preparation for burial takes place as soon as possible. The whole body is washed, preferably by same-gender close family members, making sure to respect the body at all times. The body is then perfumed and wrapped in a white shroud. Muslims gather, and a congregational prayer is performed for the dead. The body is buried soon after the prayer, usually within one or two days. The wrapped body is laid on its right side facing Mekkah at the bottom of the dug grave. A ceiling is attached to the grave so that when covered with dirt the ceiling protects the face from dirt. The family of the dead has a responsibility to fulfill any debts the person had. Visiting the graves is recommended for the living to remember death and the Day of Judgment.

It is believed that there are several stages that occur after a person dies. First, Islam views that though the person's body has died in this earthly world, the soul proceeds onto another stage. The grave life is one in which angels ask the dead about their lives, deeds, and beliefs; if they are believers who have spent their time on earth following God's commands then the grave life is comforting, but if they have done evil in their life, then the grave is torturous for them. In the grave life, the soul undergoes development that is likened to growth of the fetus in the womb, preparing for the birthing experience. Similarly, the soul prepares for the Hereafter experience, waiting to face God. The point of a Muslim's life is to be able to face the Creator and be judged according to good and bad deeds that have been written on books that will be read to a person on the Day of Judgment. A blissful Heaven is the reward for believers, while hell is the punishment for people who performed mischief and evil in the world.

Throughout life, Muslims must constantly choose between good and evil, right and wrong, and individual/self and family/society. In these choices, there should be balance created so that individuals are working in this life as though they will live forever, but also working for the Hereafter. Neither rights nor responsibility to self nor to others is denied. As the world becomes more complex, the guidelines remain the same though choices become more numerous. As long as these choices are not forbidden by God, then they are likely lawful (Al-Qaradawi, 1982).

The preceding chapter on the Islamic view of marriage and family was written so that the majority of Muslims would accept its validity. However, it is reiterated once again that some Muslim individuals may disagree with what is presented. In cases where clients present a different view of material outlined in the chapter, it will be important to check out how individuals see themselves and their faith in relation to the disputed material. For example, as the world becomes more individualistic many Muslim youth may come to believe that their choices should outweigh any prescribed parameters offered by formal religious guidelines. In this case, religious material remains valid and unchanged in today's world, but what has changed is construction of individual identity, such that persons' view of themselves as Muslims might adhere to fewer or different Islamic guidelines. Clinicians and social service helpers should assess how individuals see themselves and how important these individuals see their faith in shaping their lives and choices. It may be that some Muslims see faith as important while others may indicate that this is not the case. We should not assume that just because we are working with individuals, couples, or families who are Muslim that their faith is important in shaping their reality. For those Muslims, however, who indicate that religion is important, then it is hoped that the preceding pages provide a meaningful and useful framework from which clinicians can gauge their clients' worlds.

REFERENCES

Abdalati, H. (1993). *Islam in focus.* Indianapolis, IN: American Trust Publications.

Abdul-Rauf, M. (1995). *The Islamic view of marriage and the family* (3rd ed.). Alexandria, VA: Al-Saadawi Publications.

Albar, M. (1989). *Human development as revealed in the Holy Quran and Hadith.* Jeddah, Saudi Arabia: Saudi Publishing & Distributing House.

Al-Jibali, M. (2000). *The Muslim family 1—The quest for love and mercy: Regulation for marriage & wedding in Islam.* Arlington, TX: Al-Kitab & As-Sunnah Publishing.

Al-Qaradawi, Y. (1982). *The lawful and the prohibited in Islam* (K. El-Helbawy, M. M. Siddiqui, & S. Shukry, Trans.). Indianapolis, IN: American Trust Publications.

Dahl, T. S. (1997). *The Muslim Family: A study of women's rights in Islam.* (R. Walford, Trans.). Oslo, Norway: Scandinavian University Press.

El-Awady, N. (2003). *Homosexuality in a changing world: Are we being misinformed.* Retrieved September 26, 2005, from http://islamonline.net/english/contemporary/2003/02/article01-0.shtml

Maqsood, R.W. (2000). *The Muslim marriage guide.* New Delhi, India: Goodword Books.

Mawdudi, A. A. (1980). *Towards understanding Islam.* (K. Ahmad, Ed. & Trans.). London: The Islamic Foundation.

Mir-Hosseini, Z. (1997). *Marriage on trial: A study of Islamic family law—Iran and Morocco compared.* London: I. B. Tauris.

Omran, A. R. (1994). *Family planning in the legacy of Islam.* London: United Nations Population Fund.

Sedki, R. (n.d.). *Dying and death: Islamic view.* Retrieved September 29, 2005, from http://www.jannah.org/articles/death.html

The Holy Quran — English text, translations, and commentary (1983 ed.). (A. Y. Ali., Trans.). Brentwood, MD: Amana.

CHAPTER 7

The Practice of Marriage and Family Counseling and Buddhism

JHAMPA SHANEMAN

DEFINING MARRIAGE

Marriage is a special commitment between two people. Friends, family, and community all share the experience via the ceremony and rituals performed. Buddhism, according to the teachings of Lord Buddha, does not actually solemnize marriages. Marriage ceremonies are a civil ceremony in the Buddhist world. Rituals are not lead by the clergy nor is the Buddha invoked to consecrate the union. The ceremony does, however carry a high emotional value and spiritual overtones. Each partner may bring spiritual qualities and feelings to the relationship.

Buddhist Stories About Marriage

There are some excellent scriptures in Buddhism demonstrating how partners can have an extensive and deep commitment even extending beyond this rebirth. The Jakata Tales are a set of such stories. These recount the past lives of Buddha Shakyamuni as a common man called the Bodhisattva Siddhartha, an individual aspiring for enlightenment. Buddha explained each Jakata Tale by describing his role and the other characters, the plot, and the lessons learned. These stories demonstrate qualities a Buddhist would wish to emulate. (See http://en.wikipedia.org/wiki/Rebirth_%28Buddhism%29.)

The particular story we will recount is a rebirth of Bodhisattva Siddhartha as a wood cutter. The Buddha's current wife, Yodhasara, also had reincarnated as the Bodhisattva and was Siddhartha's wife for that rebirth too. The story explains that Bodhisattva Siddhartha was a humble man living in the forests of India. Each morning he would cut firewood and sell it in the neighboring villages. His wife tended their small hut and prepared his afternoon meals, which she would serve on his return (Lodan, 1993, p. 491).

One day, after the Bodhisattva Siddhartha had departed to the forest, an Indian Holy Man came by the hut. Bodhisattva Yodhasara had just cooked bread and vegetables for the afternoon meal. It is traditional in India that wandering religious practitioners beg their daily meal. She was moved by the man's quiet and respectful manner. She saw the light of realization in his eyes and so with great faith she gave him all the food of the day. The man retired to the edge of the forest to eat. At that moment the Bodhisattva Siddhartha returned from his work. He was tired and hot. He realized immediately his meal was gone and that a despicable looking beggar was eating it. He was furious. He scolded Bodhisattva Yodhasara and berated her for giving food to such a dirty and worthless individual. His frustration grew and he started to yell at the holy beggar. He cried, "You have no right to eat this food. You are ugly and dirty and look no better than a burnt piece of wood! Black and filthy! How dare you eat my hard earned food?"

People in India believe in karma. Karma is created by positive and negative actions and returns in the future as effects similar to the cause. In fact East Indians believe the strongest karma one can create is with holy people. This is because holy people embody purity and universal love. So the Bodhisattva Siddhartha had just made a huge error. Not only did he collect bad karma by yelling at his wife, he also accumulated an enormous amount of negative karma by swearing at the wandering holy man. Bodhisattva Yodhasara realized this as soon as Bodhisattva Siddhartha started yelling. She quickly offered a prayer to help counteract the bad karma her ignorant husband was creating. Her prayer was, "Just as my husband will have to take a rebirth and bear the ripening karmic effects of swearing at this holy man, may my prayer create a positive karmic connection with him. When Bodhisattva Siddhartha is born in a future existence with skin that looks like a black burnt stick because of cursing the holy man, may I again meet him and not be repelled by his ugliness. May I come to love him, marry him and be able to heal his skin condition with herbs and ointment." So Bodhisattva Yodhasara was able to create positive karma in spite of her husband's errors. The story continues to say the beggar also offered prayers to help them both attain enlightenment. The Bodhisattva Siddhartha realized his error and apologized to them both, thus lessening his karma load. He promised not to let attachment and anger dominate his thoughts. The saint gave them spiritual instruction and they lived out their lives in peace and harmony (Dhargave, personal communication, 1974).

This is an excellent example of the Buddhist view of marriage. It incorporates basic Buddhist principles about past and future lives, the law of cause and effect, and compassion. Although each Buddhist country will have its own special ceremony to celebrate marriage, still all these countries have this belief system underlying the ceremony.

Courtship and Arranged Marriages

The Buddha is quoted to have said, "If a man can find an understanding and suitable wife and a woman can find an understanding and suitable husband, both are fortunate indeed" (Dhammananda, 1987). Culturally courtship in the Buddhist world has many expressions. Generally courtship has parental supervision and the parents can even require an arranged marriage. The more traditional the family the more this is the case. Nowadays with the relaxation of traditional values many Buddhist families are open-minded and allow marriage to be based on mutual attraction and love.

There is one form of arranged marriage that we may not be familiar with in the west. This is the marriage of several brothers to one woman. I knew of a young Tibetan Buddhist man who was destined to marry the wife of his three older brothers. The reason for this arrangement was to ensure no division of the family estate. The logic was if all the brothers were to father their children through one woman then the land remained intact. Due to the Chinese invasion of Tibet in 1959 some of the family members fled to India as refugees. This freed the young man from his marriage constraints and he ended up marrying the woman of his choice. He confessed to me privately he was happy in a small way for the Chinese invasion.

One facet of Buddhist courtship is the use of astrology. Interested Buddhist partners will seek astrological compatibility and harmony between their birth years and months. The basis of the astrology chart is not the western zodiac. Buddhists use either a lunar calendar or the Chinese system of astrological calculation. The Chinese system breaks time into 5 cycles of twelve years. Each year is assigned an animal image and these twelve animals are further grouped by five elements to equal a total cycle of sixty years. Eligible marriage couples approach an astrologer to discover if there are any great astrological obstacles to their relationship and marriage. If they get a favorable indication then they will ask for an auspicious date for the marriage. After more astrological calculations the proper date and time are set and the marriage is announced.

Buddhism has a definition for courtship eligibility. The term is "un-owned" and this means the man or woman is free from the following constraints. They are either no longer a minor under the care of their parents or they are not in an existing committed relationship. This means they are free and un-owned and thus available to enter into a potential relationship. Although different Buddhist cultures do apply guidelines to courtship and cohabitation, strictly speaking the above definition is the only one prescribed by the Buddha.

The readers may not be aware that the Buddha in his early years was a crown prince. He had free access to the many concubines of the court during this time of his life. This was customary in ancient India and so one can assume the Buddha prior to his enlightenment and life as a monk had a good sexual education (http://en.wikipedia.org/wiki/Kama_Sutra). Premarital sex between consenting couples is not explicitly barred in Buddhist countries but again this custom can vary from culture to culture.

MARRIAGE CEREMONIES

Buddhist marriage requirements and ceremonies vary greatly. An example of cultural variance is Thailand. All mature Thai men must by law spend three months in a monastery as a monk before they marry. This ensures they have an opportunity to know the monk's life of peace and contemplation. Buddhist monks and nuns are taught worldly life is mixed with suffering. The teachings state that if the mind is deluded then the causes of suffering exist. The monk's or nun's life is an alternative. Those with ordination are living a life free of attachment and are on a path to lead them to freedom from disturbing emotions and delusions. If the eligible young man finds religious life satisfying then he can remain in the monastery. Men who do not like monastic life and its discipline are free to return to lay life and marry. The removal of the ordination is accomplished with a small ceremony where the precepts are returned to the abbot. The man does three prostrations, states that he does not wish to live within the disciplines of the ordination and by returning the robes of ordination to the abbot the precepts are removed.

Buddhist marriage ceremonies are a celebration of the couple's commitment or union. Although religious officials are not present for the marriage, often a small religious blessing is arranged prior to the wedding. The monks and nuns of a local temple are asked to offer prayers for each individual's health, wealth, and happiness. Therefore couples go to a local temple, make three prostrations to the altar, and receive a blessing prayer. After the prayers the couple returns to a secular location to celebrate the marriage.

Marriage ceremonies differ as much as cultural groups and communities differ. Generally a local government official will register the marriage or the families of the bride and groom will enter into a legal agreement. Concluding these formalities the families celebrate much as they would in any western culture.

MARRIAGE COUNSELING

Buddhism promotes the ideal of self-liberation. To become enlightened one must personally strive for realization. The same rule applies to worldly life.

If one wishes to be happy one must personally cultivate the causes of happiness. The body, speech, and mind must harmonize with virtuous intentions and positive action. Therefore marriage partners do not seek the assistance of the Buddhist clergy as a couple. They seek advice and comfort on a personal level. A monk or nun would give them a discourse of the Buddha and inspire them on an individual basis. The Buddhist monk or nun, bound by rules of celibacy, cannot comment on techniques to help the couple maintain their marriage. In fact Buddhist monks and nuns have precepts that explicitly forbid them from making such comments. Rather the clergy advises each person as an individual to seek a resolution to the problems they face. The main advice monks offer is to be patient, thoughtful, and compassionate.

True to Buddhist tradition, councilors, who can be ordained or lay Buddhists, will offer specific advice and support to people seeking assistance. A lay councilor can also be more explicit regarding marital problems whereas a monk or nun cannot. An individual is first asked by the councilor to be personally responsible for their actions. Happiness is created by each person individually. This is the rule of karma. A person is the product of his or her own actions and cannot lay blame at the feet of others (wikipedia.org). If a marriage partner has a problem they must look within to see what role or part they have played in the situation. They are asked to reflect on the intentions they brought to the situation. Are their intentions and expectations realistic or not? Have they created an expectation based on an illusion? After suitable personal contemplation and meditation the client is offered various meditation techniques to resolve the issues.

One of the fundamental ideals in Buddhism is the Four Noble Truths. (See http://en.wikipedia.org/wiki/Four_Noble_Truths.)The first is the Noble Truth of Suffering. This leads to the second fundamental Buddhist thought of the Noble Truth of the Cause of Suffering. This develops into the third Noble Truth, the Cessation of Suffering, and that leads to the path to accomplish this goal, the fourth Noble Truth of the Path Leading to the Cessation of Suffering. All Buddhist teachings lie on these foundation principles.

A Buddhist councilor may utilize this format of the Four Noble Truths to help the client realize and resolve the problems in their marriage. For example, the First Noble Truth states there is suffering. In the case of a marital problem there would be the sufferings of desire, being separated from the object of desire, not attaining the object of desire, and although attaining the object of desire not being satisfied. (See wikipedia.org, Four Noble Truths.) These sufferings all agitate the mind and cause unhappiness.

The Second Noble Truth states there is a cause to this suffering. The three primary causes as explained by the Buddha are ignorance, attachment, and anger (Berzin, 2002). If the client does not understand their ignorance then the councilor will delineate what type of ignorance the client is possibly being effected by. The main misunderstanding the client may have is to not comprehending the nature of the continuity of cause and effect. This is the ignorance of karma and means the client does not realize that from negative intentions and actions follow suffering. The counselor may use the analogy that a fruit seed produces fruit and a poisonous seed produces poison. If an action is initiated by delusion or anger, then it will produce effects related to its motive and similarly if the action is motivated by positive intentions then happiness will follow. The client comes to see they have used unskillful or negative intentions and actions to deal with their spouse. The marital problem and related suffering is the outcome of the deluded activity.

The Third Noble Truth is the Cessation of Suffering. This truth inspires the client to understand there is freedom from suffering and the causes of suffering. Traditional Buddhist terminology refers to this attainment as nirvana (wikipedia.org, Nirvana), but it can also be redefined in terms relevant to the client, in this case freedom from marital problems. The client understands there is the possibility of freedom from the sufferings of ignorance, delusion, and unhappiness.

The Fourth Noble Truth is the path leading to the cessation of suffering. The councilor encourages the client to familiarize themselves with the law of cause and effect to ensure their actions are positively motivated. This would include a contemplative meditation where the client reviews the Buddha's teachings on karma. The path to resolution of marital conflict may also include meditation instruction on how to develop a calm and peaceful mind. The meditation technique generally used in Buddhist therapy is a mindful awareness of the breath. The client is taught to be attentive of their inhalations and exhalations at the area of the nostrils. This will lead to a calm and alert mind that in turn can assist the client to be mindful in daily activity. Mindful awareness helps the client not to fall back into old negative habit patterns and to maintain a positive intention throughout the day.

The essence of these two Buddhist techniques is the instruction concerning the law of cause and effect and a simple breathing meditation with mindfulness. The councilor can add to these Buddhist teachings further instructions to inspire the client such as the benefits of a good heart and the actions of love and compassion.

We do find in Buddhist scripture advice on the responsibilities of married couples. The Buddha's teachings are called Discourses or Suttas. One such teaching is called the *Sigalovada Sutta, The Discourse to Sigala (Buddha Sakyamuni, 500 BC*, Narada Thera, Trans.). It prescribes a layperson's code of discipline. This Sutta was translated from the Pali by Narada Thera and is paraphrased below.

Thus have I heard: On one occasion the Exalted One was dwelling in the Bamboo Grove in the Squirrels' Sanctuary near Rajagaha. Now at that time, young Sigala, a householder's son, rising early in the morning, departing from Rajagaha, with wet clothes and wet hair, worshipped with joined hands the various quarters—the East, the South, the West, the North, the Nadir, and the Zenith.

The Sutta continues and Sigala meets the Buddha. The Buddha gives advice to Sigala regarding his conduct as a layman. The key advice for marriage now follows.

In five ways, young householder, should a wife be ministered to by a husband:

1. by being courteous to her,
2. by not despising her,
3. by being faithful to her,
4. by handing over authority of the household to her,
5. and by providing her with adornments.

The wife thus ministered to show her compassion to her husband in five ways:

1. she performs her duties well,
2. she is hospitable to relations and attendants,
3. she is faithful,
4. she protects his income,
5. she is skilled and industrious in discharging her duties.

It appears that although the Buddha would not talk about marriage itself, he does talk about the responsibilities of each partner. Interestingly the Sutta comments that a husband should give authority to his wife regarding maintenance of the home and family. Many cultures are considered patriarchal and a woman is considered chattel in a marriage. Buddhism stresses the interdependent relationship of the two people. If they both support each other then the family will prosper. This advice naturally will gain acceptance or rejection in different Buddhist countries depending on the cultural setting. Buddhism does not have a dogma for the faithful. Buddhism stresses self-realization and enlightenment. Therefore counselors may direct the individual to respect their spouse and thus collect positive karma.

CHILDBEARING, BIRTH CONTROL, AND ABORTION

Buddhism promotes an attitude of loving-kindness. Buddhists believe in past and future lives and that the fetus is a person from the moment of conception. Buddhists feel conception has three factors: the semen, the ovum, and the consciousness of the person taking rebirth. The child is not considered to have a clean state of being or mind but rather possess previously established tendencies or potentialities. Buddhists do consider it important to supply the newborn with the best circumstances possible for his or her development.

In a recent Mind Life Conference (The 8th Mind and Life Conference, 2000) with His Holiness the Dalai Lama, the importance of love for children in the family was clearly demonstrated. His Holiness said loving-kindness was an important principle in Buddhism, but having listened to the research material at the conference he was even more convinced of the great need for love in the early years of children.

Traditionally birth control is considered an obstacle for sentient beings (living beings) to take a rebirth. It is considered bad karma to stop the possibility of a child's conception. His Holiness the Dalai Lama has commented on this Buddhist ideal. He said with the current state of the world it is irresponsible to uncontrollably produce children. The world cannot support the needs of unlimited human beings. Buddhism has no dogma and so it utilizes common sense on religious issues as a mechanism to address concerns such as birth control. The onus is also placed on individuals to take personal responsibility and to use compassionate intelligence in all decisions.

As for the use of birth control Buddhism does have a comment. If birth control was to be used for unlimited sexual activity in noncommitted relationships, Buddhism would consider this a cause of delusion and an action of self-gratification. The individual is seeking pleasure for the sake of pleasure alone and thus the activity increases desire, which is a cause of suffering and dissatisfaction. This is in harmony with the first and second noble truths of suffering and the cause of suffering because the action is motivated by lust and will result in a dissatisfied and suffering mind. In contrast the use of birth control as a means to stop unwanted pregnancy in a developing or committed relationship would be considered common sense for a Buddhist. Birth control is not judged in a positive or negative manner; rather, the stress is placed on the motivation underlying its use.

Abortion is considered murder in Buddhist terms. This again is subject to the above criteria of motivation. Generally Buddhists promote a pro-life position for themselves as individuals. If asked how they felt about abortion a Buddhist would express deep concern for the unborn fetus. Regarding abortion for others through Buddhism would be pro-choice. People have the right to collect karma and do as they wish. To categorically close the door on abortion is too broad a rule. Each situation has its merits and demerits and a person could have an abortion for humane and compassionate reasons. Buddhism would not hide the fact that abortion entails the collection of negative karma because the life force of the fetus is stopped. This is not categorically classed as bad karma though as it may be an action for needful or compassionate reason. Karma is always proportionate to the motive that creates the action. (See wikipedia.org/wiki/Karma.) If one were to have an abortion with a callus and uncaring attitude then the full negative results of murder would be collected. Motive creates the wide diversity of karmic seeds and ripening effects (Lodan, 1993).

Teenage pregnancy or pregnancy out of wedlock is not a religious issue. Marriage is not religiously institutionalized so it is more an issue for the conceiving parents and the culture. There is encouragement from Buddhism to respond in a thoughtful and compassionate manner if someone becomes pregnant. Each person is responsible for the role they play in the pregnancy. Each is collecting karma proportionate to the way they acted and are acting. Buddhism sponsors care and love for the fetus and the child, irrespective of who takes responsibility for the upbringing (The 8th Mind and Life Conference, 2000).

DISSOLVING RELATIONSHIPS, DIVORCE, AND ANNULMENT

Buddhism is pragmatic regarding the legalities of marriage and divorce. All the issues of separation and divorce are dealt with by the laws of the land or by responsible members of the community. Marriages in Buddhist countries are based on a marriage contract and this is either written by the families or is preset by law. Thus all issues in a divorce are handled by the courts.

The Buddhist faith does have commentary on how an individual might deal with the failure of a relationship. The initial teachings of Buddhism state that worldly life is fraught with pain and suffering. This is the first noble truth of suffering. Although all beings strive for happiness there is no guarantee of attaining it. Happiness or suffering is related to one's current attitude and the ripening effect of the past accumulation of karma. If one has a positive attitude and a wealth of past positive karma then life will be pleasant and fulfilling. If one has a poor attitude and an accumulation of negative past actions then happiness will be difficult to attain. Happiness is a subjective experience and for some a painful situation does not have to entail suffering. Buddhism says physical pain and mental anguish are one way to respond to a difficult situation but it is not inherent to the experience of difficulty.

Attitude plays a significant role regarding happiness. An enlightened attitude views a divorce or separation with personal responsibility. The person reflects and meditates on what role they played in the failure of the relationship. Anger and ill will are negative karmic responses irrespective of how justified the person may feel. The use of anger just guarantees the separation will be painful, in fact more painful than it has to be. A Buddhist approach to divorce is the patient acceptance of suffering, feeling compassion toward the partner, and a personal review of the causes for the breakdown of the relationship. This is an enlightened Buddhist attitude.

Naturally divorce in Asia and with Buddhist families is as painful as it is in any culture. No one wishes to feel pain and suffer. A good practitioner of Buddhist philosophy and meditation has ample tools to resolve interpersonal problems. There are many Buddhist teachings on the suffering nature of life and how to use that dissatisfaction constructively to maintain balance and composure. The onus is on the individual to seek solutions and come to peace with life's unpleasant events. This is reflected in the fourth noble truth of the path leading to the cessation of suffering.

DEATH AND DYING

Buddhism has a wealth of material for individuals to use as death approaches. Therefore a practicing Buddhist would be well prepared for death. There are three primary meditations used to familiarize the individual with impermanence and death. These three meditations state that death is definite, the time is indefinite, and nothing material helps at the time of death. The last meditative point includes reflections on the nature of relationships. The Buddha said, "All that is born will die, all that rises will fall, all that is gathered will scatter and all that meets will part" (Lodan, 1993, p. 405). So inherent in all relationships is a final parting. This fact of life is not hidden in Buddhism.

An individual is encouraged to incorporate the reflections on impermanence into daily life. This actually has a positive impact. If one is not eternally with a lover or spouse then it is important to express and not postpone positive feelings and actions for that person. Love and support are positive karma activities. Often individuals postpone intimate interactions because of being busy or thinking there will be time at a later moment. There is no guarantee for anyone that there will be a later moment. Although everyone likes to think death will not happen today or within the foreseeable future, this again is just a hope and actually has no factual basis (Lodan, 1993, p. 246). The realization of the fragile nature of life helps inspire individuals to be more present and forthcoming in a relationship. Thus the awareness of impermanence and death is an asset to a healthy relationship.

When death does arrive in a relationship Buddhism offers various rituals and prayers. There are a set of prayers in Tibetan Buddhism called *The Tibetan Book of the Dead* (Thurman, 1994). This book specifies prayers can be beneficial in the first 49 days after a death. The book describes how to pray for the deceased while they are in the intermediate state between death and their next rebirth. These prayers also help those left behind deal with their feelings. Buddhist prayers offer an opportunity for the living to do something positive for the deceased.

The death of a loved one is a traumatic event. One of the primary qualities of a religion is to offer comfort to those with suffering. Buddhism suggests that living beings cycle through rebirth and death in a constant manner. The quality of any one rebirth is based on the karmic accumulations of the being. The story at the beginning of this chapter is an example of the Buddhist belief in karma and rebirth. Bodhisattvas Siddhartha and Yodhasara took several births together and assisted each other many times in their pursuit of both mundane and spiritual happiness. In the final rebirth of Siddhartha where he became the Buddha, he explicitly sought out Yodhasara after his enlightenment and gave her teachings on liberation. It is said that she attained personal liberation. This is seen as Buddha's final gift to his wife of many rebirths.

Individuals often see a relationship as a one lifetime event. Buddhism and Buddhist counselors offer a different perspective. Buddhism says clearly that a relationship can span several rebirths as with the story of Siddhartha and Yodhasara. A councilor if dealing with a divorce could express the idea that if the couple do not rectify or purify the bad karma created in a current life's divorce that they will most likely meet again in a future life and continue the conflict. Although it is a hypothetical situation it could motivate both parties to resolve hurt feelings and forgive each other. When someone's death is the termination of the relationship the ones left behind can feel comforted that they may meet the deceased again in a future existence and continue to have good relations.

HOMOSEXUALITY

Traditional Buddhism recognizes homosexuality as a choice arising from past karmic tendencies. (See http://en.wikipedia.org/wiki/Homosexuality#Middle East_and_Central_Asia.) There is no quote specifically about homosexuality but it can be understood within the principles of karma. The Buddha's only instruction about homosexual activity in his discourses was for the ordained spiritual community not to accept homosexual individuals as monks or nuns. (See http://www.thubtenchodron.org/Publications/PreparingForOrdination/ PFO_Appendix2.html.) Regarding comments for lay individuals, it appears to have been left up to personal choice.

The same Buddhist principles about life, its suffering, and its solutions can be applied to all, irrespective of sexual orientation. Considering the Buddha explicitly did not comment about marriage but rather talked about personal responsibility, one can assume the same suggestions apply to homosexual relationships. For example, in the ordination precepts of celibate monks it explicitly states to not insert the penis in any orifices of the body. It does not comment or judge the activity; rather, the precepts merely define it as inappropriate activity for ordained individuals.

In pure terms of Buddhist philosophy and tenets each individual is solely responsible for the karma they accumulate. If an individual acts in a virtuous and compassionate manner they gather positive karma. The definition of virtue in Buddhism is the avoidance of causing harm to oneself or others. Thus irrespective of one's sexual orientation this tenet can be applied equally. It seems inappropriate to say that a heterosexual encounter is virtuous and a homosexual one is non-virtuous. If both people act in a courteous manner then both are virtuous. If either individual acts in a disrespectful or hurtful manner then they accumulate negative karma. The main factor is motivation.

CONCLUSION

Relationship and marriage is a bond between two people willing to make a strong commitment to each other. Buddhism offers a frank and objective view about marriage. It is a civil event and a union between two people. It is a personal choice for the marriage couple to bring spiritual qualities to the relationship. It can be assumed the intention of spiritual and religious beliefs is to benefit all. A good Buddhist would bring positive qualities to his or her marriage. Each individual is responsible for how he or she acts in the marriage. Buddhist principles of mindfulness, wisdom, and compassion enhance the possibility of a successful marriage.

This chapter has covered a wide variety of subjects related to relationship and marriage. I will close with a quote from His Holiness the Dalai Lama, verbal teaching translated by Jhampa Shaneman (1978),

> I do not care if you believe in the Buddha. Do not care if you believe in past and future lives. I do not care if you believe in karma but I do care that you believe in compassion. This is because if you take compassion to heart then you will accumulate positive karma. This will then give you a good rebirth and you will actually accomplish what the Buddha wished of you. Therefore compassion is the root of all virtues and happiness.

REFERENCES

Berzin, A. AB. (2002). Mind and mental factors: The fifty-one types of subsidiary awareness description of root and secondary delusions in Buddhism. Retrieved May 12, 2006, from mind and mental factors http://www.berzinarchives.com/sutra/sutra_level_4/mind_mental_factors_51.html/ mindmentalfactors51.html

Buddha, sayings regarding the First Noble Truth of Suffering

Buddha, quote for the sexual experience of the Buddha as a youth. Retrieved June 23, 2006, from http://en.wikipedia.org/wiki/Kama_Sutra

Dalai Lama (2000, March 20-24). The 8th Mind & Life Conference, Dharamsala, India. His Holiness the XIV Dalai Lama (March 2000). The 8th Mind and Life Conference (bi-annual conference with HHDL held either in India or abroad. Participants are the leading educators or scholars related to the subject of each conference.

Dhammananda, Ven. K. Sri (1987). Source: Published by The Buddhist Missionary Society, 123. Jalan Berhala, 50470 Kuala Lumpur, Malaysia. Transcribed from the print edition in 1995 by Mark Blackstad under the auspices of the DharmaNet Dharma Book Transcription Project, by arrangement with the publisher. Copyright © 1987 Ven. K. Sri Dhammananda, Access to Insight edition © 2005 For free distribution. This work may be republished, reformatted, reprinted, and redistributed in any medium. It is the author's wish, however, that any such republication and redistribution be made available to the public on a free and unrestricted basis and that translations and other derivative works be clearly marked as such.

Dhargave, G. N. (1974). Verbal story in Dharmsala, India. (Source is a verbal story told at the Tibetan Library of Works and Achieves in Dharmsala, H. P. India.)

Lodan, T. (1993). *Path to enlightenment in Tibetan Buddhism (How to utilize death and impermanence in a constructive manner).* (1st ed., pp 225-253). Australia: Tushita Publications.

Sigalovada, Sutta. (1995). *The discourse to Sigala.* (Narada Thera, Tran.) May 12, 2006.

Thurman, R. (Trans.) (1994). *The Tibetan Book of the dead (Mystical classics of the world).* Huston Smith (Intro.). New York: Bantam Book.

Wikipedia. Definition of 4 Fundamentals in Buddhim. From http://en.wikipedia.org/wiki/Four_Noble_Truths

Wikipedia. Definition of Homosexuality. From http://en.wikipedia.org/wiki/Homosexuality#Middle_East_and_Central_Asia

Wikipedia. Definition of Karma. From http://en.wikipedia.org/wiki/Karma

Wikipedia. Definition of Nirvana. From http://en.wikipedia.org/wiki/Nirvana

Wikipedia. Ordination Rules. From http://www.thubtenchodron.org/Publications/PreparingForOrdination/PFO_Appendix2.html

Wikipedia. Definition of Rebirth in the Buddhist World. From http://en.wikipedia.org/wiki/Rebirth_%28Buddhism%29

Wikipedia. Reference for Sutta or discourses of the Buddha. From http://en.wikipedia.org/wiki/Buddhist_texts#Sutta

The Practice of Marriage and Family Counseling and Hinduism

JAYAMALA MADATHIL AND DAYA SINGH SANDHU

[HINDU MARRIAGES (*VIVAHA*)]
HINDUISM AND MARRIAGE

Hinduism, a term that was first used by the West Asian Muslims to distinguish non-Muslim inhabitants of the subcontinent, is one of the oldest living religions of the world. Hinduism constitutes a wide range of philosophy and practices ranging from monotheism, polytheism, as well as henotheism (choosing one deity for special worship, while acknowledging the divinity of others), to animism and even agnosticism and atheism (Vanita, 2004). Marriage is one of the most important social institutions in India. It is not only a union of two individuals but also an alliance between two families and thus starting a new network of relationships. Marriage is considered to be a sacred duty, and according to the Hindu religious scriptures, the main purpose of marriage is the performance of dharma, a religious duty, as well as a contribution to the family and the lineage (Sheela & Audinarayana, 2003). Hindu marriage is a sacrament and the ceremony is only complete after the performance of several sacred rites. It is a sacred and lifelong commitment. The individual is expected to make the marriage a success by adjusting and

119

compromising (Kapadia, 1966). Hindu marriage is a combination of rituals and traditions that not only joins the lives of the bride and the groom but also creates a strong bond between the two families.

It is important that helpers working with Hindu couples and families in the United States be aware of the Hindu practices and expectations so they can conceptualize the issues presented by the couple or family in a cultural context and provide services in a culturally relevant manner.

In India, as in the majority of the world's cultures, marriages are arranged by family members, not by the bride and groom (Skolnick, 1987). In his theory of love and marriage across cultures, Goode (1959) argued that in cultures with traditions of strong kinship networks and strong family ties, romantic love is viewed as irrelevant or even disastrous to marriage. In these cultures, romantic love would disrupt the tradition of family-approved and often arranged marriage choices. According to Bhopal (1999), arranged marriages are seen as an agreement between two families rather than two individuals, and are based on a contract where both sides have to fulfill their obligations. Bhopal also stated that arranged marriages are considered to be ritual and sacramental unions, and have been the customary norm for centuries among South Asian people. In Indian societies parents have a huge role in finding matrimonial alliances for their children. Freedom of selection in this process might be restricted for men and women depending on the family's culture.

Marriage and family counselors, therapists, and other mental health professionals working with individuals, couples, and families who follow Hindu religion must realize that the mate selection process, as well as the expectations between partners, might be considerably different from what is seen in a marriage of choice in the United States. This information is relevant so that helpers working with these individuals and families might recognize that the Western theories of mate selection or family functioning might not apply in these situations. The danger of not recognizing these differences could result in pathologizing behaviors that are culturally appropriate. For instance, living in a joint family can be misdiagnosed as enmeshment or arranged marriages can be interpreted as the individual having no personal freedom.

Hindu *vivaha* (marriage) is a very important ritual and formality through which an individual has to go, to be able to start his or her life in the *Grihastashram* (householder's life; Prabhu, 1963). The Sanskrit word *vivaha* means to support or to carry. The vivaha ceremony is a sacred union between a man and a woman that is meant to carry them through the journey of life. Among the Hindus it is considered as obligatory. For a Hindu, marriage is a way to continue the family and thus pay one's debts to the ancestors. Begetting a son, who will perform the social and religious rites as prescribed by the scriptures, is the primary goal of Hindu marriages. Orthodox Hindus believe that only the son can perform the rites and thus save the father from entering hell, called *putt* in Sanskrit. The son is therefore called a *putra*, who saves his father from putt. A man who dies without having a son is believed to become a ghost (*bhut*) after death and is believed to wander around without rest (Nair, 1978).

While one may or may not agree with the preference for having a son, it is necessary to understand the cultural and religious context of this expectation. This awareness could help the counselor to focus on certain core beliefs without further victimizing the client.

Banerjee (1999) has argued that although marriage is regarded as a social obligation for both men and women, and both sexes are expected to marry, the rules governing marriage differed for men and women historically and contemporarily and that it differed also between the upper and lower caste strata. Historically, while men of all social strata were permitted to remarry following the death of a wife, women were not allowed to remarry following the death of their husband. Historically, there have also been inequalities between men and women socially, educationally, and economically. Men usually receive more education than women. Usually, women are encouraged to marry someone with more education and men are encouraged to marry someone with less education (women marry up and men marry down). Traditionally, among most subgroups, after marriage, the woman joins her husband's patriarchal home. However, there are some exceptions to this custom, where among a small group of "matrilineal" communities, such as the Nairs and Menons of Kerala, the girl does not become part of the husband's family.

Indian women currently are expected to marry by their early to mid-20s and the norm is to marry men who are older. It is still considered the family's responsibility to find a suitable match for the young man or woman. Premarital chastity is strictly observed and any illicit sexual relationship or love affair could become an issue as the parents look for a suitable partner for their child (Nair, 1978). This is generally more true in the case of unmarried women. Men and women still experience pressure from their parents, family, and society to marry at an acceptable age.

Hindu marriages are said to have three main goals: *dharma* (duties), *praja* (progeny), and *rati* (pleasure). The most important goal was for the individual to have a partner for fulfilling religious duties (*dharma*), followed by the need to have a child, especially a male child as part of fulfilling one's duty to the family and the community (*praja*), and thirdly pleasure (*rati*), and emotional support.

Women's average age at marriage has risen from around 13 years in the early 1900s to around 18 in the early 1990s (Banerjee, 1999). The Child Marriage Restraint Act (1929) defined a child as a person who, if a male, has not completed 21 years of age and if a female, has not completed 18 years of age. A qualifying age to contract a marriage was set at 18 years for a girl, and 21 years for a boy. Banerjee (1999) has also argued that while the minimum age for marriage has increased, so has the demand for dowry payments. She has also noted that historically, dowry was only one of the several types of marriage payments and that it was restricted to the propertied upper caste groups in the Indian society.

Indian marital relationships tend to involve less personal autonomy among partners and appear to be derived from more objective criteria from parents or from the family (Sastry, 1999). Most Indian adults live in a collectivist and sexually conservative society where interdependence is encouraged and self-identity and expressions of strong feelings of love and romance are inhibited (Sinha, 1984). Group identity and group cohesiveness are emphasized, and young people are expected to become submissive, obedient, and cooperative. Love marriages, marriages in which partners fall in love first and then choose to marry, are discouraged because it is believed that these might interfere with family closeness and prescribed familial obligations (Medora, Larson, Hortacsu, & Dave, 2002).

Generally, while selecting a prospective mate, both cultural and societal norms are followed. Endogamy, marriage among the members of one's own caste/subcaste, is still a norm, especially among the Hindus of India (Sheela & Audinarayana, 2003). In the traditional Indian context, the oldest girl among all of the female siblings will get married first, and the second next, and so on. For the younger daughter to be married before the older one is mostly discouraged. Traditionally, a larger age difference between the bride and the groom was acceptable, where the groom is older. This is with the expectation that the bride would be obedient to the husband and her in-laws. However, in today's society, the preference is to have smaller age difference (two to five years, the husband being older; Sheela & Audinarayana, 2003). In general, families also prefer to select a prospective bride or groom from families that live closer to them geographically.

It is important for the marriage and family therapists to be aware of these cultural variations in love and romance; otherwise, the risk of mislabeling the relationship as loveless increases. In addition, it is also important that the helper recognize the differences between individualistic and collectivistic societies regarding marriage and family. A helper who directs the client to move toward an individualistic perspective may in fact be doing a disservice to the client who might be living or had been born and raised in a collectivistic system. It is also helpful for the counselors to become educated about these differences so that they can be aware of their own values and be intentional in not presenting one's own system as better than the client's system.

Kalra (1980) examined the current arranged marriage system in India and concluded that arranged marriages in the late 20th century had not departed significantly from the traditional method of mate selection. Most Indian marriages continue to be arranged by the individual's extended family and reflect economic, religious, political, and social considerations. Romantic love is considered ridiculous, unnecessary, and dangerous, whereas companionship and practical love is seen as a more legitimate form of affection and bonding between spouses (Desai, McCormick, & Gaeddert, 1989). According to cultural expectations, Indian marriages are based more upon a duty to one's parents and ancestors rather than personal desire for intimacy and social support. Young adults are socialized to have more practical and realistic expectations, so that they can accept the partner their parents select for them and still live happily (Medora, Larson, Hortacsu, & Dave, 2002). Yelsma and Athappilly (1988) suggested that marital bonds between married couples in India are based on a sense of filial piety and commitment and an adherence to cultural tradition rather than on spousal intimacy. Tewari (2000) reported that the rationale for choosing a potential mate who shares many of the same personal characteristics is to have a greater chance of maintaining a lasting, healthy, and happy marriage.

According to Lessinger (2002), however, even traditional arranged marriages are not devoid of love and romance. It is assumed that young couples of similar background and interests gradually would develop love and respect for each other after marriage, and that these feelings will be solidified by the responsibilities of parenthood and running a household. In collective societies, intimacy is likely to be diffused across a network of family relationships (Dion & Dion, 1993). Interestingly, these researchers have speculated that as aspects of traditionally collective societies change in the direction of greater individualism, the importance of psychological intimacy in marriage for marital satisfaction and personal well being also will increase. Sachar (1991) has suggested that arranged marriages might lead to higher degrees of marital satisfaction because of the congruency between expectations and actual married life. Yelsma and Athappilly (1988) reported that wives in Indian arranged marriages were more satisfied with their marital relationships than the wives in marriages of choice in the United States. These researchers suggested that a contributing factor to the lower divorce rate in Middle and Far Eastern cultures is the steadfast commitment expected from two persons in a pragmatic, institutional relationship, rather than an emotionally charged, romantic relationship. Since most Indian families are patriarchal and patrilocal, the bride after marriage moves to the husband's family home and is expected to perform multiple roles in accordance with societal expectations. These roles may include caring for the husband's parents or any other family members who might be living in the same household.

DATING AND COHABITATION

Even within Indian society, there are different cultural variations to the process of finding a mate. Mate selection may vary from autonomous, in which individuals select their own spouses, to arranged, in which some party, usually family elders, selects and negotiates for spouses for their marriageable children. There are many gradations between the extremes, and probably no systems that fully satisfy all conditions of either type (Goode, 1959). Stopes-Roe and Cochrane (1990) suggested a typology of arranged marriages among Asian groups that consisted of (a) traditional pattern, where parents and elders of the family choose the spouse; (b) modified traditional pattern, where the individual has the power to make the final choice; and (c) cooperative traditional pattern, where either the young person or the parents might make the selection depending upon the timing of events. Even in the cooperative traditional pattern, although the actual decision to marry is made cooperatively, the agreement of parents is essential. Medora et al. (2002) suggested that there also might be cultural differences in romantic beliefs. For example, it has been found that individualistic cultures assigned greater importance to love as a basis for marriage than collective cultures, and that Eastern cultures such as India and China ascribed the least importance to romantic love (Desai et al., 1989; Levine, Sato, Hashimoto, & Verma, 1995).

Human sexuality has never been discussed much in public in India. In the traditional family, sexual behaviors follow a rigid code enforced by customs, symbols, and communal rituals (Abraham & Abraham, 1998). Researchers have argued that marriage in India is related more to the family, and not so much based on meeting sexual needs, and that procreation is related to marriage, rather than to feeling of attraction and emotional love (Ross & Wells, 2000). While Hindu traditions view sexual desires as problematic and justifiable only for procreation, several texts represent Kama, god of love and desire, as a universal principle of attraction. While most Hindu texts identify procreation as the sole aim of sexual activity, the fourth century Kamasutra, also a sacred text, emphasizes pleasure and joy of sex (Vanita, 2004). However, even in the modern Indian society, it is safe to say that dating is very limited and very few couples in India engage in cohabitation. Marriages by individual choice are becoming prevalent in India these days. However, these marriages many times lead to conflicts between families and many times end in the social outcasting of the couple by one or both of the families. Cohabitation before marriage is extremely uncommon in India. However, recently, there has been some discussion about this type of living arrangement in the media and in the soap opera shows on the popular television serials.

Counselors must keep in mind that most of the theories used by helpers in the Western world focus on individualism and consider dating and mate selection as a natural part of their developmental experiences (e.g., Erik Erikson's psychosocial theory). However, if we apply these theories to someone who is in an arranged marriage (or is considering it), it may seem "abnormal" and "pathological." Therefore, it is necessary that these experiences are viewed in their cultural and religious contexts only.

DOWRY (STRIDHAN)

Giving of dowry is an ancient custom in India. Traditionally, the practice was meant to transfer a daughter's share of the family's wealth to her at the time of her marriage. This practice was socially and religiously approved (Chacko, 2003), and a daughter who was given a proper amount of dowry reflected well on her father and his social standing. Although a Dowry Prohibition Act of India in 1961 has made it a crime to take or give dowry, it is still prevalent throughout India (Banerjee, 1999) and includes cash, automobiles, household appliances, real estate, jewelry, and clothes. In many instances, dowry is demanded by the groom's family and the sum of dowry (cash, goods, etc.) is decided upon before the marriage is finalized.

The Dowry Prohibition Act was amended in 1984 by raising the limits of fine as well as period of imprisonment for this crime. However, this still has had minimum impact on this practice (Chacko, 2003). Dowry demands under pressure have escalated in many communities and are increasingly associated with domestic violence against women (Banerjee, 1999). The dowry system is widespread in India across caste, class, and religion and the percentage of individuals who are not associated with this practice is very small. While communities that engaged in dowry giving rationalize the practice as the appropriate transfer of wealth to a woman, there is evidence that the money does not remain with the bride. Chacko (2003) has further stated that in most cases the money is used by the husband or his family to pay off loans, start a new business, or even help pay the dowries of unmarried women in the groom's immediate family. Thus, instead of financially empowering the woman, this practice could further limit the woman's financial freedom.

Unfortunately, domestic violence is often linked to dowry. Physical violence, emotional trauma among women, and even death can be often traced to disputes over dowry (Chacko, 2003) and dowry deaths are triggered by unsatisfied demands for goods and money by the husband or his family members.

This information could be helpful for counselors working with individuals from certain communities. Of course, not all Hindu marriages involve dowry. But at the same time, there are numerous situations where dowry is generally the root cause of concerns and discords in the marital relationship. It is also important for the therapist to be aware of the dynamics regarding this issue. The therapist must also be able to assess the relationship for any domestic violence.

After gaining independence from the British in 1947, after 59 years, the India government has finally just enforced the Protection of Women from Domestic Violence Act (PWDVA; 2005) on October 26, 2006. It has already brought to the open domestic violence as one of the scourges of Indian society. An employee of the public sector from Chennai has become the first person to be arrested under this recently introduced Domestic Violence Act (*The Times of India,* Oct. 28, 2006). It is hoped that PWDVA (2005) will have a far-reaching positive implication for Indian women's empowerment movement both in the country and abroad.

HAVING CHILDREN AND CHILDLESSNESS

Living in a country where status of the women depends on motherhood, childlessness becomes a huge and very serious issue for the women (Riessman, 2000). From the standpoint of total population, childlessness in India should not be a problem. However, in a culture where the individual's status in this world, as well as in the afterlife, depends on his or her status as a parent, the meaning of childlessness becomes very personal and painful. For this reason, Indian women's status depends on their ability to bear children, especially a male child. Inability to conceive can become a big issue for Hindu women. Jindal and Gupta (1989) have found that these women tended to blame themselves for not having children and felt guilty about it. Most of them faced abandonment and experienced strained relationships from their husbands.

There are some couples who choose to be childless, but that number is relatively very small. Based on the social structure, it is safe to assume that even these individuals face a considerable amount of pressure from family and friends to have children. They may also experience the stigma of not having children. While childlessness can be stigmatizing, having only girl children can also be a reason for stress for many Indian families. Researchers (e.g., Jha et al., 2006) have stated that prenatal sex determination and selective abortion accounts for 500,000 missing female births a year in India. They have estimated that since access to ultrasound became common in the last two decades, 10 million female fetuses have been aborted in the last 20 years. They also concluded that it is socially and emotionally accepted to have a daughter, if the couple already has a son, but a daughter's arrival is often unwelcome if the couple already has daughters.

Prenatal sex determination has been illegal in India since the passage in 1996 of the Prenatal Diagnostic Techniques (Regulation and Prevention of Misuse) Act 1994 (Imam, 1994). However, it is an open secret that prenatal sex determination is still performed by many doctors, because of the huge demand for baby boys (Malpani, 2002). Registrar General of India (2000) reports that although abortion is legal for a range of indications in India, illegal abortions outnumber legal procedures and account for approximately nine percent of all reported maternal deaths in the country. In spite of a liberal abortion law in India (Medical Termination of Pregnancy Act of India 1971), of the 6.7 million induced abortions every year, only 10% are conducted under safe conditions (Dhillon, Chandhiok, Kambo, & Saxena, 2004). These researchers in their study of 1,851 women in India also found that although awareness of contraception is high, lack of availability of spacing methods, misinformation, and apprehension about the different contraceptive options prevented widespread use of contraceptive use and that abortion was used as an alternative to contraception. Female/male sex ratio indicates that there are 927 females per 1,000 males in India (Census of India, 1991). All of these cultural expectations have psychological ramifications for the individual and families.

Therapists working with individuals and families following the Hindu tradition would be able to help the clients better by probing deeper into the issues related to some of these expectations and the individual's sense of responsibility. These cultural expectations could result in intergenerational conflict among family members. Inability to meet certain cultural expectations could also cause anxiety, guilt, or shame in Hindu clients.

DIVORCE

Divorce in India is highly stigmatizing and objectionable (Rao & Sekar, 2002). There are limited empirical research studies on divorce in India. Possible reasons for this are the lower divorce rates and lack of sufficient data (Amato, 1994). In the Vedic society marriage was considered indissoluble by humans. The popular, although controversial code of Manu (Manusmruti) declared that a wife could remarry if the previous marriage was not consummated. Several social reforms in the form of legislations were introduced in the later centuries. The civil marriage act of 1872 enforced monogamy. The Special Marriage Act of 1954 and the Hindu Marriage Act of 1955 accorded legal sanction to Hindu couples to divorce, which prior to their enactment was only customary (Rao & Sekar, 2002). The amendment to the Hindu Marriage Act in 1976 introduced divorce by mutual consent. Since then, there has been an increase in divorce in India.

Rao and Sekhar (2002) also have stated that education level of women is an important variable associated with divorce. Although not always, women with a higher level of education were more likely to end marital incompatibility by divorce. Amato (1994) pointed out that in the Indian society, the woman faces much more social and economic burden after a separation or divorce than a man. Rao and Murthy (1990) in a study of matrimonial advertisements found that only 257 out of 5,785 advertisements sought remarriage. Rao and Shekar (2002) have suggested that in modern times due to social and technological advancements, increase in awareness levels, and increase in availability of options, unhappy marriages are terminated through divorce, which of late has emerged as a rational choice and has been acquiring greater acceptance. The ideal of a *pativrata* (extreme loyalty to the point of worshipping a husband) has been addressed by the Hindu mythologies and the writers. They implied devotion and fidelity to husband as the highest values a Hindu woman could possess. Hindu scriptures believe marriage to be a religious bond not only in this life but also in the lives to come through reincarnation. This is based on the belief that a marriage unites both the body and the soul. Death may separate two bodies, but it cannot separate two immortal souls that always remain intact, even after the death of one or both spouses.

These expectations have an influence on the individual's cognitive, affective, as well as behavioral experiences. These religious expectations might make it difficult for an individual to consider divorce as an option even when the marriage is unsatisfactory. In addition, an individual who may have experienced a divorce might be dealing with additional feelings of guilt and shame as a result of these beliefs. A counselor who is aware of these cultural and religious norms might be able to meet the needs of these clients in a culturally appropriate manner.

DEATH OF A SPOUSE AND REMARRIAGE

The Hindu notion of death and rebirth are the expression of a cyclical view of the world. Hindus see their lives as one of many, and death as the gateway to the next life. The dead body is cremated and in most instances, the ashes are sprinkled on the surface of water of a sacred river. Sometimes, the ashes are put in the earth. It is believed that the fire purifies the mortal body, which returns to the water as ashes and enters the eternal cycle of the universe (Ellinger, 1996). Varanasi is considered to be a sacred place of great spiritual significance through which the sacred river, the Ganges, flows. Hindus believe that taking a dip in the river Ganga will wash them of their sins and purify their souls.

The orthodox Hindus prohibited widow remarriage. A widow who performed *sati*, self-immolation at the funeral pyre of her late husband, was considered to be doing a sacred and meritorious act. The practice of sati was banned by law in 1829. Widow remarriage has become a more acceptable custom in India. However, the opportunities for finding a suitable husband for a widow might be more limited, while families of widowed men might find it easier to find suitable partners for remarriage. Death of a husband changes the status of the wife. Traditionally, a widow was considered to be a *bad omen* and was not allowed to participate in joyous occasions such as at weddings or at the birth of a baby. Traditionally, in most communities widows were expected to dress solemnly and wear no jewellery or *bindis*, the red dot on the forehead (Gupta, 1974). Many widows still follow these customs. In addition, in certain communities, widows were also expected to shave their head. Even now, some of the older women follow this practice. Once a man dies, the oldest son takes on the responsibility of the head of the household. The death of a spouse has a significant impact on any individual's life.

The marriage and family therapists working with Hindus who have experienced loss of a spouse need to remember the religious significance of this experience and the cultural norms and expectations related to the experience of losing a spouse. A therapist who considers the significance of the cultural context is more likely to have a better understanding of the grieving process of the individual who has lost a spouse. If one does not look at the religious significance of this experience, there is risk of pathologizing the surviving partner's behaviors and reactions to the experience.

HOMOSEXUALITY

There is limited research done on the topic of homosexuality in India. Sexuality in itself is not discussed in the public contexts and individuals are expected to follow a traditional role in their sexual behaviors. Indian attitudes toward sex and love were radically transformed during the colonial era (Vanita, 2004). The British rulers imported homophobia into India and they enshrined it into the Indian penal code in 1860. In India, homosexuality is illegal and imprisonable under Section 377 of India's penal code that prohibits carnal relations against the course of nature. It makes homosexuality involving anal sex a criminal offence, for which punishment may be imprisonment for 10 years to life. The offender may also be fined. Public display of homosexual acts is also a criminal offense. While gays are not directly prosecuted, the penal code is used to threaten and blackmail gay individuals who seem to be more visible in India than the lesbians. OLAVA (Organized Lesbian Alliance for Visibility and Action) was created in 1999 as a support network and also for political activism (Baird, 2004). (Vanita, 2004) have argued that fear and anger toward homosexuals were expressed occasionally in precolonial India, but during the colonial period in India fear and anger became quite prevalent against the homosexuals. They have argued that the reasons for the shift included the ruler's elevation of companionate monogamous heterosexuality as the only norm and the assumption that one's emotional and sexual needs should be fulfilled within marriage. In ancient Indian literature, homosexuality has been documented by different authors (Abraham & Abraham, 1998) and archaeologists have found prehistoric cave drawings depicting homosexual acts. According to the Hindu sage Vatsayana, author of the treatise on love, the Kamasutra, homosexual practice is allowed with a few exceptions. Although this practice has been referred to in the traditional Hindu literature, the general attitude toward homosexuality has been not been very favorable. Based on the religious and cultural norms among Hindus, it can be argued that homosexuality would be a difficult topic to discuss for most of the Hindus living in the United States. Therapists working with individuals who may be exploring their sexual orientation might consider helping them deal with the experience in their own cultural context. Therapists might also be able to help family members by including them in the process and modeling unconditional acceptance and connecting them to resources in the local community.

A NEW CHALLENGE FOR MARRIAGE AND FAMILY COUNSELORS AND THERAPISTS

Before 1965 South Asian immigration to the United States was quite isolated and minuscule. However, with the passing of Immigration and Naturalization

Services Act of 1965, this group has become one of the fastest growing ethnic groups in the United States.

According to the U.S. census data, there are over two million South Asian Americans living in the United States (U.S. Census Bureau, 2000). This group constitutes approximately 20% of the total Asian population in the United States. Among the South Asians, Asian Indians are the largest group (16%) of the total Asian population. In fact, Asian Indians rank third behind Chinese (23%) and Filipino (19.9%) populations among the general grouping of all Asians/Pacific Islanders. According to the U.S. Department of International Religious Freedom Report (2004) the numbers of Hindus in the United States has already shot up to 1,478,670 and their population is certain to grow even more in the United States because of the Family Reunification Act.

Since Hindus as an ethnic group are one of the most recent arrivals, there seems to be little awareness about them both among the general public and helping professionals. Because of such lack of awareness, many stereotypes and misconceptions exist and are being perpetuated. For instance, cow worship, snake charming, and the caste system in Hindus have been over-emphasized. The individual, family, and marriage related counseling needs and other psychological problems of Hindus are clearly a challenge for mental health professionals who know very little about them. Some recommendations for marriage and family therapists follow.

SOME IMPLICATIONS FOR MARRIAGE AND FAMILY THERAPISTS

Marriage and family are historically considered an integral part of the human experience. However, different meanings and significance are attached to a marriage and family by different clients that reflect the cultural milieu of a particular society in which these clients are born and raised (Suggs & Miracle, 1993). Further, after the migration when cultural contexts change, values change, priorities change, and behaviors change (Sandhu, Kaur, & Tewari, 1999). Thus adaptation to the new cultural norms, behaviors, and values of the dominant group generally cause unavoidable psychological distress for the newly arriving immigrants and their children (Sandhu, Portes, & McPhee, 1996). Naturally, a clash of values takes place between immigrant parents and their children in the new land. From the perspective and significance of acculturative experiences, we recommend that practicing marriage and family therapists and counselors should consider the following as the important guidelines when working with their Hindu clients.

Cultural Contexts

As pointed out earlier, mental health professionals must consider the behaviors, values, and priorities relating to family relations, dating practices and premarital sexual relations, marriage, and sex role expectations in the context of cultural backgrounds of their clients (Inman, Ladany, Constantine, & Morano, 2001). Conflictual acculturative experiences between the parents and their children become salient issues that would warrant the attention of the practicing counselors and therapists. For instance, for newly arriving Hindu parents, marriage is generally viewed as an alliance between two families but their children may see it as close personal relationship between the two individuals. The perspective of *emic* rather than *etic* (Triandis, 1994) that ideas, behaviors, items, concepts are culture specific is more relevant here. Mental health professionals must not conceptualize client issues through their own cultural lenses and perspectives (Inman & Sandhu, 2002).

Discussion About Sexual Matter

Counselors may need to learn when and how sex related issues are explored and discussed in Hindu families. Also, they should know to what extent the discussions about sexual matters are typically accepted or repressed in this culture. Discussions about sexual matters in Hindus are considered private and are not generally discussed with strangers, including the mental health professionals. We strongly suggest that counselors should also become aware whether or not sexual issues are expressed within clients' family directly or indirectly, or if they have the potential of becoming a discord and nonconformity problem for their family. If the counselors are not sensitive, they can expect premature termination of their clients.

Acculturation Levels

One of the most important caveats for counselors, psychotherapists, and other mental health professionals who work with Hindu clients is to recognize the acculturation levels of their clients. These acculturation levels generally guide, determine, and help plan the initiation and termination of counseling relationships, make the necessary referrals, and recommend group therapy sessions (Sandhu, & Madathil, in press). The Cultural Adaptation Pain Scale (Sandhu, et al., 1996) is one of the many useful tools that can be used to assess Hindu parents and their children's acculturation levels.

Changing Perspectives

In addition to the acculturation levels of their clients, counselors and therapists should keep themselves abreast of the new developments and constantly changing influences on their Hindu clients. Currently, there are dramatic economic, political, social, and cultural changes happening in India that might have direct impact on Hindus and their children, even on those who are living in or migrating to the United States. There has been a social and cultural revolution in India for the last decade, which is having a great impact even on marriages, family relationships, and matters relating to sex. A most recent example about the Protection of Women from Domestic Violence Act (2005) has been cited earlier. Counselors also should examine other changing aspects of their Hindu clients' lives including, religious conversions, feminist movements, modernization, and Westernization (Inman & Sandhu, 2002).

SUMMARY

In this chapter we have discussed various practices and norms related to marriage and family among the Hindus. Counseling and therapeutic implications for working with individuals and families who follow Hinduism are also addressed. It is also extremely important to keep in mind that Hinduism is a way of life and it is difficult to generalize customs and norms of all Hindus living in the United States. It is our hope that the ideas presented in the chapter would serve as an overview and that mental health professionals would pay further attention to the particular client's definition of what it means to be a Hindu for that particular individual or family.

REFERENCES

Abraham, K. C., & Abraham, A. E. (1998). Homosexuality. *Ecumenical Review, 50*(1), 22–29.

Amato, P. R. (1994). The impact of divorce on men and women in India and United States. *Journal of Comparative Family Studies, 25,* 207–221.

Baird, V. (2004). Interview with OLAVA. *New Internationalist, 373,* 33–33.

Banerjee, K. (1999). Gender stratification and the contemporary marriage market in India. *Journal of Family Issues, 20*(5), 648–676.

Bhopal, K. (1999). South Asian women and arranged marriages in East London. In R. Barot, H. Bradley, & S. Fenton (Eds.), *Ethnicity, gender and social change.* (pp. 117–134). New York: St. Martin's Press.

Chacko, E. (2003). Marriage, development and the status of women in Kerala, India. *Gender and Development, 11*(2), 52–59.

Desai, S. R., McCormick, N. B., & Gaeddert, W. P. (1989). Malay and American undergraduates' beliefs about love. *Journal of Psychology and Human Sexuality, 2*(2), 93–116.

Dhillon, B. S., Chandhick, N., Kambo, I., & Saxena, N. C. (2004). Induced abortion and concurrent adoption of contraception in the rural areas of India (an ICMR task force study). *Indian Journal of Medical Sciences, 58*(11), 478–484.

Dion, K. K., & Dion, L. K. (1993). Individualistic and collective perspectives on gender and the cultural context of love and intimacy. *Journal of Social Sciences, 49*(3), 53–69.

Ellinger, H. (1996). *Hinduism.* Valley Gorge, PA: Trinity Press International.

Goode, W. J. (1959). The theoretical importantce of love. *American Sociological Review, 24*(1), 38–47.

Gupta, G. R. (1974). *Marriage, religion and society: Pattern of change in an Indian village.* New York: John Wiley and Sons.

Imam, Z. (1994). India bans female feticide. *British Medical Journal, 309,* 428–428.

Inman, A.G., Ladany, N., Constantine, M, G., & Morano, C.K. (2001). Development and preliminary validation of the cultural values conflict scale for South Asian women. *Journal of Counseling Psychology, 48* (1), 17-27.

Inman, A.G., & Sandhu, D. S. (2002). Cross-cultural perspectives on love and sex. In L. D. Burlew and D. Capuzzi (Eds.), *Sexuality counseling* (pp. 41–62). Huntington, NY: Nova Science.

Jha, P., Kumar, R., Vasa, P., Dhingra, N., Thiruchelvam, D., & Moineddin, R. (2006). Low male-to-female sex ratio of children born in India: National survey of 1.1 million households. *The Lancet, 367*(9506), 211–218.

Jindal, U. N., & Gupta, A. N. (1989). Social problems of infertile women in India. *International Journal of Fertility, 34*(1), 30–33.

Kalra, S. (1980). *Daughters of tradition.* Birmingham, AL: Third World Publications.

Kapadia, K. M. (1966). Marriage and family in India (3rd ed.). Calcutta, India: Oxford University Press.

Lessinger, J. (2002). Asian Indian marriages-arranged, semi-arranged, or based on love? In N.V. Benokraitis (Ed), *Contemporary ethnic families in the United States: Characteristics, variations, and dynamics* (pp. 101–104). Boston: Allyn & Bacon.

Levine, R., Sato, S., Hashimoto. T., & Verma, J. (1995). Love and marriage in eleven cultures. *Journal of Cross Cultural Psychology, 26*(5), 554–572.

Malpani, A. (2002). Preimplantation genetic diagnosis for gender selection for family balancing: a view from India. *Reproductive Biomedicine Online, 4*(1), 7–10.

Medora, N. P, Larson, J.H., Hortacsu, N., & Dave, P. (2002). Perceived attitudes towards romanticism: A cross cultural study of American, Asian Indian, and Turkish young adults. *Journal of Comparative Family Studies, 33*(2), 155–182.

Nair, P. T. (1978). *Marriage and dowry in India.* Columbia, MO: South Asia Books.

Prabhu, P. H. (1963). *Hindu social organization: A study of socio-psychological and ideological foundations* (5th ed.). Bombay, India: Popular Prakasan.

Rao, A. B. S. V. R., & Murthy, R. (1990). The trend of remarriage in South India: A socio-demographic anylysis of matrimonial advertisements. *Indian Journal of Social Work, L 14:* 670–678.

Rao, A. B. S. V. R., & Sekar, K. (2002). Divorce: Process and correlates, a cross-cultural study. *Journal of Comparative Family Studies, 33*(4), 81–104.

Registrar General of India, Vital Statistics Division, Government of India. (2000). *Sample Registration System Bulletin, 33*(1): 8–8.

Riessman, C. K. (2000). Stigma and everyday resistance practices: Childless women in South India. *Society & Gender, 14*(1), 111–135.

Ross, M. W., & Wells, A. L. (2000). The modernist fallacy in homosexual selection theories. Homosexual and homosocial exaptation in South Asian Society. *Psychology, Evolution & Gender, 2*(3), 253–262.

Sachar, R. (1991). His and her marital satisfaction: The double standard. *Sex Roles, 25*(7), 451–467.

Sandhu, D. S., Kaur, K. P., & Tewari, N. (1999). Acculturative stress experiences of Asian and Pacific Islander Americans: Considerations for counseling and psychotherapy. In D.S. Sandhu (Ed.). *Asian and Pacific Islander Americans: Issues and concerns for counseling and psychotherapy* (pp. 3–19). Commack, NY: Nova Science Publishers.

Sandhu, D. S., & Madathil, J. (in press). South Asian Americans. In G. McAuliffe (Ed), *Culturally-alert counseling.* Thousand Oaks, CA: Sage.

Sandhu, D. S., Portes, P. R., & McPhee, S. (1996). Assessing cultural adaptation: Psychometric properties of the Cultural Adaptation Pain Scale. *Journal of Multicultural Counseling and Development, 24*(1), 15–25.

Sastry, J. (1999). Household structure, satisfaction, and distress in India and the United States: A comparative cultural examination. *Journal of Comparative Family Studies, 30*(1), 135–152

Sheela, J., & Audinarayana, N. (2003). Mate-selection and female age at marriage: A micro level investigation in Tamil Nadu, India. *Journal of Comparative Family Studies, 34*(4), 497–508.

Sinha, D. (1984). Some recent changes in the Indian family and their implications for socialization. *Indian Journal of Social Work, 45,* 271–286

Skolnick, A. S. (1987). *The intimate environment: Exploring marriage and the family.* Boston: Little, Brown.

Stopes-Roe, M., & Cochrane, R. (1990). *Citizens of this country: The Asian British.* Clevedon: Multilingual Matters Ltd.

Suggs, A. N., & Miracle, A. W. (1993). *Culture and human sexuality: A reader.* Pacific Grove, CA: Brooks/Cole Publishing.

Tewari, N. (2000). *Asian Indian American clients presenting at a university counseling center: An exploration of their concerns and a comparison to other groups.* (Unpublished doctoral dissertation, University of Northern Illinois, IL.)

Times of India (2006, October 28). New act: Government employee arrested. http://timesofindia.indiatimes.com/articleshow/201626.cms

Triandis, H. C. (1994). *Culture and social behavior.* New York: Penguin Books.

U.S. Census Bureau: United States Department of Commerce (n.d.). *Profiles of General Demographic Characteristics 2000.* Retrieved March 5, 2006, from http://www.census.gov/prod/cen2000/dp1/2kh00.pdf

U.S. Department of State (2004). *International religious freedom report for 2004.* http://www.state.gov/g/drl/rls/irf/

Vanita, R. (2004). Wedding of two souls. *Journal of Feminist Studies in Religion, 20* (2), 119–135.

Yelsma, P., & Athappilly, K. (1988). Marital satisfaction and communication practices: Comparisons among Indian and American couples. *Journal of Comparative Family Studies, 19*(1), 37–56.

CHAPTER 9

The Practice of Marriage and Family Counseling and Judaism

ELLIOT N. DORFF

THE SOURCES AND FORMS OF JUDAISM

The holy scriptures of Judaism are the Hebrew Bible, especially the Torah (that is, the five books of Moses). Like Christianity and Islam, however, Judaism is not equivalent to its scriptures but is rather a continuing tradition. The very choice of which books were to be part of the Bible, as well how it was to be interpreted and applied, were all in the hands of the classical rabbis in the first through the fifth centuries C.E.[1] (who played a role in Judaism similar to that of the church fathers in Christianity and the early imams in Islam) and then rabbis from that time to today. The tradition has also been critically shaped by the beliefs and practices of the people who were living their lives by it, so that Judaism as we know it is a product of the ongoing *interaction* between Jews and their rabbinic leaders.

The primary literary sources of Judaism are these: the Hebrew Bible; the Mishnah (edited c. 200 C.E.); the Babylonian Talmud (edited c. 500 C.E.); the Midrash (dating from as early as the first century C.E., or possibly even earlier, but edited and published in various forms between the 5th and 12th centuries); medieval and modern codes, especially Maimonides' *Mishneh Torah* (1177 C.E.) and Joseph Caro's *Shulhan Arukh* (1565); rabbinic rulings (*teshuvot*, responsa) over the last 1,500 years; and Jewish theology and literature. In addition, the customs that have evolved from popular practice have shaped what we know as Judaism.

There are several forms of Judaism in North America, each interpreting and applying the Jewish tradition in its own distinctive way. Only 46% of American Jews belong to a synagogue. Of those 39% affiliate with a Reform synagogue, 33% with a Conservative one, 21% with an Orthodox one, 3% with a Reconstructionist one, and 4% with other types (*National Jewish Population Study 2000-2001*, 2003, p. 7). For a description of their approaches, see Dorff, 1996, chapter 3 and Dorff, 2005, chapter 7. Some Jews who have not joined a synagogue nevertheless see themselves as religiously Jewish and others ("secular Jews") identify with Jewish culture and values, including many about the family described below, but not Jewish religious beliefs.

DEFINITION OF MARRIAGE

Companionship

In addition to multiple stories of families, the Torah contains two commandments that articulate its understanding of marriage. The first is "Be fruitful and multiply" (Gen. 1:28). The second, Exodus 21:10, asserts that when a man marries a woman, "her food, her clothing, and her *onah* he may not diminish." The rabbis interpreted *onah* to mean her conjugal rights. Thus *companionship and procreation* are the two divinely-ordained purposes of sex within marriage.

These are independent commandments. Thus regardless of their intention or ability to procreate, the couple has the duty to care for, support, and interact with each other, "for it is not good that a person be alone" (Gen. 2:18), and "so although a man may have many children, he must not remain without a wife" (B. *Yevamot* 61b; M.T. *Laws of Marriage* 15:16; S.A. *Even Ha-ezer* 1:8).[2] Sex is one of the ways in which the companionship between husband and wife is expressed, and so the rabbis structure the laws of marriage such that both spouses have rights to sex with regularity within marriage.[3] Moreover, within the bounds of modesty, Jewish law permits couples to have sex in any way they want (S.A. *Even Ha-ezer* 25:2).

On the other hand, when sex becomes a tool for control, a marriage ceases to be the partnership that it is intended to be. The rabbis forbade marital rape (M.T. *Laws of Marriage* 14:15; S.A. *Even Ha-Ezer* 25:2) long before most legal systems did; and, conversely, they disdain either spouse "rebelling" against the other by denying sex (see endnote 3). One need not agree to engage in sexual relations each time that one's spouse wants to do so, and a refusal to have conjugal relations must be respected. This should not last for long without due reason, however, for each partner is entitled to the sexual expression of companionship in marriage.

From the biblical period to the early 20th century, marriages were arranged by parents, sometimes with the help of a matchmaker, known to many through *Fiddler on the Roof.* This mode of finding a spouse bespeaks the tradition's understanding of what to expect in marriage. Unlike contemporary American conceptions, marriage is not primarily for purposes of happiness and sex, although it certainly includes those. It is rather to care for each other, raise a family, and build lives together. As the couple in that musical sing after 25 years of marriage, articulating that they love each other "doesn't change a thing, but it's nice to know."

Procreation

The rabbis determine that the command to be "fruitful and multiply" is fulfilled when the couple has borne two children, specifically, a boy and a girl (M. *Yevamot* 6:6 [61b]; M.T. *Laws of Marriage* 15:4; S.A. *Even Ha-Ezer* 1:5). If a couple cannot reproduce, the commandment to procreate no longer applies, for it makes no sense logically or legally to command people to do what they cannot do. Nevertheless, infertile couples may use modern technology to help them procreate.[4] If that does not work, they should seriously consider adoption, converting the child to Judaism if he or she was not born to a Jewish woman. (Jewish law defines a Jew as a person born to a Jewish woman or converted to Judaism.) The Talmud states that adopting and raising children are "as if one has given birth to them," and that adoptive parents "follow the Lord at all times" (B. *Megillah* 13a; B. *Ketubbot* 50a).

Traditional Jewish sources see children not only as an obligation but as a blessing, maintaining that Jews should strive to have more than the minimal number of two (B. *Yevamot* 62b; M.T. *Laws of Marriage* 15:16). Modern rabbis emphasize this even more, for nothing less than the future of the Jewish community and of Judaism depends upon that. The Jewish community lost a third of its members in the Holocaust, and we are now less than a quarter of 1% of the world's population (in contrast to Christians, who are a full 33% of the world's humans, and Muslims, who are 20%). Furthermore, contemporary Jews are not producing enough children to even maintain their present numbers. Add to these factors the high rate of intermarriage and assimilation among Jews today, and it becomes clear that Jews are in serious demographic trouble as a people. One needs a Jewish education to become an informed, practicing Jew, of course, but people can only be educated if they exist in the first place. The duty to procreate, like all other commandments, does not apply to those who cannot fulfill it, but infertile people should consider adoption. Having more children through either propagation or adoption is literally a matter of life and death for Jews, not only as individuals and as families, but as a people.

Educating Ourselves and Our Children

The importance of marriage, within the Jewish tradition, is not only for reasons of propagation and companionship, as important as they are; it is also to educate children in the Jewish tradition so it can continue across the generations. Abraham, the Patriarch of the Jewish people, is already charged with teaching his children (Gen. 18:19). The commandment for each one of us to do likewise appears several times in the Torah, including the first two paragraphs of the *Shema* (Deuteronomy 6:4–9; 11:13–21), a prayer that Jews recite twice daily. No schooling, however, can be adequate; family education is the key to the continuation of the Jewish heritage. Parents must therefore continue to educate themselves as they seek to teach their children, for the Jewish duty to study the tradition is lifelong. This includes the children's education in all aspects of Judaism, including its morals (including its sexual morals), rituals, associations, customs, history, and hopes.

DATING AND COHABITATION

Until the last century, most Jewish marriages were arranged by the parents of the bride and groom. Both the man and the woman had to agree to marry each other, but, like the author's own grandparents, they may not have met until the day they were married.

Among other things, this guaranteed that Jews would marry Jews, in accordance with Jewish norms from biblical times to our own.[5] During most of the last two millennia Jews were kept from interfaith marriages not only by their own laws and customs but also by the laws and anti-Semitism of the people among whom they lived.

Now, however, when Jews are accepted as full citizens, interfaith dating and marriage are common. Jewish leaders perceive this as a major problem for two reasons: (a) The chances of divorce are considerably less in intrafaith marriages than in interfaith ones (Phillips, 1998, 64–65); (b) The likelihood that a couple's children will be raised as Jews is much greater if both adults are Jewish. Studies indicate that as many as 82% of children of interfaith couples involving one Jewish partner are not raised as Jews (Phillips, 1998, 49). As a result, despite centuries of Jewish practice that disdained missionizing and even made it hard for a non-Jew to become Jewish, contemporary denominations of Judaism are engaged to varying degrees in welcoming Jews by choice, especially if they are married to Jews. Rabbis are simultaneously encouraging Jews to date and ultimately marry Jews.

This is a delicate balance to strike for both rabbis and counselors, for how do you explain the risks of intermarriage to both couples and the Jewish people and discourage interfaith marriages while at the same time trying to convince interfaith couples to raise their children as Jews and involve themselves and their children in synagogue life? The *keruv* (bringing close) programs of both the Conservative and Reform movements have created programs and materials to help rabbis and counselors do that, but undoubtedly it is the Jewish Outreach Institute (www.joi.org) that has produced the most in this area.

While dating, what expressions of affection are permissible? Here the denominations differ. In Orthodox Judaism, a man may not even touch a woman to whom he is not married. Conservative and Reform Judaism, in contrast, deem holding hands, hugging, and kissing as perfectly natural and healthy expressions of both a budding romance and a long-term one. This follows the Bible's example, where not only parents and children, but brothers and sisters, friends and lovers embraced and kissed.[6] One must, however, take due regard for the sense of modesty and privacy that Judaism would have us preserve in expressing our romantic feelings, and so the more intense forms of these activities should be reserved for private quarters.[7] The biblical book of Kohelet (Ecclesiastes) says this (at 3:5): "There is a time for embracing and a time for shunning embraces."

What about sexual intercourse outside of marriage? While the Torah prescribes the death penalty or excommunication for those who engage in adultery (Lev. 20:10; Deut. 22:22), incest (Lev. 18:16–29; 20:11–12, 14, 17), or rape (Deut. 22:23–27), it prescribes a fine for a man who has consensual sex with an unmarried woman (Deut. 22:28–29). That alone indicates that while Judaism does not approve of sex outside of marriage, it does not see it as an offense nearly as serious as those other forms of prohibited sex. This is especially true when the relationship is long-term.

Still, only sex within marriage can attain the religious and communal sanction of *kiddushin*, holy matrimony. That is not just an old-fashioned norm or prudish severity on the tradition's part; it is, instead, wise moral planning. After all, it is the marital context that holds out the most promise for people's intimate relations to embody fundamental Jewish views and values, such as love, fidelity, mutual responsibility, modesty, health and safety, honesty, and holiness. Furthermore, in marriage the couple has the best chance of attaining the threefold purposes for marital sex described above; namely, companionship, procreation, and the education of the next generation. While non-marital sex can provide companionship as well as physical pleasure, especially in the context of a long-term relationship, unwillingness to get married usually signifies that the couple is not ready to make a life-long commitment to each other or undertake the responsibilities of having and raising children.

Nevertheless, because people today become physically mature long before they are prepared to marry, and because some have experienced the death of a spouse or divorce and need some transitional relationships before being ready to remarry, many cohabit outside of marriage. People who have sex outside of marriage are not fulfilling the Jewish ideal. We often, though, act in ways that are less than ideal. In sex, as in all other aspects of life, failing to live up to the ideal does not free people from incorporating as much of the ideal as possible into their lives. That is, Jewish norms in sexual matters, like Jewish norms in other arenas, are not an "all or nothing" thing. In fact, precisely because a cohabiting couple does not have the structure of marriage to reinforce the morality of their relationship, they have to be especially careful to fulfill these Jewish norms as much as possible. Rabbis and counselors should therefore not strive to make unmarried couples feel guilty about their sexual activity; they should rather encourage them to carry on their relationship in a way that expresses Jewish values, like the ones listed above, as much as possible.[8]

ROLES WITHIN MARRIAGES AND FAMILIES

Spousal Duties

Traditional Jewish law presumes sharply differentiated roles for husbands and wives. Men earn a living (Ex. 21:10; M. *Ketubbot* 5:8–9; M.T. *Laws of Marriage* 12:10, 11, 14, 15; 13:3–6; S.A. *Even Ha'ezer* 154:3) and deal with communal matters. Women raise the children, especially before age six, and take care of the household (M. *Ketubbot* 5:5). Before the couple had children and after the children had grown, women often helped their husbands earn a living, but that was not their primary task. Men and women shared responsibility for satisfying each other sexually and for the upbringing of the children after the age of six. This is indicated by the provision in Jewish law that if the couple divorces, unless the welfare of the particular child requires some other arrangement, sons of age six and above should live with their father and daughters with their mother so that each could model for their children of the same gender what is to be a grown man or woman.[9]

In contemporary times, the roles of husbands and wives have become much more flexible. Women often work outside the home, whether from financial need or choice. Many men take an active role in raising their children, with some having primary responsibilities for that task. During their working hours outside the home, parents use day care, nannies, and pre-schools to take care of their children.

In response to such innovations, many synagogues offer preschools of their own. In sharp contrast to secular American values, where one's "net worth" is a function of one's material wealth, Judaism privileges family over work (*Tanhuma Mattot* 1:7 [on Num. 32:16]; *Numbers Rabbah* 22:9; Dorff 2003, 109–111). Work is important and necessary, but only as a means to support one's family and contribute to society at large, not as an end in itself. Thus modern Jews need to ensure that their work does not become an idol, to which they devote almost all of their time, energy, and skill. They must instead make decisions about their work that enable them to have the time and energy to play an important role in raising their children and in deepening their relationship to each other. This runs against the grain of contemporary American culture, so rabbis and counselors need to be quite assertive in pointing out that work and money need to take second place to one's spouse and family, not only in what a person says and intends, but also in what he or she actually does. This includes helping people to readjust their priorities and giving them some practical tools to ensure that they will have time and energy for their spouses and family. One such device is Jewish rituals; as Rabbi Edward Feinstein of Congregation Valley Beth Shalom in Los Angeles once put it in a sermon, the Jewish Sabbath can be the most effective antidote to the ills of modern American civilization.

Parental Duties[10]

Traditionally, fathers had the duty to support their children. This was especially true for daughters, for if the family were really destitute, boys could go begging without endangering themselves as much as girls would (B. *Ketubbot* 43a, 67a, 108b; B. *Bava Batra* 139b, 140b). Fathers also had specific duties toward their sons, as the Talmud specifies:

> Our Rabbis taught: A man is responsible to circumcise his son [on the eighth day after birth unless the boys medical condition does not permit that], to redeem him [from Temple service if he is the first born by paying a kohen five silver dollars, "pidyon ha-ben"], to teach him Torah, to marry him off to a woman, and to teach him a trade, and there are those who say that he must also teach him to swim. Rabbi Judah says: Anyone who fails to teach his son a trade teaches him to steal. (B. Kiddushin 29a)

In contrast to Orthodox Judaism, Conservative and Reform Judaism from their beginnings have inculcated girls and women in the same curriculum taught to boys and men in coed classrooms. With the ordination of the first female Reform rabbi in 1973 and the first female Conservative rabbi in 1985, this now applies even to rabbinical school. Thus in practice these movements make the duty to teach one's children Torah incumbent on both parents, and it applies to children of both genders. Similarly, the duty to prepare boys for a career now applies to girls as well, when training for modern jobs requires much more in the way of time and resources than preparing for a career did in the past. Finally, although Jews no longer arrange marriages, parents can and should see it as their duty to help their adult children find mates, especially after college or graduate school, when there is no obvious and easily available place to meet people they might marry.

In addition to these positive parental duties, Jewish law also bans certain parental actions. The Torah decrees excommunication for anyone who sexually abuses his or her children (Lev. 18:6, 22, 29). While some Jewish sources permit parents to spank their children as part of educating them in what is correct behavior, the Conservative Movement's Committee on Jewish Law and Standards has ruled that hitting children is ideally to be avoided altogether. Applying force to a child with a closed fist, a belt, or any other weapon is, according to the Committee, always forbidden. At most parents may give a light smack on the child's buttocks, one that does not leave a mark—but even that is discouraged. Rabbis, teachers, and counselors who see evidence of physical or sexual abuse are required by most states to report it to governmental authorities; they are not usually mandated reporters for verbal abuse. Still, in all forms of abuse, these professionals can and should play a major role in extricating the victim from the abusive situation and in the process of healing, and they may also play a significant role in curing the perpetrator of the need to abuse (Dorff, 2003, chapter 5, esp. 166–171 and 190–206).

Filial Duties

Two of the Torah's commandments frame the relationship of children to their parents: the command to honor one's parents (Ex. 20:12; Deut. 5:16) and the command to respect them (Lev. 19:3). While both sound like a demand that children have specific attitudes toward their parents, the Talmud, as is its common practice, translates those attitudes into specific actions (B. *Kiddushin* 31b; see M.T. *Laws of Rebels* 6:3; S.A. *Yoreh De'ah* 240:2, 4; 228:11:

> Our Rabbis taught: What is respect (*mora*) and what is honor (*kavod*)? Respect means that he [the son] must neither stand in his [the father's] place, nor sit in his place, nor contradict his words, nor tip the scales against him [in an argument with others]. Honor means that he must give him food and drink, clothe and cover him, lead him in and out.

Note several things about this source. First, although young children should certainly be taught to honor their parents, they are not legally responsible for anything. The rabbis therefore understood the commandment to govern primarily the relations of adult children with their elderly parents. This makes the commandment especially critical nowadays, when parents live long lives and often far away from their children, and when children find themselves balancing their duties to their parents, their children, and to each other.

Second, another rabbinic passage on the same page of Talmud requires that, as an act of reverence, one not address parents by their first names but rather call them, "My father (mother), my teacher." Moreover, the Torah itself says that "He who curses his father or his mother shall surely be put to death" (Ex. 25:17); "He who insults his father his father or mother shall be put to death" (Lev. 20:9); and "Cursed be he who dishonors his father or his mother" (Deu. 27:16). Jewish law maintains that these requirements of honor and respect also apply to one's mother-in-law and father-in-law and to one's grandparents, although to a lesser degree than they apply to one's parents (S.A. *Yoreh De'ah* 240:24 [with gloss]; 374:6).

Obviously, it is best if children honor and respect their parents as a natural outgrowth of their love for them. Because that does not always characterize parent-child relationships, however, Jewish law determines what is minimally required of children, even if they do not like their parents. Some authorities exempt children from these duties if the parents abandoned their children in their childhood or abused them, but unless that is the case, these duties apply. This gives good guidance to rabbis and counselors who are trying to help adult children deal with elderly parents they do not like, for it suggests that the children need not feel obligated to pretend to feel deep love for their parents if they do not feel that, but they do need to provide for them in specific ways, if necessary through hiring others to perform these tasks.

CHILD BEARING, BIRTH CONTROL, ABORTION, TEENAGE PREGNANCY

As indicated above, Judaism understands procreation to be one of the three prime purposes of marriage. The rabbis determined that the Torah's command to procreate is fulfilled once one has a boy and a girl, but those who can produce more children should not stop at two. In recent times, with the loss of a third of the world's Jews in the Holocaust and with a low reproductive rate among Jews, rabbis are emphasizing this commandment as absolutely critical to the future of the Jewish people. At the same time, those who cannot produce children are exempted from the commandment but are encouraged to adopt children.

The Mishnah asserts that a man should marry at 18 (M *Avot* 5:21), and the Talmud records other opinions ranging from 16 to 24 (B. *Kiddushin* 29b–30a). Presumably the woman would be in her mid-to-late teens. Now, however, high percentages of Jews go to college and graduate school, with the result that few outside the Orthodox community marry before their late twenties. They then try to have children in their 30s. Biologically, though, humans are primed for procreation in their late teens and 20s, and so those who wait to have children until their 30s all too often discover that they cannot. This causes tremendous tension in the marriage, if not divorce. For the sake of the couples themselves as well as the future of the Jewish people, then, rabbis increasingly encourage young people to look for a spouse in college and, if one finds a suitable mate, to marry and begin procreating while in graduate school.

Although contraceptives were known in earlier times, it was not until the 1950s that truly effective modes of birth control were available. Thus the question of using contraceptives for family planning was not a serious question until then. Moreover, because until recently any couple who wanted at least two or three children to survive to adulthood had to have five or six, and because Judaism emphasizes both the imperative to procreate and the blessings of children, Jews used birth control only to protect a person at risk. Specifically, a second-century rabbinic source recorded in the Talmud (T. *Niddah* 2; B. *Yevamot* 12b, 100b; etc.) prescribes that contraceptives be used in three cases: (a) if a girl under the age of 12 is married (to prevent her from endangering herself through pregnancy); (b) if a woman is pregnant (presumably to protect the fetus during intercourse, but they were medically wrong in thinking that intercourse poses a danger to the fetus); or (c) if the mother is nursing an infant (lest the mother become pregnant and her milk dry up, thus depriving the infant of nourishment). Still, some medieval rabbinic sources permit the use of birth control by other women as well

(Feldman, 1968, chaps. 9–13, esp. 185–187). Based on that line of sources, some rabbis permit a newly married couple to use contraceptives for awhile, but not for too long lest their increased age makes them infertile.

If couples are going to use contraceptives, Jewish law prefers those forms that prevent conception in the first place over those that abort an already fertilized egg. That is because in most cases Jewish law forbids abortion. For most of gestation, the fetus is considered "like the thigh of its mother" (B. *Hullin* 58a). Because our bodies are God's property, neither men nor women are permitted to amputate their thigh except to preserve their life or health. Thus Jewish law *requires* abortion when the pregnancy poses a clear threat to the woman's life or physical or mental health; it *permits* abortion when the risk to the woman's life or health (again, physical or mental) is greater than that of a normal pregnancy but not so great as to constitute a clear and present danger to her; but otherwise it prohibits abortion (Feldman, 1968, chaps. 14 and 15).

"Mental health" as a ground for abortion, however, has not been interpreted nearly as broadly in Jewish sources as it has been in American courts. It would not include, for example, the right to abort simply because the woman does not want to have another child, even due to economic pressures. Reform, Conservative, and some Orthodox rabbis, however, use the danger to the mother's mental health to justify an abortion when tests show that the child will be severely malformed or have a lethal genetic disease, or when the pregnancy resulted from rape or incest.[11]

Thus from the point of view of Jewish law the most favored form of contraception is the diaphragm, for it prevents conception and has little, if any, impact on the woman's health. If the contraceptive pill, contraceptive implant or "patch," or the "morning after pill" is not counter-indicated by the woman's age or body chemistry, those are usually the next most favored forms of contraception. RU486 and any other contraceptive that retroactively aborts an embryo should be used only when pregnancy would threaten the mother's physical or mental health, as defined in the preceding paragraphs.

The only non-permanent, male form of contraception currently available is the condom. Because Jewish law makes the male legally responsible for propagation, he should refrain from using contraception at least until he has fulfilled that duty. Condoms, moreover, sometimes split or slip off, and even if they remain intact and in place, they do not always work. Nevertheless, condoms must be used if unprotected sexual intercourse poses a medical risk to either spouse, for condoms do offer some measure of protection against the spread of some diseases, and the duty to maintain health and life supersedes the positive duty of the male to propagate. So, for example, if the history or condition of either partner suggests the possibility of HIV infection, the man must use a condom, and both partners must take a blood test. If either one tests positive for the HIV virus, the use of condoms is not enough. Abstinence is necessary, for life must take precedence over the joys of sex (Gold, 1992, 112ff; Dorff, 2003, 115–116).

Jewish law does not permit abortion simply because the mother is unmarried or does not want a child. It prefers that the mother carry to term and give the child up for adoption if she cannot or will not raise the child herself. Counselors who are consulted by unwed, pregnant Jewish women about what they should do should take into account the nature of the woman's Jewish commitments, for Orthodox women will be far less likely to abort (and far more conflicted if they do decide to abort) than secular Jewish women, with Conservative and Reform women coming somewhere in between. If the woman is close to her rabbi, the counselor may suggest consulting with him or her as well.

FINANCES

The traditional Jewish marriage document, the *ketubbah*, specifies the financial duties that the husband is assuming. Furthermore, Jewish sources require a man to support his wife and children (M.T. *Laws of Marriage* 12:10–15; 13:3–6), and they spell out in detail what happens to property that the woman brings into the marriage (M. *Ketubbot* 8:1; M.T. *Laws of Marriage* 16:1–2; 22: 7–9). Judaism thus recognizes that finances are a crucial part of any marriage and that disagreement about finances is a prime cause of divorce. Jews now are no longer governed by Jewish law on these matters. Still, these provisions in Jewish law indicate clearly that Judaism wants couples to understand that setting their finances in order will play an important role in fostering their relationship. Thus if either or both parties are bringing substantial assets into the marriage or are supporting the other through school, these financial aspects of traditional Jewish marriage law would suggest writing a legally binding prenuptial agreement.

DISSOLVING RELATIONSHIPS THROUGH DIVORCE OR ANNULMENT

Although divorce is always sad, Judaism does not consider it a sin. In fact, the Torah itself provides some instructions about the form of a divorce (Deut. 24:1–3), and the Mishnah and Talmud include an entire section on divorce law (*Gittin*). If the couple agrees to the divorce, they need not supply any justifications; incompatibility is enough. Still, traditional Jewish divorce proceedings intentionally take time to ensure that the couple has thought long and hard about going through with this. Nowadays, because the civil divorce must precede the Jewish divorce proceeding, by the time the latter takes place a number of months have elapsed, and the rabbinic court does not delay things further.

Traditional Jewish law as practiced in the Orthodox and Conservative Movements requires that the couple be divorced in Jewish law in addition to civil law; neither suffices without the other. Traditional Jewish law requires the husband to give his wife a writ of divorce (a *get*); the wife cannot initiate the proceeding. In a small minority of cases, even when the couple has divorced in civil law, the husband refuses to give his wife a *get*. Unless the husband has good reason for this (e.g., the woman is not granting him access to their children in accordance with the civil court's decree), rabbis will first try to convince him to give his wife a *get*, then they will put pressure on him through his friends and employer. Finally, if necessary, Conservative rabbis will annul the marriage so that the woman can remarry.

MANAGING FAMILY AFTER SEPARATION AND/OR DIVORCE

Part of what makes divorce sad is the dashed hopes and dreams that the couple must now mourn. If the divorce is anything but amicable, divorce also involves fights over money and/or child custody, and that itself takes a large toll. Still, sometimes divorce is the right thing to do.

Traditional Jewish law specifies that the husband must give his wife a sum of money specified in their marriage document to support her for about a year after the divorce or until she is remarried, whichever is earlier. In addition, as we have seen, it requires the husband to support his minor children; it spells out how the couple's assets are to be divided; and it determines custody of the children.

Civil law now has jurisdiction over all these matters. Still, the Jewish tradition would urge divorcing couples to separate as cleanly and amicably as possible and to support each other in raising their children. The assignment of daughters to women and sons to men in Jewish law indicates that it was sensitive to the fact that children need an adult model of their own gender to teach them how to become a woman or man. Thus if only one parent is raising a child, it is important that he or she involve an adult of the opposite gender in the child's life. This could be a family member (a grandparent, an uncle or aunt) or a volunteer in a program such as Jewish Big Brothers or Jewish Big Sisters. As recent studies have shown, in contemporary society this is especially important for American boys, 40% of whom, by some counts, live in homes without a father or another adult male.[12]

DEATH AND DYING

For a general treatment of how Judaism deals with medical aspects of dying and death, including the many new medical decisions that have to be made, such as withholding or withdrawing life support and organ transplantation, see Dorff, 1998, chapters 8 and 9. In short, some rabbis require that everything be done to keep a person's body functioning. Most rabbis would permit withholding machines or medication when they are unlikely to cure the patient, and many of those would permit withdrawing such interventions if once started. Some rabbis would also endorse withholding or withdrawing artificial nutrition or hydration. Most rabbis permit hospice care when doctors have determined that cure is impossible, and most urge that people make their organs available for transplant upon their demise.

After death, the body is cared for by a group of people especially trained to prepare the body for burial according to Jewish custom. Modesty is preserved in death, so men deal with a male body and women with a female body. The body is washed and clothed in linen shrouds. Someone remains with the body overnight, usually reciting selections from Psalms. The body is buried in a closed casket the next day or as soon thereafter as possible (excepting Sabbaths and festivals) after a funeral service in which the rabbi, family members, and sometimes friends eulogize the deceased. Conservative and Orthodox Judaism do not permit cremation.

After the funeral and interment, the official mourners, that is, the spouse, children, parents, and siblings of the deceased, engage in a seven-day period of intense mourning (*shiva*), during which they stay home. Community members come to the house morning and evening to constitute a prayer quorum for the morning, afternoon, and evening services, during which the mourners recite a special prayer, the *Mourner's Kaddish*, in addition to the regular liturgy. People come throughout the day to take care of the family's physical needs (food, carpool for the children, etc.) and to help them talk about their memories of the deceased. Men do not shave during this period. From the eighth day through the thirtieth after the funeral (the period of *sheloshim*), people go back to work but attend services in the synagogue morning and evening, where they continue to recite the *Mourner's Kaddish*. Although a spouse, parents, and siblings may continue this practice longer than that, they are not required to do so. Children, however, are required to recite the *Mourner's Kaddish* morning and evening through eleven months after the death and to refrain from joyous events such as weddings during that time as a part of their duty to "Honor your father and mother" (Ex. 20:12). Contemporary Jews vary widely in how much of these traditional practices they practice, and so counselors should not be surprised at the variation. On the other hand, many Jews who do not adhere to traditional Jewish law normally want to carry out these traditional practices in mourning because matters of life and death of loved ones strike home in a very dramatic way.

HOMOSEXUALITY IN COUPLES AND FAMILIES

The Torah (Lev. 18:22 and 20:13) prohibits a man to "lie with a male as a man lies with a female; it is an abomination." It does not define exactly what it is prohibiting for men, and it says nothing about women. The rabbis, however, defined the biblical prohibition to ban anal sex between males, and on their own authority they forbade other forms of both male and female homosexual sex.

This has become the object of immense debate in all denominations of Judaism. Orthodox rabbis maintain that all of the traditional prohibitions apply. Some, though, distinguish the sin from the sinner, allowing gay men to have honors within the synagogue. Although some Orthodox leaders at one time argued that there are no homosexual Orthodox Jews, the movie *Trembling Before God* demonstrated that all segments of Orthodoxy include gays and lesbians. The Reform movement has gradually endorsed synagogues with specific outreach to gays and lesbians (1973), ordination of gays and lesbians (1990), and commitment ceremonies (2002).

The most heated debate, then, continues in the Conservative movement. What is not debated in that movement is four assertions that were passed as identical resolutions by both the rabbinic and synagogue organizations of the Conservative Movement (i.e., the Rabbinical Assembly and the United Synagogue of Conservative Judaism) in May 1990 and November 1991, respectively. Those resolutions stated that the Conservative Movement (a) opposes any violence against gay men or lesbians; (b) supports full equality for gay men and lesbians in civil law (which includes no discrimination in employment, housing, or health care, and also, as subsequent resolutions stated, support for civil marriages); (c) welcomes gay or lesbian Jews as members of Conservative synagogues; and (d) urges rabbis and synagogues to teach Conservative Jews about Jewish sexual ethics in general and about homosexuality in particular. Conservative Jews are not at one, however, on two main issues: ordination of gay men or lesbians as rabbis or cantors, and celebrating homosexual unions through newly created Jewish commitment ceremonies (or marriages). Dissonance also remains on what to call homosexual unions and how to structure them, if they are permitted altogether. In March 1992, the Committee on Jewish Law and Standards (CJLS) proclaimed that Conservative rabbis should not publicly celebrate homosexual unions in a Jewish ceremony and that Conservative seminaries should not accept gay men or lesbians in rabbinical or cantorial school. In January 2004, however, the president of the Rabbinical Assembly and the president of the United Synagogue of Conservative Judaism both asked the CJLS to revisit the issue. It is now in the process of doing that, and in December 2006, will vote on a number of rabbinic rulings that range from reaffirming the 1992 position to narrowing the ban to male anal sex (that is, that which the Torah prohibits but not the later rabbinic expansions of that prohibition) to legislation (a *takkanah*, literally, a fixing of the law) to uproot even the biblical prohibition.

Counselors helping gay or lesbian Jews should know about these differing stances within the denominations in order to tailor their aid to the religious convictions of the particular person they are helping. Counselors also should know that within each denomination there are groups of gay and lesbian Jews who can help to provide a supportive community for their client. Further, an increasing number of rabbis nowadays are aware of the religious, psychological, and social issues involved in being gay or lesbian and can help homosexual Jews deal with those issues and feel more at home in the Jewish community as they help heterosexual Jews overcome their stereotypes and welcome homosexual Jews into their community and, sometimes, their family.

CONCLUSION

The Jewish tradition sees marriage and family as the ideal contexts for human development. Many resources of both traditional and modern Jewish communities are devoted to helping people find mates, and rabbis, cantors, and educators, as religious ideals for the community, are very much encouraged to be married and to have children. In our own day, education takes much longer than in the past, and so marriage is often postponed to the late twenties, with the result that Jewish couples are having too few children to maintain Jewish numbers and some cannot procreate altogether. That threat to the Jewish future is made worse by assimilation and intermarriage. Among Jews, as among many groups of Americans, divorce is much more prevalent than in the past, and the Jewish community includes many singles, single parents, blended families, homosexual families, and elderly people marrying after the death of their first spouse. Many Jewish norms need to be stretched to apply to these new circumstances, and contemporary Jews are doing that. The fundamentally positive Jewish view of the body, marriage, children, education, and family life, however, continues to be a reservoir for moral guidance and Jewish family strength.

ENDNOTES

1. C.E. = A.D., and B.C.E. = B.C. Jews do not believe that Jesus is Christ. Therefore referring to dates as "in the year of our Lord = *anno domini* (= A.D.) or Before Christ (=B.C.) makes no sense for Jews. I am therefore using the more religiously neutral terms, "Before the Common Era" (= B.C.E.) and "in the Common Era (= C.E.), but the years designated are the same as those intended by Christians when they say "B.C." and "A.D."

2. In this and all other notes, M. = Mishnah (edited c. 200 C.E.); T. = Tosefta (c. 200 C.E.); B.= Babylonian Talmud (c. 500 C.E.); M.T. = Maimonides' code, the *Mishneh Torah* (1177); and S.A. = Joseph Caro's code, the *Shulhan Arukh* (1565), with glosses by Moses Isserles to indicate where the practice of Northern European (Ashkenazic) Jews differed from that of Jews living in the countries surrounding the Mediterranean Sea (Sephardic Jews).

3. The wife's rights to sex within marriage: M. *Ketubbot* 5:6; M.T. *Laws of Marriage* 14:4–7, 15; S.A. *Yoreh De'ah* 235:1, *Even Ha-ezer* 76; 77:1. The husband's rights to sex within marriage: M. *Ketubbot* 5:7; M.T. *Laws of Marriage* 14:8–14; S.A. *Even Ha-ezer* 77:2–3.

4. For more on Judaism and infertility, see Dorff, 1998, chapters 3 and 4.

5. Abraham arranges that his son, Isaac, would marry a woman from among his extended clan (Gen. 24), and Rebekah and Isaac saw to it that Jacob did likewise (Gen. 27:46–28:5). The Bible records the Rebekah and Isaac's great displeasure when Esau marries Hittite women (Gen. 26:34–35), so great that Esau then takes an additional wife from the clan to placate

his parents (Gen. 28:6–9). Jews were not to marry Canaanite women (Ex. 34:16; Deut. 7:– 4; Josh. 23:12). The Bible records a number of cases when Israelites, including leaders such as Moses and kings, married foreign women (e.g., Gen. 38:1–2; 41:45; Ex. 2:21; Judg. 3:6, 2 Sam. 3:3; 11:3; etc.). Endogamous marriages, however, were clearly preferred. In line with that, Ezra and Nehemiah forced those returning to Jerusalem from the Babylonian exile to divorce their foreign wives (Ezra 9–10; Neh. 13:13–30).

6. For example, Genesis 27:26–27; 29:11, 13; 31:28, 55; 33:4; 45:14–15; 48:10; Exodus 4:27; 18:7; 1 Samuel 20:41; 2 Samuel 14:33; 15:5; 19:40; Ruth 1:9, 14; and many, many times, of course, in the love poetry of Song of Songs — e.g., 1:2; 2:6; 8:3.

7. Note that even in the Bible's book of love poetry, The Song of Songs, the lover (at 8:1) *wishes* that her lover were her brother so that she could kiss him in public without reproach, but the fact that he is not prevents her from doing so:

> If only it could be as with a brother,
> As if you had nursed at my mother's breast:
> Then I could kiss you
> When I met you in the street,
> And no one would despise me.

8. For a fuller discussion of Jewish sexual ethics, see Dorff, 2003, chapter 3.

9. B. *Eruvin* 82a; B. *Ketubbot* 65b, 122b–123a; M.T. *Laws of Marriage* 21:16–18; S.A. *Even Ha'ezer* 82:6–8. For a demonstration that these were only the presumptive rules of custody but that the welfare of the child trumped this presumption, see Schochetman, 1992, and Bryode, 1994.

10. For a fuller discussion of the topics of this subsection and the next, see Dorff, 2003, chapter 4.

11. For the official Reform approach to abortion, see Washofsky, 2001: 242–245. For the official Conservative approach, see Mackler, 2000: 293–232. Orthodox Jewry is too splintered to have an official position, but Orthodox rabbis tend to be less permissive in this, as in most matters, reserving abortion for clear threats to the physical life or health of the mother.

12. This is the number quoted in the Public Television program, "Raising Cain," first aired on January 12, 2006.

REFERENCES

Bryode, M. (1994). "Child custody in Jewish law: A pure law analysis." In S. M. Passamaneck and M. Finley (Eds.). *Jewish Law Association Studies VII: The Paris Conference Volume.* (pp. 1–20). Atlanta: Scholars Press.

Dorff, E. N. (1996). *Conservative Judaism: Our ancestors to our descendants.* New York: United Synagogue of Conservative Judaism.

———. (1998). *Matters of life and death: A Jewish approach to modern medical ethics.* Philadelphia: Jewish Publication Society.

———. (2003). *Love your neighbor and yourself: A Jewish approach to modern personal ethics.* Philadelphia: Jewish Publication Society.

———. (2005). *The unfolding tradition: Jewish law after Sinai.* New York: Aviv Press (Rabbinical Assembly).

Feldman, D. M. (1968). *Birth control in Jewish law.* New York: New York University Press.

Gold, M. (1992). *Does God belong in the bedroom?* Philadelphia: Jewish Publication Society.

Mackler, A. L. (Ed.). *Life and death responsibilities in Jewish biomedical ethics.* New York: Jewish Theological Seminary of America, 2000.

The National Jewish Population Survey 2000–01. (2003). New York: United Jewish Communities.

Phillips, B. A. (1998). *Reexamining intermarriage: Trends, textures, and strategies.* Boston: Wilstein Institute of Jewish Studies, and New York: American Jewish Committee.

Schochetman, E. (1992). "On the nature of the ruled governing custody of children in Jewish law." In *The Jewish Law Annual X.* (pp. 115–158). Boston: The Institute of Jewish Law, Boston University School of Law.

Washofsky, M. (2001). *Jewish living: A guide to contemporary reform practice.* New York: UAHC Press (Union of American Hebrew Congregations, now renamed the Union of Reform Judaism).

CHAPTER 10

The Practice of Marriage and Family Counseling and Native Religions

GORD BRUYERE

The Anishnabe Family: A Native American Culture's Values and Beliefs in Transition

At first there was nothing and the Creator was alone. The Creator sent out the first thought, but nothing came back. So the Creator decided to make something so that thoughts could be reflected and return back. The Creator decided to make a family, starting with Nee-ba-gee'-sis, Grandmother Moon and Gee'-sis, Grandfather Sun. Then the Creator made Ah'ki, a female child who would be the mother of us all and she was given many names, including Earth. This is a good reminder that woman preceded man in the life of human beings, and that Mother Earth and all women are givers of life. Water is Ah'ki's blood, the rocks are her bones, and the rich loam is her flesh. All living things are her children and because we all come from one mother, we are all related.

—(Benton-Banai, 1988, p. 2)

INTRODUCTION

Anishnabe people are one of the largest groups of indigenous peoples in North American (Encyclopedia Britannica Online, 2005), generally residing in Canada and the United States around the Great Lakes. Anishnabe people are a member of the Algonquian language family and are related linguistically and culturally to numerous other indigenous peoples (McCutchen, 1993) such as the Cree or Micmac, but are also distinct in values, beliefs, and practices that comprise their way of life. Also known as Ojibwa or Chippewa people, "Anishnabe" is the preferred indigenous language name (Peacock & Wisuri, 2001) and the most respectful means of identification.

This chapter will discuss the traditional values and beliefs concerned with aspects of family life, including aspects of the making and dissolving of marriages, family roles, death and dying, and sexual orientation. These traditional beliefs will also be contextualized by illustrating the ways in which they have been affected by the process of colonization of Anishnabe territories by European settlers and the emergent dominance of American society. The chapter will conclude with ways in which a marriage and family counselor may develop culturally respectful relationships with Anishnabe and other Native American peoples.

At this point in our shared history, where understanding of racial, ethnic, and cultural diversity is flourishing, we must be careful to not assume that all North American indigenous cultures are the same or that they are even similar. There are no monolithic Native American or American Indian beliefs about marriages and families, and to speak as if there are or were would be inaccurate and disrespectful. Anishnabe histories, and cultural values, beliefs, and practices have similarities with many other indigenous cultures, but there are also many differences. There are even variations and subtleties of dialect and beliefs among the Anishnabe themselves. Finally, the ways in which indigenous knowledges are recorded, interpreted, and told also often differ from the approaches to knowledge of nonindigenous people who work with or study us. It is most safe to assume that what is conveyed here is the present understanding of one Anishnabe person about his own culture.

TRADITIONAL BELIEFS

In order to work with Native American peoples in a contemporary context, and to better understand Anishnabe people in particular, traditional customary beliefs and practices related to marriage and family life are described. It is important to understand that while traditional beliefs and practices continue to this day, often times Anishnabe and other Native American people have been affected such that these traditional beliefs and practices may be unevenly evident in contemporary individuals, couples, and families.

Definition of Marriage

There was no definition of marriage in the legal sense, but there was a strong custom of the practice or institution of marriage. Marriage among Anishnabe people would today be called common-law unions. There were no formal marriage vows but there was ceremony. The couple could be wrapped together in a blanket or have the hems or sleeves of their garments sewn together (Johnston, 1976). Such an act symbolized the union of two people and was followed by a feast hosted by the two joined families.

Young women were considered of a marriageable age after puberty. Young men were considered marriageable once they were able to consistently demonstrate their skills to provide for their families, and such proficiency usually did not develop until a man was in his early 20s. So it was not uncommon for there to be some age difference in a couple marrying for the first time (Hilger, 1998).

Anishnabe people generally organized their society into clans. The clan system was a way to organize relationships and identify roles within Anishnabe society (Benton-Banai, 1988). Johnston (1976) says that the first question two strangers would ask each other was, "What is your clan?" followed by, "Who are you?" (p. 59). The clan system functioned such that if you were a Bear clan member, you were considered a direct or close relative to all Bear clan members wherever they were. This meant that wherever a person went in Anishnabe territory, he or she could very likely count on finding welcome as family. The names and number of clans could vary but it was generally accepted that a person would not marry into his or her own clan (Johnston, 1976). This protocol functioned to strengthen bonds between family groups living across great distances, and ensure peaceful relations among Anishnabe people who might be vying for use of the same natural resources. It also ensured genetic diversity within a family group or community.

Kohl (1985) witnessed Anishnabe men who married more than one wife. This situation, he said, only occurred if the husband was able to provide adequately for more than one wife, and the husband was duly considered to be a man of some means and worthy of communal respect.

DATING AND COHABITATION

There are some indications of the practice of arranged marriages although no documentation exists to corroborate this. Most often, a young man was required to approach a young woman's family to first seek permission to initiate courtship. If the young woman and her family agreed, then the young couple could spend time together in the young woman's family home under the supervision of one of her family members, most often her grandmother. To keep company without the presence of elders was taboo (Hilger, 1998).

One of Hilger's (1998) informants offered this example of how courtship might unfold:

A young man who wished to call on a young maiden talked first with the older people who lived next to her lodge. He then entered the girl's lodge and talked with the girl in a low tone. She was not, however, permitted to leave the lodge with him. If he happened to call late in the evening, and the embers were low, the mother or grandmother stirred up the fire so that it burnt brightly, filled her pipe, and sat up and smoked. The young man felt that he was being watched at all times. He might on an evening play his courting flute somewhere near the lodge, but the girl was never allowed to leave the lodge in response to it. (p. 61)

After marriage, the couple would often live in the home of the woman's parents for up to a year. As soon as a child was born or if the couple mutually agreed, then they would set up their own home.

ROLES WITHIN MARRIAGES AND FAMILIES

The primary unit of social organization of Native American cultures is the family or clan. Family is understood to include aunts, uncles, cousins, and grandparents in a close-knit integrated unit that at least parallels the bonds of the conventional nuclear family. The term "extended family" would be nonsensical because of the inclusive definition of "family." Traditionally, children are considered to be gifts of the Creator. We do not own children but we do own the responsibility to guide and protect them. Traditionally, entire communities were organized around that ethic and principle.

The traditional parenting of children was shared among relatives. For example, parents might have gender-specific responsibilities for children depending on the child's development and maturity. In this way children would be exposed to and educated in cultural gender relations. Parents had specific roles in shaping the behavior of their children. Parents could be the main source of instilling discipline by prescribing or admonishing behavior or that role might fall to aunts or uncles, leaving the parents to mainly focus on immediate needs for affection, sustenance, or safety. Grandparents and great-grandparents would always have a principal role in conveying teachings about history, ceremonies, philosophies, and values. Cousins or siblings were expected to play a child care role according to their abilities and subject to the supervision of adult family members.

The main point here is that the responsibility for children was shared within families, clans, and communities and this responsibility was a primary source and measure of community well-being. This point is often difficult to comprehend for individuals, such as those in mainstream American society, who have been socialized within nuclear families and who have come to expect "universal" and "neutral" mechanisms of the social welfare system to support them.

It was common custom for grandparents to "adopt" one or two grandchildren. There was no formal arrangement and children often moved back and forth between the parental and grandparental homes as they wished. The arrangement was a practical way to ensure continuity of care of the grandparents and to ensure continuity of knowledge transmission as the grandparents would often choose to share medicinal, ceremonial, historical, or other kinds of knowledge with the adoptive grandchildren.

Two-parent families organized labor and other responsibilities along gender lines. Women were primarily responsible for gathering plants and medicines, preparing food, making clothing and home utensils, and caring for children, while men were primarily responsible for protecting the community, tool making, and hunting. Men were often leaders, seen as the voices of the community. However, women were also seen as the power behind the voices. While division of roles was along gender lines, cultural values held that the roles were equally respected. Roles were clearly delineated but Anishnabe family roles were not inflexibly carried out, as it was common for men and women to take on whatever roles were necessary for family functioning.

ABORTION, BIRTH CONTROL, CHILD BEARING

Children were considered gifts of the Creator and were understood to be the primary source around which family roles were organized. Hence, abortion was uncommon but it was not unheard of. Abortion was facilitated by medicine people skilled in herbalism, usually female in these instances, and the method consisted of ingestion of plant concoctions. Birth control methods were limited to abstinence. In precolonial times, survival and proliferation of clans, communities, and the people as a whole was so vital that abortion and birth control were not issues. This also helps explain the sacredness of children.

With the understanding that women could enter into a marriage anytime after puberty, and that the birth of a child was an accepted hallmark of a successful union, it was not uncommon for teenaged women to give birth. However, there was no concept of adolescence as a discrete stage of human development: after puberty, human beings were considered adults. Therefore, there was no concept of or stigma attached to teen pregnancies. A teenaged mother would also be supported by family (extended family in common parlance), particularly her mother, aunts, and grandmothers.

The birthing process usually did not involve men. Births were usually facilitated by older female family members experienced in midwifery and personal experiences of child birth. A child's birth was considered sacred and there were many prenatal and postnatal ceremonial and symbolic acts to protect the child and manifest a healthy life for the child, but their description is beyond the scope of this chapter.

DISSOLVING RELATIONSHIPS

Separations were allowed but there were no formal divorce proceedings. However, Johnston (1976) states that dissolution of marriages was uncommon. The marriage ceremony was taken very seriously and not undertaken without a strong commitment by the couple. On the other hand, if after a year or so of living together the couple could not live together agreeably or if no children were born, they could separate. The separating couple would simply move back into the homes of their respective parents. If a man and woman had children, either one could leave the family home or both were free to remarry.

DEATH AND DYING

When death occurred, the deceased would usually be kept by family members for four days to allow the person's spirit to break free of its physical form. Both Johnston (1976) and Densmore (1979) allude to the Anishnabe belief that the deceased person's spirit lingers near its body before finally traveling on the path or road of souls.

During the four days before burial, family and community members would accompany the deceased. Kohl (1985) also describes customs regarding grieving the loss of a family member. He described how the Anishnabe people he observed blackened their faces with charcoal ash after a death of a family member and cut off their hair. Kohl (1985) noted that grieving in this manner was more elaborate and palpable when women (as life bearers) died than when men died.

The deceased would often be buried with the feet pointing west, toward the path of souls, and buried with a few personal items for the four day journey. Family members would often keep personal items of the deceased, and wear particular clothing to demonstrate mourning for up to one year. Kohl (1985) also discussed how the family kept a number of objects that belonged to a deceased child or that signified that child to the family. These items were kept for a year. This practice was a way to maintain a connection to the child during a period of grieving that was resolved ceremonially after one year. After burial of any deceased, the family would host a community feast in honor of the deceased and in order to help the deceased along the path of souls.

HOMOSEXUALITY IN COUPLES AND FAMILIES

There is no literature available to describe how homosexuality or other nonheterosexuality was accommodated within pre-contact Anishnabe society. Oral tradition asserts that non-heterosexual men and women were respected and included within Anishnabe society and were not always expected to ascribe to conventional gender roles. Oral tradition also asserts that homosexual individuals were considered to have particularly unique spiritual gifts that served a medicinal or spiritual role in the life of the community. Beyond these generalities, little information is available.

COLONIZATION AND DECOLONIZATION

From the time of the initial influx of European settlers to the late 20th century, the Anishnabe way of life, which is based on a holistic system of values and beliefs, has been systematically denigrated, attacked, and eroded. However, our way of life has survived and is currently enjoying an uneven, complex process of renewal and revitalization in a social and political context that differs greatly from much of the history of our people (Bruyere, 2003).

Colonization refers to the systemic denigration, attack, and erosion of a people's way of life, including cultural beliefs and values and concomitant relationships and social structures or institutions. The colonization of Native American people has consisted of three primary prongs of attack including (a) the dislocation and removal from traditional lands, (b) the forced participation in state boarding schools and the insinuation of Christianity, and (c) over-representation in state child welfare systems.

The dislocation from traditional lands during the treaty signing period of American history resulted in the decay of the hunting and harvesting practices that comprised the basis of Anishnabe economies. The tracts of land set aside as reservations are, for the most part, not rich in natural resources or particularly amenable to agriculture or of enough size, minimizing the land's economic viability. Dislocation from traditional territories also meant abrogation of the sovereign right to make economic and political decisions to determine and develop suitable and sustainable economic practices. Isolation on reservations and racial discrimination prohibited integration into the larger American economy and led to widespread poverty and morbidity. Also, "federal laws requiring relocation of Native people have had significant impacts on the sacred relationship between native people and the land" (Tsosie, 2001).

The late 19th century and the first half of the 20th century the federal American government, in conjunction with various Christian denominations, instituted one of the most deleterious and harmful means of colonization experienced by Native American people. Residential or boarding schools were created with the express purpose of removing children from the influence of their parents and communities, and to "civilize" them into Christianity and a final denial of all traces of Native American cultural identity. Many boys and girls were emotionally and physically abused for merely speaking their language; many were sexually abused by priests, nuns, and lay personnel. Children did not have the benefit of consistent loving, patient guidance, nor did they see it modeled for them.

State-run boarding schools began to close down beginning in the mid-20th century with the creation of tribal education systems. Yet the third means of colonizing Anishnabe people took hold and child welfare agencies picked up where the residential schools left off. As the residential school system declined, the large-scale removal of Native American children from their families and communities by child welfare agencies constituted "a new modality of colonialist regulation" (Kline, 1992, p. 382).

Child welfare authorities clearly saw the poverty reflected in poor infrastructure, overcrowded housing, ineffectual tribal governance that resulted from dislocation from traditional territories and impaired participation in the American wage economy. They also saw the social disintegration such as substance abuse, family violence, and crime that resulted from the residential or boarding school period in Anishnabe history. What they did not see was the long-term effects of the large-scale removals of Anishnabe children that they perpetuated.

In many Native American cultures, it is a common precept that everyone in a community is related to one another as family. The intimacy of community relationships as a whole is structured upon how community members relate to one another *through relationships with children*. Without children, it is impossible to have parents, aunts, uncles, cousins, grandparents. Clan designations among the Anishnabe may prescribe relationships but even the internal workings of a clan are recognized according to family structure.

As a consequence, if a child is removed from a family, it affects the relationships within a family, within a clan, within an entire community. If large numbers of children, perhaps even the majority of children are removed from a community, the ways in which family, clan, and community relationships are affected are profound.

Whether it was through residential schools or child welfare practices, generations of Anishnabe children have been removed from the care and influence of their families. Children were thus irregularly exposed to the Anishnabe language, spiritual teachings and practices, or traditional economic pursuits. Some children grew to shy away from or mistrust these aspects of an Anishnabe worldview because of their indoctrination at residential schools. Parents sometimes made conscious decisions to avoid teaching these things to children because of the racism faced by anyone who presented as an Anishnabe person. Thus, these dynamics have created an individual and collective denial of Anishnabe cultural identity.

The removals of Anishnabe and other Native American children by these modalities of colonial regulation cannot simply be understood as an absence of cultural identity. Residential schools and child welfare practices have resulted directly in social disintegration characterized by multigenerational dysfunctions such as addictions, family violence, sexual abuse, and suicide. These dysfunctions interweave with poverty, poor economic development or employment opportunities, poor health, and poor education. Children who became parents in turn taught their own children the harmful or dysfunctional lessons forced upon them.

Children did not have healthy parenting modeled for them. Parents who rarely saw their children would, out of guilt or grief, often overcompensate for that absence by being impractically indulgent when children were in their care. Individuals who grew up in residential schools or foster/adoptive homes where affection (physical, emotional, or verbal) was not demonstrated did not learn how to demonstrate the love they felt to their own children. Those who were exposed to violence as children also learned to be violent toward their own children and helped to perpetuate a cycle of violence across generations. Children who experienced residential schools were so highly regimented in their day-to-day lives because they lived in an institution, that they had difficulty forming their own codes of self-discipline or formed inordinate expectations of discipline when they became parents.

Over successive generations Anishnabe families inconsistently applied the parenting ethics and practices of their traditional cultures because of the absence of their children and the interweaving of above-named social forces. In this way, the cultural ethics, beliefs, and practices slowly broke down over time. Further, because of the removal of the *axis mundi* of Anishnabe social organization, those ethics, beliefs, and practices concerning governance and redistribution of resources also broke down.

Generation upon generation of individuals in families or communities were hammered with racist beliefs about the inherent inferiority of Native American peoples and can come to believe stereotypes, accept discriminatory practices, or simply not work to find it within themselves to address their life situations. These manifestations of multigenerational effects can also be referred to as internalized racism or internalized colonization.

However, the story of Anishnabe people does not end with a description of traditional values and beliefs that were horrendously affected by colonization. With a perspective influenced by the writer on African decolonization Franz Fanon, Waubageshig (1970) asserts that where colonization occurs, decolonization also occurs, a situation that leads to cultural, social, political, and economic revitalization. Keeping in mind that colonization took place over decades and even centuries, decolonization is also a slow, uneven, and complex process. That process refers to the initiatives of Anishnabe people to reclaim and revitalize the Anishnabe language, spiritual beliefs, cultural practices, and social and political autonomy within a contemporary context.

THE ROLE OF HELPERS

What about the role of mainstream Americans and what about those agencies or helpers mandated to assist Native American or Anishnabe peoples? Maurice Moreau, in his structural approach to social work, reconceived the role of a helper. The goal was not to help people to adjust to the prevailing socio-economic arrangement but to essentially work in solidarity to challenge prevailing social conditions (Carniol, 1990).

Working in solidarity may mean demonstrating a willingness to step back from being part of the change process within Anishnabe communities and instead focus upon the nature of the relationship Anishnabe communities have with mainstream American social service agencies and political bodies. On an individual level it means challenging racist or patriarchal assumptions of other workers or supervisors that unjustifiably question the ability of Native American people to determine the solutions to their own problems. It also means that a counselor must be aware of how Anishnabe or Native American people's experience of residential schools or child welfare authorities may make them especially sensitive to issues of social or political power in relationships with mainstream Americans.

Demonstrations of solidarity also shine through in consistent, respectful attempts to ask questions regarding culturally appropriate actions, despite the possibility of facing mistrust, anger, or frustration from Native American colleagues or clients. What is culturally appropriate depends on the degree of acculturation an individual, couple, or family has experienced. Witko (2006) states that there at least four types of American Indian families that each require a different response from helpers or counselors. A family that adheres to traditional values and beliefs may prefer the help of an Anishnabe healer or medicine person. A nontraditional, bicultural family who has adopted many mainstream styles of living may accept contemporary forms of treatment and relate well to mainstream service professionals, while having a strong Anishnabe cultural identity. The pan-traditional family that struggles to redefine and reconfirm traditional beliefs and practices often rejects mainstream forms of treatment and instead desires to recapture the traditional Anishnabe cultural heritage and look to that system for solutions to any issues of family wellness. The experiences of an urban family that strives to adhere to Anishnabe cultural norms while trying to function in mainstream city life are characterized by tensions between openness to assistance from mainstream service professionals with strong preference for services that reinvigorate their fragmented sense of Anishnabe cultural identity. If a helper wants to develop effective therapeutic relationships with Anishnabe or other Native American people in the 21st century, he or she must be willing to share in the emotional legacy of our shared history.

Part of that emotional legacy is the shame in one's Anishnabe heritage that can indicate internalized racism. It is a delicate matter, but one that in the long run may constitute a beautiful gift, for a helper to gently accompany an Anishnabe person to shed that kind of shame. Joseph Gone (2006) outlines four broad strategies for counselors to consider for this process:

1. Consider that psychological difficulties experienced by urban Indian clients are existential in origin and expressive of conflicts in cultural identity.
2. Continuously assess and (re)formulate the cultural identity status of zurban Indian clients in the context of therapeutic goals.
3. Harness the social process of the therapeutic relationship to support distressed urban Indian clients in reconstituting cultural identity as a path to wellness.
4. Recognize the limitations of the conventional or consultative relationship, and venture out of the clinic into urban Indian communities that you desire to serve. (p. 72)

The colonization of Anishnabe and other Native American peoples means that there is wide variation in how individuals, couples, and families affiliate themselves with traditional values, beliefs, and practices. Revitalization or reinvigoration of an Anishnabe cultural identity may or may not be a client-identified goal for counseling. Whatever the goals, which a counselor and client agree to, it is crucial to understand that every Native American person has been affected by colonization and to consider measures to sensitively create an effective therapeutic relationship with Anishnabe or other Native American people.

These measures involve courage; yet it is not the same courage that it has taken for Anishnabe people to survive. These acts in solidarity require the courage to undertake the development of relationships in a manner that should have happened hundreds of years ago. That may be the redeeming aspect of the way Anishnabe people traditionally viewed life as a wheel or a circle:

> By reading our own footprints we could always tell where we had come from. But there were never any footprints into the future. In fact we had no future. In our language, the closest word we had to "future" was sort of an arc or circle. Our going was part of the arc of a circle. So was our coming: we were so dumb we didn't know that progress takes place straight ahead. We walked in circles I guess. Our footprints out of yesterday were also footprints into tomorrow. (Pelletier, 1972, p. 10)

REFERENCES

Benton-Banai, E. (1988). *The mishomis book: The voice of the Ojibway.* Hayward, WI: Indian Country Communications.

Bruyere, G. (1999). The decolonization wheel: Social work practice with Aboriginal peoples. In R. Delaney, K. Brownlee, & K. Zapf (Eds.), *Social work practice with rural and northern peoples* (pp. 170–181). Thunder Bay: Centre for Northern Studies, Lakehead University.

Bruyere, G. (2003). Lessons in the blood: Reflections on protecting Aboriginal children. In D. Champagne and I. A. Saad (Eds.), *The future of indigenous peoples: Strategies for survival and development.* Los Angeles: UCLA American Indian Studies Center.

Carniol, B. (1990). Structural social work: Maurice Moreau's challenge to social work change. *Journal of Progressive Human Services, 3*(1), 1–20.

Densmore, F. (1979). *Chippewa customs.* St. Paul, MN: Minnesota Historical Society Press.

Encyclopedia Britannica Online. (2005). *Ojibwa.* (http://www.britannica.com/ebc/article-9373944?query=ojibwe&ct=) accessed October 1, 2005, 9:40 am

Gone, J. P. (2006). Mental health, wellness, and the quest for an authentic American Indian identity. In Tawa M. Wikto (ed.), *Mental health care for urban Indians: Clinical insights from native practitioners* (pp. 55–80). Washington. American Psychological Association.

Hart, M. A. (2003). *Seeking mino-pimatisiwin: An aboriginal approach to helping.* Halifax, NS. Fernwood Books, Ltd.

Hilger, I. M. (1998). *Chippewa families: A social study of white earth reservation.* 1938. St. Paul, MN: Minnesota Historical Society Press.

Johnston, B. (1976). *Ojibway heritage.* Toronto, ON: McClelland and Stewart Ltd.

Kline, M. (1992). Child welfare law, "Best interests of the child" ideology, and first nations. *Osgoode Hall Law Journal, 30*(2), 375–425.

Kohl, J. G. (1985). *Kitchi-gami: Life among the Lake Superior Ojibway.* St. Paul, MN: Minnesota Historical Society Press.

McCutchen, D. (1993). *The red record: The wallam olum: The oldest native North American history.* Wayne, NJ: Avery Publishing Group.

Peacock, T., & Wisuri, M. (2001). *Ojibwe Waasa Inaabidaa: We look in all directions.* Afton, MN: Afton Historical Society Press.

Pelletier, W. (1972). Dumb Indian. In Ralph Osborne (Ed.), *Who is the chairman of this meeting?* (pp. 1–10). Toronto: Neewin Publishing.

Tsosie, R. (2001). Land, culture and community: Envisioning Native American sovereignty and national identity in the 21st Century. *Hagar International Social Science Review, 2*(2), 183–200.

Waubageshig. (1970). The comfortable crisis. In Waubegeshig (Ed.), *The only good Indian: Essays by Canadian Indians* (pp. 65–89). Toronto: New Press.

Witko, T. M. (2006). A framework for working with American Indian parents. In Tawa M. Wikto (ed.), *Mental health care for urban Indians: Clinical insights from native practitioners* (pp. 155–171). Washington. American Psychological Association.

CHAPTER 11

The Practice of Marriage and Family Counseling and Humanism

DAVID R. KOEPSELL AND DENISE MERCURIO-RILEY

INTRODUCTION: SECULAR HUMANIST WORLDVIEW

Secular humanism is not strictly a set of beliefs or tenets so much as it is a philosophical methodology that tends to lead to certain principles. The term has become a popular term describing, generally, philosophical naturalism, together with certain generally accepted precepts. There are secular humanist "manifestos" and "affirmations," as well as secular humanist meeting groups and organizations, one of which I am currently executive director. But under the broad umbrella term, there are myriad individual sets of beliefs and opinions regarding every issue under the sun.

Paul Kurtz (1979) writes of some "common moral decencies," which he says form the core of moral behavior in every culture and religion, and which secular humanists likewise should accept. However, among secular humanists, there is broad disagreement as to not only the source or even the existence of "morality" but also what moral precepts there may be or ought to be.

Yet, secular humanism is regarded as a worldview, ascribed to by perhaps millions worldwide. So how shall we account for their particular human needs in family matters, and counsel them in a consistent and coherent fashion when they seek advice? This chapter considers certain nearly universally held secular humanist principles, and discusses roles, responsibilities, expectations, and obligations broadly conceived from the humanist perspective.

Counseling secular humanists requires understanding their worldview and working within it to develop rational, reasoned, and emotionally satisfying methods of treating problems. Because secular humanists reject dogma and authority perceived as irrational, unsound, or contradictory to their fundamental beliefs, we must first look at the common features of their worldview in order to steer secular humanist clients toward greater authenticity.

There are commonalities among secular humanists, and we can at least approach an understanding of the worldview, which I argue is more methodology than belief system. But because this worldview is characterized by, among other things, resisting dogma, none of these characteristics is itself cast in stone, nor is this list exhaustive.

Rejecting Dogma

Secular humanists almost always reject dogma. They generally abide by a naturalist epistemology, which insists on evidence before accepting or holding a belief in all but the most basic truths of experience. Thus, they question all prescriptive or normative judgments for which there is no evidence, and only accept such judgments when given proper evidence. Dogmatic belief systems or worldviews, or statements based upon them, are rejected immediately as unscientific. Dogma is also anathema to a strand of libertarianism peculiar to free-thought movements such as secular humanism.

Rejecting dogma means that suggestions or strategies to solve problems are not based on revelation, nor even untested human authority. Humans develop dogmas too when they state supposed truths that go untested. Instead, empiricism constantly checks currently accepted belief. As opposed to dogma, pragmatic knowledge about the world is always open to falsification. New evidence may always emerge, which challenges accepted empirically based beliefs and forces altering or supplanting current theory.

Secular humanists are unlikely to accept advice on the base of mere authority; applying the empirical method to their own lives means they want to see the evidence, and if what you say conflicts with the evidence, then it is likely you are wrong and are just spouting dogma.

Appreciation of Science

Given that most secular humanists consider themselves to be philosophical naturalists, they typically prefer scientific methodology to speculation. This means that propositions or judgments, once hypothesized, are subject always to being tested and must also be capable of being falsified. The sciences, which use empirical methods, are considered therefore to be the best sources of opinion, and their conclusions are more deserving of belief than those of, say, speculative philosophy, metaphysics, or religion.

Science is based upon empiricism, developed in the sciences and applied by secular humanists in all areas of human endeavor. Thus, for even practical life choices or problems, adjustments and changes are best made according to the evidence presented.

Free Inquiry

Because all new knowledge is acquired by testing the limits of human experience, and experiments at the bounds of current understanding, secular humanists tend to encourage and engage in inquiry into everything, without limit, and without prejudice. All great revolutions, in both society and science, have come from those who dare to test the limits of current thinking, and push beyond the boundaries of accepted belief. Free inquiry into moral, social, political, scientific, and cultural assumptions or norms is necessary to lead to each new human revolution. Free inquiry knows no limits.

The principle of free inquiry requires us to challenge even our most treasured and fundamental beliefs. Every principle is contingent, open to falsification, and constantly undergoing scrutiny, verification, and adjustment. There is no disrespect in a counselor suggesting that a secular humanist rethink his or her principles or assumptions given those principles should themselves be founded upon inquiry, and open themselves to introspection and adjustment in the face of new evidence.

Concern About Morality

While secular humanists tend not to agree on the foundation, basis, or even existence of "the good," in a metaphysical sense, they nonetheless respect the fact that civil society must be guided by principles, whether they are merely normative, or whether rooted in some real meta-ethical basis such as Kant's categorical imperative. Being free inquirers, and having a general concern with the world (unlike, for instance, nihilists or radical existentialists), they are generally concerned with inquiry into the possible basis for moral behavior or at least utilitarian foundations for good acts.

Morality is real, and there are good choices and bad choices. Although secular humanists may differ about their approach to morality at the meta-level, they nonetheless apply the principles above to moral choice. Namely, morality is open to free inquiry, testing by the evidence, and should be free from dogma. In other words, even moral decision making abides by empiricism, and morality is founded in natural principles rather than authority or dogma (Kurtz, 1997).

DEFINITION OF MARRIAGE

Marriage is historically both a legal and social institution, often devised by states and sometimes churches. Where church and state are intermingled, marriage is often both a church-sponsored and state-sponsored institution.

It is important to note that marriages differ from culture to culture, and often over time within the same culture, in their structure and sanctions of authority. In the West, particularly in Anglo-Saxon cultures over the past 300 or 400 years, the common-law marriage has been generally recognized to confer many if not all of the same benefits as other form of marriages, whether state- or church-sanctioned.

Whether marriages are church-defined or state-defined, the legitimacy or authority for a valid marriage confers also some cultural and legal responsibilities regardless of culture. Over time, the balance of those responsibilities has thankfully shifted. At one time in the West, the marriage relationship was extremely one-sided, favoring men, and creating a property relationship akin to that of property owners over their chattels. The property relationship as well as legal and church sanctions for a subordinate role of women in Western cultures have largely disappeared in our institutions. Even now, however, numerous fundamentalist religious cultures maintain a disparity in the power relationship and expectations from the marriage relationship. Examples include certain branches of fundamentalist Christianity and Islam.

In contrast to the historical nature of marriage relationships, secular humanists embrace a free-thinking notion of individual relationships in general. Most secular humanists accept that individuals ought to be able to enter into personal relationships unburdened by the expectations or demands of culture or religion, or even the state. What this implies is a great variety of acceptable configurations of personal relationships that often challenge traditional notions of marriage. Because secular humanists do not abide by religious dogma nor ideological authoritarianism, this leaves them free to experiment with and explore new paradigms of marriage, union, cohabitation, polyandry, and other nontraditional forms of combinatorial lifestyles.

In defining the nature of these relationships structurally, they are likewise free to define them contractually as they please. Some overarching principles held in common by most secular humanists will generally apply. Among these are the importance of individual dignity, tolerance, and equality among the sexes. Within these broad parameters, couples (or groups for polyamorous relationships) should feel generally free as consenting adults to define the reciprocal duties and responsibilities within the marital relationship. Another generally accepted condition to the marital or other similar union is love. Secular humanists generally accept that the underlying basis for entering into unions, whether marital, cohabiting, same-sex, polyamorous, or other, is mutual love and respect, and when relationships lack one or both of these, they often fail in the long run.

Working Within the Definition

As many counselors know, marital and other unions often break down when those involved either come to realize that the nature of the relationship no longer matches expectations that were held before entering the relationship, or the expectations change during its course (Kurtz, 1997). The first thing we should realize is that this is common to contractual relationships of all kinds. The marriage relationship is, at heart, a contractual relationship, albeit one founded upon values often not present in other contractual relationships. Nonetheless, the presuppositions and expectations are the same: Parties have mutual obligations, duties, and expectations, and failures to abide by them are a breach of the agreement.

Ideally, parties to any agreement enter into them with full understandings of the obligations and expectations of the contract. When consenting adults enter into agreements freely, without duress, and with full knowledge of the terms, then they are expected to abide by those terms. Failing to do so is called a "breach" and the breaching party becomes liable for some sort of damages in commercial agreements. In a marriage or civil union, similar expectations arise. Agreements do not mean much without some sort of "consideration" or loss upon one's breach. However, marriages are unlike other sorts of agreements largely because of the term of the agreement, which is typically expected to last a lifetime. Over a lifetime, people change considerably, and the pressures and situations of a union cannot be predicated over the course of a lifetime. There are a number of ways to deal with changed conditions and expectations in a marital or other committed relationship without resorting to breach, but one way to avoid much of these potential hardships is to define the nature of the union with specificity from the start.

Secular humanists do not rest upon the authority of the state or a church for the validity of the marriage or other union. Rather, they accept the freedom and dignity of the contracting parties to enter into adult relationships and abide by agreements. Because no dogma dictates the nature of those agreements, nor does any law sanctify them, the parties have maximal freedom in defining the bounds of their own marriages or unions. Nonetheless, agreements mean nothing without some expectation of abiding by them. One way to avoid breaking agreements is to rely upon the dignity and autonomy of the contracting parties in discussing the inevitable changes of conditions that occur, rather than forcing the issue through a breach. In other words, because neither a god nor the state will punish the breach, and because the authority for the contract in the first place comes from the parties, the parties should strive to relate any issues that challenge the original agreement as soon as possible. If something changes, discuss it. If the original agreement will no longer do, see if it can be altered. If the parties enter a formal contractual relationship with the understanding that conditions and expectations change naturally over time, and accept the autonomy and dignity of their partner or partners, then they can accommodate changing needs and expectations in others, or should at least strive to do so.

Many secular humanists choose to deal with these issues up front, by explicit agreements, rather than allow the pressures and expectations of others to define the nature of their marriage and possibly undermine the relationship subtly in the process. Written, explicit contracts at the start can help avoid this. The parties can explicitly state the nature of the relationship, agree to it up front, and even accommodate the necessity for changes down the road. By doing so, again, maximal autonomy and dignity of the contracting parties is maintained.

The role of the counselor is best kept to helping the parties elucidate their own values, concerns, desires, and anxieties, and to developing rational means of resolving differences, communicating, and planning according to the individual and joint needs of the clients (Corey, 2005). Secular humanists assume that they are motivated by emotions and desires, but that reason can help them guide themselves in ways that are respectful of their partners and families, and beneficial to their future development to our full human potentials.

Maximizing Freedom

Essential to the secular humanist definition of marriage is the role of individual autonomy and dignity in defining the nature of the relationship. At the crux of this is individual freedom and willingness on the part of individuals who love and value one another to subvert their personal freedoms to the wills and necessities of their loved ones. When parties wish to commit their lives to one another, they can do so while maximizing their freedoms by open lines of communication during every stage of the agreement. As well, respect throughout for one's partner's needs for honesty, and the mutual benefit of love, dignity, and freedom, enable the contract to adjust and grow as time goes on. According to recent research, the most common reasons for married couples to seek therapy were problematic communication and lack of emotional affection (Doss, Simpson, & Christensen, 2004). Counselors should therefore employ effective communication building techniques such as honing listening skills, giving and accepting feedback, and enacting problem solving (Corey, 2005).

Ultimately, the definition of the institution of marriage, for secular humanists, is extraordinarily flexible as compared to most faith traditions and even the definitions of the state. Because of this, secular humanist unions may be stronger than if they were merely sanctioned by states, dogma, or churches because the value of the agreements in such relationships comes not from the threat of punishment by a god or a state upon a breach, but rather from the freedom, worth, and dignity of the parties to the agreement. Since individual autonomy is a focus in secular humanist marriage, the counselor should work with married persons as a couple and as individuals.

DATING AND COHABITATION

Secular humanists, as discussed above, value dignity, tolerance, and freedom because these original values give worth and meaning to our relationships with others and the world in general. Without dignity, tolerance, or freedom, our individual choices and lives mean little to humanity or the world. So for example, persons are no longer "ends in ourselves" but rather means to other persons' ends. These principles are good for guiding all individual relationships with others and with groups. Maximizing dignity, tolerance, and freedom means allowing others to make choices, treating others as we would wish to be treated, and imposing few restrictions on the behaviors of others, especially where those behaviors do no harm to ourselves. These principles can guide individuals and couples in dating, selecting mates, and cohabitating, whether in a marital relationship or not.

As with the marital relationship, the parties whom are dating, mating, and cohabitating are free to define the terms. Doing so ensures a maximal amount of freedom, tolerance, and dignity. These principles should also generally define the bounds as well. As with other agreements, there may be agreements that are void on their face, especially where general but essential principles are violated. For example, one cannot bargain away one's freedom (Rawls, 1971). Similarly, one cannot bargain away one's dignity as a human being. These foundational principles define the bounds of dating, mating, cohabitating, and marriage.

Dating, mating, and cohabitating then must be centered upon the balancing of the principles of maximizing individual autonomy and freedom, tolerance for the needs and opinions of others, and the inherent dignity of all human persons. Being upfront about these principles at the start of a relationship, and standing by these principles as fundamental to all human relationships, can help avoid undue discord later on.

Of course, these general principles leave plenty of room for potential mates or dating partners to define their roles, expectations, and duties to one another. It does not violate any of these principles, for instance, for someone to hold the door for the other on every occasion, if each deems it appropriate and worthwhile. When issues or concerns arise, open lines of communication, regardless of the type of relationship, and open discussion of needs, expectations, obligations, and responsibilities, can help to avoid major blow-ups in the future. This also ensures that the foundational principles discussed above are respected. If counseling is sought in these relationships, counselors should employ strategies similar to those practiced with married couples. By working on the relationship's weaknesses with each person as an individual and the couple as a whole, the counselor will be able to see the differences and intersections of two lifestyles and help foster ways to improve and strengthen the relationship (Corey, 2005).

ROLES WITHIN MARRIAGES AND FAMILIES

The survival and improvement of our species depends in the first instance upon parenting. Because modern pregnancy is a choice due to the ready availability of contraceptives and birth control measures, the decision to follow through with a pregnancy and a birth, and to become a parent, involves concomitant responsibilities. The primary responsibility of parents is maintaining the physical and emotional health of a new child, and rearing children with the skills and ethical judgment to survive well in the world and to do good. Because of this responsibility, parents must be able to both maximize freedom and encourage respect, while protecting children while they form their survival skills and ethical judgments.

Consistent with the principles of tolerance and dignity, children who are raised to view parents as a source of wisdom and guidance will seek them out in times of need, and value and respect their parents' advice. Mutual respect does not mean complete democracy, and indeed as a child develops, autonomy will increase, but parents and children cannot be equals. Rather, because of a natural imbalance in responsibilities, children must begin by respecting their parents' authority and earn the right through demonstrating the ability to be independent in making judgments to act more and more autonomously.

Ideally, a family can grow into a democracy of sorts, with a measured amount of "filial piety" of the sort urged by Confucians, but ultimately due deference should be paid to the role of successive elders in rearing and raising younger generations. Numerous problems may develop as parents cede too much autonomy to children ill equipped to make wise decisions. However, by stressing the duty and necessity of a sound education in survival skills and moral reasoning, children may be encouraged to act more responsibly and to seek the guidance and approval of parents who return respect for good decision making.

The family is clearly not a complete democracy, as parents must exercise a certain amount of discipline and control over infants, and remain responsible for non-emancipated adolescents. However, among adult members of a family, democracy is preferable, and most conducive to the tolerance, dignity, and autonomy so valued by secular humanists (Kurtz, 1979). Thus, decisions about finances, allocation of resources, living accommodations and choices, and other similar decisions should generally be made democratically. Of course, adults can consent to variations on the hierarchy however they see fit, as long as the result is not totalitarian, and does not demean individual autonomy of any one person.

Counselors dealing with parenting concerns can help parents to discern their parenting philosophies, and help them to develop strategies for dealing with difficulties that may arise consistent with that philosophy. Children can be brought into the process by discussing their difficulties, under the assumption that they too are rational members of the family, capable of developing family life in concert with their parents and siblings.

Family finances may be treated in any number of ways consistent with reason, autonomy, and liberty. Members may choose to contribute to joint and combined accounts, which is indeed a fair choice given that the family shares joint resources. However, it is perfectly conceivable and consistent to demand of those who are able to contribute more, and provide for those who are not able to contribute a fair share. Indeed at the microeconomic level, the family resource model may be reasonably either socialist or capitalist, consistent always with secular humanist principles. In other words, freedom and responsibility should always be maximized consistent with individual autonomy. Within this framework, there are clearly unacceptable and irresponsible behaviors. For instance, gambling the family's fortune away invades the choice and dignity of other members. Even poor financial planning, failure to save within one's means, and spending only for immediate pleasure or satisfaction falls short of abiding by reason and dignity and autonomy of other members of the family.

FAMILY PLANNING

As secular humanists respect autonomy, dignity, and tolerance, the ultimate responsibility for each new person, in this day of available contraception and birth control, rests with parents. Although that responsibility rests with consenting adults, the ultimate decision as to whether to bear a child naturally lies with the mother whose womb will be home to the developing fetus for 9 months. Women have a disproportionate role in the bearing and birthing of children, and their bodies and thus their autonomy are more clearly implicated in the process than the father's, and so the final decision as to whether to proceed with a birth rests with the mother (Singer, 2001). Nonetheless, there is a shared responsibility for the pregnancy in the case of mutual consent, and so the desires of the prospective father ought to be taken into due consideration.

Unlike many faith traditions, secular humanists see no moral qualms in using contraceptives nor generally, though not universally, in abortion. Most secular humanists also accept the science that suggests populational pressures are exacting a toll on the environment and upon human wealth and well-being. It is no surprise, then, that these values, combined with respect for individual autonomy and personal dignity generally, require that the choice for whether or not to bring a pregnancy to term is up to prospective mother, and that the state, family, or church has little to nothing to say in the matter.

Moreover, the prospective dignity of potential persons is at stake when unwilling or unable mothers are forced to carry their children to term. Quite simply, even while both the law and reason afford less than full personhood status to fetuses, respecting and preserving their future dignity means that, if they cannot be raised in a loving and providing home, by no fault of their future parents, then it may be more dignified and compassionate to prevent their birth. Life, to secular humanists, does not have an inherent value above non-life, but rather derives its value from its circumstances. Thus, unlike faith traditions that may value human lives as meaningful due to "ensoulment" or simply by virtue of their creation, secular humanists see a difference in value between mere "human beings" and full-fledged persons.

Persons are full, rights-bearing human beings with intentionality, consciousness, at least the appearance of free-will, obligations, and responsibilities. Their rights and interests outweigh non-persons, and must be measured accordingly in planning a family. Potential persons, including fetuses, have rights that develop over time, but are not the same as those of full-fledged persons. Because of the necessity to respect the autonomy of persons, and to tolerate the individual choices of women over their bodies, young adults and teenagers should be made aware of the responsibilities and risks associated with sex, and the duties and obligations of parenthood, and thus given the choice to terminate unwanted and unplanned-for pregnancies.

Secular humanist ethics emphasize the individual, and freedom of choice is a central feature of these ethics (Addleson, 1990). Individuals and families facing choices regarding family planning or pregnancy should first consider their values regarding the status of fetuses and infants. Their choices will be irrational if they conflict with those initial values. It is perfectly conceivable that secular humanists are rationally pro-life, and thus choices should not conflict with that fundamental moral position. It is also conceivable that secular humanists are pro-choice, and thus their decisions about family planning, abortion, and adoption will necessarily be guided by different values, even where their ultimate decisions may coincide.

DISSOLVING RELATIONSHIPS

Ending a loving relationship is always difficult, emotionally, practically, and often financially. Loving relationships, whether marriages, civil unions, or cohabitation, ought not to be entered into lightly nor dissolved frivolously. They are presumptively serious and founded upon authentic emotion and genuine love when developed, and those values are essential to their maintenance. Inevitably, they sometimes end, but many such ends can be avoided by promoting an atmosphere of trust and communication early, and nurturing it throughout. Counselors facing secular humanists who are considering ending a relationship should consider the depth and importance not just of reason, but emotions such as love and desire and their role in maintaining a relationship. These are values of empirical fact (Christensen & Heavey, 1999; Doss et al., 2004). Marriages and other relationships thrive with communication of emotional need, and authentic desire of each partner to fulfill those needs. Recognizing that couples do not seek counseling unless they wish to work through a problem, it makes sense first to seek out the root causes and discover means of salvaging the relationship rather than jettisoning it right away.

Sometimes relationships cannot be salvaged. Comparisons of scientific literature suggest that therapy will increase marital satisfaction more than no treatment at all. However, there are instances where a couple will simply not function well together and the only positive outcome for the individuals involved is dissolution of the relationship (Christensen & Heavey, 1999). When this happens it is up to the parties to determine how to part, consistent with their autonomy, liberty, and dignity and that of their mates and families. Anger and hate are irrational and unproductive when dissolving a relationship that was built originally on love, and can seriously undermine the future development of relationships with children, if any. Counseling professionals should be aware that the stress of looming divorce can bring out latent emotions in otherwise stable adults (Ellis, 2000). Counseling secular humanists through a divorce or other negotiated end of a relationship involves facilitating understanding and patience among the parties. By doing so, counselors and clients can be ensured that the choices made are authentic and founded upon truly held principles. Further, such patience helps parents to plan for the future of the relationship with any children after the dissolution of the legal bonds. Children must continue to be nurtured, and all empirical evidence so far indicates that they thrive best when parents remain involved in their lives following divorce (Kurtz, 1997). Parents who choose divorce ought to be counseled to develop a plan for fulfilling their parental duties as best they can following divorce.

Again, consistent with autonomy and maximal personal liberty, parties to a dissolved relationship ought also to respect the choices of their former partners, and to accommodate their needs as much as possible and be fair in dissolving the formal relationship. Where possible, family and friends should be counseled to be respectful of choices to end the relationship and not to interfere with their own personal religious or moral views, to take sides, or to physically involve themselves in defying the individual choices of those ending the relationship.

DEATH AND DYING

Death, for the secular humanist, is not an entry into a better world, or another phase of existence. It is a finality, an end point (Baggini & Pym, 2005). Without any idea or concern about a soul surviving one's material existence, existence itself ends with the death of a human organism. Dying is a natural process with a natural conclusion. The value of a human life is in the joy, love, creativity, fulfillment, friendships, discovery, and family one is able to fashion during our time here on earth. The capacity for developing and maintaining these values and goods, that comprise the essence of human existence, is what makes ongoing life worthwhile (Kurtz, 2004). When these capacities disappear, or are incapacitated beyond repair, then the value of life proportionally diminishes. In other words, life itself, as measured by the mere beating of a heart, has only ongoing value if it is accompanied by the goods and values noted above. If they are not available, it is within an individual's autonomous choice, or that of an informed family or loved ones, to help terminate one's existence. Death can be a legitimate choice.

Short of euthanasia, or assisted suicide, the quality of one's life ought to be a consideration in any long-term care or hospice decisions, and that quality is legitimately measured by the above factors, and not mere heartbeats. Secular humanists do not have fewer needs than religious believers, but they are inherently different needs, which should be respected by counselors, physicians, and family alike (Baggini & Pym, 2005). Those facing difficult choices with a loved one's long-term care, or facing the possibility of euthanasia, ought to be counseled to consider the loved-one's autonomy and respect his or her own values and decisions. Choices must reflect not the selfish desires of the surviving family, but the authentic values of the dying family member.

Grief is inevitable in the face of losing one's loved one and should certainly be embraced as part of the dying process. But grief among survivors is overcome in time, and will pass. Although secular humanists have no concept of an otherworldly afterlife, there are ways in which loved ones survive naturalistically. They survive in their deeds, in the love they shared here while alive, in their families, in our memories most of all. Secular humanist families facing death can be counseled to embrace these lasting, enduring, natural goods as they approach a family member's or loved-one's death.

In order to clarify individual preferences for end of life care, or hospice, or even decisions relating to terminal illness, coma, or vegetative state, individuals and family members should be encouraged to discuss these issues and leave written instructions, living wills, powers of attorney, and proxy instruments for trusted family members who can see to it that their desires are accommodated.

HOMOSEXUALITY

Homosexuality is, according to most scientific evidence, a biological phenomenon rather than a choice (Holden, 1992). Even, however, were it a choice, it is a valid choice. The basic secular humanist principles of dignity, autonomy, and freedom require persons to accept any manner of cohabitation, dating, or marriage that people wish to pursue. These principles embrace all methods and manner of adult, considered, and reasoned forms of living together, dating, or marriage. The critical factors are that members of any relationship freely choose to enter into the relationship, have used their intellects and authentic emotion to enter into the relationship, and treat themselves and their mates with dignity.

COUNSELING SECULAR HUMANISTS

In general, secular humanism embraces individual autonomy and decision making, and respects the liberty, dignity, and ability of each of us to forge our paths in this world. Individuals choose their values, guided as they are by natural endowments, and social situations. Secular humanists are imbued with a sense of the good and the right that enables them, using their reason, emotion, and considered judgments, to live with each other in societies, and in families. Understanding the foundational nature of these secular humanist values, the counselor can only guide clients to make their decisions more authentically, more in keeping with the values of naturalism, empiricism, and secular humanist ethics.

In many ways, this process is similar to *philosophical counseling*, which seeks to help clients to decide their working "philosophy" of life, and to enable them to better coordinate their actions with that philosophy, and make their lives more coherent. The idea is that coherence and authenticity make one's life thoroughly examined, and thus, as the philosopher says, most worth living.

REFERENCES

Addelson, K. P. (1990). Some moral issues in public problems of reproduction. *Social Problems, 37*(2), 1–17.

Baggini, J., & Pym, M. (2005). End of life: The humanist view. *The Lancet, 366*(9492), 1235–1237.

Christensen, A., & Heavey, C.L. (1999). Interventions for couples. *Annual Review of Psychology, 50,* 165–190.

Corey, G. (2005). *Theory and practice of counseling and psychotherapy.* Belmont, CA: Brooks/Cole.

Doss, B., Simpson, L., & Christensen, A. (2004). Why do couples seek marital therapy? *Professional Psychology: Research and Practice, 35*(6), 608–614.

Ellis, E. (2000). *Divorce wars.* Washington, DC: American Psychological Association.

Holden, C. (1992). Twin study links genes to homosexuality. *Science, New Series,* 255(5040), 33.

Kurtz, P. (1979). *Exuberance.* Amherst, NY: Prometheus.

Kurtz. P. (1997). *Forbidden fruit: The ethics of humanism.* Amherst, NY: Prometheus

Kurtz, P. (2004). *Affirmations: Joyful and creative exuberance.* Amherst, NY: Prometheus.

Rawls, J. (1971). *A theory of justice.* Cambridge, MA: Harvard University Press.

Singer, P. (2001). *Writings on an ethical life.* New York: Harper Collins.

SECTION III

Religion and Relationships

Many aspects of religious practice are illustrated within relationships. In fact, it is within relationships where religious values, faith, and commitment might best be illustrated. Through the next three chapters, ways in which religion can benefit relationships will be discussed as well as how it may cause challenges or rifts in relationships, specifically in some cases of inter-faith marriages.

In the twelfth chapter, Centore and Clinton focus on the effect of religion on relationship problems. They also describe ways in which relationships with others and with God have found to be strengthened through religious-related activities such as being part of a religious community, meditation, and prayer. The authors review related activities, as well as provide guidelines for practitioners as they consider such faith factors within their family and couples counseling practice.

Next, Holeman sheds light on the role of forgiveness in religious life and within marriage and family relationships. Conflict and disagreements within relationships are common. Being able to forgive an offending partner often is tied to one's religious commitment. Holeman reviews beliefs about forgiveness within particular religious faith perspectives.

Finally, inter-faith marriages are discussed in the last chapter of this section. Lara and Onedera review the salient issues related to married partners whom come from different religious backgrounds. Each partner's activity of practice in their affiliated religion can affect the relationship differently. For example, individuals often enter into mixed marriages at a time when one or both of the individuals was not active in their religion. As a result, the difficulties of maintaining a relationship with significantly different religious beliefs and practices may not have been foreseen. On the other hand, many married partners struggle from the beginning of their relationship in attempting to balance the faith perspectives and related traditions of both religious backgrounds. The authors will offer suggestions for mental health practitioners working with inter-faith couples.

CHAPTER 12

Benefits of Religion on Recovery From Relationship Problems

ANTHONY J. CENTORE AND TIM CLINTON

Today's relationships are under more stress and duress than probably any other time in history. Domestic violence, drug abuse, infidelity, homicides, and suicides (which are occurring in populations and ages never before imagined) only reflect an epidemic of relational pain in today's world. Moreover, marriages and families today are facing extraordinary challenges as financial debt, terminal illness, mental disorder, aging parents, blended homes, marital discord, separation, and father absence engulf in blazes what we thought would be a safe haven. Consider the following statistics about relationship problems today:

Marital Discord

Studies show 35% of persons who marry get a divorce, and 18% of those divorced are divorced multiple times. Currently, for African Americans, single-parent households outnumber married-couple families (Population Reference Bureau, 2000). In addition, almost half (46%) of persons from the baby boomer generation have undergone a marital split, and millions more are expected to divorce in the next 10 years (Barna, 2004).

The religious are far from exempt. According to the Barna Group (2004), although churches try to dissuade congregants, rates of divorce among Christians are about the same as the non-Christian population. Moreover, data show such divorces occur *after* the married persons have accepted Christ as their Savior. Also, multiple divorces are common among born again Christians, for 23% are divorced two or more times!

It should be noticed that the destruction of the American family is troubling kids too. Reportedly, many children 10 to 15 years after the divorce of their parents continue to battle with resulting unhappiness (Wallerstein & Blakeslee, 1995). In addition, younger generations are likely to reach record heights of divorce and it is estimated that somewhere between 40-50% of marriages that begin this year will fail (Scott Stanley, Personal Communication, 2001).

Fatherlessness

Each night, nearly 40% of children fall asleep in homes where their fathers are not present (Blackenhorn, 1995). The deterioration of fatherhood in America is considered our most serious social ill. Encumbering the development of youth, fatherlessness is associated with crime, suicide, teenaged pregnancy, drug and alcohol abuse, and incarceration (National Center for Fathering, n.d.; O'Neill, 2002). Research shows youth from single-parent homes have more physical and mental health problems than children living with married-parents, and are two to three times as likely to develop emotional and behavioral problems. In addition, almost 75% of children living in fatherless homes will experience poverty, and are 10 times as likely as compared to children living with two parents to experience extreme poverty (National Center for Fathering, n.d.).

Sexual Abuse and Assault

The present evidence of widespread sexual abuse is daunting. By age 18, one in three girls and one in six boys will be sexually abused by someone they love or should be able to trust (Bagley, 1990; Finkelhor, Hotaling, Lewis, & Smith, 1990). Moreover, according to a national survey of high school students, approximately nine percent reported having been forced to have sexual intercourse against their will (National Center for Injury Prevention and Control, 2005).

Domestic Violence

Violence at the hand of an intimate partner occurs across all populations, irrespective of economic, religious, social, or cultural affiliation—and accounts for 20% of all nonfatal violent crime against women. The occurrence of nearly 5.3 million acts of domestic violence each year (among women 18 and older) results in almost two million injuries and 1,300 deaths. These deaths are not without warning; a staggering 44% of women murdered by their intimate partner enter emergency care within two years prior to the homicide, 93% seeking care for an injury (National Center for Injury Prevention and Control, 2005).

With the current state of affairs, it is not surprising that some believe this era will witness the full decimation of marriage and family. Even today the healthy family unit is fast becoming the exception to the norm, and the brokenness and dissension of spouses and family members a normal state of affairs. However, therapeutic interventions that incorporate religious faith and practices show great promise in the healing of marriage and family problems.

WHAT IS A RELATIONSHIP PROBLEM?

What is a relationship problem? In one regard, it is some aspect of a couple's relationship or family's dynamic that drains affection and tears at love, potentially leading persons to a place of emotional bankruptcy or despair. The problem could be a lack of mutual love, respect, acceptance, or forgiveness. The problem could be an issue of conflict styles or love languages. Relationship problems can stem from social ills such as pornography or infidelity; or from life issues such as money problems, extra-effort children, a chronic illness, or intrusive in-laws. In addition, husband and wife often bring with them wounds from their pasts—the effects of old relationship problems. These past experiences can affect their relational beliefs about their self and others, as well as the way they engage present relationships. These are, of course, just a few of the issues that marriage and family therapists (MFTs) deal with on a daily basis.

THE FAITH FACTOR

Until recently, the study of religion was generally neglected in medical, social, and behavioral sciences. However, there has been a recent surge of religious interventions such as Christian cognitive-relational therapy (McMinn, 2003), Christian hope-focused marriage counseling (Worthington, 1999), emotion-focused couples therapy (Hart & Hart-Morris, 2003), and Christian family systems approaches that serve to strengthen family "attachment bonds" (Diamond, Siqueland, & Diamond, 2003). While between 1986 and 1992 only 13 articles were published in major marriage and family journals regarding religious and spiritual issues (Stander, Piercy, McKinnon, & Helmeke, 1994), a review of quantitative research studies published between 1995 and 1999 found a dramatic increase: 13.2% of articles included a measure of religion (Weaver et al. 2002). Also, in treatments across the board, religion is increasingly seen as a positive correlate to therapeutic success. The evidence in regards to health issues, especially mental health issues, has manifested considerably. Moberg (2005) writes, "There are 'heaps' of anecdotal, clinical, historical, and theological evidence on the importance of spirituality and religious faith to health and well-being" (p. 22).

Regarding this evidence, research shows religious practices correspond with recovery-enhancing activities, empowerment, and improved quality of life (Yangarber-Hicks, 2004). For example, with women in physically abusive relationships, religious commitment protects against the onset of post traumatic stress disorder (Astin, Lawrence, & Foy, 1993). For disaster survivors, religious coping practices are positively correlated with effective adjustment (Smith, Pargament, Brant, & Oliver, 2000). Hence, religion is among the most significant means for dealing with crises of both life and death (Paragament, 1997). Taking into account our relational nature, this should not be surprising for Christians, coping with troubling times is much easier when they perceive Jesus as "by one's side," "holding one's hand," or "holding one in His arms" (Kirkpatrick & Shaver, 1990, p. 319). Regarding marriage and family issues specifically, evidence strongly suggests religion improves both marital satisfaction and family life.

Marital Satisfaction

Though the Barna Group (2004) paints a bleak picture, concluding that Christian couples are just as likely as non-Christians to divorce, other studies conclude the contrary. For example, in a national survey of 4,587 married couples, spouses who regularly attend church services were found to be at lowest risk of divorce (Call & Heaton, 1997). Other research findings contend that religious involvement not only lowers the likeliness of divorce, it is positively associated with marital harmony, satisfaction, adjustment, commitment, and happiness (Amato & Rogers, 1997; Hansen, 1992; Kaslow & Robinson, 1996; Robinson, 1994). One meta-study found that married couples who attend worship services report lower levels of jealousy, infidelity, irritating habits, moodiness, foolish spending, and drug or alcohol use (Weaver et al., 2002).

Family Life

Most persons in the United States believe religion strengthens their families (Abbott, Berry, & Meredith, 1990). In fact, the most common prayer of the American public is for their respective family's well-being (Gallup & Lindsey, 1999). Religion has been found to be helpful to family members when coping during times of family crisis (Pargament, 1997). For example, studies have found that families caring for older family members with dementia or terminal cancer, or for children with cancer or a birth defect, cope more effectively if a strong faith is present (Cayse, 1994; Rabins, Fitting, Eastham, & Zabora,1990; Samuelson, Foltz, & Foxall, 1992).

Regarding children and adolescents, a random sample of 13,000 students found those involved in religion were less likely to use substances such as alcohol, marijuana, or amphetamines (Bahr, Maughan, Marcoc, & Li, 1998). Other studies of minors have found that religious involvement was positively associated with lower sexual activity (Perkins, Luster, Villarruel, & Small,

1998; Whitbeck, Yoder, Hoyt, & Conger, 1999). Lastly, one study has found that parental religious involvement promotes teens' church attendance, belief in the importance of religion, and positive perceptions of God (Bao, Whitbeck, Hoyt, & Conger, 1999).

DEVELOPING A THEOLOGY OF CAREGIVING

When looking at religion in the recovery from relationship problems, we must have a theology of caregiving that incorporates both the creation and redemptive visions of God, and that is applicable to problems in relationships (Clinton & Ohlschlager, 2005). Consider this value as expressed in The Wisdom of Solomon:

> I called for help, and there came to me a spirit of wisdom. I valued her above sceptre and throne, and reckoned riches as nothing beside her ... I loved more than health or beauty, I preferred her to the light of day ... So all good things together came to me with her, and in her hands was wealth beyond counting, and all was mine to enjoy, for all follows where wisdom leads. (7:7–12)

McMinn (1996) recently called attention to the importance of theology in counseling when he stated: "Effective Christian counselors also consider theological perspectives at the same time that they engage in the various psychological tasks of counseling. Historical and systematic theology, biblical understanding, and Christian tradition are all valued and considered essential components of counseling." Effective counselors, in McMinn's view, are those given to "multitasking" the ability to utilize insights and skills gained from the study of theology, psychology, and spirituality simultaneously and appropriately for the benefit of the client.

Also, Bergin (1991) and Worthington (1988), among others, have clearly displayed that one cannot divorce counseling from its moral, theological, and philosophical roots. All counseling and psychotherapy, even that which denies it, is deeply values-based. This makes it a given that counselors are incorporating *some sort* of theology or religion when they practice counseling.

Counselor competence is greatly enhanced when it is built from a solid theological foundation. Our hope is that counselors will learn and impart to their clients a *living, caring, and experiential theology* revealing the truth of God's person and desire for healthy relationship with us, and us with each other.

ETHICAL ISSUES FOR INCORPORATING RELIGION

It is important to note that counselors have a right to practice religious interventions, and that this right is protected in current law and ethics. George Ohlschlager (2006), author of the ethics code for the American Association of Christian Counselors (AACC), writes in a syllabus for "Protecting Spiritual Interventions in Professional Clinical Practice,"

> It is now clear in all latest revisions of the major mental health codes of ethics that concern/demand for "multicultural respect" and "cultural competency" in practice translates to respect for client religious beliefs and competency in doing spiritual assessment and intervention according to client direction. Furthermore, if the therapist is unable to connect with client religious beliefs and language, or experiences a negative countertransference due to their own unbelief or rejection of childhood beliefs themselves, they are obligated to make appropriate referral to therapists who can connect. (para. 10)

Hence, religious counselors are to contend that clients possess the right to have both their religious beliefs and values integrated into the therapeutic process. These rights are explicitly stated in the 6th foundation statement of the AACC code of ethics: "The biblical and constitutional rights to Religious Freedom, Free Speech, and Free Association protects Christian counselor public identity, and the explicit incorporation of spiritual practices into all forms of counseling and intervention" (AACC, 2004).

Concerning the ethical provision of incorporating religion into therapy, Bergin, Payne, and Richards (1996) provide ethical guidelines for counselors:

1. Define clear boundaries and distinguish counselors from religious leaders.
2. Obtain training and skills for incorporating religion into therapy.
3. Be aware of counselor values, and values of the client.
4. Observe the fine line between exploring a client's views and being judgmental.
5. Obtain informed consent to address the religious or spiritual realm.

In further discussion of this last guideline, when a competent adult client (or clients, as in couples counseling) consents to religious practices, that are informed and properly conducted, there is little legal power that can overrule such practices. Informed consent is the ethical-legal expression that protects the right of clients to determine, within legal limits, in what direction therapy will go and what goals will be pursued (Ohlschlager, 2006). The AACC code of ethics identifies two types of consent for incorporating religious practices in counseling:

1-330 Consent for Biblical-Spiritual Practices in Counseling
Christian counselors do not presume that all clients want or will be receptive to explicit spiritual interventions in counseling. We obtain consent that honors client choice, receptivity to these practices, and the timing and manner in which these things are introduced: prayer

for and with clients, Bible reading and reference, spiritual meditation, the use of biblical and religious imagery, assistance with spiritual formation and discipline, and other common spiritual practices.

1-331 Special Consent for More Difficult Interventions

Close or special consent is obtained for more difficult and controversial practices. These include, but are not limited to: deliverance and spiritual warfare activities; cult de-programming work; recovering memories and treatment of past abuse or trauma; use of hypnosis and any kind of induction of altered states; authorizing (by MDs) medications, electro-convulsive therapy, or patient restraints; use of aversive, involuntary, or experimental therapies; engaging in reparative therapy with homosexual persons; and counseling around abortion and end-of-life issues. These interventions require a more detailed discussion with patient-clients or client representatives of the procedures, risks, and treatment alternatives, and we secure detailed written agreement for the procedure.

It is important to note the distinction between "common" consent for the more fundamental practices such as prayer and Bible referencing and "special" consent, which is required for practices that are more controversial, or laden with clinical risk such as spiritual warfare or reparative therapy. The latter necessitates a more detailed discussion of the procedure, including the potential for processes to go wrong, and protocol of what will be done if therapy does not transpire as planned (Ohlschlager, 2006).

When Religious Interventions Should Not Be Used

Be aware, also, that clients can and do remove consent in the midst of the counseling process. Consent is not simply a function of understanding and signing a document. When a client begins to back-peddle from their given consent, the counselor must review the concerns of that client and, if consent is not regained, move in a new direction that the client agrees to. This is particularly an issue when more than one client is present such as in marriage counseling for the counselor must be attuned to the ongoing consent of both parties. The moment a counselor pushes religious interventions, while a client is resistant, is precisely the moment unethical imposition of values begins (and not before then). In addition, there are numerous situations in which counselors should refrain from incorporating religion in the counseling process. These include:

1. When the client states they do not want religious practices as part of counseling
2. When the client discloses fear or resistance to such offerings
3. When the client discloses that a former session went badly or turned out poorly

4. When the client is in the midst of a psychotic break
5. When the client is in crisis and displays intense emotionality
6. When the client is intoxicated or is not rationally oriented to their surroundings
7. When the client reveals a hostile or angry reaction to the name of God or Christ (Ohlschlager, 2006, p. 6)

In concluding this brief ethical review, it is important for clinicians to remember they have the legal and ethical right to incorporate religious interventions into their clinical work, with the right client, and at the proper time.

RELIGIOUS DISCIPLINES AND INTERVENTIONS

A study of 299 clinical social workers (CSWs) surveyed attitudes toward the use of spiritual-religious interventions. Participants were asked if they considered each of 16 identified interventions "appropriate" or "inappropriate" for clinical work. The practices that were viewed by the majority as appropriate were as follows:

1. Doing religious/spiritual assessment
2. Recommend helpful beliefs
3. Reflect on death and its meaning
4. Recommend spiritual support groups
5. Use religious language/spiritual direction
6. Reflect on spiritual meaning
7. Recommend spiritual journaling
8. Help client develop/practice rituals
9. Praying silently for client
10. Read/recommend Bible & religious books
11. Pray openly with clients
12. Share own beliefs

The interventions viewed by the majority as inappropriate were recommending forgiveness, participating in client rituals, using "touch" for healing purposes, and engaging in exorcisms/spiritual warfare (as cited in Moody, 2005).

Though many religious interventions are viewed as appropriate by CSWs, MFTs may be the most receptive of all mental health professionals in regards to incorporating religious-spiritual interventions, for in a recent study 95% of MFT participants reported believing an important relationship exists between spirituality and mental health (Carlson, Kirkpatrick, Hecker, & Killmer, 2002). When 153 MFT participants were asked whether a specific intervention for therapy was "appropriate," the majority were more positive than negative about whether a counselor can

1. Ask a client about his/her spirituality
2. Help a client develop spirituality

3. Discuss a client's spiritual experiences
4. Use spiritual language
5. Discuss a client's spiritual symbols
6. Recommend a spiritual program
7. Pray for a client
8. Meditate with a client
9. Recommend spiritual books
10. Discuss the meaning of life
11. Refer a client to a 12-step program (Carlson et al., 2002)

With only two variables were MFTs more negative than positive: praying with a client, and the counselor discussing his/her own spirituality.

Now that numerous religious interventions used in marriage and family therapy have been identified, the last section of this chapter will address a few of the most common, and some of the more controversial, religious practices in more depth.

BEGINNING A DEEPER INVESTIGATION OF RELIGIOUS PRACTICES

God gave us religious disciplines for a reason. Fasting helps us to endure suffering at the core of what we *think* we need. Prayer helps us to humble ourselves and teaches us to ask for help when it is needed. Confession helps us to ask another for forgiveness. Forgiveness strengthens relationships and removes from us the cancer that is bitterness and unforgiveness. In sum, religious practices (1) facilitate profound reparative psychological processes in relationships, and (2) encourage opportunity for the miraculous healing power of God in our relationships.

Religious Community

For the church to help persons recover from relationship problems, it must be a source of positive and supportive relationships itself. London and Wiseman (2005) write with wisdom, "The church attracts dysfunctional people because —at least ideally—it represents acceptance, love and belonging. But when dysfunctional people come to Christ they bring their problems with them, and they look to the church for hope and healing" (p. 47).

Fortunately, religious communities and church-based support groups are often ideal settings for hurting persons to share experiences within the safety, cohesion, and empathy of others. As group members achieve greater understanding of their relationship situations, they often feel more confident regarding the integrity of themselves and those who they are in relationship with. They experience, and thereby learn how to have, healthy interpersonal interactions. And as persons share difficult feelings of shame, guilt, anger, fear, doubt, sorrow, regret, and self-condemnation, they directly confront present anxieties. This enables and encourages persons to cope with troubling aspects of their lives such as relationship problems (American Psychiatric Association, 1999; Yalom, 1995).

Prayer and Meditation

Many people turn to prayer during times of stress and trouble (Argyle & Beit-Hallahmi, 1975). Soldiers pray more frequently in combat (Allport, 1950); and during times of death, divorce (Parkes, 1972), serious illness (Johnson & Spilka, 1991), emotional crises (James, 1902/2002), relationship problems (Ullman, 1982), and other negative events, people seek God as a safe haven.

A meta-analysis of 35 studies on the relationship between prayer and health found that in eight studies subjective well-being was positively related to the frequency of prayer and the presence of religious experience during prayer (McCullough, 1995). Similarly, 18 studies found prayer to be useful for coping with a variety of issues including the death of a spouse (see also Ai, Dunkle, Peterson, & Bolling, 2000; Ai, Dunkle, Peterson, & Bolling, 1998). In a study comparing the results of persons using relaxation techniques with those utilizing devotional meditation and prayer (and a no-treatment contro group), six weeks of biweekly sessions resulted in the lowest levels of anger and anxiety among the devotional group (Carlson, Bacaseta, & Simanton, 1988).

One study investigating the benefits of prayer in couples counseling suggests that benefits include reduction of emotional reactivity; the de-escalation of negativity, contempt, and hostility during conflict; increase of relationship and partner orientation and behavior; and increased couple responsibility for reconciliation and problem solving (Butler, Stout, & Gardner, 2002). The researchers contend that clinicians who work with couples "may be remiss if they fail to appropriately consider and encourage inclusion of prayer solutions in religious couples' repertoire of conflict management tactics" (Butler et al., p. 33).

Forgiveness

The Bible is replete with God's forgiveness (Jer. 31:34; Ps. 103:12; Heb. 8:12; 10:17). Jesus displayed forgiveness even while dying on the cross when He said, "Father, forgive them, for they do not know what they are doing" (Luke 23:34). In Matthew 6:14–15, Christ teaches that one is held accountable for the amount which one forgives; "If you forgive men when they sin against you, your heavenly Father will also forgive you. But if you do not forgive men their sins, your Father will not forgive your sins." Similarly, the Apostle Paul admonishes us to "get rid of all bitterness, rage and anger, brawling and slander, along with every form of malice. Be kind and compassionate to one another, forgiving each other, just as in Christ God forgave you" (Eph. 4:31–32).

Hence, Christians are to reflect on God's example on the cross, for if God can forgive us our sins, how can we not forgive each other, thus allowing for the healing and recovery of relationships to transpire? It is said Christ's example empowers us to forgive, when left to our own accord we would not overcome our own anger, resentment, vengeance, or fear (Worthington, 2001a, 2004). However, despite these important examples and admonishments, forgiveness is still a complicated emotional process. Worthington (2005) defines forgiveness as "the emotional replacement of (a) hot emotions of anger or fear that follow a perceived hurt or offense, or (b) unforgiveness that follows ruminating about the transgression by substituting positive emotions such as unselfish love, empathy, compassion, or even romantic love" (p. 46).

Emotional replacement takes place when persons think on the transgression against them while at the same time experiencing strong positive emotions that overpower the negative. Though some think of forgiveness as an act of effort and will, a mental activity, or an action that preludes a feeling, Worthington (2003) argues that one cannot experience true forgiveness until they are able to change their emotions (i.e., their embodied experiences). For this, Worthington (2001b, 2006) provides a five-step model for changing these emotions called "REACH," which includes recalling the hurt, empathizing with the transgressor, giving an altruistic gift of forgiveness, committing publicly to forgive, and holding on to forgiveness during times of doubt. The effect of forgiveness in the recovery from relationship problems is so widespread it is self-evident!

Scriptural Truth

Stated earlier, those who have endured past pains from bad relationships may carry with them destructive beliefs about one's self or others that hinder developing healthy relationships in the present day. However, God's Word counteracts these false-negative assertions. The Bible is replete with truth, especially relational truth. Hence, persons benefit relationally from the religious discipline of studying God's Word. Below is a brief chart that counters common irrational beliefs (lies) persons hold about themselves and others with biblical truth.

SELF TALK (LIES)	GOD'S TALK (TRUTH)
This is impossible.	With my help, all things are possible. (Matthew 19:26)
I am weak.	You can do all things with my strength. (Philippians 4:13)
I am not smart enough.	I will give you wisdom. (Ecclesiastes 2:26)
I cannot forgive myself.	I forgive you. (Numbers 14:20)
I cannot go on.	I will strengthen and uphold you. (2 Thessalonians 3:3)
I cannot manage.	I will supply all your needs. (Philippians 4:19)
I am worried.	Cast your anxieties on me, and I will give you peace. (1 Peter 5:7)
I am alone.	I will never leave you or forsake you. (Deuteronomy 31:8)
I am unlovable.	Nothing can separate you from my love. (Romans 8:37–39)

DELIVERANCES AND EXORCISMS

Deliverances and exorcisms are by far the most controversial of religious practices, and the most difficult for any professional clinician to justify. Hence,
many Christian counselors simply refuse to engage in such practices. Though
this topic cannot be addressed suitably within the bounds of this chapter, it is
foremost recommended that a clinician prescribing such an act never perform
it alone, and always seek first to refer a client to another professional experienced in its practice (Ohlschlager, 2006). A clinical follow-up and attentive
aftercare is always necessary for a client who has undergone treatment for
release or deliverance from demonic oppression of any kind.

CONCLUSION

This chapter has addressed the benefits of religion on recovery from relationship problems. To begin, the current prevalence of problems in marriage and
family relationships were surveyed, and a diverse set of issues from divorce,
to fatherlessness, to abuse, and past pains were found to affect many persons
today. Next, it was discussed that though for many years the importance of religion in the process of personal and relational well-being has been neglected,
current trends stress its importance; and recent empirical research studies
display religion's positive associations with marriage and family health.

The issue of developing a theological foundation for caregiving was
addressed, and several religious therapy models were mentioned. Also, the
issue of ethically and legally incorporating religion into therapy was discussed
and numerous guidelines were detailed.

Finally, specific religious practices, namely, being part of a religious community, prayer and meditation, forgiveness, scripture reading, and others,
were found to have a positive impact on the recovery from relationship problems, and on one's relationship with God (who will never leave you or forsake
you [Deut. 31:6], and who's love cannot be separated by distance, time, death,
or even the strongest of celestial beings [Rom. 8:38–39]).

Continued investigation into the healing effects of religious faith, practices, and community is recommended in order to further understand the
effects of religion on recovery from relationship problems.

REFERENCES

Abbott, D. A., Berry, M., & Meredith, W. H. (1990). Religious belief and practice:
A potential asset in helping families. *Family Relations, 39,* 443–448.
Ai, A. L., Dunkle, R. E., Peterson, C., & Bolling, S. F. (1998). The role of private prayer
in psychological recovery among midlife and elderly patients following cardiac
surgery, *The Gerontologist, 38*(5), 591–601.

Ai, A. L., Dunkle, R. E., Peterson, C., & Bolling, S. F. (2000). Spiritual well-being, private prayer, and adjustment of older cardiac patients. In J. A. Thorson (Ed.). *Perspectives on spiritual well-being and aging* (pp. 98–119). Springfield, IL: Charles C Thomas Publisher.

Allport, G. W. (1950). *The individual and his religion.* New York: McMillan.

Amato, P. R., & Rogers, S. J. (1997). A longitudinal study of marital problems and subsequent divorce. *Journal of Marriage and the Family, 59,* 612–624.

American Association of Christian Counselors (2004). *AACC code of ethics.* Forest, VA: Biblical-Ethical Foundations of the AACC Ethics Code.

American Psychiatric Association. (1999). *Let's talk facts about posttraumatic stress disorder.* Accessed June 20, 2005, from http://www.psych.org/public _info/ptsd .cfm: Author.

Argyle, M., & Beit-Hallahmi, B. (1975). *The social psychology of religion.* London: Routledge and Kegan Paul.

Astin, M. C., Lawrence, K. J., & Foy, D. W. (1993). Posttraumatic stress disorder among battered women: Risk and resiliency factors. *Violence and Victims, 8,* 17–28.

Bagley, C. (1990). Development of a measure of unwanted sexual contact in child hood for use in community mental health surveys. *Psychological Reports, 66,* 401–402.

Bahr, S. J., Maughan, S. L., Marcoc, A. C., & Li, B. (1998). Family, religiosity and the risk of adolescent drug use. *Journal of Marriage and the Family, 60,* 979–992.

Bao, W., Whitbeck, L. B., Hoyt, D. R., & Conger, R. D. (1999). Perceived parental acceptance as a moderator of religious transmission among adolescent boys and girls. *Journal of Marriage and the Family, 61,* 9–25.

Barna Group. (2004, September). Born again Christians just as likely to divorce as non-Christians. The Barna Update. Retrieved May 2005, from http://www .barna.org/FlexPage.aspx?Page=BarnaUpdate&BarnaUpdateID=170

Bergin, A. E. (1991). Values and religious issues in psychotherapy and mental health. *American Psychologist, 46,* 394–403.

Bergin, A. E., Payne, I. R., & Richards, P. S. (1996). Values in psychotherapy. In E. P. Shafranske (Ed.), *Religion and the clinical practice of psychology* (pp. 297–325). Washington, DC: American Psychological Association.

Blackenhorn, D. (1995). *Fatherless America: Confronting our most urgent social problem.* New York: BasicBooks.

Butler, M. H., Stout, J. A., & Gardner, B. C. (2002). Prayer as a conflict resolution ritual: Clinical implication of religious couples' report or relationship softening, healing perspective, and change responsibility. *The American Journal of Family Therapy, 30,* 19–37.

Call, V. R., & Heaton, T. B. (1997). Religious influence on marital stability. *Journal for the Scientific Study of Religion, 36*(3), 382–392.

Carlson, C. R., Bacaseta, P. E., & Simanton, D. A. (1988). A controlled evaluation of devotional meditation and progressive relaxation. *Journal of Psychology and Theology, 16,* 362–368.

Carlson, T. D., Kirkpatrick, D., Hecker, L., & Killmer, M. (2002). Religion, spirituality, and marriage and family therapy: A study of family therapists' beliefs about the appropriateness of addressing religious and spiritual issues in therapy. *The American Journal of Family Therapy, 30*:157–171.

Cayse, L. N. (1994). Fathers of children with cancer: A descriptive study of the stressors and coping strategies. *Journal of Pediatric Oncology Nursing, 11*(3), 102–108.

Clinton, T., & Ohlschlager, G. (2005). Introduction to Christian counseling: The 21st-century state of the art. In T. Clinton, A. Hart, & G. Ohlschlarer (Eds.), *Caring for people God's way: Personal and emotional issues, addictions, grief and trauma* (pp. 137–409). Nashville: Thomas Nelson.

Diamond, G., Siqueland, L., & Diamond, G. M. (2003, June). Attachment-based *family* therapy for depressed adolescents: Programmatic treatment development. *Clinical Child & Family Psychology Review, 6*(2), 107–127.

Finkelhor, D., & Browne, A. (1986). Impact of child sexual abuse: A review of the research. *Psychological Bulletin, 99*, 66–77.

Finkelhor D., Hotaling G., Lewis I.A., & Smith C. (1990). Sexual abuse in a national survey of adult men and women: Prevalence, characteristics, and risk factors. *Child Abuse and Neglect, 14*(1), 19–28.

Gallup, G. H., & Lindsey, D. M. (1999). *Surveying the religious landscape: Trends in U.S. beliefs.* Harrisburg, PA: Morehouse Publishing.

Hansen, G. L. (1992). Religion and marital adjustment. In J. F. Schumaker (Ed.), *Religion and mental health* (pp. 189–198). New York: Oxford University Press.

Hart, A. D., & Hart-Morris, S. (2003). *Safe haven marriage.* Nashville: Thomas Nelson.

James, W. (1902/2002). *The varieties of religious experience: A study in human nature, centenary edition.* New York: Routledge.

Johnson, P., & Spilka, B. (1991). Religion and the breast cancer patient: The roles of clergy and faith. *Journal of Health and Religion, 31,* 21–33.

Kaslow, F., & Robinson, J. A. (1996). Long-term satisfying marriages: Perceptions of contributing factors. *The American Journal of Family Therapy, 24*(2), 153–170.

Kirkpatrick, L.A., & Shaver, P.R. (1990). Attachment theory and religion: Childhood attachments, religious beliefs, and conversion. *Journal for the Scientific Study of Religion, 29*(3), 315–334.

London, H. B., & Wiseman, N. B. (2005). *The shepherd's covenant: For pastors.* USA: Regal.

McCullough, M. E. (1995). Prayer and health: Conceptual issues, research review, and research agenda. *Journal of Psychology & Theology, 23*(1), 15–29.

McMinn, M. R. (1996). *Psychology, theology, and spirituality in Christian counseling.* USA: Tyndale.

McMinn, M. R. (2003). Cognitive-relational therapy with adults. *Helping people live the life.* Forest, VA: American Association of Christian Counselors.

Moberg, D. O. (2005). Research in spirituality, religion, and aging. *Journal of Gerontological Social Work, 15*(1/2), 11–40.

Moody, H. (ed.). (2005). *Religion, spirituality, and aging: A social work perspective.* Binghamton, NY: Haworth Social Work Practice Press.

National Center for Fathering. (n.d.). *National surveys on fathers and fathering.* Retrieved June 2005, from http://www.fathers.com/research

National Center for Injury Prevention and Control. (2005, April). *Sexual violence: Fact sheet.* Retrieved May 19, 2005, from http://www.cdc.gov/ncipc/factsheets/svfacts.htm

Ohlschlager, G. (2006, October). *Protecting spiritual interventions in professional clinical practice*, syllabus of presentation given at the *Society for Christian Psychology* in Chattanooga, TN.

O'Neill, R. (2002, September). *Experiments in living: The fatherless family.* Retrieved June 2005, from http://www.civitas.org.uk/pubs/experiments.php?PHPSESSID= 04a5571963443f822 81d8c0bd4332322#Results: The Institute for the Study of Civil Society.

Pargament, K. I. (1997). *The psychology of religion and coping.* New York: Guilford.

Parkes, C.M. (1972). *Bereavement: Studies of grief in later life.* New York: International Universities Press.

Perkins, D. F., Luster, T., Villarruel, F. A., & Small, S. (1998). An ecological, risk-factor examination of adolescent sexual activity in three ethnic groups. *Journal of Marriage and the Family, 60,* 660–673.

Population Reference Bureau. (n.d.). 2000 census data: Living arrangements profile for United States. *Analysis of data from the U.S. Census Bureau, for the Annie E. Casey Foundation,* Retrieved May 2005, from www.aecf.org

Rabins, P. A., Fitting, M. D., Eastham, J., & Zabora, J. (1990). Emotional adaptation over time in care-givers for chronically ill elderly people. *Age and Aging, 19,* 185–190.

Robinson, L. C. (1994). Religion orientation in enduring marriage: An exploratory study. *Review of Religious Research, 35,* 207–218.

Samelson, J. J., Foltz, J., & Foxall, M. J. (1992). Stress and coping in families of children with myelomeningocele. *Archives of Psychiatric Nursing, 6*(5), 287–295.

Smith, B. W., Pargament, K. I., Brant, C., & Oliver, J. M. (2000). Noah revisited: Religious coping by church members and the impact of the 1993 Midwest flood. *Journal of Community Psychology, 28,* 169–186.

Stander, V., Piercy, F. P., Mckinnon, D., & Helmeke, K. (1994). Spirituality, religion and family therapy: Competing or complementary worlds? *American Journal of Family Therapy, 22*(1), 27–41.

Ullman, C. (1982). Cognitive and emotional antecedents of religious conversion. *Journal of Personality and Social Psychology, 43,* 183–192.

Wallerstein, J. S., & Blakeslee, S. (1995). *The good marriage: How & why love lasts.* New York: Houghton Mifflin.

Weaver, A., Samford, J., Morgan, V., Larson, D., Koenig, H., & Flannelly, K. J. (2002). A systematic review of research on religion in six primary marriage and family journals. *The American Journal of Family Therapy, 30,* 293–309.

Whitbeck, L. B., Yoder, K. A., Hoyt, D. R., & Conger, R. D. (1999). Early adolescent sexual activity: A developmental study. *Journal of Marriage and the Family, 61,* 934–946.

Worthington, E. (1988). Understanding the values of religious clients: A model and its application to counseling. *Journal of Counseling Psychology, 35*(2), 166–174.

Worthington, E. L., Jr. (1999). *Hope-focused marriage counseling: A guide to brief therapy.* Downers Grove, IL: InterVarsity Press.

Worthington, E. L., Jr. (2001a). Unforgiveness, forgiveness, and reconciliation in societies. In Raymond G. Helmick & Rodney L. Petersen (Eds.), *Forgiveness and reconciliation: Religion, public policy, and conflict transformation* (pp. 161–182). Philadelphia: Templeton Foundation Press.

Worthington, E. L., Jr. (2001b). *Five steps to forgiveness: The art and science of forgiving.* New York: Crown Publishers.

Worthington, E. L., Jr. (2003). *Forgiving and reconciling: Bridges to wholeness and hope.* Downers Grove, IL: InterVarsity Press.

Worthington, E. L. (2004). Forgiveness: Laying the emotional foundation. *Christian Counseling Today, 12*(3), 44–49.

Worthington, E. L. (2005). Helping people forgive: Getting to the heart of the matter, In T. Clinton, A. Hart, & G. Ohlschlarer (Eds.), *Caring for people God's way: Personal and emotional issues, addictions, grief and trauma* (pp. 121–144). Nashville: Thomas Nelson.

Worthington, E. L. (2006). *Forgiveness and reconciliation.* New York: Routledge.

Yalom, I. D. (1995). *The theory and practice of group psychotherapy.* New York: Basic Books.

Yangarber-Hicks, J. (2004). Religious coping styles and recovery from serious mental illnesses. *Journal of Psychology and Theology, 32*(4), 305–317.

CHAPTER 13

The Role of Forgiveness in Religious Life and Within Marriage and Family Relationships

VIRGINIA TODD HOLEMAN

Earlier chapters explored the impact of religion on family relationships. Particular religious beliefs and practices that are associated with forgiveness merit specific attention. Richards and Bergin (1997) observe that "from a religious perspective, forgiveness is viewed as an act that has important spiritual consequences" (p. 212). It is also an act with the potential to heal fractured family relationships. This chapter outlines the shape of forgiveness in the five major world religions (presented in alphabetical order) and then it explores how these conceptualizations of forgiveness may affect family relationships.

A BUDDHIST UNDERSTANDING OF FORGIVENESS

Buddhism does not espouse a concept that directly corresponds with common conceptualizations of forgiveness (Rye, et al., 2000). Nevertheless, one can find aspects of the Buddha's teaching that are congruent with it. First, *karma* is the moral law of cause and effect. This assures Buddhists that the universe is fair and just because thoughts and behaviors are actions that have consequences across and beyond space and time. For example, the offenses one experiences today may be the result of wrongdoing from a previous birth or from negative actions on the part of one's ancestors. When injured parties blame or condemn an offender they add to the suffering of the offender. *Karma* asserts that these negative thoughts toward the transgressor may bring additional suffering upon the injured party who harbors these thoughts. Conversely, positive acts such as forgiveness contribute to the reduction of suffering for self and others. Second, Buddhists are encouraged to develop loving-kindness (*maitri* or *metta*), compassion (*karuna*), sympathetic joy (*mudita*), and equanimity (*upeksha* or *upekkha*), better known as the Four Immeasurable Minds (Nhat Hanh, 1998). As Buddhists nurture the Four Immeasurable Minds, they relinquish their attachments to the things and people they love by accepting the impermanent nature of all forms. This produces forbearance toward offenders and a sense of peacefulness for the self. Third, Buddhists hold a particular understanding of suffering (i.e., Four Noble Truths). Buddhists believe that (a) All life is suffering; (b) Cravings and desires are the origins of suffering; (c) The elimination of cravings, desires, and attachments is the solution to suffering; and (d) the Eightfold Path is the process by which one may end suffering (Anderson, 2004). The Eightfold Path is a middle way between self-indulgence and self-mortification. It includes right view, right intention, right speech, right action, right livelihood, right effort, right mindedness, and right concentration.

In addition to these beliefs, a number of Buddhist practices help one to release anger and bitterness without contributing to the suffering of the offender. Compassion seeks to empathize with the suffering of others, including one's offender, and then to ease their pain and suffering. Maguire (2001) offers five precepts for compassionate living. First, avoid causing harm to other sentient beings. Second, avoid taking anything that is not freely given. Third, avoid sexual misconduct. Fourth, avoid untruthfulness. Fifth, avoid clouding the mind with drugs. Forbearance involves refraining from reacting to an offense in a harmful way. "The Buddhist traditions are in general agreement that one must be rather strict in controlling one's own emotions and actions, but at the same time quite tolerant and understanding of the actions of others, especially those who hurt us" (Rye et al., 2000, p. 37). Forbearance seeks to decrease or eliminate a desire for revenge, and to reduce anger and resentment.

As a Buddhist practice, repentance is an act that recognizes "the emptiness of all things—doer, deeds, and karma" (Chappell, 2004, p. 723). One may repent for immoral behavior or from wrongful attitudes, perceptions, and understandings. Indian Buddhism teaches at least two forms of repentance, insight and metaphysical. Insight repentance seeks to eliminate wrongs that are known and past wrongs that are presently unknowable. Practitioners of insight repentance meditate on each of the sense organs and then recite a ritual repentance meditation three times. Through this form of repentance personal transformation may occur as one realizes the emptiness and impermanence of all things. Metaphysical repentance refers "to unexpiated guilt resulting from unknown or unremembered past wrongs, and [is]a plea for forgiveness to alleviate suffering and harm in the present life" (Chappell, 2004, p. 722). Metaphysical repentance seeks to avoid the larger karmic consequences of wrongful actions.

Meditation involves stilling oneself physically and emotionally. Through meditation one regularly seeks more open awareness of one's thoughts and feelings, freeing oneself from judgments and rationalizations that daily impinge on one's thoughts. Regarding forgiveness, Buddhists can use meditation to reframe the wound they have suffered, and to experience compassion and forbearance for the offender. Finally, mindfulness is a state in which the body and mind learn how to be fully present at any given moment (Maguire, 2001). Through mindfulness, one may be aware of anger and resentment that one has toward an offender, and then release those negative emotions, replacing them with compassion and forbearance.

A CHRISTIAN UNDERSTANDING OF FORGIVENESS

For many Christians, "forgiveness" captures the essence of the biblical narrative, which unfolds the story of God, the Divine injured party, in loving pursuit of unfaithful humanity, and ever seeking to reconcile these sinful people to Godself through forgiveness (Holeman, 2004). Christians believe that God gives the ultimate gift of forgiveness to humanity through the life, death, and resurrection of Jesus Christ (Volf, 2005). Forgiven persons become imitators of Jesus' life and teachings. Forgiving one another as God has forgiven them is central to the imitation of Christ within the Christian community (Jones, 1995).

Behind this basic formulation lay the theological concepts of sin, salvation, and repentance. More than a violation of a moral code, sin is a form of relationship betrayal (McClendon, 1992). Christians believe that humanity's betrayal of God is so great that no individual or corporate human action could ever repair the breach. So God had to do it. According to the New Testament, Jesus Christ proclaims the message of God's forgiveness to all people who repent and believe the good news that he preached (Mk. 1:15). Jesus' life of self-giving, other-centered love ultimately results in his execution by crucifixion (Gorman, 2001; Green & Baker, 2000). New Testament writers claim that Christ's death and resurrection demonstrate the greatness of God's love and offer of forgiveness to sinful humanity (Green & Baker, 2000; Volf, 2005). Christianity does not make repentance a *condition* for forgiveness. Instead, repentance is seen as a *consequence* of forgiveness (Volf, 2005). Grasping the full implications of Jesus' life, death, and resurrection, Christians can do little else but repent and receive God's gift of forgiveness. The New Testament subsequently links the believer's forgiveness by God with their forgiveness of one another (e.g., Matt. 5:9–15; Matt. 18; Col. 3:12–14; Holeman, 2004). Based on gratitude for their own forgiveness by God, Christians are to extend forgiveness to their offenders.

Christian practices associated with forgiveness range from particular liturgical sacraments, such as communion and baptism, to more general practices such as confession and prayer. These practices serve to restore the relationship of repentant people with God and one another through forgiveness. The Eucharist is a church sacrament that reminds Christians of their own forgiveness and challenges them to practice forgiving, repenting, and reconciling with one another (Jones, 1995; Volf, 1996). Jesus Christ inaugurates the Eucharist as he hosts his final meal with his disciples. At this meal he connects the bread that they break with his body, which would be crucified for them. He also associates the wine that they drink with his blood, which would be shed during his crucifixion, "poured out for many for the forgiveness of sins" (Matt. 26:28, Today's New International Version). As a part of the Eucharist liturgy, a minister or priest declares that those who partake of the Eucharist are forgiven. Each time Christians celebrate the Eucharist they have an opportunity to seek God's forgiveness and to both give and request forgiveness from one another.

According to Bartlett (1992), "Christians believe that baptism represents the believer's repentance, as he or she dies to sin and rises again to new life" (para. 6). Therefore, baptism is an outward and visible sign of an inward transformation. As Christians witness the baptism of others, they have an opportunity to renew their own love of God. Regarding forgiveness, Jones (1995) argues that "baptism signifies that, by the grace of Jesus Christ, people are set free from patterns of sin and evil, of betrayals and of being betrayed, of vicious cycles of being caught as victimizers and victims, so that they can bear to remember the past in hope for the future. They can do so because they are given a new perspective on that past, the perspective of forgiveness" (p. 166). Confession of sins often accompanies acts of repentance. In the Protestant tradition, individuals may confess their sins directly to God, or they may confess to one another. In the Catholic tradition, confession is made to a priest, who stipulates acts of penance.

Repentance and forgiveness are often the topic of prayer (formal and informal). Prayer for forgiveness of sins is featured in the model prayer that Jesus taught to his disciples, "Forgive us our debts, as we also have forgiven our debtors" (Matt. 6:12). In this passage, forgiveness is the only aspect of the prayer upon which Jesus offers further commentary, emphasizing the importance of extending forgiveness to our offenders. Today many Christians continue to pray to God for forgiveness of their sins and for the strength to extend forgiveness to their transgressors.

A HINDU UNDERSTANDING OF FORGIVENESS

The basic foundation of Hinduism is "*ahimsa*, nonhurtfulness, physically, mentally and emotionally" (Subramuniya, 2001, para. 7). The goal of Hindu religious life is to surrender to Hindu Dharma. Dharma is the cosmic law that directs all processes in the universe, and provides the basis for Hindu morality and ethics (Ellinger, 1996). It is the essence of an ultimate purpose in life that provides balance and integrity. The path of dharma includes practices of forgiveness, righteousness, forbearance, compassion, and patience (Rye et al., 2000). According to Subramuniya (2001) contemporary Hindu Dharma entreats people to release grudges, resentment, and self-contempt, actions that result in forgiveness of self or others. Subramuniya suggests that when one has been wronged, one should let the offense "awaken compassion, kindness and forgiveness" (para. 1) instead of resentment or anger. Then one can see one's own limitations, and ultimately bring one's speech and behavior in line with Hindu Dharma.

In Hindu thought, sin (*p-pa*) is the willful or accidental transgression of Dharma. Sins arise from one's previous lives, mental or physical deformities that one inherited from one's ancestors, and sins in this life (Beck, 1997). Two categories of sin exist in Hindu thought. Major sins include the killing of a brahmana, drinking liquor, stealing, having sexual intercourse with the wife of one's guru, and association with anyone who does any of these things. Minor sins are morally degrading behaviors for which a means of expiation exists. Examples of minor sins include killing a cow, selling oneself, abandoning one's guru or parents, and breaking a vow. Normal rituals of forgiveness have no impact on the expiation of major sins so a more extreme use of pain and suffering is needed over the course of several lifetimes.

Dharma is also associated with the dutiful performance of ritual action. Failure to perform such action results in negative social and personal consequences, or sin (*p-pa;* Flood, 1996). Hindus recognize nine duties that are eternal and that are equally applied to members of the four castes. Named among the nine eternal duties are suppression of wrath, truthfulness of speech, justice, forgiveness, purity of conduct, and avoidance of quarrel (Understanding Hinduism, n.d.). Fulfilling one's duties aligns one's life with Dharma.

Like Buddhism, Hindus believe in *karma*. Actions and thoughts from previous lives create karmic limitations in one's present life, yet a person has freedom to loosen the bonds of karma by surrender to God, creation of good karma, and dissolution of bad karma (Friedrichs, 1986). Regarding forgiveness, Hindus believe that harmful deeds or negative thoughts from one's own past are the origin of offenses. Therefore, one should not harbor resentment or grudges against one's offender because such grudge-holding and anger only contributes to negative karmic effects in one's present or future life. When one forgives, however, karma will come against the offender. In the strictest understanding of karma, everyone had to experience the consequences of one's sinful behavior before the sins could be destroyed. *Prayascitta*, or the doctrine of expiation, developed as "a flexible means of confronting moral causation and social justice" (Beck, 1997, p. 81). *Prayascitta* is performed after a sin is committed and it takes away the consequences of sin. The Vedas contain prescriptions for expiations (Lochtefeld, 2002). The *Manu-Samhita* is the most important text that spells out penances for sin. Examples of expiations include confession and repentance as a preparation for expiation, fasting, acts of charity, physical asceticism, recitations, purification rituals, and travel to sacred sites.

Two Hindu practices are particularly noteworthy in the context of forgiveness. First, the festival of Mahasivaratri is closely associated with forgiveness. It focuses on austerity and occurs on the 14th day of each month according to the Hindu calendar. No revelry or joyous celebration happens on this day. Instead this festival focuses on the disciplines of *ahimsa* (non-injury), *satya* (speaking the truth), *Brahmacharya* (continence), *daya* (compassion), *Ksama* (forgiveness), and *anasuyata* (absence of jealousy) (Shastri, 2002). Second, yoga is one way many Hindus nurture compassion, renounce resentment, or cultivate forgiveness as it contributes to mastery over one's emotional self.

AN ISLAMIC UNDERSTANDING OF FORGIVENESS

Allah's character and the nature of Allah's relationship with humanity form the template for an Islamic understanding of forgiveness. Receiving forgiveness from Allah is a central theological concern for Islam. Six of Allah's 99 names relate to forgiveness. These names of Allah are: *ar-Rahm-n,* The Merciful; *ar-Rah-m,* The Compassionate; *as-Sab-r,* The Forbearing; *al-'Afuw,* The Pardoner; *al-Ghafar,* The Forgiver; and *al-Ghaff-r,* The Forgiving (Glasse, 1991). Muslims who invoke these names of Allah are reminded that Allah forgives. Allah is sovereign. Allah created humanity with the ability to reason, so people can see for themselves that Allah and his commands are just. Muslims believe that humanity was created with *fita,* an original righteousness. Allah promises to provide guidance to humanity so that Muslims can follow the Straight Path (Altareb, 1996). Individuals bear the responsibility for deepening their devotion to Allah because Allah will not prevent them from leaving his protection.

Muslims believe that people sin because they are weak and move away from Allah's protection. Islam recognizes four categories of offenses. These include offenses (a) against Allah, (b) against a person, (c) against a group of persons or society, and (d) against aspects of the created order such as animals. The Qur'an regards sin as a breach of the laws or norms, and includes sins of omission and commission. Sins are divided into major and minor sins. Major sins are those that are in direct disobedience to the Qur'an. *Shirk,* or idolatry, is the only unforgivable major sin. *Shirk* can also involve hypocrisy or preventing others from believing in Allah. Allah will overlook minor sins, which are less easily defined, if one avoids committing major sins. Good deeds, such as prayer, studying the Qur'an, treating others fairly, etc., can repay the debt of sin that one owes to Allah.

Before Allah, people are considered either repentant or wrongdoers. Sincere repentance (*tawbah*) is required for Allah's forgiveness. If one sins against Allah three things are required for *tawbah*: (a) recognize and admit the offense before Allah; (b) commit to not repeating the offence; and (c) ask Allah for forgiveness (Ali, n.d.). Sincerity is essential because with the help of Allah it protects the person from repeating the offense. Moreover, Allah will turn the punishment for the offense into a reward if one sincerely repents. If one sins against another person or society, then a fourth condition, that of atoning for the offense and seeking the injured party's forgiveness, is added.

Forgiveness from Allah is linked to a willingness to forgive others. Forgiving others subsequently results in rewards in this life and the next. Forgiveness of another must be sincere, however. Islam values interpersonal forgiveness because Allah forgives and because interpersonal forgiveness facilitates peaceful relationships (Rye et al., 2000) and reward in the after-life. However, forgiveness is a choice that victims make rather than a religious obligation or duty. Repentance is not required for interpersonal forgiveness. Reconciliation is a desirable outcome, but it is also not required.

An Islamic concept of revenge, *qi---*, deems that the actual wrongdoer alone is guilty, and may be punished. However the punishment must be equivalent to the offense. According to Glasse- (2001), "*qi---* is the very essence of justice, the recognition that consequences are contained in acts, or that effect is contained in cause" (p. 372). According to Rye and colleagues (2000), "Islam taught a middle path between turning the other cheek and never ending blood feud, that is, revenge to the extent harm done is allowed but forgiveness is preferred" (p. 31).

In addition several Islamic practices are related to forgiveness. Muslims pray *salat* five times each day (Matthews, 2002). *Salat* nurtures one's relationship with Allah and with Allah's guidance one will follow the Straight Path and thereby forsake sin. Other Islamic practices that are related to forgiveness include reading or listening to the Qur'an and meditation (Ali, Liu, & Humedian, 2004). Each of these practices seeks to draw devout Muslims closer to Allah, to aid them in renouncing all manner of sinful behavior, and to commit to following Allah's commandments fully.

The Night of Forgiveness occurs two weeks before Ramadam. This marks a time when Muslims seek forgiveness for their sins and guidance from Allah. Many Muslims believe that one's destiny for the coming year is set on this night (Lailat-ul-Barah'h, n.d.). The 27th night of Ramadam, the holy month under Islam's lunar calendar, is called the Night of Power. This night marks the date when Allah gave to the Prophet Muhammad the first verses of the Qur'an, and is a time of Allah's maximum forgiveness. This is an ideal time for individuals to repent and seek Allah's forgiveness for major and minor sins (Holy Days, n.d.).

A JUDAIC UNDERSTANDING OF FORGIVENESS

God's moral character is central to Judaic theology. This shapes Judaic ideas of repentance and forgiveness and establishes one's moral obligations in community and family life. Based on the prime commandment of the Holiness Code—"Be holy because I, the LORD your God, am holy" (Lev. 19:2), the Judaic community is to embody the attributes of God in its life together. "To the extent that Israel is to pattern its own moral life on God's example, the obligation to forgive must become one of its central moral duties. By forgiving those who hurt them, Jews draw themselves closer to God and make God's own compassion the operative force in their relations with others" (Newman, 1987, pp. 166–177).

Judaism believes that God also endowed humanity with free will to choose between good and evil. Sadly, people have a strong propensity to violate God's laws. God forgives those who repent and punishes those who do not repent. Therefore repentance (*teshuva*) is a precondition to forgiveness for offenses committed against God and one another. Because people can change for the better, offenders ought to and can accept responsibility for their actions and should be given a chance to do so (Dorff, 1998), even if this means that the injured party confronts the wrongdoer first. Only a victim has the moral right to forgive the offender (Dorff, 1998; Schimmel, 2002). However, sins against another person are also sins against God (Schimmel, 2002). Offenders cannot receive God's forgiveness until they have sought the forgiveness of the injured party. Judaism teaches that its people are members of a covenant community (Newman, 1987). A concern for peace in the house, *shalom bayit* (Korzenik, 1994) energizes a longing for reconciliation when relationships are fractured. Nevertheless, a concern for justice and the law takes precedence over the forgiveness of the unrepentant. Dorff (1998) proposes that a focus on a change of feelings for the injured party is not central to a Judaic understanding of forgiveness. Rather it is "acting on the moral duty to forgive so that community is maintained" (p. 46).

A number of Judaic practices support forgiveness. Daily prayers remind the community of their duty to repent. These prayers emphasize repentance as a prerequisite to God's forgiveness and God's character as one who longs to pardon and forgive those who return to God through repentance. In addition to daily prayers, special holy days mark the Judaic liturgical calendar. Salient to our discussion are the High Holy Days, which begin with *Rosh Hashanah*, the New Year, and end with *Yom Kippur*, the Day of Atonement.

The ten days between *Rosh Hashanah* and *Yom Kippur* are known as the Ten Days of Repentance (Strassfeld, 1985). The themes of repentance, judgment, and atonement take center stage throughout these holy days. The period before *Rosh Hashanah* is devoted to contemplating how one may repair broken relationships. Worshippers devote themselves to careful self-examination to become cognizant of how they have failed God, others, and even themselves.

Yom Kippur, the most important holy day, is the climax of the Ten Days of Repentance. It enters on seeking God's forgiveness through repentance. On the eve of the Day of Atonement, it is customary to seek reconciliation with others because God cannot forgive sins committed against another person unless that person has first forgiven the transgressor. Family members gather together to celebrate this holy day and to share the evening meal. Five services are held in the synagogue throughout the day with sin, repentance, and forgiveness as central liturgical themes. The *viddui,* confessional, is recited at each service (Strassfeld, 1985).

While the Day of Atonement focuses on seeking divine forgiveness, Dorff (1998) describes a process of return for seeking human forgiveness. The steps in the process of return are (a) acknowledgment that one has done something wrong; (b) public confession of one's wrongdoing to both God and the community; (c) public expression of remorse; (d) public announcement of the offender's resolve not to sin in this way again; (e) compensation of the victim and acts of charity to others; (f) sincere request of the injured party for forgiveness repeated up to three times, if necessary; (g) avoidance of the conditions that caused the offense; and (h) behaving differently when confronted with a similar situation. Once the offender has repented, the injured party now is under a moral duty to forgive. If the offender repents up to three times without receiving forgiveness, then the injured party carries the burden of having sinned.

IMPLICATIONS FOR COUPLE AND FAMILY RELATIONSHIPS

Religious beliefs are deeply embedded in the language that a given community uses to name and describe itself, its values, and its mores. According to Walsh (1999) these beliefs "provide faith explanations of past history and present experiences; for many, they predict the future and offer pathways toward understanding the ultimate meanings of life and existence" (p. 6). Walsh's sentiments are underscored when one reflects upon the role that forgiveness and its companion concepts play in religious and family life. Beliefs about forgiving, repenting, retaliating, and reconciling provide the scaffolding for the stories that families construct to explain why they do or do not get along (e.g., sin against God or another; bad karma). They provide motivation to heal fractured relationships (e.g., seeking a right relationship with God, blessings in this life or the next, or promoting good karma). They undergird and support the challenging tasks of releasing anger and hostility, seeking justice, or pursuing relationship restoration. With respect to forgiveness, families are not left on their own. Beliefs about forgiveness are also reinforced by the stories that the practicing religious community tells through its holy texts. Families who participate in sacred rituals and ceremonies have ready-made avenues for offering forgiveness or repentance to one another. When taken deep into a family's soul, these beliefs become embodied in the give and take of daily life.

As indicated above, *beliefs about forgiveness influence how families understand the causes and solutions to interpersonal wounds.* Hindu and Buddhist families interpret suffering through the lens of *karma.* This cyclic and cosmic view of cause and effect gives these families a wider perspective for making attributions of innocence or blame. Interpersonal wounds in this life may have resulted from one's own wrongdoing or they may have had their origins in the misdeeds of one's own past lives or of one's ancestors. Devote Hindus and Buddhists may look to the distant past for the source of their suffering and may not attribute *total* blame to the wrongdoer.

Buddhists affirm that suffering is a natural part of life. The Four Immeasurable Minds and the Four Noble Truths encourage Buddhist families to extend compassion and forbearance to their offender. Buddhists believe that if they harbor bitterness, anger, and resentment against their transgressor, they will bring injury to that person, which then binds wounded parties and their progeny more tightly to future harmful karmic effects. If this is applied to a marital affair, for example, one can imagine how compassion and forbearance would be more likely to evoke repentance and relationship restoration than hatred or grudge-bearing. In a similar way Hindus also seek to avoid contributing to the negative effects of karma by following *ahimsa* or the principle of nonhurtfulness. Hindus believe that bad karma can be averted if the wrongdoer performs expiations for the sins he or she committed. If a family member sins, the Hindu family would look to their guru for direction on the rituals that the individual or family should perform as expiation for sin.

On the other hand, Islam, Christianity, and Judaism do not interpret hurtful interactions through the lens of karma. Instead, hurtful family interactions arise from individual wrongdoing against another. Therefore an individual bears the label of guilty or innocent without undue consideration for bad behavior on the part of one's ancestors. This confines the time frame for wounding events to the family's present, not to its ancestral past. While each of these theistic religions recognize the generational impact of family betrayals, sin is more of an individual matter than a cosmic one.

Beliefs about forgiveness determine how couples and families view the relationship between forgiving, repenting, revenge, and the extent to which reconciliation is possible. In Christianity, the New Testament presents forgiveness as a command rather than a suggestion. Because repentance is not required prior to forgiveness (Jones, 1995; Volf, 1996), family members are free to keep a soft heart toward a wayward and recalcitrant relative or mate. The priority of forgiveness within Christianity may forestall ongoing cycles of retaliation because Christians believe that revenge belongs to God alone. Yet these theological dynamics also raise questions about safety when offenders return to the matrix of family relationships but are unrepentant. Will forgiveness become "cheap" when it is offered without any expectation or demonstration of changed behavior from the transgressor (Jones, 1995)? For example, Christian battered wives place themselves in grave danger when they forgive the batterer without requiring observable and sustainable changed behavior over time. Many perpetrators "repent" as part of the cycle of abuse and then demand that injured spouses forgive and reconcile. In such cases forgiveness is too often coupled with reconciliation, minus authentic repentance (Holeman, 2004).

In Islam, Muslim families strive to honor and serve Allah in all aspects of their daily life by full obedience to Islamic teachings. This includes avoiding prohibited behaviors such as telling lies, cheating, gambling, adultery, and taking advantage of others. Obviously, these actions are harmful to family well-being! However, if family members engage in such sinful actions, then returning to Allah through repentance is required of the individual. Islam does permit retaliation, but only to the degree of the harm done. The injured party is not required to forgive, but forgiveness is preferred because Allah is forgiving. When family members engage in retribution, the question arises as to the perceived appropriate degree of retaliation. It is likely that families could be locked into ongoing cycles of retribution if wrongdoers believe that injured parties exceeded the appropriate level of punishment (Baumeister, 1997).

In Hinduism self-forgiveness is the platform from which forgiveness of others flows (Subramuniya, 2001). Forgiveness of self includes accepting oneself fully and living without guilt. Subramuniya writes, "We must start with ourselves, for as long as we hold self-contempt, we are unable to forgive others, because everyone else is a reflection of ourself" (para. 4). In Hindu thought, forgiveness does not automatically lead to reconciliation. An apology is required. When offenders remain unapologetic, Hindu practice endorses affectionate detachment with the offender.

In Judaism wrongdoers know that forgiveness does not come free. Repentance (*teshuva*) is required. This compels wrongdoers of all ages to initiate repair processes with their families. In addition, transgressors are not eligible for God's forgiveness until one has repented and been forgiven by the people one has injured. However, relationship repair is not all left up to offenders. Injured parties are also obliged to give transgressors an opportunity to repent by informing them of the offense. Although Judaic teaching underscores one's duty to forgive following repentance, the Judaic emphasis of justice may compete with an obligation to forgive. In these cases, injured family members must decide which tradition takes precedence. One can easily imagine the conundrum that exists when a transgressor has completed the process of return, but the injured family member is not yet emotionally ready to forgive.

That moral duty takes precedence over emotional readiness does not diminish the family's anguish in their struggle to forgive.

As noted in this chapter, many religious people forgive because they have been forgiven by God or because this contributes to good karma. Such deeply held convictions may compel some family members to forgive prematurely. They may feel guilty, unrighteous, or unworthy if they remain unforgiving. They may fear invoking divine wrath or bad karma if they stay angry or resentful. It is at this point that families may seek counsel from their priest, pastor, rabbi, imam, or guru. If the offender is still dangerous, reconciliation may not be possible. Then religious families may lean upon concepts of ultimate justice as framed by their religious tradition.

Forgiveness is nurtured as family units participate in holy day celebrations, special prayers, and rituals. "From a spiritual perspective, acts of worship and ritual can serve a number of purposes for believers: (a) expressing one's devotion, love, and respect toward God or the gods; (b) committing or recommitting oneself to a spiritual and moral life; (c) demonstrating devotion and piety to other members of one's religious community; (d) offering penitence and sacrifice for sins or wrongdoings; (e) demonstrating one's solidarity with other members of the religious community; and (f) seeking spiritual enlightenment, guidance, and healing" (Richards & Bergen, 1997, p. 215). These holy observances remind families of their duties and responsibilities as related to forgiveness.

For many Christian families, the local church is a center of family activity. Denominations vary on the frequency with which they celebrate the Eucharist, ranging from quarterly to weekly to daily. Whatever the frequency, the family is encouraged to settle interpersonal conflicts through repentance and forgiveness at each communion service. In addition, baptism is celebrated as a family event. If the church practices infant baptism, parents make the commitment to raise their child to be a disciple of Jesus. This would naturally include the parents modeling forgiving, repenting, and reconciling. If the church practices the baptism of only adolescents or adults, then that individual is affirming his or her status as a forgiven follower of Jesus Christ. All who witness a baptism have an opportunity to reflect upon their own forgiveness and what it means to them to be a member of the body of Christ. Moreover, many parents take the discipleship of their children seriously so that training in how to be a follower of Christ begins in the home. Clearly forgiveness, repentance, and reconciliation should be included along with Bible study, prayer, and church attendance.

The community of which a particular Judaic family belongs may become involved in the family's conflict in an effort to encourage repentance. Schimmel (2002) explains: "The communitarian ethos is strong in Judaism, making every member of society responsible for one another's moral and spiritual state" (pp. 183–184). Once repentance has been made, an expectation exists that wrongdoers will be reincorporated into the community, although not necessarily into the same position they once held, and by extension into the family, taking appropriate precautions against re-violation (Dorff, 1998).

World religions set aside special holy days that revolve around the restoration of right relationship with God, others, and the cosmos. For example, Christians celebrate Easter; Hindus celebrate the festival of Mahasivaratri; Muslims celebrate Ramadam, which includes the Night of Forgiveness; Jews celebrate Yom Kippur. Couples and families who practice these holy day celebrations have regular opportunities to make peace with one another through forgiving and repenting. During these hallowed times of worship, families reaffirm their commitment to one another because observance serves as a reminder of the way to restore harmony to fractured relationships. The bond between family members is strengthened as they practice forgiving and repenting during these holy days. This would seem to affirm the saying that "The family that prays together stays together."

CONCLUSION

Obviously beliefs about forgiveness rarely are cold propositional or theological statements when couples and families face the kind of betrayals that threaten to rip them apart. At these benchmark family moments, beliefs about forgiveness serve constraining and facilitative functions. Practices of forgiving, repenting, and reconciling prevent couples and families from immediate collapse, and exert subtle and not so subtle pressure for family reunification. As religious practices, these religious beliefs help couples and families to define their problems as "solvable," their recalcitrant family member as "redeemable," and renders their relationships as "restorable." While resentment, grudge-holding, and hatred do exist even in the most committed families, teachings on forgiveness or repentance press family members toward resolution.

Religious beliefs help bring a sense of cohesion to couples and families. As individuals commit themselves to values and virtues that are greater than themselves, they gain a new perspective on painful family interactions. All of the major world religions offer the image of an individual who epitomizes their practices of forgiveness. In Buddhism, there is Sakyamuni Buddha. In Christianity, this is Jesus Christ. In Judaism, it is the Messiah. In Islam, one finds Muhammad. In Hinduism, one reads in the Vedas examples of forgiving and merciful acts of the gods and goddesses. These exemplars can inspire family members to act as "transitional figures" in their family. Bergin (1988) defines this as a person who makes a difference in their family history, by embracing the pain from past victimization, preventing its transmission into future generations, forgiving offenders, and adopting a redemptive role between previous ancestors and future family members. In this way, forgiveness is no longer a theological construct, but a lived reality that will impact the well-being of family for generations to come.

REFERENCES

Ali, M. Amir (n.d.) Forgiveness. Retrieved January 14, 2006, from http://www.iiie .net/Articles/Forgiveness.html

Ali, S. R., Liu, W. M., & Humedian, M. (2004). Islam 101: Understanding the religion and therapy implications. *Professional Psychology: Research & Practice, 35*(6), 635–642.

Altareb, B. Y. (1996). Islamic spirituality in America: A middle path to unity. *Counseling and Values, 41*(1), 29–39.

Anderson, C. (2004). Four noble truths. In R. E. Buswell, Jr. (Ed.), *Encyclopedia of Buddhismi* (Vol. 2, pp. 295–298). New York: Macmillian Reference USA.

Bartlett, D. L. (1992). Worship. In D. W. Musser & J. L. Price (Eds.), *The Abingdon dictionary of theology.* Nashville, TN: Abingdon Press. Retrieved January 9, 2006, from iPREACH database. Available from Cokesbury Libraries Web site, http:// www.cokesburylibraries.com

Baumeister, R. F. (1997). *Evil: Inside human violence and cruelty.* New York: W. H. Freeman.

Beck, G. L. (1997). Fire in the -tman: Repentance in Hinduism. In A. Etzioni & D. E. Carney (Eds.). *Repentance: A comparative perspective* (pp. 76–95). Lanham, MD: Rowman & Littlefield Publishers.

Bergin, A. E. (1988). Three contributions of a spiritual perspective to counseling, psychotherapy, and behavior change. *Counseling and Values, 32,* 21–31.

Chappell, D. W. (2004). Repentance and confession. In R. E. Buswell, Jr. (Ed.), *Encyclopedia of Buddhism* (Vol. 2, pp. 721–723). New York: Macmillian Reference USA.

Dorff, E. (1998). The elements of forgiveness: A Jewish approach. In E. L. Worthington, Jr. (Ed.), *Dimensions of forgiveness: Psychological research and theological perspectives* (pp. 29–55). Radnor, PA: Templeton Foundation Press.

Ellinger, H. (1996). *The basics of Hinduism.* Valley Forge, PA: Trinity Press International.

Flood, G. (1996). *An introduction to Hinduism.* New York: Cambridge University Press.

Friedrichs, K. (1986). Karma. In S. Schuhmacher & G. Woerner (Eds.). *The Encyclopedia of Eastern Philosophy and Religion* (p. 175). Boston: Shambhala Publications.

Glasse-, C. (Ed.). (1991). *The concise encyclopedia of Islam.* San Francisco: HarperSanFrancisco.

Glasse-, C. (Ed.). (2001). *The new encyclopedia of Islam.* Walnut Creek, CA: AltaMira Press.

Gorman, M. (2001). *Cruciformity.* Grand Rapids, MI: Eerdmans.

Green, J. B., & Baker, M. D. (2000). *Recovering the scandal of the cross.* Downers Grove, IL: InterVarsity Press.

Holeman, V. T. (2004). *Reconcilable differences: Hope and healing for troubled marriages.* Downers Grove, IL: InterVarsity Press.

Holy Days (n.d.). Retrieved January 16, 2006, from http://www.bbc.co.uk/religion/ religions/islam/holydays/index.shtml

Jones, G. (1995). *Embodying forgiveness.* Nashville, TN: Abingdon.

Korzenik, E. F. (1994). Forgiveness in Judaism. *The Living Pulpit, 3*(2), p. 22.

Lailat-ul-Barah'h (n.d.). Retrieved January 16, 2006, from http://www.bbc.co.uk/print/religion/religions/islam/holydays/lailat_ul_barah.shtml

Lochtefeld, J. G. (2002). *The illustrated encyclopedia of Hinduism*. New York: The Rosen Publishing Group.

Maguire, J. (2001). *Essential Buddhism: A complete guide to beliefs and practices*. New York: Pocket Books.

Matthews, D. (2002). Forgiveness despite repeated sins. Retrieved on January 14, 2006, from http://www.islamonline.net/servlet/Satellite?cid=1123996015606&pagename=IslamOnline-English-AAbout_Islam/AskAboutIslamE/AskAboutIslamE

McClenden, J. W., Jr. (1992). Sin. In D. W. Musser & J. L. Price (Eds.), *The Abingdon Dictionary of Theology*. Nashville, TN: Abingdon Press. Retrieved December 19, 2005, from iPREACH database. Available from Cokesbury Libraries Web site, http://www.cokesburylibraries.com

McCutcheon, A. L. (1988). Denominations and religious intermarriage: Trends among white Americans in the twentieth century. *Review of Religious Research, 29*(3), 213-227.

Newman, L. E. (1987). The quality of mercy: On the duty to forgive in the Judaic tradition. *The Journal of Religious Ethics, 15*(2), 155–172.

Nhat Hanh, T. (1998). *The heart of the Buddha's teaching: Transforming suffering into peace, joy, and liberation*. New York: Broadway Books.

Richards, P. S., & Bergen, A. E. (1997). *A spiritual strategy for counseling and psychotherapy*. Washington, DC: American Psychological Association.

Rye, M. S., Pargament, K. I., Ali, M. A., Beck, G. L., Dorff, E. N., Hallisey, C., Narayanan, V., & Williams, J. G. (2000). Religious perspectives on forgiveness. In M. E. McCullough, K. I. Pargament, & C. E. Thoresen (Eds.), *Forgiveness: Theory, research & practice* (pp. 17–40). New York: Guilford Pres.

Schimmel, S. (2002). *Wounds not healed by time: The power of repentance and forgiveness*. New York: Oxford University Press.

Shastri, A. S. S. (2002). Mahasivaratri (Magha Krsna Chaturdasi). *Hindu Encyclopedia*. Retrieved January 5, 2006, from http://saranam.com/Festivals/Mahasivarathri.asp

Snyder, C. R., Rand, K. L., & Sigmon, D. R. (2002). Hope theory: A member of the positive psychology family. In C. R. Snyder & S. J. Lopez (Eds.), *Handbook of positive psychology* (pp. 257–276). New York: Oxford University Press.

Strassfeld, M. (1985). *The Jewish holidays: A guide and commentary*. New York: Harper & Row Publishers.

Subramuniya (2001). The power called forgiveness. In *Living with Siva, Hinduism's Contemporary Culture (The Master Course, Bk 2)* (chap 41). Retreived January 5, 2006, from http://www.himalayanacademy.com/resources/books/lws/lws_ch-41.htm

Understanding Hinduism (n.d.). *Nine duties that are eternal*. Retrieved January 5, 2006 from http://www.hinduism.co.za/duties.htm#Nine%20duties%20that%20are%20eternal

Volf, M. (1996). *Exclusion and embrace: A theological exploration of identity, otherness, and reconciliation*. Nashville, TN: Abingdon.

Volf, M. (2005). *Free of charge*. Grand Rapids, MI: Zondervan.

Walsh, F. (Ed). (1999). *Spiritual resources in family therapy*. New York: Guilford Press.

CHAPTER 14

Inter-Religion Marriages

TRACY M. LARA AND JILL D. ONEDERA

Inter-religion marriage, defined as a marriage between persons of differing religions, is also known as mixed marriage, intermarriage, religious hete-rogamy, and interfaith marriage. For example, the Catholic Church (2003) defines mixed marriage as a "marriage between a Catholic and a baptized non-Catholic" and uses the term *disparity of cult* in reference to a marriage "between a Catholic and a non-baptized person" (Kelly, 2001, p. 455). On the other hand, the terms *religious homogamy* and *intrafaith* are used to describe marriages between persons of the same religious affiliation (i.e., Protestant, Catholic, and Jew).

For the majority of Americans, marrying someone who is demographically similar seems to be the norm (Gardyn, 2002). There are considerable social, cultural, and religious pressures that tend to dissuade individuals from intermarrying. "Although the ideals [of] faith are supposed [to] unite people across the great chasms carved by race and ethnicity, social scientists have long noted in a manner of speaking 'Sunday morning service is the most segregated hour in America'" (Kosmin, Mayer, & Keysar, 2001, p. 34).

"Most major religious denominations severely regulate intermarriages, often explicitly citing the difficulties of socialization [of children] as the main justification" (Bisin, Topa, & Verdier, 2004, p. 622). For example, throughout the history of the Catholic Church dispensation for the validity of a mix marriage is required (Catholic Church and Canon Law Society of America, 1983). In Jewish biblical and rabbinical law, two distinct passages from

213

the Torah historically prohibited intermarriage (Rudolph, 2003). For example, throughout early Jewish history, Jews were severely punished for cohabitating with Gentiles. Although conversionary marriages were encouraged, many Jews historically risked even death as punishment for intermarriage.

Today another perspective applies. Inter-religious marriages are more common and acceptable. Even still Evangelicals discourage intermarriage based on St. Paul's message in 2 Corinthians 6:14 (Life Application Bible): "Do not be yoked with those who are different, with unbelievers. For what partnership do righteousness and lawlessness have? Or what fellowship does light have with darkness?" This objection is founded on the difficulty inherent with the joining of people with divergent core beliefs and values. In Judaism the more literal translation of the Torah passages indicates a prohibition of marriage only between Jews and those from the seven nations of Canaan. As such, within Judaism a concern for the preservation of the Jewish culture drives resistance to intermarriage and the earlier prohibitions no longer apply. Intermarriage is allowed so long as the Gentile partner "embraces the God and people of Israel" (Rudolph, 2003, p. 32). Other reasons exist for the premium some religions (conservative Protestants, Catholics, and Jews) place on same faith marriages. Same faith marriages are strongly encouraged to maintain the integrity of marriage, to sustain the faith community through active members, and as mentioned in the case of Jews, to preserve culture and customs.

Marriage is a social as well as a religious structure and is therefore subject to the reciprocal influences of social, cultural, and political forces. Moreover, religion itself can be viewed as a sociocultural institution. "There is an entire religious culture that has had an impact, from telling one what is appropriate attire for the Sabbath to what political party to join to where holidays are spent" (Heaton & Pratt, 1990, p. 205). Musick and Wilson (1995) discussed religions as social institutions in which family and social ties overlap. As such, some religions strongly value, and therefore strongly advocate, finding a marriage partner within the same religion.

Despite these prohibitions and pressures to remain in and marry within one's faith, over 33 million American adults, or about 16% of the total U.S. adult population, indicate they have changed their religious affiliation at some point (Kosmin et al., 2001). Interestingly enough, the precise numbers who have switched for marital reasons is unknown. However, some suggest that many Americans convert to other religious denominations to harmonize their marriages (Musick & Wilson, 1995).

For those who intermarry religiously, racially, or culturally, a number of challenges tend to arise. The challenges include planning the ceremony, marriage preparation, contraception, family planning and child rearing, holiday observations, religious practices, family relations, finances, etc. Negotiating these issues with a partner who sees the world through a different lens has implications for marital happiness, satisfaction, stability, as well as the socialization of any children who are born into such a family.

INCIDENCE AND TRENDS

The incidence of inter-religion marriages in America is increasing, although it still constitutes a distinct minority of all marital unions (Kelly, 2001). Multiple sources have indicated the rise of both interreligious and intercultural marriages using national survey data such as the General Social Survey, National Survey and Families and Households, and Gallup Polls. For instance, from 1972 to 1982 an increase in inter-religion marriages was found within seven major religious denominations with the only exception being among Conservative Christians (McCutcheon, 1988). The mixed-religion rate for various religions and denominations in the United States included the following: 23% of Catholic marriages, 33% of Protestant marriages, 27% for Jewish marriages, and 21% for Muslim marriages (Kosmin et al., 2001). Further, Kulczycki and Lobo (2002) reported high rates of Arab Americans marrying non-Arabs. This statistic leaves room for one to wonder as Islamic law prohibits Muslim women from marrying non-Muslims.

The Trends

Increases in interfaith marriages seem to be impacted by the pool of possible marriage candidates available in particular religious clusters. That is, "The smaller the religious group, the more likely its members are to marry persons who belong to another group. The larger the group, the more likely its members are to marry persons who belong to the same faith" (Davidson & Widman, 2002, p. 397). Whether this is true or not, it is important to consider that during the last 40 years since the 1967 abolition of antimiscegenation laws in America, interracial marriages have significantly increased (Gardyn, 2002). Further, statistics suggest that interracial marriages increased from 321,000 in 1970 to 1.5 million in 2000.

Examining such trends in interracial and interethnic marriages is important. One might wonder, are inter-religious marriages possible because society's tolerance and acceptance is increasing? Also, such trends might imply a reflection of diversity in society. Whatever the reasons, a pluralistic society naturally precipitates and fosters marriages between individuals from diverse backgrounds (geographic, religious, racial, and cultural). Consequently, when examining and considering the impacts inter-religion has on couples, counselors are behooved to consider any relevant racial, ethnic, and cultural influences on individuals and relationships. Furthermore, marriage and family counselors might consider the impact that a family's religious orientation has on its cultural practice and belief systems (Kosmin et al., 2001). A family's or couple's religious foundation then should be treated as a multicultural phenomena; that is, not only should counselors consider how culture and ethnicity play out in family or couple dynamics, but also their religion.

Perhaps the Jewish faith best exemplifies the religious ethnic connection. In America, there is a long history of Jewish/Catholic marriages (Tvrtkovic, 2001). Drastic differences in the fundamental beliefs and practices associated with Judaism and Catholicism are a constant source of conflict and can become a formidable barrier to couple bonding (Horowitz, 1999). Fortunately, over the years support organizations and ever growing resources have been made available to these couples. By the same token, the number of Muslims in America today exceeds the number of Jews and the incidence of Muslim-Christian (of all denominations) marriages is on the rise. Further, Muslims have cultural norms that are as strict as any contemporary religious group.

> Muslim women wishing to marry Christian men face the additional worry of potential ostracism from the faith community, for although Islam permits Muslim men to marry "people of the book" (Christians and Jews), Muslim women marry only within the faith. (Tvrt-kovic, 2001, pp. 11–12)

These examples illustrate how pervasive cultural influences may be on the marriage even within our multicultural American society.

Clearly our society and the family units making up our society are constantly changing (Sherkat, 2004). The tremendous diversity in America provides many rich opportunities for counselors to learn from their clients. Rather than being daunted by the myriad of variations in religious, cultural, and ethnic marriages and the complexity they pose, counselors need to remain mindful that they are lifelong learners and have much to gain from their clients. It is important for marriage counselors to be aware of the macro and micro trends impacting marital structure and functioning.

THE PLAY OF SECULARIZATION IN RELIGIOUS PRACTICE

Caution should always be exercised in ascribing general behavior or tendencies to interfaith marriages and individuals within those marriages. Counselors are encouraged to consider the particular elements specific to religiosity including one's membership in a religious institution, participation in religious observance or worship, adherence to beliefs and doctrine, and a defined spiritual life (Goldscheider & Goldscheider, 1993). One's adherence and level of practice of particular religious beliefs, doctrine, and practices will factor into the significance of religious difference in terms of couple relations.

Religion varies in personal significance for individuals, which can affect one's practice, affiliation, and organized church participation. That is, identifying self with a particular religion is not necessarily indicative of religiosity or religious practice. Even church membership does not guarantee participation or religious related activity (Kosmin et al., 2001). For example, one can say that he is "Jewish," but may practice a more secular lifestyle while not ascribing to the major tenets of the religion through activity or rituals.

So how do these different degrees of religious affiliation and identity play out in one's life? Kosmin et al. (2001) reported that religious identification might be more of a social marker than a religious one. It also might reflect the individual's connection to community or family. Further, some Americans may have a lukewarm affiliation and only participate in worship or observance on special occasions such as weddings or holidays. Others may have not matured in their faith and lack discernment and life experience such that their religious values and beliefs have not yet crystallized to guide their behavior and choices. In some instances, religion may be a central and guiding force in the lives of individuals or religion may form the template for an individualized and personal relationship with God and others. Moreover, some people describe themselves as spiritual not religious.

Another avenue worth exploring when working with couples is how the couple or partners view the beliefs and practices of people from other religions. For example, some individuals believe their religion is the one true religion, leaving grave consequences for "non-believers, non-repentant, or the unsaved." Or in the case of Jews and Catholics, Jews suffered persecution for years at the hands of Christians and in addition to divergent beliefs between them there may be strong feelings of fear and anger directed at one by the other. To the other extreme, ecumenicism is becoming more widely accepted. As American society becomes more pluralistic, more people are embracing diversity of religion and adopting accepting attitudes and beliefs.

Nonetheless, it is important for counselors to explore how each partner identifies with his or her religious affiliation. So, for example, the counselor might ask, "If I were to see you being religious, what would I see? In your home? In the community?" The counselor also might ask, "And how does this play out in your marriage?" Finally, seeking and coming to a mutual understanding of each partner's interpretation of the meaning of their religious affiliation is advantageous to the counseling process and a must for minimal multicultural competence.

HETEROGAMY VS. HOMOGAMY: FACTORS TO CONSIDER

As mentioned previously, a growing number of American adults are shifting toward secularism (Kosmin et al., 2001). Part of this trend may be related to the assumption that interfaith marriages generally have a secularizing affect on the family. More specifically, they are perceived as representing weaker religious commitment and a resultant weaker socialization of children in a given faith (Petersen, 1986; Shehan, Bock, & Lee, 1990). However, since most Americans indicate a religious identity it can be inferred that such an identity impacts relationships. In fact, several researchers have found a link between marital satisfaction and adjustment and religiosity (Bock & Radelet, 1988; Wilson & Musick, 1996). The effects of religiosity (or lack thereof as in the case of secularization) have been studied in relation to both homogamous and heterogamous marriages.

Church Attendance

Several studies attend to the effects of church attendance within inter-religious marriages on the success rate of such marriages. For example, in 1984 Heaton found that lower levels of marital happiness attributes to decreased church attendance among interfaith couples. Since then, it has been suggested otherwise by several other researchers. In 2001, Shehan et al. found that the marital happiness of inter-religious couples (specifically when one partner was Catholic) decreases when one partner attends mass infrequently. Call and Heaton (1997) found that the risk for divorce is 2.9 times greater if the wife attends mass regularly and if the husband never attends church. Even still, divorce is more likely in the above mentioned case than if both spouses never attend church. Finally, the lowest risk for divorce occurs when both partners attend church.

Counselors might conclude from these findings that marital happiness is affected by each partner's church attendance, as well as the importance a partner places on church attendance as a part of his or her faith system. Furthermore, counselors might defer to the research indicative of the link between religious constructs (such as church attendance, homogamy, and institutional affiliation) and marital quality, adjustment, stability, and happiness (Heaton, 2002; Heaton & Pratt, 1990; Musick & Wilson, 1995; Myers, 2006; Wilson & Musick, 1996).

Shared Religious Activities

It is important to understand how a divergence or likeness in religious beliefs influences marital functioning. In homogamous marriages shared beliefs, values, and religious practices are affirmed and thus can become self-perpetuating in the relationship (Petersen, 1986). In fact, Call and Heaton (1997) described "shared participation in religious activities" as "a critical aspect of religious experience that can sustain marriages" (p. 390). However, religious activities such as attending services together may not be the unique factor in marital satisfaction. Rather, it might be the meaning founded within the joint activities that brings about greater relationship satisfaction (Fiese & Tomcho, 2001). In other words, higher frequency of church attendance may be more an indicator of shared or mutual activity, which marriage partners find satisfying (Shehan et al., 1990). The significance may be attributed to social and interaction needs of partners more so than the actual effects of religion of one's religious affiliation.

Common beliefs and values unite couples and shape their relationship behaviors in terms of commitment, interaction, shared activities, and approach to handling the daily issues of marriage and family (Lehrer & Chiswick, 1993). Even more specifically, religious orientation can impact how a couple spends leisure time, spends money, and raises children as well as other aspects of marriage satisfaction (Heaton & Pratt, 1990). Such uniting of couples on religious issues can generate family cohesiveness (Waite & Lehrer, 2003).

Finally, both religiously heterogamous and homogamous marriages benefit from couple participation in mutually satisfying joint activities, giving credence to the adage "a couple that plays together, stays together." Religious activities might include celebrating religious holidays together, praying for each other and praying together, discussing moral and spiritual issues, discussing ways in which to live out God's will, and examining God's role in marriage. Mutual participation in such activities has been associated with better marital functioning. Marriage and family counselors should assess shared activity, possibility of more shared activity, and the matter in which couples are communicating about their activities and day-to-day routine (Williams & Lawler, 2003).

Worldviews

Worldviews are obviously shaped by experience. That is, those who have had similar formative experiences through their religious traditions develop similar worldviews (Heaton & Pratt, 1990). Having similar worldviews enhances marital satisfaction because decision making and other key behaviors in the relationship are guided by beliefs and values held in common. Couples who rely on divergent worldviews to shape their decision-making processes, communication styles, and conflict resolution skills are likely to contribute to marital conflict between interfaith couples (Sussman & Alexander, 1999). Partners may fail to support and reinforce the other's particular faith perspective due to a gap in mutual shared beliefs.

When marriage and family counselors work with couples struggling to connect their unique religious orientations into the many aspects of their marriage, they should consider the social and cultural ideations permeating the essence of the marriage. Perhaps culture can serve as the uniting link, in which counselors might consider as another key dimension or factor influencing the common beliefs and values laden in the marriage (Heaton & Pratt, 1990). On the other hand, it might be the broader, cultural expectations anticipated from a spouse that are at the root of the marital conflict.

COUNSELING IMPLICATIONS

Marriage preparation for interfaith marriages is the ideal time to inform couples of potential risk factors for the relationship and how to ameliorate them. In addition, proactive marriage preparation counseling and or psychoeducational programs are fruitful in preparing all couples for the adjustment and work of marriage. Marriage enrichment programs are also useful in fostering relationship success. However, it is all too often the case that a relationship breakdown precipitates help seeking, sometimes at the order of the family court judge in divorce proceedings. A counselor's ability to assist couples in resolving their conflicts, however, relies less on when, how, or why the clients enter the session and more on the counselor's preparation and multicultural competence.

Multicultural competency enables counselors to work with couples struggling to succeed in their relationships when they possess two different worldviews. Counselors and counselors-in-training should be competent in exercising the following dimensions: (a) awareness of one's own cultural values and beliefs, (b) awareness and respect for client's worldview, and (c) interventions that are culturally appropriate (Arredondo et al., 1996). All counselors are behooved to be aware of, knowledgeable of, and skilled in the previously mentioned dimensions when it comes to working with any given client's religious orientation and belief system. More specifically, these competencies become the model for helping clients develop the knowledge and skills to successfully navigate the divergent worldviews inherent in interfaith marriages.

In this part of the chapter we will attempt to highlight some of the foundational issues, treatment goals, and possible counseling interventions related to working with couples who are inter-religiously married. In addition, we will briefly address issues related to cross–religious identity among the counselor and the partners.

Foundational Issues

The foundation of a successful marriage is the identification, awareness, and experiences associated with different aspects of the marriage. For example, counselors will want to help couples move toward an awareness and understanding of each partner's faith and practices and that of one's partner; discomfort and tension of differences, meaning, and mattering of behaviors; and each partner's personal religious identity within the coupleship. Other foundational issues worth exploring during marital counseling include how each partner experiences each other's religion and practices and how they have considered integrating religion into their relationship. Furthermore, marital counseling should provide the medium for couples to explore the following: new communication patterns, arrangements that incorporate facets of both religions, how they will create unique and mutual traditions and rituals reflective of both religious traditions. Finally, a foundational aspect of counseling inter-religious couples should include helping them solidify communication strategies to support ongoing discovery, negotiation, conflict resolution, and a deepening spiritual love relationship.

Treatment Goals

Communication

Heaton and Pratt (1990) explained that individuals assign "normalcy" to the way things are seen or handled within one's faith or culture. Therefore, alternative worldviews or approaches to tasks may be misunderstood and/or considered problematic or dysfunctional. Therefore, self-exploration, awareness, and understanding serves as an integral part in working with couples from interracial, intercultural, and interfaith marriages. In particular, assisting clients in the development of an understanding of events, circumstances, and beliefs that shape worldviews can facilitate their discovery regarding other ways of seeing the world and related influences. For example, each partner must examine how religion and faith practices have shaped his or her beliefs about marriage and how such beliefs might influence the accepted interactional style within the marriage. In order to encourage this conversation the counselor might help couples address how their religious orientation impacts expected gender roles, sanctity of marriage, and conflict resolution strategies.

Negotiation

In order to better negotiate issues grounded in religious differences, marriage and family counselors should work at helping partners separate the problem from the person (Greenstein, Carlson, & Howell, 1993). Even more specifically, the principles of the issue should be the focal point rather than the position held by either partner. Partners can work toward the adoption of a problem solving approach, which lends itself to the preservation of respect and to the relationship as a whole. For example, managing holidays and deciding how to raise children are two key areas of decision making for interfaith couples. Baptism and religious instruction are two of the most contentious issues. These issues become more manageable when the couple has adopted negotiation and commitment to respect differences and the relationship. Once the couple is aware of the areas of potential conflict they can discuss the possibilities, experiment with alternative solutions, and create their own way of handling the issue for the benefit of the relationship and family.

Mutual Participation

Very often couples coming to counseling may never have participated in the religious traditions or practices of each partner. However, if there has been some exposure to the partner's religion it is likely to have been in the event of a special occasion or holiday. Often the couple has not shared in a meaningful way what the experience means for the person whose tradition is represented. The advantage to such a situation is opportunity. That is, the opportunity arises for the couple to choose structured opportunities to participate with the other partner in a religious ritual or practice. A counselor can work with the couple in exploring possible avenues of mutual religious activity. This could be a non-Catholic attending mass followed by a discussion between the couple about the various aspects of the mass and underlying tenants of the mass. Couples could join a Bible study together and share outside of the Bible study group their feelings and reactions. After the participation in such activities, couples should be encouraged to talk to each other about their experiences and what particular meaning such experiences held. Coming together like this may provide a segue into a discussion around making decisions regarding the integration of the different religious traditions into the family.

Counseling Interventions

The Genogram

One way of assisting couples in their mutual understanding of each other's religiously based worldviews and religious differences is through a genogram. The genogram could be a useful tool in helping couples explore how their religious affiliations and practices and family traditions have permeated their expectations of each other and of the marriage (McGoldrick & Gerson, 1985). Through the use of a genogram, counselors can assist clients in sorting out which behaviors are central to the religious system and which have more secular origins. Constructing the genogram with the couple will encourage discussion about the significance of each partner's respective and divergent beliefs and ways of handling daily life tasks. Furthermore, the genogram can help partners identify how rigid their religious beliefs and practices are and how this rigidity might play out in the relationship.

The genogram also can bring enlightenment to each partner regarding any adaptive and maladaptive communication patterns existing in the religious base of their family system. The counselor can supplement this awareness by encouraging the couple to share and examine their beliefs regarding the purpose and meaning of marriage. By doing this, each partner can further distinguish the difference between their marriage and what was expected and typical within their family of origin.

The genogram technique also might highlight family members who have served as a social network to the couple, especially in time of need. Discussion of family members and friends also might conjure up persons that *could* be a source of support to the couple. Counselors should encourage couples to consider such persons that they can rely on outside of therapy (Hughes & Dickson, 2005).

The Use of Immediacy to Encourage Communication

Religious differences may impact important family decisions such as family planning and childrearing as well as daily issues such as social involvement or distance from friends and how to manage finances. Sometimes the tension is felt, yet neither spouse is equipped to identify or express concerns. However, after some examination of self and the basis of behaviors for both partners, the couple's awareness of issues and perhaps sensitivity is heightened. Thus the use of immediacy in session around these unspoken issues creates movement. Through a counselor's attention to immediacy, partners can begin to practice appropriate communication skills in order to move to greater exploration and awareness. Increased effective communication also can lead to better negotiation and resolutions of differences (Miller, Miller, Nunnally, & Wackman, 1991).

Encouraging Communication Through Other Means

Sussman and Alexander (1999) provided the following suggestions for counselors to consider while working with couples who could benefit from developing effective communication and conflict resolution skills in order to better navigate their differences.

1. Be cautious in assuming either partner is less serious or committed to their faith.
2. Be aware that husbands and wives experience marriage differently.
3. Consider both perspectives before attributing marital difficulties to religious differences.
4. Account for the role of extended family in regards to marital satisfaction.
5. Encourage couples to seek additional resources and support.

Incorporating these elements into the practice allows the counselor to foster an atmosphere for open communication. It's important to note that the couple will be vulnerable as they discuss potentially emotionally overwhelming topics. As clients disclose and face these sensitive topics, unresolved family of origin issues may arise making negotiation and resolution more complex (Eaton, 1994). It is important to keep the issues from becoming disagreements, rather to direct the couple in negotiation and conflict resolution through effective communication (Chinitz & Brown, 2001). The desirable outcomes of the process might include the following (Tvrtkovic, 2001):

1. Shared information about the varied salient aspects of their respective religion and practices
2. Identification regarding which aspects of an individual's faith may not be negotiable at that point in time
3. A mutual understanding regarding the principles under discussion
4. The development of mutual respect and appreciation for each other's differences
5. A problem-solving approach to navigating religious differences affecting daily living and interaction

Encouraging the Process of Negotiation

In order to move a couple toward negotiation of differences and of discovering ways of participating in mutually respectable joint religious activities, the counselor can point out strengths of a couple's decision-making process already in place. Further, the counselor can support already made efforts and decision making. A partner's experience of intense emotions driven by exploring alternatives as part of the decision-making process should be pointed out as normal. Partners can be guided to use their self-awareness and effective communication to work through the emotions evoked by difficult decisions. Exploring decision-making skills and helping clients identify how values and beliefs influence decisions aids the couple in understanding the decision-making process, the potential barriers, and the skills present.

Sometimes the outcomes of the decision-making process are to embrace one religious tradition. Other times some family practices become unique as they embrace different aspects of each of the couples' religious traditions. Couples are encouraged to identify and reaffirm which aspects of their religious beliefs are non-negotiable and to find a creative way to compromise when possible.

It's important to note that there might be side effects or benefits from partners exploring the meaning of their religious beliefs and consequential practices (Walker, Gorsuch, & Tan, 2004). That is, each partner's faith may be individually deepened as each examines what is believed and why in an effort to teach the other partner. This is a prime opportunity for the counselor to encourage the couple to seek additional support and resources from their religious institutions and other sources. Additionally, through interfaith marriage an opportunity for the entire family, immediate and extended, to embrace diversity is created. Prejudice may be potentially eliminated as families encounter diverse unions and through the experience alter their stereotyped views, thus changing their attitudes and behaviors (Eaton, 2001). It is important for religious and cultural identities to be maintained so their beliefs and practices can be maintained in society. Further understanding how these identities play out should be seen as an opportunity to embrace diversity rather than a reason to doubt the success of the marriage.

When the Counselor's Religious Affiliation Differs

Marriage and family counselors ingrained in the mainstream Western Christian ethic may be posed with challenges if working with families who live their lives according to a more collectivist or family-oriented cultural/religious perspective. For example, in some cultures, families may traditionally be involved in both mate selection and arrangement of marriages. This can be viewed as suspect and problematic from a Western individualist perspective. Therefore, counselors must remain sensitive to the perspectives of each partner and must allow families to openly share their cultural viewpoints and influences.

Counselors should assist clients in facilitating an open discussion of the role of family to deepen the cross-cultural understanding. Parental influence on decisions, as well as healthy or "normal" boundaries between family members, should be considered in the context of the family's culture or religious orientation. Counselors can help families brainstorm and evaluate alternatives in the context of their religious views. Counselors might also consider providing or exploring possible group counseling opportunities in order for couples to listen and share experiences with other couples facing similar issues in the same religious or cultural context (Tvrtkovic, 2001).

CONCLUSION

Religion in America is alive and well. Marriages are impacted by the individual's and couple's religious preferences and practices as well as a host of other factors (ethnicity, culture, gender roles, work, etc.). Interfaith marriages can create challenges for couples centering on the melding of divergent worldviews. Counselors can assist couples in examining religion's impact upon and within the relationship. Aiding clients in gaining a better understanding of their partner's perspective and resultant behavior contributes to marital happiness, stability, and longevity.

REFERENCES

Arredondo, P., Toporek, R., Brown, S. P., Sanchez, J., Locke, D. C., Sanchez, J., & Stadler, H. (1996). Operationalization of the multicultural counseling competencies. *Journal of Multicultural Counseling & Development, 24*(1), 42–78.

Bisin, A., Topa, G., & Verdier, T. (2004). Religious intermarriage and socialization in the United States. *Journal of Political Economy, 112*(3), 615–664.

Bock, E. W., & Radelet, M. L. (1988). The marital integration of religious independents: A reevaluation of its significance. *Review of Religious Research, 29,* 228–241.

Call, V. R. A., & Heaton, T. B. (1997). Religious influence on marital stability. *Journal for the Scientific Study of Religion, 36*(3), 382–392.

Catholic Church. (2003). *Catechism of the Catholic Church* (2nd ed.). New York: Doubleday.

Catholic Church and Canon Law Society of America. (1983). *Code of Canon Law: Latin-English Edition.* Author.

Chinitz, J. G., & Brown, R. A. (2001). Religious homogamy, marital conflict, and stability in same-faith and interfaith Jewish marriages. *Journal for the Scientific Study of Religion, 40*(4), 723–733.

Davidson, J. D., & Widman, T. (2002). The effect of group size on interfaith marriage among Catholics. *Journal for the Scientific Study of Religion, 41*(3), 397–404.

Eaton, S. C. (1994). Marriage between Jews and non-Jews: Counseling implications. *Journal of Multicultural Counseling & Development, 22*(4), 210–214.

Fiese, B. H., & Tomcho, T. J. (2001). Finding meaning in religious practices: The relation between religious holiday rituals and marital satisfaction. *Journal of Family Psychology, 15*(4), 597–609.

Gardyn, R. (2002, July/August). Breaking the rules of engagement. *American Demographics, 24*(7), 35–37.

Goldsheider, F. K., & Goldscheider, C. (1993). *Leaving home before marriage: Ethnicity, familism, and generational relationships.* Madison, WI: University of Wisconsin Press.

Greenstein, D., Carlson, J., & Howell, C. W. (1993). Counseling with interfaith couples. *Individual Psychology, 49*(3), 428–437.

Heaton, T. B. (1984). Religious homogamy and marital satisfaction reconsidered. *Journal of Marriage and the Family, 46*(3), 729–733.

Heaton, T. B. (2002). Factors contributing to increasing marital stability in the United States. *Journal of Family Issues, 23*(3), 392–409.

Heaton, T. B., & Pratt, E. L. (1990). The effects of religious homogamy on marital satisfaction and stability. *Journal of Family Issues, 11*(2), 191–207.

Horowitz, J. A. (1999). Negotiating couplehood: The process of resolving the December dilemma among interfaith couples. *Family Process, 38*(3), 303–323.

Hughes, P. C., & Dickson, F. C. (2005). Communication, marital satisfaction, and religious orientation in interfaith marriages. *Journal of Family Communication, 5*(1), 25–41.

Kelly, A. (2001). Can this marriage be saved. *U.S. Catholic, 66*(3), 18–22.

Kosmin, B. A., Mayer, E., & Keysar, A. (2001). American religious indentification survey. New York: Graduate Center of the City University of New York.

Kulczycki, A., & Lobo, A. P. (2002). Patterns, determinants, and implications of intermarriage among Arab Americans. *Journal of Marriage & Family Therapy, 64*(1), 202–210.

Lehrer, E. L., & Chiswick, C. U. (1993). Religion as a determinant of marital stability. *Demography, 30*, 385–403.

McCutcheon, A. L. (1988). Denominations and religious intermarriage: Trends among white Americans in the twentieth century. *Review of Religious Research, 29*(3), 213–227.

McGoldrick, M., & Gerson, R. (1985). *Genograms in family assessment.* New York: Norton.

Miller, S., Miller, P., Nunnally, E., & Wackman, D. (1991). *Talking and listening together.* Littleton, CO: Interpersonal Communication Programs.

Musick, M., & Wilson, J. (1995). Religious switching for marriage reasons. *Sociology of Religion, 56*(3), 257–270.

Myers, S. M. (2006). Religious homogamy and marital quality: Historical and generational patterns, 1980–1997. *Journal of Marriage and Family Therapy, 68*, 292–304.

Petersen, L. R. (1986). Interfaith marriage and religious commitment among Catholics. *Journal of Marriage and the Family, 48*(4), 725–735.

Rudolph, D. J. (2003). *Growing your olive tree marriage: A guide for couples from two traditions.* Baltimore: Lederer.

Shehan, C. L., Bock. E. W., & Lee, G. R. (1990). Religious heterogamy, religiosity, and marital happiness: The case of Catholics. *Journal of Marriage and the Family, 52*(1), 73–79.

Sherkat, D. E. (2004). Religious intermarriage in the United States: Trends, patterns, and predictors. *Social Science Research, 33*, 606–625.

Sussman, L. M., & Alexander, C. M. (1999). How religiosity and ethnicity affect marital satisfaction for Jewish-Christian couples. *Journal of Mental Health Counseling, 20*(2), 173–185.

Tvrtkovic, R. G. (2001, September 10). When Muslims and Christians marry. *America,* 11–14.

Tyndale House Publishers. (1997). *Life application Bible.* Carol Stream, IL.

U.S. Department of Labor. (1999). Futurework-Trends and challenges for work in the 21st Century. Retrieved June 1, 2006, from http://dol.gov/oasam/programs/history/herman/reports/futurework/chapter1/main.htm#4b

Waite, L. J., & Lehrer, E. L. (2003). The benefits from marriage and religion in the United States: A comparative analysis. *Population and Development Review, 29*, 255–275.

Walker, D. F., Gorsuch, R. L., & Tan, S. (2004). Therapists' integration of religion and spirituality in counseling: A meta-analysis. *Counseling and Values, 49*, 69–80.

Williams, L. M., & Lawler, M. G. (2003). Marital satisfaction and religious heterogamy: A comparison of interchurch and same-church individuals. *Journal of Family Issues, 24*(8), 1070–1092.

Wilson, J., & Musick, M. (1996). Religion and marital dependency. *Journal for the Scientific Study of Religion, 35*, 30–40.

SECTION IV

Religion and the Counselor

The remaining section of this book focuses primarily on particular techniques and interventions that counselors and counselor educators alike might find useful in their practice and instruction. For example, in chapter 15 Deaner, Pechersky, and McFadden describe the intricate relationship among religion, ethnicity, and culture. They describe the skills needed and possible intervention strategies for incorporating all of these dimensions. More specifically, the authors will discuss how McFadden's Stylistic Model can be used to best exercise cultural sensitivity when working with religious, ethnic, and cultural issues presented in counseling.

From a systemic point of view, mental health practitioners must be willing to tap into the extended system of clients in ordere to best meet their needs more specifically, practitioners are encouraged to depend on the religious community for support and guidance in their practice. In chapter 16 Onedera, Minatrea, and Kindsvatter address the relationship between mental health professionals and religious leaders. When mental health professionals take time to develop a working relationship with such religious leaders, the clients benefit the most. The authors suggest ways in which practitioners can develop these relationships, as well as potential benefits and challenges to this collaborative relationship.

The final chapter of this book addresses the importance of considering religion within the training programs of future practitioners. In this chapter, Onedera reviews the historical and current trends of how religion is incorporated in counseling training programs. Counselor educators, as well as educators of other mental health trainees, will be offered specific ways in which to incorporate religious education into their affiliated training programs. Since religion plays such an important role in the lives of our clients, mental health professionals need to be trained in such a way that they are comfortable in identifying and treating religious issues before they arise.

CHAPTER 15

Ethnicity: Religious Practice and Marriage and Family Counseling Implications

RICHARD DEANER, KARA PECHERSKY, JOHN McFADDEN

It is no secret. While Freud was instrumental in the development of psychology, he was antagonistic toward the implications concerning religion and spirituality. Freud (1939) once purported, "As if the world had enough problems, we are confronted with the task of finding out how those who have faith in a Divine Being could have acquired it, and whence this belief derives the enormous power that enables it to overwhelm Reason and Science" (pp. 193–194). In the aforementioned citation, Freud seems to acknowledge the "enormous power" of religious and spiritual faith in a pejorative manner while placing reason and science in a more esteemed position. It seems that Freud's values and perception of rational and scientific thought are highly regarded as faith and religion precludes such reasoning. For Freud, examining the faith of an individual is irrelevant as the presence of such a value system is indicative merely of a problematic phenomenon associated with terms such as *neurosis*, *repression*, and *delusions* (Freud, 1939). Imagine, if Freud's ideological value system persisted today within a counseling atmosphere. According to the Gallup Poll (Winseman, 2005), over 90% of Americans report believing in either a higher power or belief in God. Thus, fewer than 10% of Americans might feel at ease, while over 90% of the remaining Americans might feel as if their religious value system was being unfairly overlooked, criticized, and misinterpreted. Currently, it is the task of practitioners to gain an understanding of the belief systems and practices of individuals, couples, and families, which may be based on religious values (Bishop, 1992; Georgia, 1994; Shafranske & Maloney, 1996). Since it is asserted that "All behaviors are learned and displayed in a cultural context" (Pedersen, 2003, p. 31), practitioners must address these beliefs and practices within a cultural context. Indeed, the American Counseling Association (ACA) and American Psychological Association (APA) include religion as an element that practitioners need to consider in terms of cultural diversity (ACA, 2005; APA, 2002). As cultural upbringing is distinct for every individual, practitioners must be aware of the uniqueness in which religion and/or spirituality evolves and emerges within couples and families. In order to understand the cultural context of couples and families, one must gain an understanding of each individual's value system that may be rooted in religion (Bishop, 1992). According to Shafranske (1996), religion "is one of the 'webs of significance' that culture provides and that the human community constructs. It informs the creation of a sense of personal identity and provides a 'sacred canopy' under which spheres of relevancy are created that orient human values and ultimately determine behavior" (p. 2). Religion, ethnicity, and culture are profoundly intertwined. Richards, Keller, and Smith (2004) suggest, "No book on human diversity and the practice of multicultural counseling and psychotherapy would be complete without a chapter on religious and spiritual aspects of diversity" (p. 276). This notion of completion seems applicable for books concerning religion and the necessary inclusion of ethnic and cultural considerations. Examining religion and spirituality in a cultural context illuminates the "enormous power" that Freud chose to acknowledge, yet neglect with disdain. In regards to this cultural context, attention is required if the needs of the clients are expected to be met appropriately.

ETHNIC AND CULTURAL CONSIDERATIONS

Religious and spiritual culture within the United States is a rich tapestry of diversity. As stated previously, culture, ethnicity, and religion are deeply intertwined. Understanding the cultural context of ethnicity, culture, and religion is crucial for practitioners in order to appropriately measure and attend to the needs of clients. The impact of religious and spiritual diversity concerning marriage and family counseling is an inevitable reality for practitioners across the country. Sue, Arredondo, and McDavis (1992) developed the Multicultural Counseling Competencies in order to address interpersonal racism and oppression within the counseling profession. The competencies framework outlined three dimensions requiring attention in order to enhance multicultural competency within the counseling profession: awareness, knowledge, and skills. Pedersen (2003) suggests that the culturally encapsulated practitioner mistakenly interprets behavior by displaying indifference or inattention to the cultural context. The competent practitioner avoids being culturally encapsulated "by *first* increasing their awareness of culturally learned assumptions, *second* increasing their access to culturally relevant knowledge, and *third* increasing their appropriate use of culturally sensitive skills" (Pedersen, 2003, p. 31). In this manner, practitioners can choose to view religion and spirituality as an asset and resource rather than stigmatizing the elements where individuals may discover identity, meaning, hope, and strength. Increasing awareness, knowledge, and skills concerning culture, ethnicity, and religion is an essential journey for the practitioner seeking cultural sensitivity and competency.

Awareness of Ethnicity, Culture, and Religion

In 2005, the American Counseling Association (ACA) revised and updated the *ACA Code of Ethics* governing the professional conduct of counselors. Among the major updates is an emphasis on cultural considerations and sensitivity. The revision provides a definition of the term *culture* as the "membership in a socially constructed way of living, which incorporates collective values, beliefs, norms, boundaries, and lifestyles that are cocreated with others who share similar worldviews comprising biological, psychosocial, historical, psychological, and other factors" (Glossary of Terms, p. 20). In fact, terms such as *culture* (e.g., multicultural, cross-cultural, cultural, etc.) occur 44 times within the *ACA Code of Ethics* (2005). Indeed, culture is a significant factor in the shaping of worldviews for both therapist and client. Within the broader concept of culture is the term *ethnicity*. Sometimes used interchangeably with the term *culture,* the term *ethnicity* can be utilized to describe an individual's perception of personal meaning and group membership. According to McGoldrick and Giordano (1996), "Ethnicity refers to a common ancestry through which individuals have evolved shared values and customs. It is deeply tied to the family, through which it is transmitted. A group's sense of commonality is transmitted over generations by the family and reinforced by the surrounding community. Ethnicity is a powerful influence in determining identity" (p. 1). This shared sense of identity shapes thoughts, assumptions, and behaviors for individuals. Subsequently, couples inherently display two unique cultural identities of which practitioners should be aware. McGoldrick, Giordano, and Pierce (1996) cite that ethnicity "plays a major role in determining what we eat and how we work, relate, celebrate holidays and rituals, and feel about life, death, and illness" (p. ix). Religious diversity is a pervasive variable within the context of culture and ethnicity (McGoldrick, Giordano, & Pierce, 1996; Richards & Bergin, 2000). Cultural sensitivity regarding religious diversity has recently expanded to include its own elements of considerations.

A noticeable revision in the *ACA Code of Ethics* (2005) concerning cultural sensitivity includes reference to religious *and* spiritual needs of the client. For instance, practitioners should include the involvement of religious/spiritual support networks when appropriate (A.1.d), attend to the spiritual needs of terminally ill clients (A.9.a.1), avoid discriminating on the basis of religion/spirituality (C.5), and recognize religious and spiritual diversity when assessing (E.8). Therefore, counselors have an ethical obligation to understand, respect, and integrate issues related to religious *and* spiritual diversity. The supporting ethical obligation regarding understanding, respecting, and integrating religious and spiritual diversity seems applicable, given the nature of our diverse nation.

Since numerous scholars address religion and spirituality, one can imagine the scope in which these constructs are defined. While religion seems to be easier to define, spirituality is more difficult to ascribe meaning (Cashwell & Young, 2005; Wiggins-Frame, 2005). Ingersoll (1994) suggested that religion can be conceptualized as a culturally influenced framework through which the potential for spiritual expression is developed. According to Cashwell (2005), although spirituality is universal, it is highly developmental and personal as "each person defines spirituality in her or his personal way, and this changes over time so that each person defines spirituality differently at various periods in her or his life" (p. 197). Cashwell and Young (2005) believe that an individual's spirituality is more fully understood by reviewing the beliefs, practices, and experiences of the individual. At times, an individual's spirituality is based on a particular religion and, therefore, the worldview may stem from that religion. A particular religion itself may be based on cultural and ethnic variables as well. Thus, the examination of various religions provides an opportunity from which cultural sensitivity and competency is generated for marriage and family practitioners.

Religion is a valid and valuable resource for practitioners to understand values, beliefs, and worldviews of clients. According to Wiggins-Frame (2005), the postmodern movement in the 20th century acted as "a bridge over the gulf between science and religion" (p. 20) and marked a paradigm shift in the philosophical thought concerning spirituality and religion in the profession of counseling. In this shift, spirituality and religion were dependent on the perceptions, meaning, context, and worldview of the individual. Wiggins-Frame (2005) asserts that human relationships, personal meanings, culture, and language influence meaning and truth as "religious or spiritual beliefs are considered human constructions of reality" (pp. 20–21). In this manner, "Both religion and psychology contribute to an individual's construction of meaning and values" (Shafranske & Maloney, 1996, p. 573). Historical neglect, discontent, hostility, and apathy toward the inclusion of religion and spirituality in psychology and counseling is a result of "clear but discomforting factor of value judgement—the preferencing process" (Bergin, Payne, & Richards, 1996, p. 317). Since each individual has his/her own personal experiences, perception, meaning, and worldview, each individual has the capacity to impose values onto others. Currently, a practitioner who imposes a value laden system, such as Freud's aforementioned values, might experience a problematic, ineffective, and unethical situation while working with any religious and/or spiritual individual and/or family.

Indeed, recognizing the values concerning religion and spirituality of the client(s) *and* practitioner is necessary for competent cultural assessment and interventions to be constructed throughout the therapeutic process (Bergin et al., 1996; Bishop, 1992; Georgia, 1994; Shafranske & Maloney, 1996; Wiggins-Frame, 2005). For the marriage and family practitioner, self-reflection is necessary in order to recognize personal reactions regarding religious and spiritual diversity. Fukuyama (2003) purports that these "reactions can range from negative stereotyping of various religious traditions, power struggles with authority, and fear of pressure to convert or believe or act in ways that are contradictory to self" (p. 190). "Culturally self-aware professionals know their own assumptions, values, biases, and limitations" (Ridley & Thompson, 1999, p. 21) and how these variables might affect the therapeutic relationship and environment. A nonjudgmental, open-minded, respectful, and sensitive approach is required in promoting the establishment of rapport and an active understanding when working with clients (Bishop, 1992). It is crucial for marriage and family practitioners to gain awareness concerning their own biases, assumptions, and limitations prior to understanding the incalculable number of worldviews that may be different than their own. Also, reviewing the tremendous cultural diversity within the United States is necessary in order to acknowledge, embrace, and address religious and spiritual issues within the therapeutic setting.

Knowledge of Ethnicity, Culture, and Religion

A large portion of knowledge concerning the diversity of religious and spiritual identification is included in this text. It is imperative for marriage and family practitioners to learn, know, and acknowledge this diversity. Ingersoll (1994) suggested that spirituality may or may not be based on the belief system of a particular religion. Nevertheless, the study of various religions may reveal different patterns of beliefs, practices, values, and perceptions that are based on culture and ethnicity. Emmons (1999) suggested that studying religion is integral to understanding personality functioning and structure of individuals. Shafranske and Maloney (1996) assert that "it is incumbent that clinicians develop at least a rudimentary understanding of religion in its institutional expressions" (p. 566). As familial patterns shape individual identity, ethnic and cultural considerations shape familial identity. Reviewing the diversity of religion yields informative ways in which practitioners can better understand individual, couples, and family dynamics. Discussing religious diversity in its entirety is beyond the scope of this chapter. Nevertheless, a brief discussion of the five major religions in the United States and the ethnic diversity within these religions may provide a possible framework from which further investigation can be promoted. As immigration continues to augment the diverse landscape of the American population, a more comprehensive description of various world religions is required. Ethnic and cultural diversity within religious and/or spiritual identification is clearly prominent within the country.

Indeed, religious and spiritual diversity is a pervasive quality for many Americans. In the United States, Fukuyama (2003) states that "there are more than 2,000 religions and spiritual traditions" (p. 189). The Gallup Poll (Lyons, 2005) surveyed the importance of religion in the lives of participants and cited that 55% of Americans, on average, reported religion to be "very important" while another 28% reported religion to be "fairly important." Furthermore, the same Gallup Poll stated that non-whites, women, older adults, lower income individuals, Southerners, lower educated individuals, and Protestants tended to report religion as "very important" in their lives. Approximately two-thirds (66%) of Americans claim to be members of a church, mosque, or synagogue (Lyons, 2005). The American Religious Identification Survey (ARIS; Mayer, Kosmin, & Keysar, 2001) examined religious identification of the adult population within the United States by utilizing a telephone survey. The results included cited that 81% of the adult population identified with a particular religion. Approximately 77% of the population would classify themselves as Christian, a number that has dropped from 86% from 1990. Catholics and Baptists were the largest proportion respectively of this group, which also included a variety of religious affiliations. Meanwhile, non-Christian identification ("Other religion groups") has risen from 5.8 million (3.3%) to 7.7 million (3.7%). The "Other religion groups" included from largest to smallest populations: Jewish, Muslim/Islam, Buddhist, Unitarian/Universalist, Hindu, Native American, Scientologist, Baha'I, Taoist, New Age, and more. According to Mayer et al., 2001, this survey was the first to include a representative sample of the religious identification for Native Americans. Approximately 20% of Native Americans in the survey identified themselves as Baptist, 17% as Catholic, and 17% indicated no religious preference, and 3% indicated a tribal religion (or other). According to Mayer et al., the increase in Asian immigration in the previous two decades has produced a number of individuals who may not speak English. From 1990–2001, the Asian American population who identifies themselves as Christian has decreased from 63% to 43%, while the population identifying themselves as Hindu, Buddhist, Muslim, etc. has increased from 15% to 28%. Mayer et al. cite that the survey statistics may not be entirely representative as the survey was limited to phone interviews with English speaking participants. Furthermore, some respondents may perceive the act of answering questions related to religion on the telephone as risky or alien. Thus, specific differences based in culture may be impacting the religious identification (or lack of) within current surveys. Nevertheless, the changing landscape of religious and ethnic diversity within the United States continues to evolve with an incredible array of identification.

According to the American Religious Identification Survey (ARIS; Mayer, Kosmin, & Keysar, 2001), the ethnicity of the Baptist population in the United States consists of 64% White, 29% Black, 1% Asian, and 3% Hispanic individuals while the ethnicity of the Catholic population in the United States consists of 60% White, 3% Black, 3% Asian, and 29% Hispanic individuals. Mayer et al., 2001 cite Hispanic or Latino individuals are sometimes presumed to identify with the Catholic religion due to many Spanish-speaking countries having Catholicism as the established religion. Mayer et al. cite that 57% of individuals who identified themselves as Hispanic in origin also identified themselves as Catholic and 22% identified themselves as Protestant. Thus, this information seems to indicate that a significant proportion of the largest minority group in the United States includes diverse representation within Christianity.

According to ARIS (2001), the ethnicity of the Jewish population in the United States includes 92% White, 1% Black, 1% Asian, and 5% Hispanic individuals. These statistics are primarily according to religious identification. Mayer et al., 2001 indicate that 53% of the Jewish adult population reported religious identification with Judaism. Meanwhile, the remaining portion of the Jewish adult population (47%) considered themselves as Jewish for alternative reasons, identified being raised Jewish or purported to be of Jewish descent. Furthermore, Mayer et al. suggests that 1.36 million of the 5.3 million Jewish adults are estimated to adhere to a religion other than Judaism. This information seems to indicate that Jewish identification contains tremendously complex issues related to religious and cultural identity. Nevertheless, knowledge of Judaism provides possibilities for understanding cultural and religious implications.

According to ARIS (2001), the ethnicity of the Muslim/Islamic population in the United States consists of individuals who identify as White (15%), Black (27%), Asian (34%), Hispanic (10%), and Other (14%). Meanwhile, according to ARIS (2001), the ethnicity of the Buddhist population in the United States consists of individuals who identify as White (32%), Black (4%), Asian (61%), and Hispanic (2%). Although ARIS (2001) does not report the ethnicity of the Hindu population in the United States, the survey does indicate that there are approximately 766,000 Hindus in the United States. Also, the Hindu population has risen threefold since 1990. Mayer et al., 2001 suggest that the increase in Asian American immigrants seems to have impacted the increase in Asian religions. According to Keller (2000), "It is possible to be a polytheist, a monotheist, or a nontheist and still be a Hindu" (p. 48), so it is difficult to summarize the complexity and diversity within Hinduism.

Overall, the importance of religion in the lives of individuals, couples, and families demonstrates tremendous diversity and identity across ethnic, cultural, gender, generational, developmental, regional, educational, socioeconomic, sociopolitical, historical, and religious/spiritual identification. Of course, contemporary statistics merely represent a portion of ethnic, cultural, and religious diversity within the United States. There are undoubtedly ethnic and religious identifications that are not adequately represented. This information is provided in order to increase knowledge concerning cultural, ethnic, religious, and spiritual diversity represented within the United States. Pedersen (2003) asserts that "By accepting the complexity of culture, it becomes possible to manage more variables efficiently, generate more potential answers to each question, identify contrasting perspectives, tolerate ambiguity more comfortably, and recognize the diversity within each cultural context" (p. 31). Also, this information should demonstrate the necessity of avoiding assumptions based on ethnic identity and religious identity alike. The culturally sensitive and competent practitioner must recognize awareness of personal assumptions *and* knowledge concerning religious and spiritual diversity in order to transcend cultural boundaries and integrate culturally appropriate skills within the therapeutic environment.

Skills Concerning Ethnicity, Culture, and Religion

Transcultural Approach

McFadden (2003a) suggests, "Transcultural counseling theory development may represent another avenue for the interconnectedness between spirituality and psychotherapy" (p. 52). The transcultural practitioner is one who is willing to become familiar with an individual's religious and spiritual foundation within the reciprocal relationship of counselor and client. Through this mode, practitioners smoothly transcend cultural differences by engaging, understanding, and embracing external cultures from intellectual and experiential analysis (McFadden, 2003a). Religious and spiritual identity seems to impact the daily functioning for many individuals as this is a source of coping, meaning, wholeness, and strength. According to Fukuyama and Sevig (1999), "In most cultures, spirituality is not separated from the rest of life. From a holistic perspective, people's psychological well-being is inextricably intertwined with their spiritual well-being" (p. 83). In this manner, healthy spirituality can lead to psychological and spiritual growth. Therefore, attending to the religious identification of an individual may result in the discovery of a valuable resource for marriage and family practitioners. Honoring the cultural and ethnic needs of couples and families includes attending to each individual identity, which often encompasses religion and spirituality. This may lead to the exploration of religious ideals and how they are incorporated within the family system. The transcultural approach promotes an interactive understanding and sensitivity between couples, family members, and practitioners alike.

Stylistic Model

Increasing awareness, knowledge, and skills and integrating this newly discovered potential toward transcultural sensitivity regarding religious and spiritual issues are important; however, accessing this potential within a therapeutic environment is another area of concern. The Stylistic Model (McFadden, 2003b) provides a platform through which awareness, knowledge, and the integration of skills can be identified and utilized in a way that promotes cultural understanding, sensitivity, and growth regarding a variety of cultural issues including religious and spiritual concerns. McFadden (1999) asserts, "The stylistic model for transcultural counseling is introduced, therefore, as one approach to improving cultural understanding and contributing to the counseling profession's quest for focus and efficiency in meeting contemporary challenges" (p. 60).

For the marriage and family practitioner, this model includes essential components that are worthy of therapeutic exploration and provides an opportunity to address and incorporate these religious and spiritual issues within the therapeutic setting. The model is represented by 27 cubicles and is composed of three basic dimensions that include the Cultural-Historical (C-H) dimension, Psychosocial (PS) dimension, and Scientific-Ideological (S-I) dimension (McFadden, 2003b). Therefore, each dimension includes nine possible topics of cultural exploration concerning the development and identification of issues including religious and/or spiritual identity within the couple and/ or family system. Marriage and family practitioners applying this model may move through the cubical descriptors in horizontal, vertical, or diagonal move-ment regardless of cultural issue addressed. Furthermore, it may be necessary to revisit a particular dimension as the needs of the couple and/or family are addressed. However, when using the model, practitioners must remember to begin exploration of cultural issues at the C-H dimension.

The Stylistic Model is grounded in the Cultural-Historical (C-H) dimen-sion. This C-H dimension is the basis from which cultural and ethnic themes are pervasively displayed and derived by the individual, couple, and/or family. This dimension is based on the notion that our cultural background and history are profoundly contributory to the foundation of who we are as unique cultural beings. For instance, religious and spiritual issues within the family system are impacted by variables such as historical migratory patterns and exposure to different ethnic/racial groups. The nine cubicles within this dimension include possible topics of exploration such as *family patterns, value systems, cultural traditions, language patterns, dynamics of oppression, ethnic/racial isolation, leaders and heroes, monocultural memberships,* and *historical movements* (McFadden, 2003b). Each cubicle provides a possible topic of investigation in order for the practitioner to gain insight into the unique cultural identity of the couple and/or family.

For the purposes of this chapter, we will explore religious and spiritual dynamics as they relate to the cultural identity of a particular family who recently emigrated from Trinidad and Tobago. First, when working with this family, some might assume particular religions are common for various ethnic groups. As stated earlier, religious identification within the United States includes complex diversity within and between group affiliations. Also, there seems to be an influx of Asian immigrants and individuals who identify with religions such as Buddhism, Hinduism, and Islam within the United States. The practitioner, aware of this influx, may assume that these immigrants are arriving mainly from Asian nations. This practitioner, working with a family from Trinidad and Tobago, may unwittingly neglect addressing religious diversity of the homeland based on this preconceived notion. They may assume Protestant or Catholic affiliation due to the Caribbean accent. Learning about the native culture may reveal interesting aspects not yet illuminated. Further investigation with this immigrant family may reveal an East Indian heritage and Hindu religious identification. In this event, it is imperative for practitioners to avoid moving therapeutically based on assumptions. Instead, the transcultural practitioner should inquire and learn utilizing the family as a resource in a respectful manner. This is the foundation of the Stylistic Model as it seeks to identify and expose the particular "style" of the couple and/or family system.

The options of exploration are particularly essential in regards to the blending of couples, especially interfaith couples, as these individuals may present very different styles of culture, religion, and spirituality. As the navigation of possible topics within the model is negotiated within the therapeutic environment by the practitioner, the "style" of the practitioner is recognized as well. Thus, the model respects the theoretical orientation, approach, and freedom of the marriage and family practitioner. Furthermore, the model incorporates flexibility as 27 cubicles are offered in order to tailor to the "style" and needs of the individual, couple, and/or family. For instance, the practitioner may first choose to explore the cubicles within the C-H dimension related to *family patterns*, *value systems*, and *cultural traditions* of the couple. In doing so, the practitioner chooses to assess and acknowledge the values, assumptions, and traditions of each individual and how these individual perceptions impact the daily functioning and interactions of the couple. Alternatively, the practitioner may choose to investigate the *dynamics of oppression*, and *racial/ethnic isolation* within the C-H dimension in order to discern any possible formation of cultural identity within the family system in the presence of a dominant culture. For the couple and/or family immigrating to the United States, the practitioner needs to be aware of any possible *dynamics of oppression* and *racial/ethnic isolation* encountered previously within the dominant culture of Trinidad and Tobago that may impact current religious and/or spiritual functioning in the United States.

Exploring cultural and historical responses to these dynamics may provide information concerning the formation of religiously and spiritually adaptive beliefs, practices, assumptions, and behaviors in the presence of a dominant culture. For example, the family may reveal that *racial/ethnic isolation* is somewhat common in the homeland and that Christians and Catholics comprise the majority of the population; however, they may feel that this is somewhat due to historical migratory patterns of slaves and laborers to the islands. According to the family, historical settlements tended to concentrate according to mills and plantations where larger groups of Hindu families may be encountered today. Concerning *dynamics of oppression*, family members may report that Hindus were not historically allowed to congregate in temples or holy places. Instead, comfort, support, and identity were sought through the solidification of their belief system, which included inherently spiritual social interactions, rituals, and celebrations with the family. Furthermore, the interdependence and interconnectedness of the family included nuclear and extended family members. In essence, it may be that the spirituality demonstrated through rituals within the family system historically served as an adaptive form of protective resistance to the dominant culture. As a result, the societal, familial, and personal interaction may be influenced by this spiritual element, which in turn remains a critical factor concerning the development of familial interdependence, interconnectedness, and cultural identity. Here, the insight afforded by the family has revealed yet another critical element within the C-H dimension concerning *value systems*. *Values systems* related to the interdependence and unity of the family seem to be demonstrated organically through religious and spiritual practices. Indeed, scholars support the notion that religious obligations are performed through many Hindu families and are connected to the family life of Hindus (Hodge, 2004; Sharma, 2000). After discovering this crucial element of spirituality concerning the retention of familial stability and cultural identity, it is necessary for the family practitioner to explore the implications of issues within the Psychosocial (PS) dimension.

The second dimension, the Psychosocial (PS) dimension, focuses on how our social interactions and psychological responses are intertwined with our cultural base. Here, the practitioner, couple, and/or family begin to connect how social interactions and psychological responses are inextricably related to issues of culture, ethnicity, religion, and spirituality. The nine cubicles within the PS dimension include *human dignity, perception of others, self-development, personality formation, social forces, mind building, ethnic/racial identity, psychological security,* and *self-inspection* (McFadden, 2003b). In continuing with the example family, the practitioner discovered through careful inspection and discourse that familial *ethnic/racial identity* includes religious and/or spirituality as a bonding element for the tightly knit family system. The *value system* related to interdependence and unity of the family contributes to *ethnic/racial identity*. In this manner, the family's responses to having *value systems* of familial interdependence and interconnectedness, based in religious and spiritual identity, influence social interactions and psychological responses.

Now, the practitioner can access the current perceptions of family members concerning their *ethnic/racial identity* in their homeland versus the United States. By attending to the cubicle related to *ethnic/racial identity*, the practitioner can glean implications concerning the family's interactions and experiences with Hindus and/or other denominations. For instance, despite the tendency of historical ethnic isolation, family members report celebrations of diversity and a sense of collectivity as essential qualities displayed within the culture of Trinidad and Tobago, especially related to religious diversity. Members of the family may reveal that they do not feel this same sense of collectivity within the United States. It seems that the *value system* related to collectivity extends beyond the family system as a more extensive sense of interconnectedness may be related to spiritual elements within the family system. Upon further investigation, they may feel thwarted in their religious and spiritual expressions due to the loss of extended family members who were integrally involved with the family system. These family members were not able to furnish the resources to move. As a result, the immigrant family may be experiencing conflicting stress and guilt regarding their decision to move while feeling a sense of selfless responsibility regarding the desire to increase the educational opportunities for the children. Furthermore, the family realizes that resources, networks, and support systems concerning cultural and religious and/or spiritual identity is diminished as fellow Hindus are rarely encountered in their new city. Thus, it seems that the spiritual expression of family connectedness and interdependence is constrained as support systems are somewhat different and limited for the family. An implication of having this sense of loss may result in the elder family members seeking solidarity in the family unit through religious/spiritual practices that bond the family unit. Furthermore, issues related to beliefs, assumptions, expectations, and traditions of gender roles within the family may be uniquely defined and increasingly restricted by the couple. Meanwhile, younger members of the family may clash with certain familial religious/spiritual practices as they seek assimilation and enculturation in the highly Westernized culture. In this event, friction in the tightly knit family system may impact expectations, behaviors, and relationships concerning religious/spiritual responsibilities within the family system. Individual roles may change and overcompensate as the family system seeks realignment.

Regardless of the insight illuminated by the family, the marriage and family practitioner needs to understand the cultural and historical roots supporting current family expectations, attitudes, assumptions, and daily interactions. Centuries of displacement from an original destination may have contributed to a unique expression of cultural traditions, practices, and relationships regarding Hinduism displayed in Trinidad and Tobago. Attending to the uniqueness of this expression is a vital aspect within the process of effectively engaging this Hindu family. Subsequently, attending to the developmental, gender, generational, social, historical, and intellectual context of the individuals within the family system is important. Cultural history, language, identity, and experiences will vary in meaning and expression concerning religion and/or spiritual issues. A practitioner may choose to revisit the C-H dimension in order to explore possible topics such as *family patterns, cultural traditions, language patterns,* and *historical movements.* Afterward, the PS dimension provides the opportunity for the practitioner to assist family members to discover possible patterns, thoughts, expectations, and behaviors that may have been influenced by cultural themes and later solidified into an evident framework from which the family functions. In doing so, the family may be ready to move toward an increasingly active stage.

The Scientific-Ideological (S-I) is the final dimension of the model. This dimension combines all information that has been gained regarding the cultural, ethnic, religious, and spiritual identity of individuals, couples, and family members. This dimension allows clients to move from basic knowledge and assessment to a working plan. In this manner, awareness, knowledge, and skills that one gains regarding implications of culture on lifestyle can be converted into action. Here, the couple and/or family unit may find strength in acknowledging the culmination of many patterns and the possibility of being malleable in order to meet expectations and goals of the family unit while recognizing and honoring cultural, religious, and spiritual aspects of each individual. This dimension includes the nine cubical descriptors such as *economic potency, relevant programs, institutional goals, meaningful alternatives, media influences, politics, ethnic/racial relations, logic-behavioral chains,* and *individual goals* (McFadden, 2003b). Again, the practitioner is able to choose from possible topics in order to explore possible plans for the couple and/or family unit.

Within this dimension, the practitioner may assist the couple and/or family in moving from identification and connection of cultural, ethnic, religious, and spiritual themes to an action-oriented plan rich with strategies that encompass a more adaptive lifestyle. For instance, *meaningful alternatives* and *individual goals* may include elements related to the language and meaning of the couple and/or family system that is based on a particular religious and/or spiritual realm. The language and meaning undoubtedly will be uniquely based on the cultural context of the couple and/or family. For the marriage and family practitioner, the possible participation of the entire family in counseling may be emphasized as the centrality of the family unit for Hindu families is common (Hodge, 2004; Sharma, 2000). Investigating the cubicle of *meaningful alternatives* identified within this dimension, the practitioner may explore possibilities and traditions that family members prefer to share and promote within the family. Discovering *meaningful alternatives* concerning religious/spiritual practices, identification of religious/spiritual support systems, and clarification of religious/spiritual identity can be addressed. For this Trinidadian family, recognizing *meaningful alternatives* concerning the nuclear and extended family may be critical as the familial kinship may be solidified through religious/spiritual identity. However, the cubicle of *individual goals* may be included as specific roles, expectations, and behaviors concerning religious/spiritual practices are discerned. When working in a spiritually sensitive manner with Hindu clients, Hodge (2004) suggests that interventions should balance autonomy and interdependence as the centrality of the family unit is embraced. Overall, the discovery of patterns, traditions, beliefs, perceptions, and behaviors related to ethnicity, culture, and religious/spiritual issues allows the practitioner and clients to work in a collaborative manner that enhances the therapeutic process in a transcultural manner.

SUMMARY

As the counseling progression encounters an inevitably and pervasively diverse population, the necessity for attending to the ethnic and cultural dimensions is unequivocally crucial in regards to religious and spiritual diversity. Increasing personal awareness, fundamental knowledge, and culturally sensitive application of skills is integral to this cultural sensitivity. The culmination of intellectual and experiential analysis in a transculturally sensitive manner allows the marriage and family practitioner to better understand themselves and the client population in a more competent and effective manner. The Stylistic Model provides an opportunity to attend to various areas of concentration within the Cultural-Historical, Psychosocial, and Scientific-Ideological dimensions as they relate to the religious and spiritual identity of the couple and/or family. The transcultural practitioner enhances, therefore, the therapeutic process and heightens the potential for sensitivity concerning cultural awareness, knowledge, skills, and the religious/spiritual identity of the couple and/or family.

REFERENCES

American Counseling Association (2005). *Code of ethics*. Alexandria, VA.

American Psychological Association (2002). *Ethical principles of psychologists and code of conduct*. Washington, DC.

Bergin, A. E., Payne, I. R., & Richards, P. S. (1996). Values in psychotherapy. In E. P. Shafranske (Ed.), *Religion and the clinical practice of psychology* (pp. 297–325). Washington, DC: American Psychological Association.

Bishop, D. R. (1992). Religious values as cross-cultural issues in counseling. *Counseling and Values, 36*, 179–191.

Cashwell, C. S. (2005). Spirituality and wellness. In J. E. Myers and T. J. Sweeney (Eds.), *Counseling for wellness: Theory, research, and practice* (pp. 197–205). Alexandria, VA: American Counseling Association.

Cashwell, C. S., & Young, J. S. (2005). *Integrating spirituality in counseling: A guide to competent practice*. Alexandria, VA: American Counseling Association.

Emmons, R. A. (1999). Religion in the psychology of personality: An introduction. *Journal of Personality, 67*, 873–888.

Freud, S. (1939). *Moses and monotheism*. New York: Alfred A. Knopf.

Fukuyama, M. A. (2003). Integrating spirituality in multicultural counseling: "A worldview." In F. D. Harper & J. McFadden (Eds.), *Culture and counseling: New approaches* (pp. 186–195). Boston: Pearson Education.

Fukuyama, M. A., & Sevig, T. D. (1999). *Integrating spirituality into multicultural counseling*. Thousand Oaks, CA: Sage Publications.

Georgia, R. T. (1994). Preparing to counsel clients of different religious backgrounds: A phenomenological approach. *Counseling & Values, 38,* 143–151.

Hodge, D. R. (2004). Working with Hindu clients in a spiritually sensitive manner. *Social Work, 49,* 27–38.

Ingersoll, R. E. (1994). Spirituality, religion, and counseling: Dimensions and relationships. *Counseling and Values, 38,* 98–111.

Keller, R. R. (2000). Religious diversity in North America. In P. S. Richards & A. E. Bergin (Eds.), *Handbook of psychotherapy and religious diversity* (pp. 27–55). Washington, DC: American Psychological Association.

Lyons, L. (2005). Faith accompanies most Americans through life. *Gallup Poll News Service*. Retrieved November 12, 2005, from http://poll.gallup.com/content/default .aspx?ci= 16522&VERSION=p

Mayer, E., Kosmin, B. A., & Keysar, A. (2001). *American Religious Identification Survey*. Retrieved November 2, 2005, from http://www.gc.cuny.edu/studies/aris_index. htm

McFadden, J. (Ed.) (1999). *Transcultural counseling* (2nd ed.). Alexandria, VA: American Counseling Association.

McFadden, J. (2003a). Transcultural counseling theory development through the liberal arts. In F.D. Harper & J. McFadden (Eds.). *Culture and counseling: New approaches* (pp. 47–65). Boston, MA: Pearson Education.

McFadden, J. (2003b). Stylistic model for counseling across cultures. In F. D. Harper & J. McFadden (Eds.), *Culture and counseling: New approaches* (pp. 209–232). Boston: Pearson Education.

McGoldrick, M., & Giordano, J. (1996). Overview: Ethnicity and family therapy. In M. McGoldrick, J. Giordano, & J. K. Pearce (Eds.), *Ethnicity and family therapy* (2nd ed., pp. 1–27). New York: Guilford Press.

McGoldrick, M., Giordano, J., & Pearce, J. K. (1996). *Ethnicity and family therapy* (2nd ed.). New York: Guilford Press.

Pedersen, P. B. (2003). Increasing the cultural awareness, knowledge, and skills of culture-centered counselors. In F. D. Harper & J. McFadden (Eds.), *Culture and counseling: New approaches* (pp. 31–46). Boston: Pearson Education.

Richards, P. S., & Bergin, A. E. (1997). *A spiritual strategy for counseling and psychotherapy*. Washington, DC: American Psychological Association.

Richards, P. S., & Bergin, A. E. (2000). *Handbook of psychotherapy and religious diversity*. Washington, DC: American Psychological Association.

Richards, P. S., Keller, R. R., & Smith, T. B. (2004). Religious and spiritual diversity in counseling and psychotherapy. In T. B. Smith (Ed.), *Practicing multiculturalism: Affirming diversity in counseling and psychology*. (pp. 276–293). Boston: Pearson Education.

Ridley, C. R., & Thompson, C. E. (1999). Managing resistance to diversity training: A social systems perspective. In M. S. Kiselica (Ed.), *Confronting prejudice & racism during multicultural training* (pp. 3–24). Alexandria, VA: American Counseling Association.

Shafranske, E. P. (1996). Introduction: Foundation for the consideration of religion in the clinical practice of psychology. In E. P. Shafranske (Ed.), *Religion and the clinical practice of psychology* (pp. 2–17). Washington, DC: American Psychological Association.

Shafranske, E. P., & Maloney, (1996). Religion and the clinical practice of psychology: A case for inclusion. In E. P. Shafranske (Ed.), *Religion and the clinical practice of psychology* (pp. 561–586). Washington, DC: American Psychological Association.

Sharma, A. R. (2000). Psychotherapy with Hindus. In P. S. Richards & A. E. Bergin (Eds.), *Handbook of psychotherapy and religious diversity* (pp. 341–365). Washington, DC: American Psychological Association.

Sue, D. W., Arredondo, P., & McDavis, R. J. (1992). Multicultural counseling competencies: A call to the profession. *Journal of Counseling and Development, 70,* 477–486.

Wiggins-Frame, M. (2005). Spirituality and religion: Similarities and differences. In C. S. Cashwell & S. Young (Eds.), *Integrating spirituality and religion into counseling: A guide to competent practice* (pp. 11–29). Alexandria, VA: American Counseling Association.

Winseman, A. L. (2005). Does congregation membership imply spiritual commitment? *Gallup Poll News Service.* Retrieved November 12, 2005, from http://poll .gallup.com/content/ default.aspx?ci=17749&VERSION=p

Collaboration Between Licensed Mental Health Professionals and Religious Leaders

JILL D. ONEDERA, NERESA MINATREA, AARON KINDSVATTER

Under the constraints of time and hectic schedules, collaborative efforts between licensed mental health professionals (LMHPs) and religious leaders might be more about wishful thinking than something that can actually occur. In addition, the history of this relationship is one that has often been strained, specifically because of the hostility that some individuals within the helping profession have expressed toward others in the religious community. For instance, religious leaders have expressed concern about some mental health professionals who have undermined their faith perspective, as well as the persons being referred to them (Mannon & Crawford, 1996). Literature also suggests that some particular theoretical perspectives are antithetical to religious beliefs and practice, namely psychoanalytic theory (Oppenheimer, Flannelly, & Weaver, 2004).

The effects of this relationship tension may be illustrated in the trends of who religious persons seek emotional support from. Many religiously committed persons needing emotional support actually go to their pastoral counselor versus a mental health professional (Kanz, 2001). In fact, clergy are considered to be at the forefront of mental health providers (Gallup & Lindsay, 1999; Moran et al., 2005). There is reason to believe that clergy are being sought out for reasons other than those related to the relationship strain among clergy and LMHPs. First, persons seeking help might believe that their struggle is a spiritual based one rather than a psychological one. If this is the case, religious leaders or pastoral counselors are more likely to follow suit with a religiously laden intervention such as prayer and reliance on biblical scripture.

A second reason why many persons seek help from religious leaders (or clergy) is because they may not trust the motives of secular counselors. Unfortunately, reason for such apprehension is warranted. Secular counselors who have not been sensitive or trained to address religious and spiritual issues might have unintentionally or intentionally disregarded or placed little emphasis on clients' religious values or the religious context of the present problem (Burke, Hackney, Hudson, & Miranti, 1999; Plante, 2003). Disregarding this essential part of clients' lives has left persons weary of seeking help from traditional counselors.

A third reason why persons may be seeking emotional and mental help from religious leaders and/or clergy instead is because LMHPs are simply not reaching out to them. That is, LMHPs have not been doing much in the order of challenging their insulted past or advocating for how they might be able to help religious clients. Perhaps this is due to a lack of incentives for professionals to work with religious clients. A limited training background in religious and spiritual issues in counseling has put LMHPs in a place where they do not have adequate awareness, skills, and knowledge bases about particular religious groups and how to work with clients affiliated with those groups (Burke et al., 1999; Pate & Bondi, 1992). To be able to work effectively with religious clients means effort and work. The question at hand is, are LMHPs up to the challenge?

There is no longer an excuse for limitations in training or knowledge on the part of mental health professionals. It is very clear that religion plays a very important role in the lives of many Americans. In fact, according to a study by Gallup and Lindsey (1999), approximately nine in ten American adults pray to God at least occasionally. Further, about half of all Americans reported that they attend a church, temple, or mosque at least once a week. If this is the case, then it might be assumed that half of any given mental health professional's clientele is affiliated with a particular religious institution and is living a life accordingly. Furthermore, mental health professionals are ethically bound to be competent in exploring and working with clients from these various faith backgrounds. Religious beliefs in a holistic context is well documented across the various professional fields (Aten, 2004; Fallot, 2001; Getz, Kirk, & Driscoll, 1999; McMinn, 1996; Wells, 1993). Licensed mental health professionals do not have a choice; they *must* be up to the challenge of working towards increasing their knowledge, skill and awareness in working with religiously-oriented clients.

There are many ways for mental health professionals to become competent in working with persons from particular religious orientations. Seeking out information through workshops, consultation with colleagues, enrolling in a religious and spirituality counseling course, and reading literature in the area can enhance a professional's expertise. Perusing books such as this one may be helpful in providing LMHPs with a knowledge base. However, sometimes this type of information does not address the unique client situations that professionals will face. It is simply not enough. In such cases, collaborating with religious leaders is an indispensable resource. Not surprisingly, there is a good deal of support for this sort of consultation based, collaborative relationship with clergy and spiritual directors (Faiver, O'Brien, & McNally, 1998; Moran et al., 2005; O'Connor, 2002).

Not only do collaboration efforts benefit LMHPs; pastoral counselors and clergy benefit as well. For example, LMHPs can provide clergy with information regarding mental health, health, and social services that could benefit their parishioners. In addition, LMHPs might help clergy understand families better by sharing their knowledge about family systems. Further, in the case of more serious mental health issues, LMHPs can partner with clergy in order to gain additional information about individuals in order to effectively provide a wider scope of assessment, intervention, and treatment options for them. Trained mental health professionals can apply their training to identify serious mental health diagnosis, while also serving as a link to appropriate service and resources for such individuals and families.

When mental health professionals take time to develop a working relationship with religious leaders who can serve as resources for information on religious beliefs and practices, the clients benefit the most. The combination of varying training backgrounds and orientations is wrought with possibility, especially as it pertains to strengthening and enhancing the mental, emotional, and spiritual health of individuals and communities (O'Connor, 2002; Oppenheimer et al., 2002; Pate & Bondi, 1995). For the purpose of keeping a specific focus, this chapter will focus on the role of mental health professionals in this collaborative effort. The authors will address the ways in which collaboration can enhance the scope of practice among mental health professionals. In addition, the benefits as well as the challenges of this working relationship will be addressed in more detail. Finally, the authors will provide specific suggestions regarding how such collaboration might be cultivated.

THE COLLABORATIVE RELATIONSHIP: WHAT CAN HAPPEN

Collaborative efforts might occur in different contexts including but not limited to mental health treatment settings, community outreach, and in parish life (Oppenheimer et al., 2004). The authors will briefly discuss the former two contexts and what mental health professionals can do in working toward establishing such a collaborative in these specific areas.

Mental Health Treatment

Mental health professionals are called not only by their ethical codes but also by recent research to be sensitive to the possibility of a religious dimension in their clients' presenting problem and recovery. With a lack of training, they may not be prepared to fully integrate this responsibility into practice. This gap in training and skill actually provides a window of opportunity, however, for a collaborative relationship between a mental health professional and a religious leader. For example, in the case of a religious client who is expressing symptoms of a psychological disorder, the mental health professional might first consult with a religious leader representative of the client's religious affiliation in order to conceptualize the symptoms in a religious context. Collaborated efforts in such cases might include inviting the religious leader in the therapy session as a religious consultant or as a member of a reflecting team.

Collaboration in a mental health treatment context can go beyond working with any individual client. Religious leaders in the community may be asked to speak at weekly group team supervision meetings at various counseling agencies. Such leaders might be asked to provide information that could be helpful in assessment proceedings, as well as better understanding clients from particular religious affiliations. Just as there is a consulting psychiatrist at mental health agencies, efforts can be made to establish such a working relationship with various religious leaders.

Assessment and Intake Information

In the case of assessment, for example, mental health professionals should already be seeking information regarding the following during the intake process: (a) importance of religious faith in their lives; (b) how their faith has impacted their lives in the past and in the present; (c) their affiliation and/or activity with a religious or spiritual community; (d) if there are any spiritual or religious needs that they would like to address in counseling (Koenig & Pritchett, 1998); and (e) possible religious leaders that might serve as religious consultants in the process of therapy. However, religious experts can provide LMHPs with a broader religious context of possible client variables.

Client Goals and Treatment Plans

Religious leaders can be asked to speak on behalf of their affiliated theology as "representatives" of the varying religious affiliations of clients being seen in the agency. Leaders can be asked to talk about the basic tenets and belief systems that might guide how clients live their lives. Furthermore, such leaders provide mental health providers with information that might be relevant to individual treatment plans, as well as how religious beliefs might play out in a family system.

Interventions Strategies

According to the Association of Multicultural and Development competencies (Arredondo et al., 1996), counselors should be aware of and skilled in using particular interventions appropriate for any given client's culture. Exercising sensitivity in providing interventions with religious clients is no exception. Having connections with religious leaders provides LMHPs efficient access to information about relevant biblical references, as well as self-help resources that might serve clients best.

According to the literature, the incorporation of biblical references in the counseling process can be very helpful (Woodruff, 2002). However, in order to incorporate biblical scripture into the counseling process, mental health professionals must have an understanding of their clients' religious background, as well as a clear grasp on how the Bible is interpreted within the context of that religious orientation. Relationships already established with a Baptist minister in town, for example, will make it an uncomplicated and understood task for a mental health professional to make a phone consultation with this religious leader. For example, information can be gained quickly and efficiently regarding how this particular Baptist client is interpreting certain passages of the Bible and what the impact of such interpretations might be on this client's personal development. Furthermore, a collaborative effort requested by and helpful to the client might result in the inclusion of the religious leader in the session through speakerphone.

Another result of a collaborative relationship with religious leaders might be ongoing and updated lists of self-help books for clients practicing any given religion. According to the literature, the majority of professional counselors, marriage and family therapists, and psychologists use self-help books in their practice (Johnson & Johnson, 1998; McMahan, 2002). In addition, clients seem to be very satisfied with such resources. Self-help books can provide guidance to clients in areas where their counselors are unfamiliar. They can be used as a springboard for discussion in counseling, thus providing a gateway for better understanding among their counselors. In order to incorporate or suggest relevant and appropriate self-help books for religious clients, counselors are behooved to consult with religious experts on appropriate books.

These are just two examples of resources that can be used when working with clients from particular religious orientations. Mental health professionals can continue to build upon their intervention strategies by collaborating with religious leaders whom they have made contact with before or persons whom have been recommended by their clients. From the beginning of the counseling relationship, mental health professionals should exercise an open attitude about consulting religious leaders on possible intervention strategies if needed at any time during the process.

Addressing Religion in Cultural Practice: A Community Phenomena

Various authors have suggested that religion is an integral part of certain ethnic identities (Pate & Bondi, 1995). In order to connect the two, mental health professionals might consider making efforts to move beyond literature and make contact and conversation with a religious leader engaged in that particular culture and ethnic group. Consider the Native American culture. First, literature suggests that Native Americans underutilize mental health services (Trimble & Thurman, 2002). One reason may be related to the lack of knowledge and awareness that mental health professionals have about the rich practice of spirituality in the lives of many Native Americans. In order to challenge this lack of sensitivity on the part of mental health professionals, collaborative efforts might be made with Native American spiritual leaders. Such a relationship might be helpful in providing counselors with the awareness, knowledge, and skill that they need to work effectively with Native American clients throughout the therapeutic relationship (Olson, 2003). In addition, such collaborative efforts might provide the groundwork for making traditional counseling something that Native Americans could find useful and helpful. Finally, collaborative efforts might materialize into a relationship among a Native American religious leader, the mental health professional, and the client so as to found a helping relationship on trust and on a concerted effort to meet the client where he or she *really* is.

Religious leaders in the African American culture also should be key contacts among mental health professionals working in a predominantly African American community (Moore, 2003). Collaborative efforts might result in social action in the form of psychoeducational workshops, creating youth organizations, and working with school leaders in enhancing their knowledge of mental health resources in the community. The help and support of church leaders within African American communities can provide mental health professionals with the resources to make a difference in the lives of their clients, but also at the larger system level.

Interventions With Couples and Families

As noted in the previous chapters, religious beliefs provide a structure in which to understand how marriages and families work and deal with crisis or normal developmental issues. Many couples and families come to counselors when they are already unhappy or unhopeful. Perhaps, mental health professionals should take the initiative and address this pattern *before* these couples and families come to their office. Establishing contacts with leaders of community churches might provide them with the opportunity to do psychoeducational workshops on couples communication, parent education, and/or providing family support groups. In exchange for such services, religious leaders can be asked to serve as the "religious consultant" for the counseling agency or licensed professional.

Community Service Activities

In many mental health training programs, students are required to engage in a community service project (Aten, 2004). Such projects may involve a student making a concerted effort in establishing a relationship with a religious leader in the community. The initiation of this relationship might involve educating the religious leader on what and how mental health services are helping people in the community. In addition, the religious leader might be invited to serve as a consultant for the training program. Mental health community centers also might work toward the same collaborative relationship. Such centers might sponsor workshops for religious leaders in the community regarding the mental health services and resources that are available if such leaders (or clergy) need referrals.

The above mentioned collaborative efforts in no way exhaust the possibilities of what such relationships can manifest. Readers are encouraged to consider efforts that would be suitable in their settings and communities.

STEPS TOWARD INCREASING COLLABORATION BETWEEN RELIGIOUS LEADERS AND LICENSED MENTAL HEALTH PROFESSIONALS

The aforementioned addresses the possibilities regarding partnership efforts between religious leaders and mental health providers. The following section proposes specific direction for facilitating collaboration efforts between mental health professionals and faith communities. The listing is divided into three categories: (1) Licensed Mental Health Professionals, (2) Religious Leaders, and (3) Mental Health Consumers; while extensive, these items are not meant to be inclusive, only a catalyst for new ideas.

Licensed Mental Health Professionals

1. Compile a list of mental health organizations with contact numbers and services
2. Complete a practicum/internship with a local religious organization (e.g., religious school for children and adolescents, camp, refugee center, hospital) (Aten, 2004)
3. Conduct special screenings during state or national awareness times (e.g., depression, alcohol, anxiety, career, stress) for religious congregation(s)
4. Create a community-wide board of mental professionals and representation of religious leaders ensuring religious, spiritual, and ethnic diversity
   a. Assess and meet community needs (homeless, food, crisis, etc.)
   b. Identify mental health and religious/spiritual roles (Getz et al., 1999; Oppenheimer et al., 2004)
5. Facilitate a support group for a local religious organization (e.g., caring for children with physical and mental challenges, divorce, grief, living with chronic illnesses)
6. Formulate with community religious leaders a listing of self-help books addressing developmental, relationship, and/or mental health concerns (Johnson & Johnson, 1998)

7. Free admission or registration for religious leaders to regional, state, national conference (conduct a drawing of a limited number to attend the conference)

8. Increase learning and awareness of various religious values and beliefs:
   a. Attend community religious events outside the mental health providers own religious or spiritual preferences (Fallot, 2001; Olson, 2003; Oppenheimer et al., 2004)
   b. Attend different religious events within the community (Fallot, 2001; Olson, 2003; Oppenheimer et al., 2004)
   c. Interview local religious leaders (Fallot, 2001; Oppenheimer et al., 2004)
   d. Participate in a training focusing upon a specific religious and spiritual rituals or belief (Fallot, 2001; Getz et al., 1999; McMinn, Meek, Canning, & Pozzi, 2001; Olson, 2003; Oppenheimer et al., 2004)

9. Invite religious leaders to serve on boards and committees involving mental health issues (Moran et al., 2005)

10. Make available counseling services
    a. Consultation (contract for # of times)
    b. Crisis counseling (contract for # of times)
    c. Counseling session for a client and/or family (contract for a number one or two)
    d. Facilitate a group counseling session (one or more times) on a specific topic or concern (Fallot, 2001)
    e. Co-lead a group with a religious professional

11. Offer invitations and opportunities for visiting local community mental health agencies and hospitals (Moran et al., 2005)

12. Provide a counseling service during children and youth camps

13. Send a representative(s) to regional, state, or national religious conferences (Oppenheimer et al., 2004)

14. Implement a committee of community leaders (mental health, religious, hospital, police, fire, etc.) to formulate a crisis plan for the community

15. Workshops and seminars
    a. Request a list of physical and mental health issues as topics for future workshops or seminars
    b. Offer training for religious leaders
       i. Assessing, referring, and community resources (Oppenheimer et al., 2004)
       ii. Risk assessment (suicide) (Oppenheimer et al., 2004)
    c. Present workshops on special topics for a specific age group, crisis, developmental, or gender for religious and spiritual affiliations and their members

      i. Communication skills
     ii. Coping with children or adolescents
   iii. Career
   iv. Forgiveness
    v. Grief (Olson, 2003)
   vi. New parent
  vii. Parenting
 viii. Premarital
   ix. Prenatal
    x. Retirement
   xi. Self-care
  xii. Sexuality
 xiii. Spiritual self-worth
 xiv. Stress
  xv. Substance abuse and addictions
 xvi. Widowed
  d. Facilitate weekend retreats

Religious Leaders

1. Attend workshops on assessment and referrals to mental health professionals (Oppenheimer et al., 2004)
2. Compile a list of religious/spiritual organizations with contact numbers and services (Oppenheimer et al., 2004)
3. Complete religious internship with a local entity serving mental health consumers (e.g., college, group home, hospital, community based clinic, emergency room, university) (Aten, 2004; Oppenheimer et al., 2004)
4. Conduct trainings at regional and state mental health meetings and conferences (Fallot, 2001; Oppenheimer et al., 2004)
5. Construct with community mental health professionals a listing of self-help books addressing developmental, relationship, and/or mental health concerns (Johnson & Johnson, 1998)
6. Identify ways mental health professional can augment religious/spiritual services (Oppenheimer et al., 2004)
7. Lead or co-lead a group with a licensed mental health profession for individuals with mental health disorders focusing upon spirituality (Fallot, 2001)
8. Make available a spiritual advisor for yearly camps or events targeting individuals with mental chronic or severe illness (Oppenheimer et al., 2004)
9. Offer consultation to mental health practitioners
10. Participate in home visits periodically with the mental health team (Oppenheimer et al., 2004)

11. Present as a guest lecturer at a college or university discussing their area of expertise (Oppenheimer et al., 2004)
12. Provide discussion groups or trainings focusing upon various religious/spiritual philosophies (Oppenheimer et al., 2004)
13. Sit on boards of local agencies, hospitals, and programs focusing upon mental health issues (Moran et al., 2005; Oppenheimer et al., 2004)
14. Visit local agencies, group homes, hospitals providing services for individuals with mental health concerns (Moran et al., 2005; Oppenheimer et al., 2004)

Mental Health Consumers

1. Encourage and make available for individuals within mental health group homes, day care facilities, and residential centers to attend various religious and spiritual events (Oppenheimer et al., 2004)
2. Participate in a multi-religious/spiritual event increasing awareness of various practices (Oppenheimer et al., 2004)

BENEFITS AND CHALLENGES OF COLLABORATIVE RELATIONSHIPS AMONG LICENSED MENTAL HEALTH PROFESSIONALS AND RELIGIOUS LEADERS

Religious and mental health leaders fostering religious-cultural empathy through joint ventures will obtain many advantages such as enhancing the quality of life for a larger number in the community. Collaboration between religious leaders and LMHPs also facilitates the possibility of clients receiving more out of the services provided by both professions. As clients receive integrated services, there is the possibility for more comprehensive problem resolution, and therefore the potential for clients to live fuller lives. Yet, the process of collaboration between LMHPs and religious leaders is not without some tribulations. This section will explore both the benefits and the dilemmas associated with collaboration between LMHPs and religious leaders (Chung & Bemak, 2002; Getz et al., 1999; Moran et al., 2005; Olson, 2003; Oppenheimer et al., 2004).

Therapeutic Change

One need only consult counseling outcome data to understand the importance of the collaboration between LMHPs and religious leaders. The importance of LMHPs being able to engage in informed conversation with clients about their religious activities, and the inclusion of those activities in the context in counseling, is a concept that counseling outcome data would seem to support. For religious clients, religious ideals and constructs often play a significant role in the facilitation of therapeutic change. This is because factors related to clients strengths, resources, and ideas contribute so considerably to therapeutic change processes.

Assay and Lambert (1999) reported that positive counseling outcomes are attributable to four factors, referred to as the common factors of therapeutic change. These four common factors include client factors (accounting for 40% of therapeutic change), therapeutic alliance factors (accounting for 30% of therapeutic change), hope and expectancy (accounting for 15% of change), and model or technique factors (accounting for 15% of change).

Client factors are the most sizable contributor to therapeutic change. Client factors include those attributes, strengths, and resources that a client possesses when he or she presents for counseling. For religious clients these factors might include faith, regularly scheduled religious activities, inspirational stories, and membership in a caring religious community. Indeed Walters and Neugeboren (1995) noted that the involvement of mental health clients in religious communities provides multiple beneficial opportunities. Involvement in such activities allows for clients to socialize in and contribute to a community, while they avoid pitfalls to mental health such as isolation or boredom. These opportunities include the chance for increased socialization, decreased stigmatization, and the creation and enhancement of social networks. These opportunities (such as taking part in Bible studies or teaching in Sunday school) might constitute nonclinical interventions, the opportunities for which LMHPs should be aware of. Through collaboration with religious leaders, LMHPs may also be better able to recognize, understand, and utilize stories, values, and traditions that have meaning in religious client's lives, and that help them to persevere in the face of mental illness.

The therapeutic alliance is a sizable contributor to therapeutic change. The therapeutic alliance was defined by Bordin (1979) as an *agreement* between the client and the counselor on the goals and tasks of counseling within the context of a trusting and mutually respectful relationship. The concept of agreement is central to the formation of a helpful therapeutic alliance. If the client does not "buy into" the topics and process of counseling, it is unlikely that therapy will produce meaningful change. Moreover, research has demonstrated that it is the *client's* perceptions of whether an alliance is helpful that is most closely associated with positive therapeutic change, over the perceptions of the counselor (Horvath & Symonds, 1991).

In order for counselors to facilitate agreement with clients, they must be able to understand and appreciate important meanings in clients' lives. For religious clients these meanings would likely include spiritual themes. Religious leaders constitute a valuable source of information for counselors. Collaboration between counselors and religious leaders can assist counselors in understanding the importance and relevance of religious client's spiritual ideas as avenues to change. Such understandings would assist counselors in integrating these ideas into the counseling process, thus strengthening the therapeutic alliance, and increasing the likelihood of positive therapeutic outcomes for religious clients.

Hope contributes about as much to therapeutic change as do models and techniques of counseling. While models and techniques of counseling facilitate change by bringing structure and novelty to the counseling process (Hubble, Duncan, & Miller, 1999), hope contributes to clients' expectations for a more preferred future. We might consider hope as consisting of *pathways* hope and *agency* hope; that is a client's belief in a "road" to change (a series of actions steps likely to produce change), and a client's belief in his or her personal ability to engage in change (Snyder, Michael, & Cheavens, 1999).

As with the therapeutic alliance, religious clients may have spiritual elements to their lives and psyche that promote and enhance pathways and agency hope. Involvement in religious practices and communities provides counseling clients with many avenues to hope in times of psychological distress. For example, religious rituals and scripture are often designed as a means whereby a pathway to change is provided or indicated. Similarly, one's spiritual identity (i.e., as a Christian, Jew, Muslim, etc.), bolstered by inspirational religious mythology, may provide a means whereby one may find the strength (personal agency) to engage in difficult changes.

Pathways and agency hope provide potential sources of strength for religious clients that allow them to persevere in times of crisis or hardship. The more that these elements of hope can be intentionally utilized in counseling, the more counseling can be of benefit to the client. Thus, counselors can be aided in their endeavors to help religious clients through collaboration with religious leaders who are able to enlighten them as to the significance, meanings, and availability of religious materials and practices that provide a fertile ground for the cultivation of hope.

Benefits for Religious Leaders

Just as LMHPs can benefit from collaboration with religious leaders, religious leaders can benefit from collaboration with LMHPs. The roles of religious leaders in the lives of those they serve are multifaceted. Pastors and their parishioners often relate to each other in a variety of roles in carrying out the social and business functions of their churches.

Difficulties may arise when religious leaders are required to take on roles that entail in-depth counseling with parishioners with whom they are involved in duel relationships. Difficulties that arise from duel or multifaceted counseling relationships between pastors and parishioners may include the potential impairment of the pastor's clinical judgment, an increased risk of exploitation of the client, and potential conflicts of interests for both the pastor and the client (Montgomery & DeBell, 1997). Through collaboration with LMHPs religious leaders could provide distressed parishioners with a clear avenue for attaining help with issues that may require extended or intensive counseling interventions while avoiding participation in potentially awkward, or harmful, duel relationships.

Establishing a clear avenue for referral by means of collaboration with LMHPs can also be beneficial for religious leaders who may encounter parishioners with severe psychological difficulties. Although religious leaders are frequently called upon to assist parishioners with interpersonal problems, there are some issues that may be better addressed by LMHPs.

Moran and colleagues (2005) conducted a study investigating clergy's perceptions of their own competence to address mental health issues. Results indicated that clergy perceived themselves to be competent in addressing certain problems, such as issues pertaining to grief, dying, and minor marital conflict. However, clergy perceived themselves to be less prepared to assist parishioners with more severe problems including severe mental illness and suicidal ideation. Collaboration between religious leaders and LMHPs can provide a means whereby clergy can assist parishioners in receiving help with severe psychological problems.

Barriers to Collaboration

Although there are several good arguments to be made regarding how collaboration can benefit the professional endeavors of both religious leaders and LMHPs, the prospect of collaboration is not without potential barriers. Chief among these is the clash of values and ideas inherent to each profession's explanatory systems for the human struggles and problem resolution. This conflict has led to mistrust and reciprocal skepticism between LMHPs and religious leaders in some cases (Kanz, 2001).

From within certain religious traditions, emotional problems may have causes and explanations that transcend traditional psychological theory and treatment approaches (O'Conner, 2002). Psychotherapy may be viewed within such traditions as a means by which one's religious ideals can be threatened. In certain religious cultures psychotherapeutic interventions may even be viewed as satanic due to their propensity for offering nonreligious explanations and interventions for human problems and dilemmas (Kanz, 2001).

Certain traditions within psychology have trepidation about the role of religion in counseling client's lives. Within the Freudian tradition religious beliefs were viewed as a manifestation of neurosis (Kanz, 2001). Contemporary psychotherapeutic practices may likewise eschew or rebuke religious practices. Presley (1992) indicated that many LMHPs may tend to avoid religious content in psychotherapy sessions, or to view religiosity as a contributor to clients' problems.

To an extent then, religious and psychotherapeutic traditions have held contentions and explanatory paradigms that have provided each profession with structure and continuity, but that kept the two traditions from a richer history of collaboration. In a sense, some religious leaders and some LMHPs might be considered to have been engaged in monological interactions (Anderson, 1997). That is, they have adopted certain exclusive problem definitions, explanations, and realities, along with language systems that protect their traditions while excluding others. If there is a "con" to increased collaboration between religious leaders and LMHPs it is that members of both professions must be willing to venture forth from the safe and predictable waters in which their beliefs are harbored, and plunge into a rough sea of pluralism from which possibilities may emerge. In other words, each tradition must learn to accommodate realities other than its own.

Accommodation of views that fall outside of one's explanatory system is no small feat. The tendency to avoid those with differing views, as well as the tendency to avoid simplifying the views of foreign traditions, must be overcome (Gergen, 1999). To be mindful of these distancing traps, and to take risks with alternative explanations and routes to human change, is to engage in what Gergen (1999) calls "poetic activism" (p. 117).

There are many routes which religious leaders and LMHPs might take to reach a stance of poetic activism. The philosopher Paul Ricoeur (1981), in writing about the reunification of Germany with the rest of Europe following the Second World War, described adopting stances of host and guest as a means to overcome alterity (the tendency to alienate another's views). It was Ricoeur's thought that as one adopts a stance of host (engaging the other in a spirit of hospitability) then the other is invited to adopt a stance of guest (being open to receiving and reciprocating hospitable advances). It is likely that religious leaders and LMHPs would find the adoption of such linguistic hospitality to be a useful means to engender on-going efforts at collaboration.

REFERENCES

Anderson, H. (1997). *Conversation, language and possibilities.* New York: BasicBooks.

Arredondo, P., Toporek, R., Brown, S. P., Sanchez, J., Locke, D. C., Sanchez, J., & Stadler, H. (1996). Operationalization of the multicultural counseling competencies. *Journal of Multicultural Counseling & Development, 24*(1), 42–78.

Assay, T. P., & Lambert, M. J. (1999). The empirical case for the common factors in therapy: Quantitative findings. In M. A. Hubble, B. L. Duncan, & S. D. Miller (Eds.), *The heart and soul of change: What works in therapy* (pp. 33–56). Washington, DC: American Psychological Association.

Aten, J. D. (2004). The college campus ministry internship site: Interfacing religion and counseling. *Counseling and Values, 49,* 64–68.

Bordin, E. S. (1979). The generalizability of the psychoanalytic concept of the working alliance. *Psychotherapy: Theory, Research, and Practice, 16,* 252–260.

Burke, M., Hackney, H., Hudson, P., & Miranti, J. (1999). Spirituality, religion, and CACREP curriculum standards. *Journal of Counseling & Development, 77,* 251–257.

Chung, R. C., & Bemak, F. (2002). The relationship of culture and empathy in cross-cultural counseling. *Journal of Counseling & Development, 80,* 154–159.

Fallot, R. D. (2001). Spirituality and religion in psychiatric rehabilitation and recovery from mental illness. *International Review of Psychiatry, 13,* 110–116.

Favier, C. M., O'Brien, E. M., & McNally, C. J. (1998). "The friendly clergy": Characteristics and referral. *Counseling & Values, 42*(3), 217–221.

Gallup, G. G., & Lindsay, D. M. (1999). *Surveying the religious landscape: Trends in U.S. beliefs.* Harrisburg, PA: Morehouse Publishing.

Gergen, K. J. (1999). *An invitation to social construction.* London: Sage.

Getz, H. G., Kirk, G., & Driscoll, L. G. (1999). Clergy and counselors—Collaborating toward new perspectives. *Counseling and Values, 44*(1), 40–50.

Horvath, A. O., & Symonds, B. D. (1991). Relation between working alliance and outcome in psychotherapy: A meta-analysis. *Journal of Counseling Psychology, 38,* 139–149.

Hubble, M. A., Duncan, B. L., & Miller, S. D. (1999). Directing attention to what works. In M. A. Hubble, B. L. Duncan, & S. D. Miller (Eds.), *The heart and soul of change: What works in therapy* (pp. 179–200). Washington, DC: American Psychological Association.

Johnson, W. B., & Johnson, W. L. (1998). Self-help books used by religious practitioners. *Journal of Counseling & Development, 76,* 459–466.

Kanz, J. E. (2001). The applicability of individual psychology for work with conservative Christian clients. *The Journal of Individual Psychology, 57*(4), 342–353.

Koenig, H. G., & Pritchett, J. (1998). Religion and psychotherapy. In H. G. Koenig (Ed.), *Handbook of religion and mental health* (pp. 323–336). San Diego, CA: Academic Press.

Mannon, J. D., & Crawford, R. L. (1996). Clergy confidence to counsel and their willingness to refer to mental health professionals. *Family Therapy, 23*(3), 213–231.

McMahan, O. (2002). A living stream: Spiritual direction within the Pentecostal/Charismatic tradition. *Journal of Psychology and Theology, 30*(4), 336–345.

McMinn, M. R. (1996). *Psychology, theology, and spirituality in Christian counseling.* Wheaton, IL: Tyndale House.

McMinn, M. R., Meek, K. R., Canning, S. S., & Pozzi, C. F. (2001). Training psychologists to work with religious organizations: The center for church-psychology collaboration. *Professional Psychology: Research and Practice, 32*(3), 324–328.

Montgomery, M. J., & DeBell, C. (1997). Dual relationships and pastoral counseling: Asset or liability? *Counseling & Values, 42*(1), 30–41.

Moore, T. (2003). Promoting change through the African American church and social activism. *Journal of Psychology and Christianity, 22*(4), 357–362.

Moran, M., Flannelly, K. J., Weaver, A. J., Overvold, J. A., Hess, W., & Wilson, J. C. (2005). A study of pastoral care, referral, and consultation practices among clergy in four settings in the New York City area. *Pastoral Psychology, 53*(3), 255–266.

O'Connor, M. (2002). Spiritual *dark night* and psychological depression: Some comparisons and considerations. *Counseling and Values, 46,* 137–146.

Olson, M. J. (2003). Counselor understanding of Native American spiritual loss. *Counseling and Values, 47,* 109–117.

Oppenheimer, J. E., Flannelly, K. J., & Weaver, A. J. (2004). A comparative analysis of the psychological literature on collaboration between clergy and mental-health professionals—perspectives from secular and religious journals: 1970–1999. *Pastoral Psychology, 53*(2), 153–162.

Pate, R. H., & Bondi, A. M. (1992). Religious beliefs and practice: An integral aspect of multicultural awareness. *Counselor Education & Supervision, 32*(2), 108–115.

Pate, R. H., & Bondi, A. M. (1995). Religious beliefs and practice: An integral aspect of multicultural awareness. In. M. T. Burke & J. G. Miranti (Eds.), *Counseling: The spiritual dimension* (pp. 169–176). Alexandra, VA: American Counseling Association.

Plante, T. G. (2003). Psychological consultation with the Roman Catholic Church: Integrating who we are and what we do. *Journal of Psychology and Christianity, 22*(4), 304–308.

Presley, D. B. (1992). Three approaches to religious issues in counseling. *Journal of Psychology and Theology, 20*(1), 39–46.

Ricoeur, P. (1981). *Hermeneutics and human sciences: Essays on language, action, and interpretation.* (J. B. Thompson, Trans.). New York: Cambridge University Press.

Snyder, C. R., Michael, S. T., & Cheavens, J. S. (1999). Hope as a psychotherapeutic foundation of common factors, placebos, and expectancies. In M. A. Hubble, B. L. Duncan, & S. D. Miller (Eds.), *The heart and soul of change: What works in therapy* (pp. 179–200). Washington, DC: American Psychological Association.

Trimble, J. E., & Thurman, P. J. (2002). Ethnocultural considerations and strategies for providing counseling services to Native American Indians. In P. B. Pedersen, J. G. Drafuns, W. J. Lonner, & J. E. Trimble (Eds.), *Counseling across cultures* (5th ed., pp. 53–91). Thousand Oaks, CA: Sage.

Walters, J., & Neugenboren, B. (1995). Collaboration between mental health organizations and religious institutions. *Psychiatric Rehabilitation Journal, 19*(2), 51–58.

Wells, P. J. (1993). Preparing for sudden death: Social work in the emergency room. *Social Work, 38*(3), 339–342.

Woodruff, C. R. (2002). Pastoral counseling: An American perspective. *British Journal of Guidance & Counselling, 30*(1), 93–101.

CHAPTER 17

Incorporating Religion Within Marriage and Family Counseling Programs

JILL D. ONEDERA

The literature consistently supports the need to include dimensions of religion and spirituality in the training of professional counselors (O'Connor, 2004; Pate & Bondi, 1995). For the purpose of specific focus, discussion related to religion will be highlighted in this chapter. In this context religion is defined as the "social or organized means by which a person expresses spirituality" (Burke, Chauvin, & Miranti, 2005, p. 5). The term refers to beliefs and behaviors founded in a particular institution or faith tradition such as Christianity, Judaism, Islam, Hinduism, or Buddhism. Furthermore, religiosity is often expressed in group participation, whereas spirituality is expressed more privately (Myers, Sweeney, & Witmer, 2000).

The previous chapters of this book highlight the presence of possible religious phenomena within couple relationships. Counselors should be alerted to the fact that religious issues may present themselves in couples counseling, as well as in individual counseling. In fact such issues might ground or shape a client's behavior and beliefs. It would only be expected that counseling students would be trained to attend to such religious factors when working with clients. However, the majority of students in counselor education programs (marriage and family *or* mental health tracks), marriage and family therapy (MFT) programs, and in graduate psychology programs are not receiving adequate training in order to understand how to incorporate and work with religious factors in the therapy process (Kahle & Robbins, 2004; Prest, Russel, & D'Souza, 2001; Wolf & Stevens, 2001).

Attention to training in the area of religious factors needs to be addressed across a variety of programs training students to become helping professionals. However, the author will remain true to the counseling sentiment of this book. Consequently, this chapter will specifically focus on the history, as well as how counselor education programs (including both the marriage and family track and mental health/community counseling track) implement religious factors into the training of counselors. It is the author's hope, however, that helping professionals and educators in other fields can glean information from this chapter in order to address religious dimensions in their practice or affiliated programs.

IMPORTANCE OF INCORPORATING RELIGIONS TRAINING INTO COUNSELOR EDUCATION

There are several reasons why students should be introduced to religious issues related to the counseling process. For one, aspects of religion seem to fall naturally underneath the umbrella of diversity training, a very important element in counselor training programs (Pate & Bondi, 1995; Zinnbauer & Pargament, 2000). In fact, the literature suggests that there is a tie between culture and religion. One author suggests that diversity in culture "sprang from multiple religious roots" (McFaul, 2006, p. 31). That is, a client's ethnicity might be tied very closely to a particular religion (or visa versa). So if students are learning about diversity in ethnic groups, gender, age, socioeconomic status, why should they not be introduced to variances in religion?

Statistics suggest that most people are affiliated with a particular religion and are practicing their faith on a consistent basis. For example, Keller (2000) noted that 90% of Americans reported either being Protestant or Catholic. Forty percent of Americans were reported to attend religious services on a weekly basis. Further, 75% of the world's population is affiliated with a particular religion (McFaul, 2006). Not surprisingly, it would be likely that persons coming to counseling will have some sort of religious affiliation. It may not be a stretch to assume that many presenting problems will be linked in some fashion to clients' religious affiliation (Kelly, 1994). For example, Conservative Christians or persons with strong religious convictions may have increased anxieties and anticipations about seeking counseling due to their fear of members within the "secular world" (e.g., counselors) trying to impose their worldly views (Keating & Fretz, 1990; Levitt & Balkin, 2003). On the other hand, the incorporation of religious ideals and values may offer couples help with their marital conflict (Sabloff, 2002).

Research has suggested that the religious affiliations and practices of most mental health professionals are markedly lower than that of the average American population (Fukuyama & Sevig, 1997; Pate & Bondi, 1992; Walker, Gorsuch, & Tan, 2004). Further, several studies across time have confirmed that most mental health professionals in various fields including counseling, psychology, and rehabilitation counseling have limited training in the area of religion and spirituality. When religiosity is brought into the counseling process, many of these trained individuals approach the topic based on their own religious and spiritual experience, or lack thereof (Shafranske, 1996; Young, Cashwell, Wiggins-Frame, & Belaire, 2002).

WHERE RELIGION IS IN COUNSELING PROGRAMS

Few studies have been conducted on how religious training is being incorporated in counselor education programs. For example, in 1994 Kelly found that 25% of counselor education programs surveyed incorporated some type of religious or spiritual training in their programs. Later, Pate and High (1995) and Kelly (1997) found that only half of the counselor educator programs that they surveyed included religious issues in counseling within their curriculum. In 2002, Young and colleagues found that within 70% of the programs, religious and spiritual related counseling factors are attended to somewhere in the curriculum. However, only 22% of CACREP-accredited programs include a specific course addressing spiritual and religious issues in counseling.

Interestingly enough, such results are similar across training disciplines such as those accredited by the American Psychological Association (APA) and by the American Association of Marriage and Family Therapy (AAMFT) programs (Sabloff, 2002; Walker et al., 2004.) For example, in 1999 a study of 52 students taking classes in six AAFMT accredited training programs in the United States indicated that half of the participants never had any training regarding the incorporation of spirituality and religion in clinical work (Prest et al., 1999).

Despite the limitations of incorporating religious training in counselor education programs, studies indicate that the number of counselor educators and students wanting training regarding religious and spiritual client factors is on the rise (Green, Benshoff, & Harris-Forbes, 2001; Kelly, 1994, 1997; Pate & High, 1995). In addition, many students have reported feeling unprepared in the area of addressing religious concerns with clients (Prest et al., 1999; Young et al., 2002). Furthermore, both students and counselor educators have reported a need to address knowledge and skill areas related to religious and spiritual issues within the counseling curriculum (Briggs & Rayle, 2005; Burke et al., 1999; Souza, 2002).

Such interest and discussion plays an important factor in moving the counseling profession toward meeting the apparent religions gap in counseling training. In fact, at the conclusion of one recent article on the topic, the author invited readers to continue "discourse on this vital area of counselor education curriculum." He asked, "Who will accept the invitation and continue the discussion" (O'Connor, 2002, p. 238). Just recently, the American Counseling Association and related organizations have.

Ethical Codes

Discussion about the ethical ramifications in addressing religious diversity in the counseling process has been reported in the counseling literature (Lee & Sirch, 1994). In addition, the American Counseling Association (ACA) has responded to the importance of religious factors in counseling by directing its attention to the 2005 ACA Code of Ethics. For example, under Nondiscrimation (C.5.) in the Codes it is written that counselors should "not condone or engage in discrimination based on age, culture, disability, ethnicity, race, religion/spirituality ..." Under Section E.8., or Multicultural Issues/Diversity in Assessment, counselors are required to "recognize the effects of age, color, culture ... religion, spirituality ..."

The Association for Spiritual, Ethical, and Religious Values in Counseling

In 1996, the Association for Spiritual, Ethical, and Religious Values in Counseling (ASERVIC) division of ACA developed a list of nine competencies associated with the ethical integration of religion and spirituality into counseling (Miller, 1999). Although the first five listed specifically attend to religiosity, readers might consider the religious impact on the practice of any given client's spirituality. For example, ASERVIC suggests that in order for counselors to be competent in helping clients address the spiritual dimensions of their lives, they should be able to

1. explain the relationship between religion and spirituality
2. describe religious and spiritual beliefs and practices in a cultural context
3. engage in self-exploration of his/her religious and spiritual beliefs in order to increase sensitivity, understanding, and acceptance of his/her belief system
4. describe one's religious and/or spiritual belief system and explain various models of religious/spiritual development across the lifespan
5. demonstrate sensitivity to and acceptance of a variety of religious and/or spiritual expressions in the client's communication
6. identify the limits of one's understanding of a client's spiritual expression, and demonstrate appropriate referral skills and general possible referral sources
7. assess the relevance of the spiritual domains in the client's therapeutic issues

8. be sensitive to and respectful of the spiritual themes in the counseling process as befits each client's expressed preference
9. use a client's spiritual beliefs in the pursuits of the client's therapeutic goals as befits the client's expressed preference

Council for Accreditation of Counseling and Related Educational Programs (CACREP)

The Council for Accreditation of Counseling and Related Educational Programs (CACREP) also has attended to the importance of religious values within counselor education. Under the Foundation section for each of the counseling programs the 2001 CACREP Standards require curriculum experiences and demonstrated knowledge and skills related to "the role of racial, ethnic ... religious and spiritual beliefs ..."

RELIGION IN COUNSELING CURRICULUM

In 1995, Pate and Bondi reported that the "need for religious factors to be included in the training and practice of mental health professionals is well documented" (p. 170). About a decade later, literature continues to reiterate the message that counselor educators, clinicians, and students want additional training in the area (Hall, Dixon, & Mauzey, 2001). As mentioned before, ethical codes and guidelines have now been written to ensure that counselors are attending to this important dimension of counseling. It also is worth noting the potential consequences associated with limited training and knowledge about religious entities among counseling professionals. Such consequences may include the following: (a) a reluctance on the part of the counselor to even attend to their client's religious experiences and values (Weinstein, Parker, & Archer, 2002); (b) struggles to achieve rapport and demonstration of empathy (Burke, Chauvin, & Miranti, 1995); (c) limited exploration into client's worldview and cultural background (Bishop, 1995); (d) inability to manage conflicts between the counselor's beliefs and values and that of the client's (Myers & Williard, 2003); and (e) failure to meet the standards of the ACA Code of Ethics (2005) specifically regarding respect of matters related to the client's cultural background (A.2.b) and awareness of one's personal values and beliefs (A.5.b).

Such findings imply that counselors-in-training should be taught the importance of personal awareness and the relevance of attending to a client's religious values, specifically as it pertains to that client's cultural background and ethnicity (Fukuyama & Sevig, 1997; Levitt & Balkin, 2003). Counselors-in-training should have opportunities to explore their own religious and spiritual values and beliefs, as their ability to address religious and spiritual issues with clients is highly dependent on their ability to do the same in their own lives (Polanski,

2003). Finally, the research indicates a need for increased skill building during training as it relates to addressing religious issues within counseling.

For the remaining of this chapter, the author will present particular ways in which counselor education programs can begin to incorporate religious issues in counseling into the curriculum. First, the development of a course specific to religious and spiritual issues in counseling will be introduced. Ways in which to include this topic across the curriculum, specifically in diversity courses, also will be presented. Finally, ways in which to use the supervisory relationship present in practicum and internship as a medium for instilling training in religious and spiritual dimensions will be addressed.

The Religion and Spiritual Issues in Counseling Course

Readers may note that the title of this section presents a potential title of a counseling program elective course related to religion and spiritual issues in counseling. Since most professional guidelines attend to both religion and spirituality, it would make sense that such an elective would be designed around both. Since the present literature tends to focus more on incorporating spirituality in courses, the author will focus on how religious training might be infused into the course.

Course Objectives and Related Activities

The author suggests that a religious and spirituality issues course be founded on at least two premises. First, the course should address the ASERVIC spiritual competencies as presented earlier in the chapter (Cashwell & Young, 2001). Secondly, the course activities and learning activities should be developed in such a way that the course adheres to the related CACREP Standard (2001), specifically by providing students with an "understanding of the cultural context of relationships, issues, and trends in a multicultural diverse society related to such factors as … religious and spiritual values" (Section 11. K. 2).

Based on this foundation, particular course objectives can be incorporated into the course. Further, course objectives and activities might be structured around the Association of Multicultural Counseling and Development (AMCD) Competencies (Arredondo et al., 1996). The AMCD competencies are designed along the following three dimensions: (a) beliefs and attitudes, (b) knowledge, and (c) skill.

Objectives Addressing Students' Beliefs and Attitudes

One set of course objectives should address the importance of student exploration. For example, students should have opportunities to take an in-depth look at their own beliefs and attitudes about religiosity and spirituality, and how such beliefs play out in their lives. For example, related course objectives might be related to increasing student awareness and exploration of the following: (a) their own spiritual and religious development; (b) how religion structured and continues to structure their family dynamics; (c) how their religious beliefs and attitudes play out in their lives and how this might affect the counseling process; and (d) religious diversity in order to increase tolerance of other religious worldviews (Curtis & Glass, 2002; Fukuyama & Sevig, 1997; Ingersoll, 1997).

There are multiple ways in which to infuse class activities that are meant to address course objectives related to religious related beliefs and attitudes among students. For example, students might be required to attend a religious or spiritual activity different from their own tradition (Cashwell & Young, 2004.) They might be asked to journal or talk about the experience with their classmates. Other assignments aimed at stimulating self-exploration of religious and spiritual beliefs and attitudes might include a chronological timeline or a genogram. Fukuyama and Sevig (1997) suggested a series of themes that could be used as an outline for a personal exploration paper or for classroom discussion, including (a) earliest childhood memories of religion, of God, or of the sacred; (b) religious background of self and of family; (c) influences on beliefs about religion and religious values (either by a person or by experiences); (d) the impact of religious beliefs and spiritual experiences on movement through life cycle stages; (e) turning points on religious or spiritual journey; (f) present position or place on the journey; (g) any confusing or frightening moments related to religion or spirituality; and (h) recollection of a particular religious or spiritual experience.

Objectives Addressing Students' Knowledge

A second set of objectives worthy of being included in a religion and spirituality issues in counseling course should address student knowledge. For example, such objectives might be related to a knowledge base in the following areas: (a) belief systems or cultural bases of varying spiritual systems and world religions; (b) faith development models; (c) possible religious and spiritual expressions during the counseling process; (d) related ethical considerations; (e) importance of religion and spirituality to mental health; (f) relevance of religion and spirituality in the lives of families; and (g) appropriate intake, assessment, and diagnosis processes and instruments used to address a client's religious beliefs and values (Cashwell & Young, 2004; Fukuyama & Sevig, 1997; Ingersoll, 1997; Pate & Hall, 2005).

Knowledge objectives can be addressed in multiple ways within religion and spirituality issues in counseling courses. For example, students might be required to seek out a religious helper in the community for increased knowledge in a particular religious domain, as well as what aspects of this religion might be important to address in the counseling process. Furthermore, students should learn to develop working relationships with such persons for future consult on client cases (Pate & Bondi, 1992). Certainly knowledge objectives can be met through but not limited to classroom lectures, role-plays, readings, guest lecturers, and videotapes. Students also can increase their knowledge through individual and group presentations and papers on topics related to religious issues in counseling (Ingersoll, 1997). An interview with a family unrelated to the student's family that is structured around how religion plays out into this family's behaviors, belief systems, and values might serve to increase knowledge. Knowledge-based topics also may be based upon the chapters included in this book.

Objectives Addressing Students' Skills

The point at which students are ready to incorporate skills related to religion in the counseling process will be based upon their depth of awareness about how religion and spirituality play out in their own lives, as well as how such issues might play out in diverse client cases. Assuming objectives related to attitudes and beliefs and knowledge are met, skill-based objectives might be introduced. Such objectives might include (a) ability to address religious and spiritual related matters with individuals and families through the use of basic counseling skills; (b) ability to address religious and spiritual related matters in the context of specific theories; (c) competence in using specific religious or spiritual related techniques in session; and (d) ability to handle countertransference reactions (Fukuyama & Sevig, 1997; Ingersoll, 1997).

Students can become competent in addressing religious issues in the counseling process through observation of experts in the field working with such issues (i.e., videotapes, instructor role-plays), participation in classroom role-plays, and examination of case studies (Pate & Bondi, 1992). Collaborating with religious helpers in the field also will provide students with the opportunity to practice talking within and about a religious context in a formal setting.

Students might practice applying family systems theory during counseling role-plays. The application of transgenerational theory to a family can be practiced by gathering the religious identity, heritage, and traditions passed on throughout the family (Stander, Piercy, Mackinnon, & Helmeke, 1994). Students also might improve their competence in systems techniques be helping clients explore where God fits into the "client's" family system (Weld & Eriksen, 2006). Further, counselors-in-training can build upon their treatment interventions with religious couples by employing conversation about where the partners and God fit within the "divine triangle" (Butler & Harper, 1994).

Incorporating Religious Issues Into Specific Counseling Courses

In many cases it is neither likely nor feasible to infuse an entire course on religious and spiritual issues in a counseling program or any related program. Incidentally, Burke et al. (1999) suggested that issues related to religion and spirituality "pervade all aspects of counseling and human development" (p. 252) and could be infused throughout the counselor education curriculum. For example, in an appraisal course, students might practice surveying a client's religious values during the intake process and through various assessment instruments (Kahle & Robbins, 2004). Furthermore, through the use of self-exploration assessment tools, students might gain better insight and awareness about their own religious and spiritual development (Myers & Williard, 2003). Another course in which to integrate religion and spirituality is the research and program evaluation course. In addition to increasing students' competence in reading research articles, students also can increase their knowledge of religious and spirituality issues in counseling through required reading of research articles on the topic. Further, with the dearth of literature and research on the topic, doctoral students, for example, should be encouraged to explore and conduct related research topics.

The Diversity Course

Another likely option is the diversity course. In fact, many authors assert that religion and spirituality are essential components of the heritages of particular cultural groups (Bishop, 1992; Burke et al., 2005; Pate & Bondi, 1995). Consequently, counselor trainees should give thought to the potential connection between their clients' cultural identity and development and the impact their religious affiliation has had on their worldviews (Hayes & Cowie, 2005; Levitt & Balkin, 2003; Pate & Bondi, 1992).

Many examples of the cultural and religious connection can be illustrated. For instance, in order for counselors to grasp the worldviews of many African-Americans, they should have an understanding of African spirituality, the strong connection that African-Americans have with the community church, and the impact of religious beliefs on family life (Burke et al., 2005; Kahle & Robbins, 2004). In fact, the organized Black church is one of the most influential institutions used by African-Americans and is "often acknowledged as the pulse of the African-American community" (Adksion-Bradley et al., 2005, p. 147). Religion tends to permeate through the African-American system. Not surprisingly, then, knowledge of religious factors can provide counselors with a better benchmark in which to work with African-American families.

Consider the Islamic people, where religion and culture interact and thereby affect their daily behaviors and rituals. Successful interventions with families will come from knowledge about the major tenets regarding family life within the Islamic religion (Burke et al., 2005). For example, gender roles, behavioral scripts, and values within the family dynamics may be best understood within the religious context of Islam (Rasheed Ali, Ming Liu, & Humedian, 2004).

In the context of a diversity course, learning objectives related to religion and spirituality might again be in sync with the AMCD competencies. Objectives related to beliefs and attitudes might include students' exploration of the following: (a) their own religious and spiritual practices and related values; (b) how such practices reflect their cultural/ethnic group; and (c) potential dissonance with and biases about other religious and spiritual belief systems (Bishop, 1992; Briggs & Rayle, 2005; Zinnbauer & Parament, 2000). Knowledge-based objectives might include the following: (a) understanding of the different religious and spiritual traditions and rituals; (b) religious values and beliefs embedded in particular cultures and ethnicities; (c) how religion has shaped the history of a particular culture; and (d) how religious traditions impact family behavior (Hall et al., 2004; Levitt & Balkin, 2003). Finally, skill based objectives may be similar to those found in a specific religious and spirituality issues course. However, examples of more specific objectives might include the following: (a) confidence in talking about religious and spiritual issues during the counseling process and (b) ability to integrate counseling techniques and language that match the spiritual and religious needs of clients.

Practicum and Internship Courses

Exposure to religious and spiritual issues in counseling also might be presented in the practicum and internship courses. Myers and Williard (2003) suggested that students might be required to visit and participate in both Eastern and Western faith traditions. Discussions of such experiences could take place during class time. Another avenue in which to insert training and discussion about religious and spiritual issues in counseling is in the supervision process (Genia, 1994; Polanski, 2003). Supervisors should be mindful of their supervisees' attention to and knowledge of religious and spiritual factors present within the counseling process. Supervisors and supervisees have the opportunity of directly linking religiosity and spirituality into the therapeutic and supervisory relationship.

CONCLUSION

Weld and Erikson (2006) mention that religious and spiritual issues are among "the dearest to people's hearts" (p. 390). Further, religion guides the practice and behavior of institutions at all levels of the system, including individuals and families to nations. Despite the salience of religion present in the behavior, values, and outlooks of so many people, it is still very difficult for persons, both clients and counselors, to conceptualize and define. At the same time, it can have a strong presence in the counseling process, whether overtly or otherwise. Members of the counseling profession, as well as those affiliated with other related fields, are behooved to consider the ramifications of limited attention to this matter. Attention to training efforts, research, and continued professional and personal development in the area of religious issues in counseling is something all professionals should consider in order to increase their overall competence and effectiveness.

REFERENCES

Adksion-Bradley, C., Johnson, D., Lipford Sanders, J., Duncan, L., & Holcomb-McCoy, C. (2005). Forging a collaborative relationship between the Black church and the counseling profession. *Counseling and Values, 49*(2), 147–154.

American Counseling Association. (2005). *Code of ethics and standards of practice.* Alexandria, VA.

Arredondo, P., Toporek, R., Brown, S. P., Sanchez, J., Locke, D. C., Sanchez, J., & Stadler, H. (1996). Operationalization of the multicultural counseling competencies. *Journal of Multicultural Counseling & Development, 24*(1), 42–78.

Bishop, D. R. (1992). Religious values as cross-cultural issues in counseling. *Counseling and Values, 36*(3), 179–191.

Bishop, D. R. (1995). Religious values as cross-cultural issues in counseling. In M. T. Burke & J. G. Miranti (Eds.), *Counseling: The spiritual dimension* (pp. 59–72). Alexandra, VA: American Counseling Association.

Briggs, M. K., & Rayle, A. D. (2005). Incorporating spirituality into core counseling courses: Ideas for classroom application. *Counseling and Values, 50*(1), 63–75.

Burke, M. T., Chauvin, J. C., & Miranti, J. G. (2005). *Religious and spiritual issues in counseling.* New York: Brunner-Routledge.

Burke, M. T., Hackney, H., Hudson, P., Miranti, J., Watts, G. A., & Epp, L. (1999). Spirituality, religion, and CACREP curriculum standards. *Journal of Counseling & Development, 77,* 251–257.

Butler, M. H., & Harper, J. M. (1994). The divine triangle: God in the marital system of religious couples. *Family Process, 33,* 277–286.

Cashwell, C. S., & Young, J. S. (2001). Spirituality in counselor training: A content analysis of syllabi from introductory spirituality courses. *Counseling and Values, 48,* 96–109.

Council for Accreditation of Counseling and Related Educational Programs (2001). *Directory of accredited programs—2001.* Retrieved September 22, 2006, from http://www.counseling.org/cacrep/directory.htm

Curtis, R. C., & Glass, J. S. (2002). Spirituality and counseling class: A teaching model. *Counseling and Values, 47,* 3–12.

Fukuyama, M. A., & Sevig, T. D. (1997). Spiritual issues in counseling: A new course. *Counselor Education & Supervision, 36*(3), 233–244.

Genia, V. (1994). Secular psychotherapists and religious clients: Professional considerations and recommendations. *Journal of Counseling & Development, 72,* 395–398.

Green, R. L., Benshoff, J. J., & Harris-Forbes, J. A. (2001). Spirituality in rehabilitation counselor education: A pilot study. *Journal of Rehabilitation, 67*(3), 55–60.

Hall, C. R., Dixon, W. A., & Mauzey, E. D. (2001). Spirituality and religion: Implications for counselors. *Journal of Counseling & Development, 82,* 504–507.

Hayes, M. A., & Cowie, H. (2005). Psychology and religion: Mapping the relationship. *Religion & Culture, 8*(1), 27–33.

Ingersoll, R. E. (1997). Teaching a course on counseling and spirituality. *Counselor Education & Supervision, 36*(3), 224–232.

Kahle, P. A., & Robbins, J. M. (2004). *The power of spirituality in therapy: Integrating spiritual and religious beliefs in mental health practice.* Binghamton, NY: The Haworth Publishing Press.

Keating, A. M., & Fretz, B. R. (1990). Christians' anticipations about counselors in response to counselor descriptions. *Journal of Counseling Psychology, 37,* 293–296.

Keller, R. R. (2000). Religious diversity in North America. In P. S. Richards & A. E. Bergin (Eds.), *Handbook of psychotherapy and religious diversity* (pp. 27–56). Washington, DC: American Psychological Association.

Kelly, E. W. (1994). The role of religion and spirituality in counselor education: A national survey. *Counseling and Values, 33*(4), 227–237.

Kelly, E. W. (1997). Religion and spirituality in variously accredited counselor training programs: A comment on Pate and High (1995). *Counseling and Values, 42*(1), 7–11.

Lee, C. C., & Sirch, M. L. (1994). Counseling in an enlightened society: Values for a new millennium. *Counseling and Values, 38*(2), 90–97.

Levitt, D. H., & Balkin, R. S. (2003). Religious diversity from a Jewish perspective. *Counseling and Values, 48,* 57–66.

McFaul, T. R. (2006, September/October). Religion in the future global civilization. *The Futurist,* 30–36.

Miller, G. (1999). The development of the spiritual focus in counseling and counselor education. *Journal of Counseling & Development, 77*(4), 498–501.

Myers, J. E., Sweeney, T. J., & Witmer, J. M. (2000). The wheel of wellness counseling for wellness: A holistic model for treatment planning. *Journal of Counseling & Development, 78,* 251–266.

Myers, J. E., & Williard, K. (2003). Integrating spirituality into counselor preparation: A developmental, wellness approach. *Counseling and Values, 47,* 142–155.

O'Connor, M. (2004). A course in spiritual dimensions of counseling: Continuing the discussion. *Counseling and Values, 48,* 224–240.

Pate, R. H., & Bondi, A. M. (1992). Religious beliefs and practice: An integral aspect of multicultural awareness. *Counselor Education & Supervision, 32*(2), 108–115.

Pate, R. H., & Bondi, A. M. (1995). Religious beliefs and practice: An integral aspect of multicultural awareness. In. M. T. Burke & J. G. Miranti (Eds.), *Counseling: The spiritual dimension* (pp. 169–176). Alexandria, VA: American Counseling Association.

Pate, R. H., & High, J. H. (1995). The importance of client religious beliefs and practices in the education of counselors in CACREP-accredited programs. *Counseling and Values, 40*(1), 2–5.

Pate, R. H., & Hall, M. P. (2005). One approach to a counseling and spirituality course. *Counseling and Values, 49,* 155–160.

Polanski, P. J. (2003). Spirituality in supervision. *Counseling and Values, 47,* 131–141.

Prest, L. A., Russel, R., & D'Souza, H. (1999). Spirituality and religion in training, practice and personal development. *Journal of Family Therapy, 21,* 60–77.

Rasheed Ali, S., Ming Liu, W., & Humedian, M. (2004). Islam 101: Understanding the religion and therapy implications. *Professional Psychology: Research & Practice, 35*(6), 635–642.

Sabloff, J. (2002). The role of religion and spirituality in marriage and family therapy. *Journal of Pastoral Counseling, 37,* 45–49.

Shafranske, E. P. (1996). Religious beliefs, affiliations, and practices of clinical psychologists. In E. P. Shafranske (Ed.), *Religion and the clinical practice of psychology* (pp. 149–164). Washington, DC: American Psychological Association.

Souza, K. Z. (2002). Spirituality in counseling: What do counseling students think about it? *Counseling and Values, 46,* 213–217.

Stander, V., Piercy, F. P., Mackinnon, D., & Helmeke, K. (1994). Spirituality, religion and family therapy: Competing or complementary worlds? *The American Journal of Family Therapy, 22*(1), 27–41.

Walker, D. F., Gorsuch, R. L., & Tan, S. (2004). Therapists' integration of religion and spirituality in counseling: A meta-analysis. *Counseling and Values, 49*, 69–80.

Weinstein, C. M., Parker, J., & Archer, J. (2002). College counselor attitudes toward spiritual and religious issues and practice in counseling. *Journal of College Counseling, 5*, 164–174.

Weld, C., & Eriksen, K. (2006). The challenges of religious conflicts in couples counseling. *The Family Journal, 14*(4), 383–391.

Wolf, C. T., & Stevens, P. (2001). Integrating religion and spirituality in marriage and family counseling. *Counseling and Values, 46*, 66–75.

Young, J. S., Cashwell, C., Wiggins-Frame, M., & Belaire, C. (2002). Spiritual and religious competencies: A national survey of CACREP-Accredited Programs. *Counseling and Values, 47*, 22–33.

Zinnbauer, B. J., & Pargament, K. I. (2000). Working with the sacred: Four approaches to religious and spiritual issues in counseling. *Journal of Counseling & Development, 78*, 162–171.

Index